Ulrich Weisstein was educated at the Goethe-Universität in Frankfurt-am-Main and the University of Iowa and received his Ph.D. from Indiana University. In addition to scholarly articles, he is the author of books on Heinrich Mann, Max Frisch, and comparative literature and the translator of Wolfgang Kayser's *The Grotesque in Art and Literature.* He is Professor of German and Comparative Literature at Indiana University.

The Essence
of Opera

Edited and Annotated by ULRICH WEISSTEIN

The Norton Library
W · W · NORTON & COMPANY · INC ·
NEW YORK

First published in the Norton Library 1969 by
arrangement with The Free Press of Glencoe.

ML
1700
.N35

R00785 51588

W. W. Norton & Company, Inc. is the publisher of current
or forthcoming books on music by Putnam Aldrich, William Austin,
Anthony Baines, Philip Bate, Sol Berkowitz, Friedrich Blume, How-
ard Boatwright, Nadia Boulanger, Paul Brainerd, Nathan Broder,
Manfred Bukofzer, John Castellini, John Clough, Doda Conrad,
Aaron Copland, Hans David, Paul Des Marais, Otto Erich Deutsch,
Frederick Dorian, Alfred Einstein, Gabriel Fontrier, Harold Gleason,
Richard Franko Goldman, Noah Greenberg, Donald Jay Grout,
James Haar, F. L. Harrison, Daniel Heartz, Richard Hoppin, John
Horton, Edgar Hunt, A. J. B. Hutchings, Charles Ives, Roger
Kamien, Hermann Keller, Leo Kraft, Stanley Krebs, Paul Henry
Lang, Lyndesay G. Langwill, Jens Peter Larsen, Jan LaRue, Maurice
Lieberman, Irving Lowens, Joseph Machlis, Carol McClintock,
Alfred Mann, W. T. Marrocco, Arthur Mendel, William J. Mitchell,
Douglas Moore, Joel Newman, John F. Ohl, Carl Parrish, Vincent
Persichetti, Marc Pincherle, Walter Piston, Gustave Reese, Alexander
Ringer, Curt Sachs, Denis Stevens, Robert Stevenson, Oliver Strunk,
Francis Toye, Bruno Walter, J. T. Westrup, Emanuel Winternitz,
Walter Wiora, and Percy Young.

ISBN 0 393 00498 8

This book is dedicated to the memory of my wife,
Allyn, 1924-1963,
who did not live to see it in print

FOREWORD

*T*HE CULTURAL HISTORIAN Riehl once called the history of opera a martial history. Indeed, there is hardly a period in operatic history in which idealism and realism are not engaged in heavy warfare. Even the birth of opera around 1600 must be regarded as a protest against the nonrealistic tendencies of fifteenth- and sixteenth-century polyphonic music. The antithesis *bellezza/verità* prevails in the entire history of the genre and finds its most striking expression in the confrontation of recitative and aria in eighteenth-century opera. Over and again, the realistic principle asserts itself against the sensual one, with the French, as a rationalistically inclined people, insisting on a more natural use of language and the Italians on sensual beauty. As so often in musical history, the Germans occupy an intermediate position, with Gluck taking the part of the French, Mozart that of the Italians, and Wagner creating the first efficient synthesis of realism and idealism. In his correspondence with Goethe, Schiller, the foremost German author of idealistic drama, voices the following views on opera:

I have always maintained a certain confidence in opera and thought that tragedy, in its noblest form, might evolve from it, as it did from the choruses of the ancient Bacchic festivals. Opera is free from any servile imitation of nature. By the power of music it attunes the soul to a beautiful receptiveness. Here, too, pathos has greater play, because it is accompanied by music, and the wonderful which is tolerated here must, of necessity, cause indifference toward the subject matter.

What a contrast between this ideal conception of opera and those satires and invectives, like Benedetto Marcello's *Teatro alla moda,* which ridicule opera as an art form!

No wonder, then, that the fierce struggle for and against French and Italian opera, for and against *opera seria,* for and against Gluck and Piccinni, for and against opera as drama, was often a literary one and sometimes threatened to erupt in physical violence. This martial history is reflected in a vast body of literature, of which Ulrich Weisstein's anthology gives a well-rounded picture. The editor displays a thorough knowledge of the sources, and his selections span the entire range of Western cultural history from Euripides to W. H. Auden. We find documents by Rinuccini, the librettist of the first modern opera, as well as Corneille, Addison, Rameau, the French Encyclopedists, Metastasio, and such writers of the present century as Hofmannsthal, Claudel, and Brecht. We look over Mozart's shoulder as he discusses with his father the relationship of music and words in his *Abduction.* We witness how Beethoven is induced to make changes in *Fidelio* and how Nietzsche reverses his attitude toward Wagner.

This anthology meets all the conditions a documentary work on opera ought to meet. As professor of comparative literature, Weisstein was drawn to the libretto as an art form and dealt with it, perhaps for the first time, from the point of view of literary criticism ["The Libretto as Literature," *Books Abroad,* XXXV (1961), 16-22]. That he is not unaware of the practical aspects of the problem is shown by his translation of the libretto to Schubert's Singspiel *Die Zwillingsbrüder.*

The editor is overly modest when declaring that an anthology like the present one will serve as a source book for students as well as opera fans. It is the first compilation of its kind; one can reasonably expect that for many years to come it will be indispensable to cultural historians.

Paul Nettl

PREFACE

*T*HE THOUGHT OF COMPILING AND EDITING an anthology of writings on opera occurred to me while I was preparing my dissertation on the musico-dramatic structure of *Otello* and *Der Rosenkavalier*. After approximately ten years of intermittent labor I am reasonably satisfied that I have gathered material sufficiently broad in scope and representative in nature to constitute a historical introduction to what with Beaumarchais I should like to call the Poetics of Opera. In translating many of the items in the collection, several of them for the first time, I have endeavored to go back to the sources rather than relying on, often inaccurate or garbled, earlier English versions.

On numerous tricky questions in French and Italian I have had the expert advice of my colleagues, Professors Joël Hunt and Mark Musa of Indiana University. To the staff of the Interlibrary Loan Department of the university, especially to Mrs. Eleanor Rogers and Mr. Thomas Glastras, I owe a particular debt of gratitude. Without their help, I could hardly have completed my task successfully. Thanks are due also to the editors and editorial advisers of The Free Press, notably Mr. Thomas Simpson, Mrs. Barbara Brown, and Mr. Frederick Freedman, who have assisted me in the final stages of preparation; to

Mr. Hilton Kramer, who showed an active interest in the project; and to Dr. Paul Nettl, whose presence in Bloomington was reassuring. Mr. Douglas Feaver's offer to write the essay on "Words and Music in Ancient Drama" was extremely welcome. The Graduate School of Indiana University made it possible for me to have the final draft of the manuscript expertly typed. My wife, finally, shared with me most of the joys and sorrows felt in the long period of gestation.

Bloomington, Indiana   U. W.

CONTENTS

INTRODUCTION

$\mathcal{T}$HE EDITOR OF A COLLECTION like the present one, which aims at acquainting the reader with as wide as possible a variety of views on opera broached by composers, librettists, and aestheticians during the last three hundred and fifty years, cannot possibly hope to unite all the important statements bearing on that subject in a single volume. It will rather be his task to proffer the most significant samples of each of the four basic approaches to opera which evolve in the course of the history of the form. The undertaking seems doubly justified by the fact that it has no precedent and that a considerable portion of the material appears for the first time in translations from the German, French, and Italian.

The omission of relevant utterances by such eminent librettists as Quinault,[1] Apostolo Zeno,[2] Marmontel,[3] Goldoni,[4] Eugène

1. Concerning this principal librettist for Jean Baptiste Lully see Etienne Gros' *Philippe Quinault* (Paris: Champion, 1926).

2. Zeno, the predecessor of Metastasio and da Ponte, lived from 1668 to 1750. He wrote innumerable librettos for composers like Bononcini, Galuppi, Hasse, Porpora, and the Scarlattis. His letters in six volumes were published in 1785 (Venice: Sansoni).

3. Marmontel, the chief French author of librettos for comic operas in the second half of the eighteenth century (he wrote ten for Grétry and

Scribe,[5] and Gabriele d'Annunzio[6] is regrettable. But a line had to be drawn at some point and repetition would have been unavoidable. The number of first-rate and second-rate composers slighted in our anthology is naturally legion. Some of those whose works are still in the repertory (Donizetti, Bellini, Smetana, etc.) or formerly had a prominent place in it (from Cimarosa and Païsiello to Cherubini, Spontini, Meyerbeer, Gounod, and Auber) either found no occasion to verbalize their feelings about the art they practiced or merely echoed what their predecessors and contemporaries had to offer by way of comment, although some interesting material could have been drawn from the formal or informal writings of most of them. Evidence from the pen or mouth of older masters (Purcell, Hasse, Telemann, Alessandro Scarlatti) either does not exist or is extremely hard to come by. Nor did it seem desirable to burden the collection with views on comic opera. On the whole it is evident that unless they are conscious innovators or reformers, the makers of operatic music are not overly inclined to theorize about their art, except spontaneously during the creative process. Of the great masters in the field who are still acknowledged as such, Handel is the only one not directly quoted in the anthology, since his letters shed little light on his conception of opera as an art form. Haydn's annotations to his own works for the musical stage and Weber's communications with Helmina von Chézy are, unfortunately, unavailable.

five for Piccinni), lived from 1723 to 1799. He is also known for his *Essai sur la révolution de la musique française* of 1777.

4. Goldoni's *Memoirs*, trans. by J. Black, edited by W. A. Drake (New York: Knopf, 1926) contains many interesting details and anecdotes about his experiences with managers and composers, especially with Baldassare Galuppi.

5. Scribe, the most prolific librettist of them all, not only wrote thirty-eight texts for Auber but provided the librettos for Verdi's *Vêpres siciliennes*, Boieldieu's *Dame blanche*, Meyerbeer's *Huguenots, Robert le diable*, and *La Prophète*, and Halévy's *La Juive*. Verdi's *Un ballo in maschera*, Bellini's *Sonnambula*, and Cilea's *Adriana Lecouvreur* also derive from plays he wrote. Scribe's contribution is discussed by Neil C. Arvin in his book *Eugène Scribe and the French Theatre 1815-1860* (Cambridge: Harvard University Press, 1924).

6. D'Annunzio wrote the *Mystère de Saint Sebastien*, for which Debussy supplied incidental music. Their correspondence, edited by G. Tosi, was published in 1948.

One cannot help but notice that this anthology is largely composed of programmatic and quasi-programmatic statements, even though some of the selections appear to be of a strictly descriptive nature. In spite of the many disparities between intention and execution, no attempt has been made—except briefly as part of the introductory matter—to evaluate the material critically, i.e., to match an artist's theory with his practice. The reader who wishes to pursue that aspect should consult the books and articles listed in the succinct bibliographies appended to each introduction. An excellent analysis of the relationship between music and drama and its effect on operatic history, theory, and criticism is made by Joseph Kerman in his stimulating though one-sided book *Opera as Drama*. In his judgment of works for the musical stage Kerman is guided by the belief that "in opera, the composer is the dramatist and . . . the clarification of the dramatic idea and the refinement of the vision cannot be left to the librettist," a view that flatly contradicts the neoclassical concept of opera. So far nobody has written a history of the libretto, a task we consider to be a prerequisite for that history of melo-dramaturgy for which our anthology might serve as a tentative basis and for that poetics of opera which Beaumarchais envisaged in his preface to *Tarare* and which a latter-day Algarotti should perhaps be encouraged to create.

The pieces assembled on the following pages are extremely diverse. Some constitute private, some semi-private documents, while others were intended for publication. Letters exchanged between individuals engaged in creating a symbiosis of music and drama are especially valuable insofar as their content directly reflects the creative process and acquaints us with the actual intentions of librettists and composers. Monteverdi's letters to Striggio, Goethe's to Christoph Philipp Kayser, Mozart's to his father, Verdi's to his numerous collaborators, and Puccini's to Giuseppe Adami belong to this category, which is nowhere better represented than in the extensive correspondence exchanged between Richard Strauss and Hugo von Hofmannsthal. Other epistles, such as St. Evremond's letter to the Duke of Buckingham, Gluck's to de la Harpe and the *Mercure de France*, and Debussy's to the Secretary General of the Opéra Comique in Paris, are much less spontaneous. The same applies to Rossini's conversations with his biographer Zanolini and to Lorenzo da Ponte's patently apologetic memoirs.

Prefaces to, and dedications of, specific works represent a rather formal type of communication between an artist and his patrons or his audience. Gluck used his dedication of *Alceste* to Grand Duke Leopold of Tuscany as an excuse for writing a manifesto. Corneille's *Examen* of *Andromède*; Dryden's preface to *Albion and Albanius*, Beaumarchais' to *Tarare*, Berlioz' to *La Damnation de Faust*, Hofmannsthal's to *Die ägyptische Helena*, Strauss' to *Intermezzo*; Berg's observations about *Wozzeck*; and Brecht's "Anmerkungen zur *Dreigroschenoper*" fall under this heading. Examples of treatises on the genre are found in Voltaire's *Dissertation sur la tragédie ancienne et moderne*, Diderot's *Le Neveu de Rameau*, Wieland's essay on the Singspiel (his term for *opera seria*), E. T. A. Hoffmann's dialogue between poet and composer, Wagner's *Oper und Drama*, Nietzsche's pro-Wagnerian and anti-Wagnerian polemics, Busoni's *Versuch einer neuen Ästhetik der Tonkunst*, Cocteau's aphoristic *Le Coq et l'arlequin*, and Claudel's dissertation on "Modern Drama and Music." Stendhal's *Vie de Rossini* is a Romantic poetics of opera in disguise, Marcello's satire *Il Teatro alla moda* a melo-dramaturgy in reverse. Dictionary entries, like Rousseau's articles on opera and counter-sense from his *Dictionnaire de musique* and Voltaire's definition in his *Connaissance des beautés et des défauts de la poésie et de l'eloquence dans la langue française*, lay claim to greater objectivity but are by no means free of polemic overtones.

Several contributions consist of reviews of specific operas (Grillparzer on Weber's *Freischütz*, Weber on E. T. A. Hoffmann's *Undine*) and books (Shaw on Noufflard's *Richard Wagner d'après lui-même*) or, as in Addison's sarcastic *Spectator* essays, are journalistic attacks on contemporary operatic abuses. Aesthetics proper is represented in writings by Schopenhauer and Kierkegaard; and the volume concludes with a symposium on the present state of opera conducted by some of today's leading melodramatists.

Although it is quite impossible (and perhaps undesirable) to reduce the manifold views on opera to a set of clearly delimited, mutually exclusive categories, four basic approaches to melodramaturgy suggest themselves, with numerous intermediary positions completing the spectrum. A fifth approach—that which posits the absurdity of the genre "since music is unable to tell a story" (Boileau)—cannot be taken seriously by anyone concerned with enriching the repertory. The first approach, which is essentially that embraced by the classicists and neoclassicists of all nations and ages, rests on the assumption that in opera music must always remain a modest handmaiden. At its inception in the days of the Florentine *camerata*, opera was earmarked as the modern equivalent of ancient tragedy (of whose musical qualities we have only a faint idea based on, among other things, the notation of a few lines in Euripides' *Orestes*). Rinuccini, Caccini, Peri, and their contemporaries agreed that the musical ingredient should underscore, perhaps enhance, but never overshadow the spoken word. From Corneille to Beaumarchais this was the position held, with a few notable exceptions, by one generation of French critics after another. Rousseau and the Encyclopedists never ceased to think of music—or, at any rate, of song—as a kind of language; and the venerable Pietro Metastasio, reminding us of the fact that Aristotle listed music as the fifth of the six constituent parts of drama, proudly reported that his dramas—the famous *Didone abbandonata* among them— were more frequently seen as plays than as operas.

By far the staunchest defender of the neoclassical view was Christoph Willibald Gluck, who thought it his mission to "reduce music to its true function," that of "serving the poetry by means of the expression." Luckily for us, the great reformer was much too inspired a musician to let his genius be quenched, although he too cherished the notion that music "even in the most terrible situations, must never offend the ear, but must please the hearer, or, in other words, must never cease to be *music*" (Mozart)—a view that was subsequently challenged by Diderot and Berlioz and refuted *in toto* by the Expressionists. Philosophically, the neoclassical theory of opera finds support in the writings of Kant, for whom reason is the supreme guide in human affairs and who, judging the arts according to the degree in which reason partakes in their execution and reception, finds fault with music on account of its sensuousness.

The Romantic theory of opera, radically opposed to its classical antecedents, celebrates the triumph of music over drama. Stepping out of the role assigned to it by the classically minded aestheticians, music now regards literature as its slave. Mozart, although a born melo-dramaturgist, nevertheless demands that "the poetry must be altogether the obedient daughter of the music," Stendhal wants the operatic audience to dispense (or nearly dispense) with the libretto, Berlioz shows sovereign contempt for dramatic values by dispatching his Faust to the plains of Hungary, and W. H. Auden offends his muse by asserting that "the verses which the librettist writes are not addressed to the public but are really a private letter to the composer." Romantically inclined composers—but, understandably, not only those—are at times so carried away by their inspiration that they compose the music for numbers whose text has not as yet been written. This paradox, bearing out the contention *Prima la musica e poi le parole* (the title of an opera by Salieri), is mentioned in the letters of Mozart, Verdi, Strauss, and Puccini. The philosophical blessing upon Romantic melodramaturgy was bestowed by none other than Schopenhauer who, revolting against the Kantian rationalism, glorified Rossini's music as one that speaks "its own language so distinctly and purely that it requires no words and produces its full effect when rendered by instruments alone."

The two radical positions just outlined are duly complemented by two others, which hinge on the conviction that the two principal ingredients of opera are equally valuable and that neither of them should be exalted at the expense of the other. Wagner proclaimed the union of music and drama in terms of a perfect marriage contracted and consummated between male and female, whose copulation renders the *Gesamtkunstwerk* possible, whereas, breaking away from the Wagnerian style, the founders of Epic Opera were determined to provide equal but separate facilities for music and drama. Both elements are thus assured their independence. Stravinsky, Brecht, and to a certain extent Claudel are fond of alienation, whereas Alban Berg, in his *Wozzeck*, alienates music from drama *sub rosa* while emphasizing the expressive quality of his music.

Chronologically, the neoclassical view predominated in the seventeenth and eighteenth centuries (except when opera gave itself frankly as a baroque spectacle), whereas the Romantic concept prevailed in the first half, and the Wagnerian in the second half, of the following centennium. Twentieth-century melo-dramaturgy, when it avoids the charge of being conservative or reactionary, centers in the fourth approach. However, at times the rebellion against Wagner took so violent a turn that an exodus of opera from the theater to the concert hall (opera-oratorio) or music hall (Satie's *Parade*) was deemed advisable. Thus a period of operatic history is brought to a close under circumstances that bear a striking resemblance to those which led to the demise of Handelian opera under the impact of John Gay's *Beggar's Opera*.

Apart from the basic, and hence constantly repeated question concerning the true nature of the relationship between music and drama (or poetry), a limited number of topics of a more specialized nature are intermittently discussed in our anthology. Those who affirm the role of opera as an important ingredient of the aesthetic universe are naturally eager to explain what makes it a form *sui generis*. What can opera do, they ask, that the exclusively literary or musical genres find themselves barred from achieving? Those who want to undermine the foundations of opera, on the other hand, seek to prove that it can never rid itself of its inherent flaws.

The champions of opera are only too quick to point out that what the spoken drama lacks most of all is the ability to handle several strands of action or emotion simultaneously. In the musical drama, however, simultaneity comes naturally and, as Stendhal explains, "experience completely ruins the arguments" of those "poor frigid souls [who] claim [that] it is silly for five or six persons to sing at the same time." Nor do the participants in an ensemble (Weber calls it a "Janus head") have to share identical feelings, a fact most beautifully illustrated in the quartet from *Otello* to which Boito refers in his letter to

Verdi. What is more, considerable depth is gained in opera by the interplay between the singers and the orchestra, since the latter may be advantageously used to comment upon the action on stage, just as it can serve to reveal the subconscious motives and urges of the protagonists. Wagner even wants it to perform the role of historian and prophet.

Music being a mood-building art, its presence often adds a totally new dimension to the drama: the sensuousness which language, that arbitrary system of counters, lacks. In the spoken drama, mood can only be expressed negatively, for instance by means of significant pauses. In the lyrical plays of Hofmannsthal, Chekhov, and Maeterlinck, what is said often matters less than what remains unspoken, whereas Shakespeare's *Othello*—joined, perhaps, by the second part of Goethe's *Faust*—is the rare example of a play that is lyrical in the sense of aspiring to be music. Stanislavsky, I think, was right when treating it symphonically.

A further advantage enjoyed by opera, and repeatedly touched upon in our anthology, derives from the use of several levels of expression, and hence consciousness, which that art form renders feasible. The operatic composer commands a variety of means of expression—from the conversational to the symphonic, from ordinary speech via *Sprechstimme*, melodrama (of the type encountered in *Fidelio*), *recitativo secco* and *accompagnato* to full-fledged arias, ensembles, and purely instrumental music—that is unparalleled in regular drama. At best this wealth can be approximated in a poetic play like T. S. Eliot's *Cocktail Party*, where the number of stresses per line indicates the appropriate level of consciousness. This stratification, however, also has its disadvantages: for how is the composer to proceed from one level of discourse to another without breaking the continuity? Wagner fiercely attacked the fragmentation he noticed in operatic practice, a fragmentation defended by, among others, Alfred de Musset in his maiden speech at the Académie Française. Wagner insisted on writing through-composed operas, in which the levels imperceptibly merge in a continuous stream of musical progression. Today operatic abuses of the kind Wagner attacked are out of fashion and composers are no longer forced to bow to the wishes of prima donnas (as Mozart did in *Die Entführung aus dem Serail* and *Die Zauberflöte*) or the spoiled taste of a public set in its ways. To us even Puccini's striving for effect seems out of place.

What the critics of opera most violently object to in the genre is the artificiality of the conventions which gave rise to it and which make its existence possible. People don't sing in real life, these critics say; why should they do so in the theater? But, as Wieland points out astutely, the conventions of the spoken drama, and of art in general, are hardly less constraining, and the difference is, at best, one of degree. Many champions of opera, anticipating this common objection, sought to assign to it a realm sufficiently remote from ordinary life to make these conventions tolerable. The musical theater, in their opinion, should never engage in realistic modes but should restrict itself to the presentation of mythological, pastoral, or otherwise "marvelous" scenes and actions. Dryden, Wieland, Busoni, Hofmannsthal, and, in part, Beaumarchais share this view; and Schiller, in a letter to Goethe of December 29, 1797, goes so far as to express the hope that a rejuvenation of drama might be effected by way of opera.

Other weighty objections consistently raised by the foes, and difficulties encompassed by the executants, of opera, include the undue brevity of the libretto (Hofmannsthal was frightened to see "how short is the libretto of *Tristan* and how long the opera"), the amount of repetition allowed and often required by music, music's inability to convey deception, contradiction, and even humor *(Hamlet* makes a very poor operatic subject; and perhaps the best way of being humorous in an opera consists in introducing unmusical characters such as Beckmesser in *Die Meistersinger* and the male protagonist of Strauss and Zweig's *Die schweigsame Frau)*, and the often painfully noticeable unintelligibility of the singers (Richard Strauss claimed that one third of each operatic text is a total loss). These factors surely contribute to the failure of many a music drama and help to account for the excruciatingly small number of operatic masterpieces. All the more reason for us to ponder these questions anew and to sharpen our awareness of the hurdles any team of composer and librettist has to clear before it can proceed to the finish.

WORDS AND MUSIC IN ANCIENT GREEK DRAMA
DOUGLAS FEAVER

WE HAVE ALWAYS KNOWN, of course, that ancient Greek drama was set to music. Whatever misconceptions Peri and the Camerata may have had about the details of ancient music when they "invented" opera around 1600, they were fundamentally right in their realization that ancient tragedy and comedy were both fully musical productions. Music was one of the six essential constituents of tragedy which Aristotle listed in his *Poetics;* and Aristotle's work was known to Peri and his associates.

Indeed, an ancient tragedy bore more resemblance to an opera than to a stage play, and ancient tragedians were composers as well as playwrights. Euripides in particular was popular for his songs. In his *Life of Nicias,* Plutarch relates that the Athenians captured during the ill-fated Sicilian expedition won their freedom by singing Euripides' songs and teaching them to their captors. Aristophanes, in his comedy *The Frogs,* portrays Aeschylus and Euripides in the underworld competing for the "Chair of Tragic Poetry"; and much of the criticism of both dramatists turns on musical matters. Euripides brings out a kithara and, charging that Aeschylus' poetry is kitharodic in style, mocks him by quoting several Aeschylean lines interspersed with the phrase "tophlattothrat to phlattothrat."[1] Subsequently,

1. It is evident that Euripides himself is not being ridiculed for inappropriately using the *kithara* on stage instead of the *aulos,* as Regner (*Das Musikleben der Griechen,* p. 106) states. Nor, for that matter, is it implied that Aeschylus, who is the object of ridicule at this point, actually used the *kithara.* Euripides' point is that the style of these lines is more appropriate to the "ti-tum" of the *kithara.* Actually, some lines from the same strophe were earlier accompanied by the *aulos.*

Aeschylus means to call for a lyre, but changes his mind and summons the "Muse of Euripides," who appears in the guise of a courtesan playing castanets and shell rattles. The lyre and the castanets both implied that Euripides drew his music from harlot songs, drinking songs, dirges, and dance music, as Aeschylus is at pains to stress. One musical innovation introduced by Euripides particularly draws the fire of Aristophanes, namely, the setting of a single syllable to an extended melodic passage. It is clear that both the music and the text are satirized in the brilliant parody of a Euripidean melodramatic aria which follows.

Yet commentators have paid very little attention to the fact that the texts they are interpreting are, so to speak, the librettos of ancient musical dramas. And this for the good reason that little of the music has survived.[2] Only one small fragment of a few mutilated lines can make any claim to represent the music to which ancient classical drama was set. It is a papyrus fragment first published by Wessely in 1892 and containing the following lines from Euripides' *Orestes,* together with the vocal notation of the music and a few notes in instrumental notation:

> (O Zeus, is there mercy? What struggle of doom
> Cometh fraught with death-danger,
> Thrusting thee onward, the wretched, on whom
> The Erinnys-avenger
> Heapeth tears upon tears) the blood she has brought
> Of thy mother upon thee
> And thine house, that it driveth thee frenzy distraught!
> I bemoan thee, I bemoan thee!
> Not among men doth fair fortune abide,
> But as sail tempest-riven
> It is whelmed in affliction's death ravening tide
> (By the malice of heaven . . . .)[3]

2. Only about sixteen pieces of any kind of music survive from ancient Greece. Most of them are Hellenistic or Roman in date. Only the *Orestes* fragment, and perhaps the *Ajax* fragment, are from classical tragedy. Oxyrhynchus Papyrus 2436 may be a monody from a satyr play, but the music is probably Hellenistic.

3. The translation is that of A. S. Way (Loeb Classical Library), and the text in parentheses is supplied from manuscript tradition. I have discussed the passage in my article "The Musical Setting of Euripides' *Orestes,*" *American Journal of Philology,* LXXXI (1960). 1-15.

Whatever information this fragment may supply can be eked out with a consideration of another passage from the same play which Dionysios of Halicarnassos cites in his important analysis of the relationship between words and music in the treatise *Of Literary Composition.*[4] Viewing this quotation and the passage from the papyrus fragment, it seems possible that the text and the "score" of *Orestes,* or selections from it, were preserved because of some special excellence it had in the minds of ancient critics.

Before we turn to the music of *Orestes,* it will be useful to speak briefly about the music of tragedy in general. Normally, the entire drama was set to music, though Euripides sometimes calls for a word or phrase to be declaimed rather than sung whenever he wants to achieve a special effect. Yet it is clear that the kind of music set to the dialogue differed considerably in style from that set to the solo arias, the *kommoi* (dirges in the form of a duet between a soloist and the chorus), and the various choral lyrics. This is clear from the variation in meters between the individual types. Nonetheless, even though the standard meter of the dialogue, the iambic trimeter, most closely resembled the spoken language, it was by no means *vers libre.* Its strictness leads me to suppose that the melody which accompanied it was likewise similar to speech yet more formal than modern recitative.

The music of tragedy was usuallly written in either the Mixolydian or the Dorian *harmonia,* though occasionally the Phrygian *harmonia* was employed.[5] There is still no agreement among scholars as to just how the term *harmonia* is to be interpreted. Current opinion inclines to the belief that it is a traditional melodic pattern implying a scale, but not simply a scale. The musical accompaniment was supplied by a single

---

4. Trans. by W. Rhys Roberts (London: Macmillan, 1910). The relevant passage occurs on p. 129.

5. The term *harmonia* is usually translated as "mode," but its exact meaning has proven very difficult to ascertain. See Reginald P. Winnington-Ingram's *Mode in Ancient Greek Music* (Cambridge, 1936) for a brilliant survey of the literary evidence. Kathleen Schlesinger, in *The Greek Aulos* (London: Methuen, 1939), identifies them with the *aulos* scales, discussed below, but has found no followers.

player on the double *aulos* (a term widely mistranslated as "flute"). In reality, the *aulos* is a reed pipe using either a double reed like an oboe, English horn, or bassoon, or a single beating reed like a harmonica, with a tone somewhat like a modern clarinet. Aristophanes' use of the *kithara* in the *Frogs* was exceptional and meant to be comically incongruous. Whatever the meaning of *harmonia*, it is evident that the scales used in tragedy were scales playable on the *aulos*. There is good reason to assume that these scales are fundamentally different from those performed on the *kithara*. It is clear from archeological evidence that the holes of the *aulos* were equally spaced and that its bore was cylindrical. The scales produced always show intervals gradually increasing in size as one ascends the scale, no intervals of which are equal. The Pythagorean school expressed this mathematically in the formula $n/n+1$ (i.e. 12/11, 11/10, 10/9, etc.). Such scales can contain a wide range of intervals, from micro-tones to intervals larger than a whole tone. Their very nature precludes the possibility of harmony and counterpoint but makes available a whole palette of scale ethos unknown to Western music.[6] $\rightarrow n+1/n$

The music of the *aulos* supported the vocal line, perhaps embellishing it with figures and ornaments. For special effect it might play alone (as at lines 1263-64 of the *Frogs*); but there were no elaborate instrumental overtures, interludes, or *entr'-actes*.

It is now clear that the ancient tragedians faced in some form the central problem of the operatic composer: how to fit the words to music. This problem had both a technical and an

6. Scales formed by equal division are valid scales and have different characters to which the Greek term *ethos* can be applied. To that extent Schlesinger, in her controversial book, is right, as can be shown by repeating some of her experiments with reconstructed *auloi* and on the monochord, as I have done. That these *aulos* scales are the famous *harmoniae* about whose ethos Plato and Aristotle argued cannot be proved. Most Greek theory is derived from Aristoxenos and his school, who conceived only of scales built on the principle with which we are familiar, that is, a *gamut* of fourths and fifths filled in with tones and semitones equal in size and supposedly commensurate with each other. This type of scale is natural to the *kithara*, which was tuned in fourths and fifths by the "up and down" principle. See Curt Sachs, *The Rise of Music in the Ancient World* (New York: Norton, 1943), p. 73 and note 19.

aesthetic aspect. Because of the nature of the Greek language, however, the problem took a form different from that familiar to Western musicians. There was no difficulty in relating musical beat to poetic beat, because for the most part the poetic meter *was* the meter of music as well. It was possible to mark variations from the poetic meter by special signs, but these were rarely, if at all, used in the fifth century B.C.

The problem did arise at another point, namely, that of pitch accent. Ancient Greek had three accents: an acute, marked in ordinary speech by a rise in pitch (amounting, according to Dionysios, to a fifth), a grave marked by a fall in pitch, and a circumflex which combined both in a rise and fall. Thus the movement of the melody had to be related in some way to the natural rise and fall of the pitch accents of the words. The evidence furnished by most of the pieces of Greek music which have survived indicates that the note sung to an acute syllable was high, that of a grave syllable low, and that of a circumflexed syllable either high or a two-note falling phrase.

It is, then, somewhat perplexing that Dionysios, who raised this problem, flatly declares that the music "demands that the words submit to the melodies and not the melodies to the words." As an example he quotes three lines from Euripides' *Orestes:*

> Hush ye, O hush ye! light be the tread
> Of the sandal; no jar let there be!
> Afar step ye thitherward, far from his bed. (140-42)

"In these lines," Dionysios continues, *"sîga sîga leukòn* are sung to one note; and yet each of the three words has both low pitch and high pitch. And the word *arbúles* has its third syllable sung at the same pitch as its middle syllable, although it is impossible for a single word to take two acute accents. The first syllable of *títhete* is sung to a lower note while the two that follow it are sung to the same high note. The circumflex accent of *ktupêite* has disappeared, for the two syllables are uttered at one and the same pitch. And the word *apopróbate* does not receive the acute accent on the middle syllable but the pitch of the third syllable has been transferred to the fourth." Dionysios, in other words, indicates the places where, in his opinion, the music contradicts the pitch accents of the words.

Scholars have been led by this assertion to examine the relationship between the pitch accents and the melody as found in the papyrus fragment; and most of them have asserted that this fragment likewise exhibits a disregard of the pitch accents by the melody. A theory has been advanced to explain the alleged phenomenon; namely, that it was only in later Hellenistic times that the relationship between pitch accent and melody was observed.[7]

In my article in the *American Journal of Philology*, I ventured to challenge this view, pointing out that the evidence is not conclusive. Five acute accents in the fragment *do* agree with the melody, only three do not. One circumflex accent is sung to a high pitch, another to a low. Of more importance is the fact that when the melody, which in the papyrus is set to the *antistrophe* of the aria (or the second stanza, as it were), is matched with the *strophe*, six acute accents conform to the melody and the circumflex is set neatly to an otherwise anomalous two-note falling phrase. Only two acute accents do not conform. Thus I believe it is clear that there is a certain degree of correspondence, higher in the *strophe*, but detectable in both *strophe* and *antistrophe*.

In a passing reference to my article, Borthwick declared himself not yet convinced, since I had not dealt with the passage from a strophe cited by Dionysios. This is not the place to analyze the evidence, which is too technical for our present purpose. I believe, however, that such an analysis will show several things. First of all, Dionysios does not discuss all the accents involved; and those he omits probably contradict his thesis. In several instances he quotes as a violation practices—such as the extension of the high note of an acute to the following note, or the setting of a circumflex to a single high note—which are licenses observed throughout Greek music. Several other cases are resolved when the better manuscript tradition is followed, since the version quoted by Dionysios is certainly

7. See Sedgwick's article in *Classica et medievalia*, XI (1950), 222 ff.

corrupt. We are, then, left with the case of the opening line, which is sung, according to Dionysios, at the same pitch. But when we examine the meaning of the words, it is obvious that this treatment has a valid dramatic purpose: the words mean "hush, hush . . . ," and the music must surely be intended to suggest a whisper.

This is not to imply that Dionysios may not have had any justification for remarking that, at times, musical considerations took precedence over verbal ones. Euripides, for one, did not feel absolutely bound to observe accentual correspondence. What is clear is that even for the classical period the pitch accent of the text played a normative role in shaping the line of the melody.

This leads us to the second aspect of the problem of the relationship between music and words, namely the aesthetic one. To what extent, that is to say, does the music enhance or modify the meaning of the text? Dionysios does not raise this question; nor can we deal with it except by a few scattered observations.

We have already commented on the dramatic appropriateness of the whispered "hush, hush" in the quotation from Euripides. Let us look at one or two examples from the papyrus fragment as well. As I have pointed out in the above-mentioned article, the music here is more melodically formal than is attested for other pieces of Greek music. Its central musical idea is the ringing of the changes of the enharmonic *pukna* (a group of notes separated by very small intervals). There is no denying the mournful effect of this, which is in complete accord with the melodramatic content of the words. One word, "murderous," is declaimed rather than sung, and the effect is quite dramatic.[8] It is immediately followed by a few notes on the *aulos*, then by a high, poignant quarter tone quaver on the word "alas!," which could have been electrifying when sung effectively.

These are but scattered hints, but they are clear enough to make it certain that consciously or, more probably, uncon-

---

8. The same applies to the *deinôn pónon* ("woe for the dreadful labors") in the *antistrophe*.

sciously, the Greek dramatists composed music which enhanced the mood and meaning of their incomparable texts. In fact, for the Greeks all the Muses were one Muse and Tragedy was Poetry was Dancing was Music.

THE CAMERATA

THE HISTORY OF MODERN OPERA begins in the last quarter of the sixteenth century, with the first two decades constituting a kind of prelude. The artists and connoisseurs gathering regularly between 1580 and 1589 at the house in Florence of Giovanni Bardi, Conte di Vernio, and later at the home of Jacopo Corsi, constituted the *camerata*. They were strongly preoccupied with the reconstruction and revival of classical drama, of the musical nature of which they were keenly aware. One of their number, the composer Vincenzo Galilei (Galileo's father), is credited with the invention of the cantata, the first specimen being a setting of the Ugolino episode from Dante's *Inferno*. In 1594 another step toward the creation of opera was taken with the "madrigal opera" *L'Amfiparnasso* of Orazio Vecchi (who was not a member of the *camerata*). But the first opera worthy of that name—Jacopo Peri's *Dafne*, based on a libretto by Ottavio Rinuccini—did not appear until three years afterward. However, it is the same authors' *Euridice*, performed on the occasion of the wedding of Henri IV of France with Maria de' Medicis in 1600, that is the first opera to have survived, and it is usually cited as the fountainhead of opera as we know it. It is in these two works that the *stile rappresentativo*, which closely resembles our recitative, was first consistently and effectively used. Peri's *Euridice* was followed, in the same year, by Giulio Caccini's setting of the same libretto; and, still in 1600, Rome witnessed a performance of Emilio de' Cavalieri's *La rappresentazione di anima e di corpo*. None of these works are familiar to contemporary audiences, and the average opera buff conceives of Monteverdi's *Orfeo* of 1607 as the first opera in a line that stretches, almost without interruption, over a period of three hundred and fifty years.

In addition to Peri's and Rinuccini's forewords to their *Euridice*, the following items (all found in Solerti's anthology) are especially relevant to this earliest phase of operatic history: Caccini's preface to *Euridice* (1600), his introduction to *Le nuove musiche* (1601, 1614, 1615) and Giovanni Bardi's thumbnail sketch of the activities of the *camerata* contained in a letter to G. B. Doni of 1634.

A. Solerti, ed., *Le origini del melodramma* (Turin: Bocca, 1903); R. Rolland, *Histoire de l'opéra en Europe avant Lully et Scarlatti* (Paris: Boccard, 1931); D. J. Grout, *A Short History of Opera* (New York: Columbia University Press, 1947), pp. 29-59.

Preface to *Euridice* (1600)
OTTAVIO RINUCCINI

To the Most Christian Maria di Medici, Queen of France and Navarre

IT HAS BEEN THE OPINION of many, most Christian Queen, that the ancient Greeks and Romans sang their entire tragedies on the stage. But until now this noble art of recitation has neither been revived nor, as far as I know, attempted by anyone; and it seemed to me that this was due to the defect of the modern music, which is far inferior to the ancient. But this notion of mine was altogether dispelled by Signor Jacopo Peri who, when hearing of mine and Signor Jacopo Corsi's intention, composed the fable of *Dafne*—which I had written merely to give simple proof of what the song of our age could accomplish—with so much grace that it gave excessive pleasure to the few listeners present on this occasion.

Whence, mustering courage, Signor Jacopo improved the same fable and, once again, had it produced at his house, where it was praised not only by the entire nobility of this favored country but also by the illustrious Grand Duchess and the cardinals Dal Monte and Montaldo.

But much greater praise and favor were lavished upon the *Euridice* composed with great skill, not much used by others, by the same Peri, and found worthy by the graciousness and munificence of the Grand Duchess to be performed on a most noble stage in the presence of Your Majesty, the Cardinal Legate, and numerous Princes and noblemen of France and Italy.

Whereupon, beginning to realize with how much favor such representations in music would be received, I wished to publish these two so that others, more accomplished than myself, could employ their talents in increasing the quantity and improving the quality of poems of this kind, in such a way that they would no longer envy those ancients whom the great writers praise so highly. Some may feel that I have been overly bold in changing the end of the fable of Orpheus; but so it seemed fitting to me at a time of such rejoicing, especially in view of the example furnished by Greek poets in the case of other fables. And our Dante dared maintain that Ulysses had drowned on his voyage, even though Homer and the other poets had told differently. And similarly I have followed the authority of Sophocles in his *Ajax* by prescribing a change of scene, since the entreaties and lamentations of Orpheus could not have otherwise been represented. May Your Majesty recognize in these my small labors my humble devotion to You, and may You live long and happily in order to receive from God each day greater graces as well as favors.

Preface to *Euridice* (1600)
JACOPO PERI

To the Readers:

BEFORE PRESENTING TO YOU, gracious readers, these compositions of mine, I thought it fit to explain what caused me to invent this new way of singing; because the reason must be the beginning and source of all human actions. And he who cannot supply a reason promptly makes one think that he has acted by chance.

Although Signor Emilio di Cavaliere[1] was, as far as I know,

---

1. Emilio de' Cavalieri (1550-1602) was organist in Rome from 1578 to 1584, Inspector General of the Arts in Florence from 1588 to 1596, member of the *camerata*, and composer of *intermedii* and *favole pastorali*, some of them based on works by Tasso and Guarini. He is best known for *La rappresentazione di anima e di corpo.*

the first to make our music heard upon the stage, with marvelous skill, it yet pleased the Signors Jacopo Corsi and Ottavio Rinuccini in the year 1594 to have me, using it in a different manner, compose the story of *Daphne*, which Signor Ottavio had written, in order to furnish simple proof of what the song in our age could accomplish. Whence, seeing that I had to do with dramatic poetry and that, accordingly, I had to reproduce speech by song (and, surely, no one ever spoke in song), I thought that the ancient Greeks and Romans—who, in the opinion of many, sang the entire tragedies on stage—used a kind of harmony which, going beyond ordinary speech, remained so far below the melody of song that it constituted an intermediate form. And this explains why they used the iambic meter in these poems, since it is not as exalted as the hexameter but exceeds the limits set to ordinary discourse. And therefore, forsaking every other manner of singing heard so far, I concentrated on finding a manner of imitation suited to these poems.

I noticed that the kind of speech which the ancients assigned to song and which they called *diasistematica*, i.e., sustained and suspended, could in part be quickened, thus taking a middle course between the slow and suspended movement of song and the fast and rapid movement of speech, thereby adapting it to my purpose (as they, too, adapted it when reciting their lyrics and epics) and bringing it close to the other kind of speech, which they called *continuata*, i.e., continuous. This latter our moderns, although perhaps with different intentions, have already done in their compositions.

I also knew that in our speech certain words are intoned in such a way that harmony can be based on them, and that in the course of speaking one passes through many others that are not intoned, until he returns to another conducive to a new consonance. And having considered which modes and accents we use to express pain, joy, and related feelings, I made the bass move in time with these, either fast or slow, according to the emotions to be expressed, and held to this firmly through right and wrong proportions until, progressing through different notes, the voice of the speaker arrives at that which, being intoned in ordinary speech, paves the way for a new harmony. And this not only in order that the ear may not be offended by the flow of the speech (as though tripping in meeting with reiterated chords and too frequent consonances) but also in order that it might not seem, as it were, to dance to the movement of the bass, and especially in sad or grave subjects, the more cheerful ones being naturally suited to a faster progression, as well as because the use of the false proportions would either diminish or cancel out whatever advantage was gained by the necessity of intoning every note. Of which necessity the compositions of the ancients may well have been altogether free.

And thence, even though I do not claim that this was the song used in Greek and Roman tragedies, I believed that it was the only one that would lend itself to our music by adapting itself to our speech. Having imparted my opinion to these gentlemen, I demonstrated to them this new way of singing, which greatly pleased not only Signor Jacopo, who had already composed beautiful airs for this play, but also Signor Pietro Strozzi, Signor Francesco Cini, and other most learned gentlemen (for music today flourishes among the nobility) as well as that excellent lady who may be called the Euterpe of our age, Signora Vittoria Archilei. The latter has always made my compositions worthy of her art by adorning them not only with those turns and long trills of the voice, both single and double, which by the liveliness of her talent she constantly invents—more to comply with the usage of our time than because she thinks that in them lies the beauty and strength of our song—but also with those charms and graces which cannot be put into notation and, if put into notation, cannot be deciphered. . . .

Receive it, then, graciously, courteous readers; and if I have not accomplished what I considered possible, the awe of novelty having restrained my course, accept it in every way. It may happen that on another occasion I will show you something more perfect than this. For the time being, I will have done enough if I have paved the way for the talent of others to march in my footsteps toward that fame which it was not given me to achieve. And I hope that my discreet use of the false proportions, played and sung forthrightly, having pleased so many distinguished gentlemen, will not displease you, particularly in the gravest and most mournful airs for Orfeo, Arcetro and Dafne, which latter part was sung with so much grace by the young Jacopo Giusti from Lucca. And live joyously.

Translated by Ulrich Weisstein from the text as printed in Angelo Solerti, *Le origini del melodramma* (Turin: Bocca, 1903).

CLAUDIO MONTEVERDI (1567-1643)

BORN IN CREMONA, where he spent his youth, Monteverdi served Duke Vincenzo of Mantua from 1590 until 1612, and in the following year was appointed musical director at St. Mark's in Venice, a post he occupied until his death. Only six of the master's fifteen operas have been preserved *in toto* (two from each major period). The best known of these is the earliest one, *La favola d'Orfeo* (1607). Having been inactive as an operatic composer for many years, Monteverdi conceived a new interest in the genre when the first public opera house was opened in 1637. *Il ritorno d'Ulisse in patria* and the famous *Incoronazione di Poppea* were written in the years immediately following this event. In addition to being the first great melodramatist, Monteverdi was one of the greatest composers of madrigals and wrote a great deal of religious music. The following letter is addressed to Monteverdi's librettist Striggio, who was chancellor at the court of the Duke of Mantua (the "Highness" referred to repeatedly on the following pages). The composer's attitude toward the subject of the projected, but never executed, opera about Peleus and Thetis shows him to have been the first operatic realist. Several passages in the letter remain obscure even to Italianists.

L. Schrade, *Monteverdi: Creator of Modern Music* (London: Oxford University Press, 1951); H. F. Redlich, *Claudio Monteverdi* (New York: Oxford University Press, 1953), Kerman, *Opera as Drama*, pp. 28-38.

Letter to Alessandro Striggio
Concerning the Opera *Le Nozze di Tetide* (1616)
CLAUDIO MONTEVERDI

IF HIS HIGHNESS approves of this subject, I shall find it both beautiful and appropriate. But if you bid me speak, I am reverently and speedily at the command of His Excellency, although I am cognizant of the fact that my opinion in this matter counts for nothing. I am one, after all, who, being of little worth, yet is at the same time, a person who honors all talent, especially that of the poet in question, whose name I do not know. Since the art of writing poetry is not mine, I shall say at your behest, with all due respect, that, generally, music wants to be mistress of the air, and not only of the water. I want to say in my language that the music required by such a plot is altogether of too low a level and too close to the earth. It is greatly lacking in beautiful strains, since the harmonies are entrusted to the wind instruments, which are much too rude for the air of the scene, and have to be treated in such a way that they can be heard by everybody and played on the stage. As regards this matter, I leave it to your fine taste and intelligence to judge that, in order to make up for this deficiency, three *chitarones* will be needed instead of one, three harps instead of one, and so forth. In the place of a delicate singing voice we shall need a strong one. In addition, the proper imitation of speech should, in my opinion, be accompanied by wind instruments rather than delicate stringed ones. The strains of the Tritons and other sea gods should be accompanied by trombones and cornets rather than lyres, harps, or clavichords. And since the action centers in the sea, it will take place outside of the city. But Plato teaches that the kithara [lyre] belongs to the city and the *thibia* [flute] to the country; so either the delicate instruments would be inappropriate or the appropriate ones indelicate. Moreover, I have noticed that the speakers are winds: Amoretti, little Zephyrs, and Sirens, which means that many sopranos will be needed. And there are even more winds that are to sing, namely Zephyrs and Boreals. How, my dear Sir, can I imitate the language of winds, which do not speak? And how can I, through these winds, affect an audience? Ariadne moves us because she is a woman, and Orpheus because he is a man, not a wind. The harmonies imitate their like (and not by way of speech): the noise of the winds, the bleating of sheep, the neighing of horses, and so forth. But they do not imitate the speech of the winds, because it does not exist. Furthermore the dances, which occur at different places throughout the action, do not have the proper dance meters. The whole plot, as far as my ignorance can make it out, does not affect me in the least. I understand it with difficulty and do not feel that it leads me in a natural way toward a goal that moves me. Ariadne inspires me to a just lament and Orpheus to a just prayer; but this tale inspires me to nothing. What would His Excellency have music do under these circumstances?

Nevertheless, I shall with due respect and without any further objection fully accept whatever Your Excellency is pleased to order. If Your Highness orders that this plot be set to music (since more than one deity speaks in the piece, and since I like to hear the deities sing graciously), I would say that the three sisters, that is, Signora Andriana and the others, could sing as well as compose their parts. The same applies to Signor Rasco, Signor D. Francesco, and the other gentlemen. This would be in imitation of Cardinal Mont'Alto, who wrote a comedy in which each character wrote his own part. If this were something that tended toward a single end, like *Ariadne* and *Orpheus!* But then there is also the need for a single hand, that is, one that would tend toward the singing of speech and not, as here, toward the speaking of song. I also think that those parts where the Sirens and certain other minor characters speak are too lengthy. Please forgive me, dear Sir, if I have said too much. But I have spoken not in order to make denunciations but merely to obey your orders. If you should ask me to compose this piece, Your Excellency, I hope, will take my remarks into consideration.

Translated by Mark Musa and Ulrich Weisstein from Francesco Malipiero, *Claudio Monteverdi* (Milan: Treves, 1930).

PIERRE CORNEILLE (1606-84)

THE BEGINNINGS of opera in France can be traced to Mazarin's efforts on behalf of the Barberinis, the principal patrons of opera in Rome, who emigrated to Paris upon the election of Pope Innocent X in 1644. They were accompanied by a number of musicians. The first operatic performance in Paris was that of Luigi Rossi's *Orfeo* in 1647.[1] Approximately three years later Corneille was to write a "tragédie à machines," *Andromède*, with whose success he credited the ingenious stage designer Torelli (another Barberini protégé) rather than Charles d'Assoucy,[2] who had furnished the music and later claimed that it was he who had brought the piece to life. In 1659 Corneille wrote another tragedy, *La toison d'or*, in which music and spectacle played an important part. But this, too, was hardly an opera in the strict sense of the word. It is, then, not to Corneille, who was so skeptical with regard to the function of music in the theater that he pledged "to have nothing sung that is necessary for the comprehension" of a play, that we owe the first flowering of native French opera.

J. Ecorcheville, *Corneille et la musique* (Paris, 1906); A. R. Oliver, "Molière's Contribution to the Lyric Stage," *Musical Quarterly*, XXXIII (1947), 350-364.

Preface to *Andromède* (1650)
PIERRE CORNEILLE

AS FOR THE CHANGE OF SCENE, it is handled in such a way that each act, as well as the prologue, has its own setting and at least one flying machine along with a piece of music, which I have merely used to enthrall the ears of the spectators while their

1. Luigi Rosso (ca. 1598-1653) wrote two operas: *Il palazzo d'Atlante incantato* (libretto by Giulio Rospigliosi after Ariosto's *Orlando furioso*) and the above-mentioned *Orfeo* (libretto by Buti).
2. Charles d'Assoucy (1605-77) was a writer as well as a composer. Only fragments of his music for *Andromède* survive.

eyes are busy watching the descent or reascent of a machine or are focused on something that keeps them from paying attention to what the actors might say, such as the combat between Perseus and the monster. But I have seen to it that nothing is sung that is necessary for the comprehension of the play, because usually the words that are sung are only poorly understood by the audience. On account of the confusion created by the diversity of voices pronouncing them simultaneously, they would have caused great obscurity in the body of the work if they had had to inform the audience of anything important.

Translated by Ulrich Weisstein from Corneille's *Oeuvres* (Paris: Janet & Cotelle, 1821).

JEAN-BAPTISTE LULLY (1632-87)

LULLY, who was born in Florence, went to Paris when he was twelve years old. He and Molière created the genre of the comédie-ballet between 1663 and 1672. In the latter year Lully wrested from Pierre Perrin the privilege of administering a French national opera, which the latter had acquired from the king a decade earlier. Lully developed the genre of serious French opera.

Lully's principal librettist was Quinault, who collaborated with him on a dozen operas composed between 1670 and 1685. How they proceeded is shown by Nicholas Boindin in his *Lettres historiques sur tous les spectacles de Paris* of 1719:

Quinault . . . suggested several operatic plots. He and Lully presented these to the king [Louis XIV], who selected one. Quinault then prepared a scenario and an outline of the action, of which he gave a copy to the composer. Seeing what each act was about and to what goal it tended, the latter added interludes, ballets, choruses of shepherds, sailors, etc., at his discretion, whereupon Quinault wrote out the scenes. As soon as he had finished some, he showed them to the Academy, of which he was a member. Lully examined the screened and corrected poetry word by word, made emendations and cut out half of the lines, until he was satisfied. And there was no appealing his verdict. He returned the libretto of *Phaëton* (1683) twenty times, in order to have entire scenes changed, although the Academy had passed on them.

Quinault, unfortunately, had many enemies among his colleagues and, especially, among the ladies at court. When the opera *Alceste* met with the disapproval of the Parisian public in 1674, Madame de Thianges prevailed upon Lully to commission a libretto from La Fontaine, the writer of fables. However, the composer rejected the finished work, *Daphne*, because it was "only a pastoral unworthy of the king," who preferred the heroic genre. La Fontaine took revenge by writing "Le Florentin," a satirical poem he was naturally unable to publish before Lully's death. Madame de Thianges herself found the piece too harsh, a criticism which caused the poet to address to her an apologetic verse epistle. La Fontaine and Lully were outwardly reconciled in 1684, but the former's views on opera, as summed up in the phrase "The good actor never ought to sing," did not change appreciably.

H. Prunières, "La Fontaine et Lully," *La Revue Musicale*, II (1921), 97-112; R. Rolland, *Musiciens d'autrefois* (Paris: Hachette, 1908), pp. 107-202.

The Florentine (ca. 1674)
JEAN DE LA FONTAINE

THE FLORENTINE FINALLY SHOWS of what he is capable. He resembles the wolves one feeds, and fares well. For a wolf always ought to stick to his nature, just as a sheep sticks to his. I was forewarned. People had told me: "Beware! Whoever deals with him, takes a risk. You don't know the Florentine yet. He is a rake, a cur who seizes, tears up and devours everything. He has a triple throat. Give him things, stuff him, and the glutton wants more. The king himself can hardly satisfy him." In spite of all these warnings, I let myself be talked into working for him. The rake went off to arouse a child of nine sisters [the Muses], a child with grey beard who should by no means have been duped. But duped he was and shall always be. I feel myself born to be the butt of dirty tricks. Let another cheater come, and I'll act the same way. That one told me: "Would you like to write, quickly, quickly, an opera, but a good one? Your Muse will be rewarded before the notary. Here is how we shall divide our gains: we'll make two lots, one for the money, the other for the lampoons. I'll take the money, and you the songs. You will hear your praises chanted, and I'll bag the coins. I'll gladly pay in jumps. I have eight or ten tricks up my sleeve. Add that to the honor of working for me; and you'll be *grandseigneur*." Perhaps this is not what he actually said. But if he didn't utter these words with his tongue, he certainly harbored them in his mind. He persuaded me. Rightly or wrongly he asked for sweetly cloying stuff and other nonsense, for small talk, amorous phrases, and honey cakes. In short he deceived me.[1] I spared no pains to suit his purpose and satisfy him. My friends were to help me. If necessary, I could have made use of their talents.[2] "Friends," said the glutton, "do you have any? These fellows will cheat you by cutting out what is good and putting in what is bad." Such is the mind of the Florentine: suspicious, trembling, uncertain, never sufficiently sure of his profit, whatever one says or does to him. In vain I released him a hundred times from his obligations. The wretch had sworn to lead me by the nose for six months. He fell short by two. My friends mercifully saved me by sending him to where, I think, he's better off without me or them. This is the gist of the story. As for the details, which are well worth relating, I could dwell a whole year on them. I would then resemble that man from Florence, who deserves a long account, if anybody in France does. Everybody would like to see him in Abraham's bosom. His architect, his publisher, his neighbor, his colleague, his father-in-law, his wife, his chil-

---

1. La Fontaine, by using the verb *enquinauder* ("to deceive"), creates a *double entendre;* for *enquinauda* can also be understood to mean "talked me into writing like Quinault."

2. The friends are Racine and Boileau, who were designated as Lully's collaborators in 1677 but never finished the projected libretto of an opera, *Phaëton.*

dren, and all mankind, big and little, in their morning and evening prayers, ask the Lord, in His mercy, to rid them of the Florentine.

Translated by Ulrich Weisstein from La Fontaine's *Oeuvres complètes,* ed. P. Clarac (Paris: Bibliothèque de la Pléïade, 1948).

LA BRUYERE (1645-96)

JEAN DE LA BRUYERE was the greatest French moralist of the seventeenth century after La Rochefoucauld, whose *Reflexions* appeared in 1665. He translated the *Characters* of the Greek philosopher Theophrastos of Eresos and published his own reflections on contemporary life and manners in a book entitled *Les caractères ou Les moeurs de ce siècle* (1688). (According to Webster, a "character" is a "description of the traits or qualities of a person or type.") La Bruyère, who had studied law at the University of Orleans, became tutor of the young Duke of Bourbon in 1684. Nine years later he was elected to the French Academy. The reflections on opera here presented occur in the section "Des ouvrages de l'esprit" of his book. They clearly betray the classical bent of their author's mind.

Les caractères (1687)

LA BRUYERE

IT IS APPARENT that opera is the mere outline of a great spectacle; it gives one an idea of what this spectacle could be like.

I don't see how opera, with such perfect music and truly royal expenditure, succeeds in boring me. There are operatic passages that make one wish for others like them. And sometimes one forgets to wish that the spectacle were over, and that on account of the stage effects, the action, and other things that hold our interest.

To this day opera is not a poem but a collection of verses. Nor is it a spectacle in the true sense of the word, since the machines have disappeared through the economy practiced in *Amphion* and other works of that kind.[1] It is rather a concert where the voices are supported by instruments. One is mistaken and shows poor taste if one says, as people do, that machines are there only for the amusement of children, and that they are only suited for marionettes. In reality they enhance and embellish the fiction and maintain in the audience that sweet illusion which is at the heart of all theatrical pleasure. To them the marvelous is added. There is no need for flights, chariots, and change of scenery in *Bérénice* or *Pénélope;* but there is in opera.[2] It is fitting for that genre to charm our mind, our eyes, and our ears with equal magic.

Translated by Ulrich Weisstein from La Bruyère's *Les caractères de Théophraste traduits du Grec avec Les caractères ou Les moeurs de ce siècle* (Paris: Garnier, 1872).

SAINT-EVREMOND *(1613-1703)*

SAINT-EVREMOND (Charles de Marguetel de Saint-Denis-le Guast, Seigneur de Saint-Evremond sur l'Olson) was a professional soldier with a distinguished military career that came to a sudden end around 1660, when some imprudent remarks he had made about his superior made it advisable for him to leave his native country. In 1661 he established permanent residence in London, where Charles II became his patron (he was officially employed as keeper of decoy ducks at St. James' Park in London). In France he had already gained a reputation as a writer and moralist. He was a passionate lover of music and an amateur composer to boot. Since opera was not formally introduced in France until the late fifties, he could hardly have had any first-hand

1. The reference to *Amphion* is usually taken to apply to the reforms wrought by Lully and his school, although Lully himself composed no opera by that name.

2. Both Corneille and Racine authored a *Bérénice* in 1670. *Pénélope* is the title of a drama by the Abbé Genest performed in 1684.

acquaintance with it before his emigration. In England he must have attended the performances of both *Pomone* and *Ariane* (with music by Cambert),[1] the first French operas to be staged in that country. Shortly afterward he

composed an Idyll, which he set himself to music and sang at Mme. Mazarin's before a great many persons of distinction. The conversation turned afterwards on plays with musical entertainments, and particularly upon operas, which made then so much noise in France. M. Saint-Evremond gave but an indifferent character of these compositions; but not having had time to speak all his thoughts about them, he wrote a discourse upon that subject, which he inscribed to the Duke of Buckingham, who had his share in that discussion.[2]

This is the origin of the famous letter of 1677 (or 1678) to the Duke of Buckingham, in which opera is defined as a "bizarre mixture of poetry and music where the writer and the composer, equally embarrassed by each other, go to a lot of trouble to create an execrable work." Saint-Evremond's definition is perfectly in keeping with the French neoclassical position taken also by La Bruyère, Boileau, and Voltaire (in his letter to Cideville). Soon after composing the letter, Saint-Evremond wrote a comedy, *Les Opéra*, in which he satirized the genre.

I. Lowens, "Saint-Evremond, Dryden and the Theory of "Opera," *Criticism*, I (1959), 226-248, Q. M. Hope, *Saint-Evremond: The Honnête Homme as Critic* (Bloomington: Indiana University Press, 1962).

Letter to the Duke of Buckingham (1677)
SAINT-EVREMOND

FOR SOME TIME NOW, Mylord, I have wanted to tell you what I think about opera in general and the difference between French and Italian opera in particular. . . . I begin by frankly stating that I am not especially fond of the comedies in music now in vogue. I admit that I enjoy the magnificence of the spectacle,

1. In collaboration with the Abbé Pierre Perrin (1625-1675) Robert Cambert (1628-1677) created three of the first French operas: *La Pastorale d'Issy* (1659), *Ariane* (1661, but not performed until 1674) and *Pomone* (1671).

2. From the Introduction to the 1726 edition of Saint-Evremond's works by Des Maizeaux and Silvestre.

that the machines provide a modicum of surprise, that the music occasionally affects me, and that the whole seems marvelous. But I must also confess that the marvels soon grow boresome; for where the mind has so little to say the senses needs begin to languish. After the initial pleasure engendered by the surprise, the eyes look their fill but soon grow tired of the constant attachment to objects. At the beginning of concerts, one notices the appropriate use of sounds and misses none of the many ingredients which combine to produce the sweetness of the harmony. A little later, the instruments begin to deafen us and the music seems to the ears but a confused noise in which one can distinguish nothing. And who can endure the boredom of a recitative, which possesses neither the charm of the song nor the forcefulness of the spoken word? The soul, fatigued by the prolonged attention which does not involve the feelings, seeks in itself some secret movement that will affect it. The mind, which has vainly lent itself to impressions from the outside, begins to indulge in daydreams or is annoyed by its own uselessness. At last the boredom becomes so great that one thinks only of leaving; and the only pleasure which is left for the languishing audience is the hope that the spectacle will soon be over.

The languor which ordinarily overcomes me at the opera is caused by my never having seen one that didn't seem censurable on account of the handling of its subject matter and its poetry. The ear is flattered and the eye charmed in vain if the mind remains dissatisfied. My soul, more closely linked to my mind than to my senses, forms a secret resistance to the impressions it might receive or, at least, fails to give its approval, without which even the most voluptuous objects cannot please me very much. A farce embellished with music, dances, machines, and decorations remains a farce, if a magnificent one. It is a rotten core beautifully clothed to which I penetrate with great disdain.

There is another thing in opera that is so unnatural that it stuns my imagination. It is the fact that the whole piece is sung from beginning to end, as if the characters on stage had conspired to present musically the most trivial as well as the most important aspects of their lives. Can one imagine that a master sings when calling his servant or when giving him an order?

That a friend confides a secret to another musically? That deliberations in a council of state are sung? That commands are chanted, and that people are killed melodiously in battle? To arrange things in this way means to violate the spirit of drama, which takes precedence over that of music, which latter ought to be used solely as accompaniment. The great dramatists, accordingly, have added music as an embellishment instead of making it intrinsically important. They have first taken care of the action and the language. But in most operas the composer seems to be more important than the hero; and Luigi, Cavalli, and Cesti are called to our attention.[3] Since it seems unreasonable that a hero should sing, one fastens on the one who makes him sing; and one can't deny that at the performances in the Palais-Royal the audience thinks of Lully a hundred times more often than of Theseus and Cadmus.

I do not claim, however, that singing in general should be banished from the theater. There are things that ought to be sung and can be sung without offense to propriety and reason. The vows, the sacrifices, and, generally speaking, all that concerns the cult of the Gods, has always and in all nations been sung. The tender and mournful passions are naturally expressed by a kind of chant: the expression of a budding love, the irresolution of a soul torn between two conflicting emotions, are subjects suited to measured poetry and, hence, to singing. Everybody knows that the Greeks employed choruses in their dramas; and one must admit that they could equally well be used in ours. This, in my opinion, is the domain of song. All that is conversation and debate, intrigue and business transaction, deliberation and advice belongs to the actors and sounds ridiculous in the mouth of singers. The Greeks fashioned good tragedies with intermittent song; whereas the Italians and the French make bad ones, where all is sung.

If you want to know what an opera is, I tell you that it is

---

3. Francesco Cavalli (1602-76) composed more than forty operas, most of them for Venetian theaters. Pietro Cesti (1623-69), the composer of the famous *Pomo d'oro* (1667), spent many years in the service of Archduke Ferdinand of Austria at Innsbruck, and from 1666 until his death was active in Vienna.

a bizarre mixture of poetry and music where the writer and the composer, equally embarrassed by each other, go to a lot of trouble to create an execrable work. Granted that one finds in many operas pleasant words and beautiful musical numbers; but one is sure in the end to come upon passages that show how the writer's genius has been constrained, or others in which the composer has indulged in unduly extended melisms. If I felt capable of giving advice to the gentlemen who work for the theater, I would ask them to go back to our comedies, where dances and music are used without harming the action. In them, a prologue with pleasant musical accompaniment is chanted. In the interludes the song enlivens words that mirror the mood of the action. At the end, an epilogue or some reflection on the greatest beauties of the work is sung. Thus the impression gained from the play is strengthened and the content of the latter endeared to the audience. In this way one can satisfy both the mind and the senses, since one no longer desires the charms of music in the action proper nor longs for action in the extended musical passages.

It remains now for me to state a rule that should be applied to all comedies that are set to music: namely, that the poet should be given the principal authority in all matters concerning the work. The music must be there for the sake of the poetry, not the poetry for the sake of the music. The composer must obey the orders of the poet so that he may know the passions and penetrate even further into the heart of man. Lully alone should be exempted. . . .

I do not want to conclude my discourse without saying something about the low esteem which our operas enjoy in Italy, and vice versa. The Italians, who concentrate wholly on the action, cannot tolerate that we call opera a sequence of dances and music that does not hang together and is only loosely related to the principal subject. The French, accustomed to the beauty of their overtures, the charm of their musical numbers and their instrumental interludes, rebel against the poor use which is made of the orchestra in Venetian operas and refuse to listen to the long recitatives which grow boring on account of their lack of variety. I can't tell you exactly what their recitatives are like; but I know that they are different from either singing or declamation. They are of a type unknown to the ancients and definable as a grave abuse of both song and language. . . . The major flaw of our operas lies in their having too little text. One expects to witness an action, and nothing happens. One goes to view a comedy, and one finds not a shred of the comic spirit.

Translated by Ulrich Weisstein from Saint-Evremond's *Oeuvres Melées*, edited by Charles Giraud (Paris: L. Techener fils, 1865).

JOHN DRYDEN (*1631-1700*)

IN THE ENGLAND OF THE RESTORATION PERIOD, the lines between spoken and musical drama were no longer clearly drawn. Many of Shakespeare's plays, for example, were now given in such a manner as to resemble operas. John Dryden, the leading writer of the period, was himself responsible for a musical version of *The Tempest*, staged in 1667. (It was later followed by Shadwell's opera on the same subject).[1]

Dryden's attitude toward the operatic genre was decidedly ambivalent. Like Saint-Evremond (whose definition he did not embrace) he witnessed the first performances of French opera on the island, and in his "Prologue Spoken at the Opening of the New House, March 26, 1674" he scornfully mentioned the "French machines" that "have never done England good." However, he himself was not above creating the libretto of a work conceived in the very same manner. In 1685 he decided to expand what had originally been intended as a prologue to the musical drama *King Arthur* into a full-length opera, which he entitled *Albion and Albanius*. The music for this work was written by one Lewis Grabu, a French composer of meager talent then active in the British capital.[2] E. J. Dent called this

1. Thomas Shadwell's adaptation of *The Tempest* was performed in 1674. Matthew Locke (1630-77) provided the instrumental music and John Banister (1630-79) most of the Ariel songs for that version.

2. Lewis Grabu (exact dates unknown), a French composer, came to England in 1665 and stayed at least until 1694. He had a hand in the pro-

opera a "monument of stupidity," and a contemporary wit ascribed its failure to the fact that Dryden had written the music and Grabu the words. Having heard Purcell's *Dido and Aeneas* and *Dioclesian*—both performed about 1690—Dryden wished to work with that composer, and he finished his libretto of *King Arthur*, not without making some concessions to Purcell. The opera was successfully performed at the Dorset Gardens Theatre in the late spring of 1691. Purcell subsequently wrote the music for Dryden/Howard's play *The Indian Queen* and Dryden/Davenant's version of *The Tempest*, and also furnished incidental music for several other of Dryden's stage works.

E. J. Dent, *Foundations of English Opera* (Cambridge University Press, 1928); J. Mark, "Dryden and the Beginnings of Opera in England," *Music & Letters*, V (1924), 247-252; I. Lowens, "St. Evremond, Dryden and the Theory of Opera," *Criticism*, I (1959), 226-248.

Preface to *Albion and Albanius*, an Opera (1685)

JOHN DRYDEN

IF WIT HAS TRULY BEEN DEFINED, "a propriety of thoughts and words," then that definition will extend to all sorts of Poetry: and, among the rest, to this present entertainment of an opera. Propriety of thought is that fancy which arises naturally from the subject, or which the poet adapts to it. Propriety of words is the clothing of those thoughts with such expressions as are naturally proper to them; and from both these, if they are judiciously performed, the delight of poetry results. An opera is a poetical tale, or fiction, represented by vocal and instrumental music, adorned with scenes, machines, and dancing. The supposed persons of this musical drama are generally supernatural, as gods, and goddesses, and heroes, which at least are descended from them, and are in due time to be adopted into their number. The subject, therefore, being extended beyond the limits of human nature, admits of that sort of marvelous and surprising conduct which is rejected in other plays. Human impossibilities are to

duction of Cambert's *Ariadne* in 1674 and, thirteen years later, furnished the instrumental music for Waller's adaptation of Beaumont and Fletcher's *Maid's Tragedy*.

be received as they are in faith; because, where gods are introduced, a supreme power is to be understood, and second causes are out of doors. Yet propriety is to be observed even here. The gods are all to manage their peculiar provinces; and what was attributed by the heathens to one power ought not to be performed by another. Phoebus must foretell, Mercury must charm with his caduceus, and Juno must reconcile the quarrels of the marriage-bed. To conclude, they must all act according to their distinct and peculiar characters. If the persons represented were to speak upon the stage, it would follow, of necessity, that the expressions should be lofty, figurative, and majestical, but the nature of an opera denies the frequent use of these poetical ornaments; for vocal music, though it often admits a loftiness of sound, yet always exacts an harmonious sweetness; or, to distinguish yet more justly, the recitative part of the opera requires a more masculine beauty of expression and sound; the other, which, for want of a proper English word, I must call the *songish part*, must abound in the softness and variety of numbers; its principal intention being to please hearing rather than to gratify the understanding. It appears, indeed, preposterous at first sight, that rhyme, on any consideration, should take place of reason; but, in order to resolve the problem, this fundamental proposition must be settled, that the first inventors of any art or science, provided they have brought it to perfection, are, in reason, to give laws to it; and, according to their model, all afterundertakers are to build. Thus, in Epic Poetry, no man ought to dispute the authority of Homer, who gave the first being to that masterpiece of art, and endued it with that form of perfection in all its parts that nothing was wanting to its excellency. Virgil therefore, and those very few who have succeeded him, endeavoured not to introduce, or innovate, anything in a design already perfected, but imitated the plan of the inventor; and are only so far true heroic poets as they have built on the foundations of Homer. Thus Pindar, the author of those Odes which are so admirably restored by Mr. Cowley in our language, ought for ever to be the standard of them; and we are bound, according to the practice of Horace and Mr. Cowley, to copy him. Now, to apply this axiom to our present purpose, whosoever undertakes the writing of an opera (which is a modern invention, though built indeed on the foundation of ethnic worship) is obliged to imitate the design of the Italians, who have not yet invented, but brought to perfection, this sort of dramatic musical entertainment. I have not been able, by any search, to get any light, either of the time when it began, or of the first author. But I have probable reasons, which induce me to believe that some Italians, having curiously observed the gallantries of the Spanish Moors, at their *zambras*, or royal feasts, where music, songs, and dancing were in perfection, together with their machines, which are usual at their *sortijas*, or running at the ring, and other solemnities, may possibly have refined upon those Moresque divertisements, and produced this delightful entertainment, by leaving out the warlike part of the carousels, and forming a poetical design for the use of the machines, the songs, and dances. But however it began (for this is only conjectural), we know that, for some centuries, the knowledge of Music has flourished principally in Italy, the mother of learning and of arts; that Poetry and Painting have been there restored and so cultivated by Italian masters that all Europe has been enriched out of their treasury; and the other parts of it, in relation to those delightful arts, are still as much provincial to Italy as they were in the time of the Roman empire. Their first operas seem to have been intended for the celebration of the marriages of their princes, or for the magnificence of some general time of joy; accordingly the expenses of them were from the purse of the sovereign, or of the republic, as they are still practised at Venice, Rome, and at other places, at their carnivals. Savoy and Florence have often used them in their courts, at the weddings of their dukes; and at Turin particularly, was performed the *Pastor Fido*, written by the famous Guarini, which is a pastoral opera made to solemnize the marriage of a Duke of Savoy.[3] The prologue of it has given the design to all the French; which is a compliment to the sovereign power by some god or goddess; so that it looks no less than a kind of embassy from heaven to

---

3. Antonio Bertali (1605-69) had composed several intermezzi for a performance of Battista Guarini's pastoral play *Il pastor fido* (written in the 1580's).

earth. I said in the beginning of this preface that the persons represented in operas are generally gods, goddesses, and heroes descended from them, who are supposed to be their peculiar care; which hinders not but that meaner persons may sometimes gracefully be introduced, especially if they have relation to those first times, which poets call the Golden Age; wherein, by reason of their innocence, those happy mortals were supposed to have had a more familiar intercourse with superior beings; and therefore shepherds might reasonably be admitted, as of all callings the most innocent, the most happy, and who by reason of the spare time they had, in their almost idle employment, had most leisure to make verses, and to be in love; without somewhat of which passion no opera can possibly subsist.

It is almost needless to speak anything of that noble language in which this musical drama was first invented and performed. All who are conversant in the Italian cannot but observe that it is softest, the sweetest, the most harmonious, not only of any modern tongue, but even beyond any of the learned. It seems indeed to have been invented for the sake of Poetry and Music; the vowels are so abounding in all words, especially in terminations of them, that, excepting some few monosyllables, the whole language ends in them. Then the pronunciation is so manly, and so sonorous, that their very speaking has more of music in it than Dutch poetry and song. It has withal derived so much copiousness and eloquence from the Greek and Latin, in the composition of words and the formation of them, that if, after all, we must call it barbarous, 'tis the most beautiful and most learned of any barbarism in modern tongues; and we may at least as justly praise it, as Pyrrhus did the Roman discipline and martial order, that it was of barbarians (for so the Greeks called all other nations), but had nothing in it of barbarity. This language has in a manner been refined and purified from the Gothic ever since the time of Dante, which is above four hundred years ago; and the French, who now cast a longing eye to their country, are not less ambitious to possess their elegance in Poetry and Music; in both which they labour at impossibilities. 'Tis true, indeed, they have reformed their tongue, and brought both their prose and poetry to a standard; the sweetness, as well as the purity, is much improved, by throwing off the unnecessary consonants, which made their spelling tedious, and their pronunciation harsh; but, after all, as nothing can be improved beyond its own *species,* or farther than its original nature will allow; as an ill voice, though ever so thoroughly instructed in the rules of music, can never be brought to sing harmoniously, nor many an honest critic ever arrive to be a good poet; so neither can the natural harshness of the French, or their perpetual ill accent, be ever refined into perfect harmony like the Italian. The English has yet more natural disadvantages than the French; our original Teutonic, consisting most in monosyllables, and those encumbered with consonants, cannot possibly be freed from those inconveniences. The rest of our words, which are derived from the Latin chiefly, and the French, with some small sprinkling of Greek, Italian, and Spanish, are some relief in Poetry, and help us to soften our uncouth numbers; which, together with our English genius, incomparably beyond the trifling of the French, in all the nobler parts of verse, will justly give us the pre-eminence. But, on the other hand, the effeminacy of our pronunciation (a defect common to us and the Danes), and our scarcity of female rhymes, have left the advantage of musical composition for songs, though not for recitative, to our neighbours.

Through these difficulties I have made a shift to struggle in my part of the performance of this opera; which, as mean as it is, deserves at least a pardon, because it has attempted a discovery beyond any former undertaker of our nation; only remember, that if there be no North-East Passage to be found, the fault is in Nature, and not in me; or, as Ben Jonson tells us in *The Alchymist,* when projection had failed, and the glasses were all broken, there was enough, however, in the bottoms of them to cure the itch; so I may thus far be positive, that if I have not succeeded as I desire, yet there is somewhat still remaining to satisfy the curiosity, or itch of sight and hearing. Yet I have no great reason to despair; for I may, without vanity, own some advantages which are not common to every writer; such as are the knowledge of the Italian and French language, and the being conversant with some of their best performances in this kind; which have furnished me with such variety of measures, as have given the composer, Monsieur Grabut, what occasions he could wish to show his extraordinary talent in diversifying the recitative, the lyrical part, and the chorus; in all which, not to attribute anything to my own opinion, the best judges, and those too of the best quality, who have honoured his rehearsals with their presence, have no less commended the happiness of his genius than his skill. And let me have the liberty to add one thing, that he has so exactly expressed my sense in all places where I intended to move the passions that he seems to have entered into my thoughts and to have been the poet as well as the composer. This I say, not to flatter him, but to do him right; because amongst some English musicians, and their scholars, who are sure to judge after them, the imputation of being a Frenchman is enough to make a party who maliciously endeavor to decry him. But the knowledge of Latin and Italian poets, both which he possesses, besides his skill in music, and his being acquainted with all the performances of the French operas, adding to these the good sense to which he is born, have raised him to a degree above any man who shall pretend to be his rival upon our stage. When any of our countrymen excel him, I shall be glad, for the sake of old England, to be shown my error; in the meantime, let virtue be commended, though in the person of a stranger.

If I thought it convenient I could here discover some rules which I have given to myself in the writing of an opera in general, and of this opera in particular; but I consider that the effect would only be to have my own performance measured by the laws I gave; and, consequently, to set up some little judges, who, not understanding thoroughly, would be sure to fall upon the faults and not to acknowledge any of the beauties; an hard measure, which I have often found from false critics. Here, therefore, if they will criticize, they shall do it out of their own fond; but let them first be assured that their ears are nice; for there is neither writing nor judgment on this subject without that good quality. 'Tis no easy matter, in our language, to make words so smooth, and numbers so harmonious, that they shall almost set themselves. And yet there are rules for this in Nature, and as great a certainty of quantity in our syllables, as either in the Greek or Latin; but let poets and judges understand those first, and then let them begin to study English. When they have chawed a while upon these preliminaries, it may be they will scarce adventure to tax me with want of thought and elevation of fancy in this work; for they will soon be satisfied that those are not of the nature of this sort of writing. The necessity of double rhymes, and ordering of the words and numbers for the sweetness of the voice, are the main hinges on which an opera must move; and both of these are without the compass of any art to teach another to perform, unless Nature, in the first place, has done her part by enduing the poet with that nicety of hearing that the discord of sounds in words shall as much offend him as a seventh in music would a good composer. I have therefore no need to make excuses for meanness of thought in many places: the Italians, with all the advantages of their language, are continually forced upon it, or, rather, affect it. The chief secret is the choice of words; and, by this choice, I do not here mean elegancy of expression, but propriety of sound, to be varied according to the nature of the subject. Perhaps a time may come when I may treat of this more largely, out of some observations which I have made from Homer and Virgil, who, amongst all the poets, only understood the art of numbers, and of that which was properly called *rhythmus* by the ancients.

The same reasons which depress thought in an opera have a stronger effect upon the words, especially in our language; for there is no maintaining the purity of English in short measures, where the rhyme returns so quick, and is so often female, or double rhyme, which is not natural to our tongue, because it consists too much of monosyllables, and those, too, most commonly clogged with consonants; for which reason I am often forced to coin new words, revive some that are antiquated, and botch others; as if I had not served out my time in poetry, but was bound apprentice to some doggrel rhymer, who makes songs to tunes and sings them for a livelihood. It it true, I have not been often put to this drudgery; but where I have, the words will sufficiently show that I was then a slave to the composition, which I will never be again: it is my part to invent, and the musician's to humour that invention. I may be counselled, and will always follow my friend's advice where I find it reasonable; but will never part with the power of the militia.

I am now to acquaint my reader with somewhat more particular concerning this opera, after having begged his pardon for so long a preface to so short a work. It was originally intended only for a prologue to a play of the nature of *The Tempest;* which is a tragedy mixed with opera, or a drama, written in blank verse, adorned with scenes, machines, songs, and dances, so that the fable of it is all spoken and acted by the best of comedians; the other part of the entertainment to be performed by the same singers and dancers who were introduced in this present opera. It cannot be properly called a play, because the action of it is supposed to be conducted sometimes by supernatural means or magic; nor an opera, because the story of it is not sung. But more of this at its proper time. But some intervening accidents having hitherto deferred the performance of the main design, I proposed to the actors to turn the intended prologue into an entertainment by itself, as you now see it, by adding two acts more to what I had already written. The subject of it is wholly allegorical; and the allegory itself so very obvious that it will no sooner be read than understood. It is divided, according to the plain and natural method of every action, into three parts. For even Aristotle himself is contented to say simply that in all actions there is a beginning, a middle, and an end; after which model all the Spanish plays are built.

The descriptions of the scenes and other decorations of the stage I had from Mr. Betterton, who has spared neither for industry, nor cost, to make this entertainment perfect, nor for invention of the ornaments to beautify it.

To conclude, though the enemies of the composer are not few, and that there is a party formed against him of his own profession, I hope, and am persuaded, that this prejudice will turn in the end to his advantage. For the greatest part of an audience is always uninterested, though seldom knowing; and if the music be well composed and well performed, they who find themselves pleased will be so wise as not to be imposed upon and fooled out of their satisfaction. The newness of the undertaking is all the hazard. When operas were first set up in France they were not followed over eagerly; but they gained daily upon their hearers, till they grew to that height of reputation which they now enjoy. The English, I confess, are not altogether so musical as the French; and yet they have been pleased already with *The Tempest*, and some pieces that followed, which were neither much better written nor so well composed as this. If it finds encouragement, I dare promise myself to mend my hand by making a more pleasing fable. In the meantime, every loyal Englishman cannot but be satisfied with the moral of this, which so plainly represents the double restoration of His Sacred Majesty.

Reprinted from John Dryden, *Dramatic Poesy and Other Essays* (London: J. M. Dent; New York: E. P. Dutton, 1912).

JOSEPH ADDISON (1672-1719)

OPERA "after the Italian manner" was introduced into England in 1705, thirty years after the first French operas had reached that country and fifteen years after the première of Purcell's *Dido and Aeneas* at Josias Priest's boarding school for young ladies in Chelsea. Before Handel's arrival in London—which occurred in 1710—close to a dozen Italian operas were staged in that city, the first one being a work called *Arsinoe, Queen of Cyprus* and originally performed in Bologna with music by Franceschini. Immediately, a heated controversy began to rage, and the writers of the day at length discussed the pros and cons of melodramas like *Camilla, Thomyris, Pyrrhus and Demetrius, Clotilda, Almahide, Hydaspes,* and *Etearco*. Pamphlets were issued, and the two leading weeklies, Richard Steele's *The Tatler* (1709-11) and Joseph Addison's *The Spectator* (1710-12), contributed their share. The attacks grew increasingly violent as the managers became less inclined to have the Italian librettos translated into English. The recitatives of *Pyrrhus and Demetrius* were sung in Italian, and *Almahide* (1710) was the first wholly Italian production. The tide could not be stemmed by Addison's and Thomas Clayton's English opera *Rosamond*, which was unsuccessfully given in 1707. Thanks to the genius and ceaseless effort on its behalf by George Frederic Handel, opera in the Italian manner survived for another twenty years, until Gay's *Beggar's Opera* swept it off the stage.

As for Addison's musical criticism, it is far from being professional or technical. In the words of E. Betz, "For the authors of the *Spectator* papers opera was not, like the drama, a thing to be analyzed and discussed according to a well-known, recognized tradition, but rather a popular institution, a social phenomenon within the scope of any intelligent gentleman's judgment and condemnation."

A. Nicoll, "Italian Opera in England: The First Five Years," *Anglia*, XLVI (1922), 257-281; E. Betz, "The Operatic Criticism of the *Tatler* and the *Spectator*," *Musical Quarterly*, XXXI (1945), 318-330.

The Spectator
JOSEPH ADDISON

No. 18, March 21, 1710:

It is my design in this paper to deliver down to posterity a faithful account of the Italian opera, and the gradual progress which it has made upon the English stage; for there is no question but our great grand-children will be very curious to know the reason why their forefathers used to sit together like an audience of foreigners in their own country, and to hear whole plays acted before them, in a tongue which they did not understand.

Arsinoe was the first opera that gave us a taste of Italian music. The great success this opera met with produced some attempts of forming pieces upon Italian plans, which should give a more natural and reasonable entertainment than what can be met with in the elaborate trifles of that nation. This alarmed the poetasters and fiddlers of the town, who were used to deal in a more ordinary kind of ware; and therefore laid down an established rule, which is received as such to this day, "That nothing is capable of being well set to music, that is not nonsense."

This maxim was no sooner received, but we immediately fell

to translating the Italian operas; and as there was no great danger of hurting the sense of those extraordinary pieces, our authors would often make words of their own which were entirely foreign to the meaning of the passages they pretended to translate; their chief care being to make the numbers of the English verse answer to those of the Italian, that both of them might go to the same tune. Thus the famous song in *Camilla*[1] "Barbara si t'intendo" ("Barbarous woman, yes, I know your meaning") which expresses the resentments of an angry lover, was translated into that English lamentation "Frail are a lover's hopes." And it was pleasant enough to see the most refined persons of the British nation dying away and languishing to notes that were filled with a spirit of rage and indignation. It happened also very frequently, where the sense was rightly translated, the necessary transposition of words, which were drawn out of the phrase of one tongue into that of another, made the music appear very absurd in one tongue that was very natural in the other. I remember an Italian verse that ran thus, word for word: "And turn'd my rage into pity," which the English for the rhyme sake translated "And into pity turn'd my rage." By this means the soft notes that were adapted to pity in the Italian, fell upon the word rage in the English; and the angry sounds that were turned to rage in the original, were made to express pity in the translation. It oftentimes happened likewise, that the finest notes in the air fell upon the most insignificant words in the sentence. I have known the word "and" pursued through the whole gamut, have been entertained with many a melodious "the," and have heard the most beautiful graces, quavers, and divisions bestowed upon "then," "for," and "from"; to the eternal honour of our English particles.

The next step to our refinement was the introduction of Italian actors into our opera; who sung their parts in their own language, at the same time that our countrymen performed theirs in our native tongue. The king or hero of the play generally spoke in Italian, and his slaves answered him in English. The lover frequently made his court, and gained the heart of his princess, in

---

1. Antonio Maria Bononcini's *Camilla, regina de' Volsci* was first performed in Naples in 1696. It was brought to London in 1706.

a language which she did not understand. One would have thought it very difficult to have carried on dialogues after this manner without an interpreter between the persons that conversed together; but this was the state of the English stage for about three years.

At length the audience grew tired of understanding half the opera; and therefore, to ease themselves entirely of the fatigue of thinking, have so ordered it at present, that the whole opera is performed in an unknown tongue. We no longer understand the language of our own stage; insomuch that I have often been afraid, when I have seen our Italian performers chattering in the vehemence of action, that they have been calling us names, and abusing us among themselves. But I hope, since we put such an entire confidence in them, they will not talk against us before our faces, though they may do it with the same safety as if it were behind our backs. In the mean time, I cannot forbear thinking how naturally an historian who writes two or three hundred years hence, and does not know the taste of his wise forefathers, will make the following reflections: "In the beginning of the eighteenth century, the Italian tongue was so well understood in England, that operas were acted on the public stage in that language."

One scarce knows how to be serious in the confutation of an absurdity that shows itself at first sight. It does not want any great measure of sense to see the ridicule of this monstrous practice; but what makes it the more astonishing, it is not the taste of the rabble, but of persons of the greatest politeness, which has established it.

If the Italians have a genius for music above the English, the English have a genius for other performances of a much higher nature, and capable of giving the mind a much nobler entertainment. Would one think it was possible (at a time when an author lived that was able to write the *Phaedra and Hippolitus*) for a people to be so stupidly fond of the Italian opera, as scarce to give a third day's hearing to that admirable tragedy? Music is certainly a very agreeable entertainment; but if it would take the entire possession of our ears, if it would make us incapable of hearing sense, if it would exclude arts that have a much greater tendency to the refinement of human nature; I must confess I would allow it no better quarter than Plato has done, who banishes it out of his commonwealth.

At present our notions of music are so very uncertain, that we do not know what it is we like; only, in general, we are transported with anything that is not English; so it be of a foreign growth, let it be Italian, French, or High Dutch, it is the same thing. In short, our English music is quite rooted out, and nothing yet planted in its stead.

When a royal palace is burnt to the ground, every man is at liberty to present his plan for a new one; and though it be but indifferently put together, it may furnish several hints that may be of use to a good architect. I shall take the same liberty in a following paper, of giving my opinion upon the subject of music; which I shall lay down only in a problematical manner, as to be considered by those who are masters in the art.

No. 29, April 3, 1710:

There is nothing that has more startled our English audience, than the Italian *Recitativo* at its first entrance upon the stage. People were wonderfully surprised to hear generals singing the word of command, and ladies delivering messages in music. Our countrymen could not forbear laughing when they heard a lover chanting out a billet-doux, and even the superscription of a letter set to a tune. The famous blunder in an old play of "Enter a king and two fiddlers solus," was now no longer an absurdity; when it was impossible for a hero in a desert, or a princess in her closet, to speak anything unaccompanied with musical instruments.

But however this Italian method of acting in recitativo might appear at first hearing, I cannot but think it much more just than that which prevailed in our English opera before this innovation: the transition from an air to recitative music being more natural, than the passing from a song to plain and ordinary speaking, which was the common method in Purcell's operas.

The only fault I find in our present practice is the making use of the Italian recitativo with English words.

To go to the bottom of this matter I must observe, that the

tone, or (as the French call it) the accent of every nation in their ordinary speech is altogether different from that of every other people; as we may see even in the Welsh and Scotch who border so near upon us. By the tone or accent I do not mean the pronunciation of each particular word, but the sound of the whole sentence. Thus it is very common for an English gentleman when he hears a French tragedy, to complain that the actors all of them speak in a tone: and therefore he very wisely prefers his own countrymen, not considering that a foreigner complains of the same tone in an English actor.

For this reason, the recitative music, in every language, should be as different as the tone or accent of each language; for otherwise, what may properly express a passion in one language will not do it in another. Every one who has been long in Italy knows very well, that the cadences in the recitativo bear a remote affinity to the tone of their voices in ordinary conversation, or to speak more properly, are only the accents of their language made more musical and tuneful.

Thus the notes of interrogation, or admiration, in the Italian music (if one may so call them) which resemble their accents in discourse on such occasions, are not unlike the ordinary tones of an English voice when we are angry; insomuch that I have often seen our audiences extremely mistaken as to what has been doing upon the stage, and expecting to see the hero knock down his messenger, when he has been asking him a question; or fancying that he quarrels with his friend, when he only bids him good-morrow.

For this reason the Italian artist cannot agree with our English musicians in admiring Purcell's compositions, and thinking his tunes so wonderfully adapted to his words; because both nations do not always express the same passions by the same sounds.

I am therefore humbly of opinion, that an English composer should not follow the Italian recitative too servilely, but make use of many gentle deviations from it, in compliance with his own native language. He may copy out of it all the lulling softness and "dying falls" (as Shakespeare calls them),[2] but should still remember that he ought to accommodate himself to an

2. See the Duke's speech in the first scene of *Twelfth Night.*

English audience; and by humouring the tone of our voices in ordinary conversation, have the same regard to the accent of his own language, as those persons had to theirs whom he professes to imitate. It is observed, that several of the singing birds of our own country learn to sweeten their voices and mellow the harshness of their natural notes, by practising under those that come off from warmer climates. In the same manner I would allow the Italian opera to lend our English music as much as may grace and soften it, but never entirely to annihilate and destroy it. Let the infusion be as strong as you please, but still let the subject matter of it be English.

A composer should fit his music to the genius of the people, and consider that the delicacy of hearing, and taste of harmony, has been formed upon those sounds which every country abounds with. In short, that music is of a relative nature, and what is harmony to one ear, may be dissonance to another.

The same observations which I have made upon the recitative part of music may be applied to all our songs and airs in general.

Signior Baptist Lully acted like a man of sense in this particular. He found the French music extremely defective, and very often barbarous. However, knowing the genius of the people, the humour of their language, and the prejudiced ears he had to deal with, he did not pretend to extirpate the French music, and plant the Italian in its stead; but only to cultivate and civilize it with innumerable graces and modulations which he borrowed from the Italians. By this means the French music is now perfect in its kind; and when you say it is not so good as the Italian, you only mean that it does not please you so well; for there is scarce a Frenchman who would not wonder to hear you give the Italian such a preference. The music of the French is indeed very properly adapted to their pronunciation and accent, as their whole opera wonderfully favours the genius of such a gay airy people. The chorus in which that opera abounds, gives the parterre frequent opportunities of joining in concert with the stage. This inclination of the audience to sing along with the actors, so prevails with them, that I have sometimes known the performer on the stage do no more in a celebrated song, than the clerk of a parish church, who serves only to raise the psalm, and is afterwards drowned in the music of the congregation. Every actor that comes on the stage is a beau. The queens and heroines are so painted, that they appear as ruddy and cherry-cheeked as milk-maids. The shepherds are all embroidered, and acquit themselves in a ball better than our English dancing-masters. I have seen a couple of rivers appear in red stockings; and Alpheus, instead of having his head covered with sedge and bullrushes, making love in a full-bottomed periwig, and a plume of feathers; but with a voice so full of shakes and quavers, that I should have thought the murmurs of a country brook the much more agreeable music.

I remember the last opera I saw in that merry nation was the *Rape of Proserpine*,[3] where Pluto, to make the more tempting figure, puts himself in a French equipage, and brings Ascalaphus along with him as his valet de chambre. This is what we call folly and impertinence; but what the French look upon as gay and polite.

I shall add no more to what I have here offered, than that music, architecture, and painting, as well as poetry, and oratory, are to deduce their laws and rules from the general sense and taste of mankind, and not from the principles of those arts themselves; or in other words, the taste is not to conform to the art, but the art to the taste. Music is not designed to please only chromatic ears, but all that are capable of distinguishing harsh from disagreeable notes. A man of an ordinary ear is a judge whether a passion is expressed in proper sounds, and whether the melody of those sounds be more or less pleasing.

From Joseph Addison, *Works*, edited by R. Hurd (London: Bell, 1888), II, 268-271; 288-291.

NICOLAS BOILEAU-DESPREAUX
(*1636-1717*)

NICOLAS BOILEAU-DESPREAUX, the most ardent champion of French classicism and bosom friend of Racine, Molière, and La Fontaine, (whom Giraudoux introduced as drinking companions in the

---

3. Probably Lully/Quinault's *Proserpine*, which was first staged in 1680.

original version of Act I of his *Madwoman of Chaillot*), was opposed to opera in principle because "music can neither tell a story nor paint the passions in their full scope, and it is frequently impossible to set to music the most sublime and grandiloquent passages." He rejected it also on moral grounds, and in his tenth Satire—which is directed against women—severely censured "the clichés of wanton morals which Lully rehashed in his music" (*Et tous ces lieux communs de morale lubrique,/Que Lully rechauffa des sons de sa musique*). However, when, in 1677, after the total failure of his opera *Isis*, Lully temporarily dismissed Quinault as his collaborator, Racine, Boileau, and Thomas Corneille were asked to fill the gap. Thomas Corneille furnished the texts for the operas *Psyché* and *Bellérophon* (in which latter Boileau is also said to have had a hand), performed in 1678 and 1679 respectively. Racine set to work on a libretto concerned with the myth of Phaëton's fall, and asked Boileau to lend him a helping hand. Reluctant as Racine and Boileau were, they did not proceed very far with the project. In 1679 Quinault succeeded in regaining the favor of Louis XIV and was promptly reinstalled as the regime's official librettist. *Phaëton*, with his libretto, was performed at Versailles in January, 1683.

Fragment of a Prologue to an Opera (1713)

NICOLAS BOILEAU-DESPREAUX

MADAME DE M. AND MADAME DE T., her sister, tired of the operas of Mr. Quinault, asked the king to have Racine write a libretto. Racine, in expressing his desire to grant their wish, momentarily forgot something on which he had repeatedly agreed with me, namely that one can never make a good opera. For music can neither tell a story nor paint the passions in their full scope, and it is frequently impossible to set to music the most sublime and grandiloquent passages. I reminded him of this when he told of his promise. He admitted that I was right; but he had already gone too far to stop. He actually began writing a libretto, whose subject was the fall of Phaëton. He even composed a number of verses, which he recited to the king, whom they seemed to please. But since Mr. Racine undertook this work only reluctantly, he told me frankly that he would never be able to finish it unless I collaborated with him. In particular he asked me to write a prologue. Although I told him how little talent I possessed for that kind of thing and that I had never before written flippant love poetry, he persisted and told me that he would let the king order me to comply with his wishes. I began to think, then, of what I would be able to do in this line if I should be forced to collaborate in the making of a work so contrary to my talent and my inclinations. By way of exercise I prepared the sketch of a prologue without mentioning this to anybody (not even to Mr. Racine); and I wrote the opening scene. The subject of that scene was a dispute between poetry and music concerning the excellence of these arts. At the conclusion of the scene, the two were about to part ways when suddenly the goddess of agreements, i.e. Harmony, descended from the sky, with all her charms and graces, and reconciled the opponents. She was subsequently to explain why she had come to earth, namely because she wanted to entertain the prince worthiest of being served and to whom she owed the most, since it was he who supported her in France, where she reigned in all things. She then added that, in order to prevent any foolhardy individual, by rebelling against so great a prince, from diminishing the fame which she enjoyed together with him, she wanted on that very day a dramatization of the fall of Phaëton to be presented on the stage. Immediately, all the poets and composers retired upon her command in order to get things ready. This, then, was the subject of my prologue, on which I worked rather disdainfully for approximately three or four days, while Racine, on his part, continued with equal disdain to work out the plan of his opera, which I helped him design. We were engaged in this miserable task, of which I don't know how we would have acquitted ourselves, when suddenly a lucky incident restored our peace of mind. Mr. Quinault having appeared before the king in tears and having told him how great would be the offense given to him if he were no longer to work for the king's entertainment, His Majesty, pitying him, told the above-mentioned ladies that he could not bring himself to do him that tort. Thus Apollo came to our aid. Mr. Racine and I then returned to our former occupations; and the opera—of which Racine had written no more than a handful of verses, which were not found among his literary remains, since he probably destroyed them in view of the fact that they dealt with love—was no longer mentioned. As for me, since there was no question of such a subject in the scene which I had composed, I not only thought it unnecessary to suppress the latter but herewith offer it to the public. I am confident that it will give pleasure to the readers, who might be interested in how I would go about sweetening the gall and vigor of my satirical poetry in accordance with the gentler style. This they can judge by the following fragment, which I present all the more confidently since, being short, if it does not entertain them, it at least will not leave them time enough to get bored.

Translated by Ulrich Weisstein from Boileau's *Oeuvres*, edited by Ch. Gidel (Paris: Garnier, n. d.).

BENEDETTO MARCELLO (1686-1739)

IN CONTRAST with Rome and Florence, where opera long remained a courtly affair, Venice was the first Italian city in which a public opera house was erected. The opening of this theater took place in 1637; and nearly four hundred operas are said to have been performed in that city by the end of the seventeenth century. One of the first contributors to the repertory was Claudio Monteverdi, whose *Ritorno d'Ulisse* and *L'incoronazione di Poppea* were performed in the city of St. Mark in 1641 and 1642 respectively. Subsequently the operatic scene was dominated by his pupil Cavalli and, one generation later, by Marc Antonio Cesti, the composer of the famous *Pomo d'Oro*, commissioned on the occasion of the marriage between Emperor Leopold I of Austria and the Infanta Margherita of Spain in 1667. Benedetto Marcello, the author of the *Teatro alla moda*, a witty satire upon operatic abuses in the early eighteenth century, was a native of Venice who rose relatively early to the high civic position of member of the Council of the Forty. To posterity he is mainly known as a composer of church and chamber music, his major work being a setting of fifty psalms, the *Estro poetico-armonico* of 1724-26. The *Teatro alla moda*— the aptness of whose irony is proved by the experiences Handel underwent during these very years in London—is broken up into numerous sections in which, one by one, the librettists, composers, singers, impresarios, dancers, prompters, copyists, and singing teachers are singled out for ridicule. The satire is partly addressed to Antonio Vivaldi, another famous Venetian writer of operas, who had just set himself up as his own impresario.

R. G. Pauly, "Benedetto Marcello's Satire on Early 18th-century Opera," *Musical Quarterly*, XXXIV (1948), 222-233.

Il teatro alla moda (1720)
BENEDETTO MARCELLO

Instructions for Librettists:

A writer of operatic librettos, if he wants to be modern, must never have read the Greek and Latin classic authors, nor should he do so in the future. After all, the old Greeks and Romans never read the modern writers.

Nor should he have the slightest knowledge of Italian meter and verse. All he might possibly admit is that he "had heard somewhere" that verses should consist of seven or eleven syllables. This will suffice, and now he can suit his fancy by making verses having three, five, nine, thirteen, or even fifteen syllables.

He should brag, however, that he has had thorough schooling in mathematics, painting, chemistry, medicine, law, etc., and then he should confess that his genius compelled him with such force that he just *had* to become a poet. Yet he need not have the slightest acquaintance with the various rules concerning correct accentuation or the making of good rhymes. He need not have any command of poetical language, and mythology and history can be closed books to him. To make up for this he will employ in his works as frequently as possible technical terms from the above-named sciences, or from some others, though they may have no relation whatsoever to the world of Poetry. He should call Dante, Petrarch, and Ariosto obscure, clumsy, and dull poets whose works, for that reason, should never, or only very seldom, be used as examples. Instead the modern librettist should acquire a large collection of contemporary writings; from these he should borrow sentiments, thoughts, and entire verses. This sort of theft he should refer to as "laudable imitation."

Before the librettist begins writing he should ask the impresario for a detailed list giving the number and kind of stage sets and decorations he wishes to see employed. He will then incorporate all those into his drama. He should always be on the lookout for elaborate scenes such as sacrifices, sumptuous banquets, apparitions, or other spectacles. When those are to occur in the opera the librettist will consult with the theater engineer in order to find out how many dialogues, monologues, and arias will be needed to stretch each scene of that type, so that all technical problems can be worked out without hurrying. The disintegration of the drama as an entity and the intense boredom of the audience are of no importance in connection with all this.

He should write the whole opera without any preconceived plan but rather proceed verse by verse. For if the audience never understands the plot their attentiveness to the very end of the opera will be insured. One thing any able modern librettist must strive for is frequently to have all characters of the piece on the stage at the same time, though nobody knows why. They then may leave the stage, one by one, singing the usual canzonetta.

The librettist should not worry about the ability of the performers, but so much more about whether the impresario has at his disposal a good bear or lion, an able nightingale, genuine-looking bolts of lightning, earthquakes, storms, etc.

For the finale of his opera he should write a magnificent scene with most elaborate effects, so that the audience won't run off before the work is half over. He should finish the opera with the customary chorus in praise of the sun, moon, or impresario. . . .

It is extremely useful for the modern librettist to include a note to the reader in which he points out that he wrote this opera back in the days of his earliest youth. He might add that it took him only a few days to write the opera—though actually he labored over it for years—for in that way he will prove that he is truly modern and no longer following the ancient maxim *Nonumque prematur in annum* (let him hold it back for nine years). At this point he might well add that he writes "only for his own amusement," as a relief from more serious work. He never dreamed of having his work published: only the urging of his friends and the wishes of his superiors caused him to do so—certainly not any desire for praise, or any financial considerations. Moreover, "the renowned talent of the composer and the skill of the extras and the theater bear will cover up the libretto's deficiencies."

When he sets down the outline of his work in a preface, the librettist should embark on a lengthy discourse on the rules of tragedy and the art of poetry, quoting heavily from Sophocles, Euripides, Aristotle, and Horace. He should not fail to add that any truly modern poet is constrained to abandon all the salient rules in order to please the taste of a decadent century, the licentiousness of the theater, the extravagance of the conductors, the presumption of the singers, and the whims of the trained bear and the extras.

Still, he must not neglect the customary explanation of the three most important aspects of any drama, namely unity of place, time, and action. Thus he might give the place as THIS OR THAT THEATER, the time as FROM SEVEN TO ELEVEN O'CLOCK AT NIGHT, and the action as THE RUIN OF THE IMPRESARIO.

The libretto's subject matter need not be historically true. As a matter of fact, since all the Greek and Roman subjects have been treated by the writers of those nations as well as by the choicest writers of the Golden Age of Italian literature, the modern librettist is faced with the task of inventing a fable and adding to it all kinds of oracles, realistic shipwreck scenes, ominous prophecies gathered by examining the flesh of a roasted animal, etc. All that is needed is to have an historical name or two on the public announcement of the work, the rest can then be freely invented and the only further thing that matters is that the number of verses must not exceed twelve hundred, arias included. To increase the opera's popularity, the modern librettist will describe in the title one of the work's principal scenes, instead of using the name of one of the characters. For instance, instead of calling it *Amadis,*[1] *Bovo,* or *Berta al Campo,* he will name it *The Generous Ingratitude, The Funerals out of Revenge, The Bear in the Bark,* and the like.

Real life is imparted to the opera by the use of prisons, daggers, poison, the writing of letters on stage, bear and wild bull hunts, earthquakes, storms, sacrifices, the settling of accounts, and mad scenes. The audience will be deeply moved by unexpected events of, that kind. If it should furthermore be possible to introduce a scene in which some actors sit down and doze off while an attempt on their lives is being made (which they conveniently thwart by waking up in time), then one would have created something so extremely admirable as has never before been viewed on the Italian stage.

The modern librettist need not worry about his literary style. He must keep in mind that his work is to be heard and understood by the crowd of common people. To render it more easily intelligible he should omit the usual articles (in front of nouns), but employ instead unusual and long phrases, and he should include an abundance of flowery language in any recitative or canzonetta.

The librettist then must have at hand a supply of old operas (by some other writer) from which he will borrow the plot as well as the stage sets. All he has to change is the meter and the names of some of the characters. He can achieve similar results by translating dramas from the French, by changing prose to verse or tragedies into comedies, adding or omitting characters according to the requirements of the impresario.

Once he has decided to write on opera he should let nothing stand in his way. If his ingenuity deserts him completely he will enlist the help of some other writer and borrow a plot from him. He will then put it into verse, and both will sign a pact that they will share equally the income derived from the dedication and from the sale of the printed libretto.

---

1. Quinault and Lully produced an *Amadis* in 1684.

One rule of prime importance is never to let a character make his exit before he has sung the usual canzonetta. This is especially appropriate if it immediately precedes that person's execution, suicide, or taking of poison.

The poet must never read the entire work to the impresario. Instead he should only show him fragments of a few scenes, but he should recite over and over again the scenes containing the poisoning, the sacrifices, the divans, the bear, the dozing off in the garden, and the reckoning scene, and he should swear that if *those* did not bring the house down he would never write another line.

A good modern librettist should be careful not to acquire any knowledge about music even though the poets of antiquity were well acquainted with it, as is related by Strabo, Pliny, and Plutarch. They make no distinction between a poet and a musician but mention a good many artists . . . who were masters in both fields.

The aria must in no way be related to the preceding recitative but it should be full of such things as sweet little butterflies, bouquets, nightingales, quails, little boats, little huts, jasmine, violets, copper basins, little pots, tigers, lions, whales, crabs, turkeys, cold capon, etc. Thus the poet will demonstrate to the world his proficiency as a natural scientist who, by his well-chosen similes, shows off his knowledge of animals, plants, flowers, etc.

Before the opera is staged the librettist should praise the music and the singers, the impresario, the orchestra, and the extras. Then, if the work should turn out to be a failure, he should start a tirade against the singers whose performance did not at all do justice to his intentions and who thought of nothing but their notes. He should censure the composer for failing to understand the dramatic force of the scenes since he paid attention to nothing but his arias, the impresario for being a miser who spent nothing on beautiful scenery and props, and the orchestra players and extras for being continually drunk. He should furthermore protest that his dramatic intentions were disregarded altogether, and that he was given direct orders by the management, the ever-dissatisfied prima donna, and the theater bear to cut out some passages and to add others. He should announce that he will insist on publication of the original version, not of that altogether disfigured present one which he can hardly recognize as his own. If anyone should have any doubts about this, let him ask the chambermaid or washwoman at his house: they were the first ones to read the work and to give a critical evaluation of the same.

During the rehearsals he must not reveal any of his dramatic intentions to the actors since he rightly assumes that they will do as they please anyway.

If the work should be such that certain characters have little to do or to sing he should immediately comply with the requests of these singers (or of their rich patrons) to add to their parts. He should always keep at hand a supply of a few hundred arias, in case alterations or additions should be wanted. He should not fail to insert many verses which can be omitted, indicating those by quotation marks.

If the plot should require husband and wife to be put into prison together, and if one of them should have to die, it is absolutely necessary to have the other one stay alive so that he or she can sing an aria of a merry character. This will cheer up everyone in the audience as it will make them realize that, after all, it is all only make-believe.

If two persons should be engaged in love-making, plotting, or conspiring, the presence of pages and extras is always required.

If a letter is to be written, a change of scenery seems called for. A writing table and a chair should be carried on the stage and after the letter has been written should be removed immediately, so that the belief cannot arise that the table might be standing in its usual place. The same applies to thrones, armchairs, canopies, and grasscovered "natural" seats.

In royal palaces he should provide for a ballet of the gardeners and in the countryside for a dance of the courtiers. . . .

The librettist might notice that the singers pronounce their words indistinctly, in which case he must not correct them. If the virtuosos should see their mistake and enunciate clearly the sale of the libretto might be seriously impaired.

If some of the actors should ask him from where they are to

go on the stage and in which direction they should make their exit, or if they have questions about acting or costumes he will tell them to do all of these things in any way they have a mind to.

The composer might express a dislike for the meter in some of the arias, in which case the librettist must change it at once. To suit the composer's fancy he might also add a breeze, storms, fog, southern, eastern, and northern winds.

A good number of the arias should be so long that it will be impossible to remember the opening bars by the time the middle has been reached.

There should be no more than six roles in the opera, and two or three of the six ought to be so unimportant that they can be left out if necessary, without any harm to the plot.

The parts of the father and of the tyrant—assuming that they are principal parts—must be given to castrati, and the bass and tenor parts should be left to such characters as captains of the guard, friends of the king, shepherds, messengers, etc.

Librettists who do not enjoy great fame or credit will make a living during the rest of the year, when the opera season is over, by taking care of legal matters, administrative affairs, by supervising other people's business, by copying parts and proof-reading, and by trying to ruin each other's reputations.

The librettist should ask the manager for a box and sublet half of its seats many months before the season begins, but especially for all first performances. The remaining half of the box he should fill with his friends whom he will smuggle in somehow, without their having to pay the customary fee at the door.

The librettist should pay frequent social calls to the prima donna, since the success of the opera generally depends on her. He should change his drama as her artistic genius may order him to do, making additions or cuts in her part or that of the bear or other persons. But he must be on his guard not to reveal to her anything about the opera's plot—the modern virtuosa is not supposed to know anything about that. He might possibly inform her most gracious mother, her father, brother, or patron, but the greatest secrecy must be used.

He should also visit the *maestro di cappella,* read him the libretto several times and point out to him where the recitative has to go slowly and where rapidly or *appassionato,* since the modern composer must not be bothered with such decisions. He will then urge him to include in the arias short *ritornelli* and embellishments (and, above all, many word repetitions) since all these add so much to the enjoyment of his work. Finally, he must pay his respects to the orchestra, to the tailors, to the theater bear, the errand boys, and to the extras, recommending his opera to their kindness.

Reprinted from R. G. Pauly, "Benedetto Marcello's Satire on Early 18th-Century Opera"; *Musical Quarterly,* XXXIV (1948), by permission of the publisher, G. Schirmer, Inc.

GEORGE FREDERIC HANDEL
(1685-1759)

AFTER FOUR YEARS of musical training in his native Halle, George Frederic Handel, the son of a barber-surgeon, was made first an assistant organist and then an organist at the *Domkirche* of that central German city. In 1703 he went to Hamburg, where he played in the orchestra of the opera directed by Reinhard Keiser. In Hamburg, his first two Italian operas, *Almira* and *Nero,* were performed. In 1706 Handel traveled to Italy, whence he returned four years later to become *Kapellmeister* at the court of the Duke of Hanover. However, shortly after his appointment he went to London on a leave of absence. His first English opera, *Rinaldo,* was staged in 1711. Beginning in 1712, Handel resided permanently in England. In the following three decades he was to write approximately thirty-five operas for the London stage. In 1719 he helped to found the Royal Academy of Music, which had the express purpose of cultivating opera "in the Italian manner." In performing this task he was assisted by his librettists Haym and Rolli. The deathblow to this Academy was dealt by the triumph of John Gay's *Beggar's Opera,* a parody of the Handelian style that had its première in June, 1728. With constantly waning success, Handel continued to present his type of opera for still another decade, but around 1740 he began to devote himself more and more exclusively to the writing of oratorios (the most famous one, *The Messiah*, dating from 1742).

None of Handel's operas now occupy a permanent place in the repertory, although Oscar Fritz Hagen initiated a Handel Renaissance in the 1920's and a number of works are intermittently revived to display the voice of some prima donna. The reason for their failure to grip modern audiences is largely that the librettos are static—they are little more than gems of arias and ensembles loosely strung together. Handel's awkward position with regard to his audience and his soloists is reflected in the following letter, which the Modenese representative at the English court, Giuseppe Riva, dispatched to the famous historian Ludovico Antonio Muratori, who had asked him whether he could get a commission for a young friend to write a libretto for the Haymarket Theatre.

O. E. Deutsch, *Handel- A Documentary Biography* (New York: Norton, 1955); R. A. Streatfeild, "Handel, Rolli, and Italian Opera in London in the Eighteenth Century," *Musical Quarterly*, III (1917), 428-445; F. Rogers, "Handel and Five Prima Donnas," *Musical Quarterly*, XXIX (1943), 214-224.

Letter to Ludovico Antonio Muratori (1725)
GIUSEPPE RIVA

THE OPERAS which are given in England, however fine as music, and however well sung, are nevertheless ruined by their poetry. Our friend Rolli, who, when the present Academy was formed, was commissioned to write the librettos, began by producing two very good ones, but he then quarreled with the directors, and they then took into their employment a certain Haym, a Roman violoncellist, a man who was little short of an idiot as far as literature was concerned. Deserting the orchestra for the slopes of Parnassus, he has for the last three years employed himself in adapting a number of old librettos for the use of the composers who write operas for the English stage, making still worse what was bad before. Our friend Bononcino, however, has been an exception. He has got his librettos from Rome, where they were written by certain pupils of Gravina. If your friend thinks of sending a specimen of his work here, I must warn him that in England people like very few recitatives, thirty airs, and one duet at least distributed over the three acts. The subject must be simple, tender, heroic—Roman, Greek, or possibly Persian, but never Gothic or Lombard. For this year and for the next two there must be two equal parts for Cuzzoni[1] and Faustina.[2] Senesino[3] takes the principal male characters, and his part must be heroic. The other three male parts should be arranged proportionately song for song in the three acts. The duet should be at the end of the second act and entrusted to the two women. If the subject demands three women, a third woman may be employed, as there is a third singer here to take part. If the Duchess of Marlborough, who gives 500 Pounds a year to Bononcini, will allow him to give the Academy an opera, it will be *Andromaca*, which is almost a translation of Racine's drama, omitting the death of Puppens, cleverly turned into an opera libretto. From it your friend can get an idea of the sort of opera that is popular in England.

Reprinted from R. A. Streatfeild, "Handel, Rolli and Italian Opera," *Musical Quarterly*, III (1917), by permission of the publisher, G. Schirmer, Inc.

JEAN-PHILIPPE RAMEAU (1683-1764)

JEAN-PHILIPPE RAMEAU, whose father was a church organist at Dijon, began his musical training in his early youth. In 1699 he was sent to Italy in order to continue his musical studies. He returned to France in 1702 and was an organist first at Avignon

1. Francesca Cuzzoni (1700-70), famous Italian soprano, in London since 1723.
2. Faustina Bordoni (1700-81), renowned singer and wife of the composer Hasse.
3. Stage name of the Italian castrato Francesco Bernardi (1680-17 ?), in London since 1720.

and then at Clermont-Ferrand, where he remained until 1705. In that year he went to Paris, where he composed a number of pieces for the harpsichord. He lived in Dijon from 1708 to 1714, and in Clermont-Ferrand from 1715 to 1721. It was in the latter town that he wrote the first of his influential and very important theoretical treatises, the *Traité de l'harmonie*, which was published in Paris, where he settled down permanently in 1722.

In 1723 he embarked on his long career as an operatic composer, in the course of which he wrote approximately thirty-five works for the lyrical stage. As the letter here included indicates, success did not come easy: only in the mid-thirties, with such pieces as *Les Indes galantes* and *Castor et Pollux*, did Rameau begin to gain a modicum of popularity. In 1745, with the production of *La Princesse de Navarre*, for which Voltaire had supplied the libretto, he finally became a national figure.

His position was unshaken until 1752, when the arrival of an Italian troupe led to the outbreak of the so-called *guerre des bouffons*,[1] in which Rameau was attacked by Rousseau and his fellow-Encyclopedists for having exalted harmony at the expense of melody. Rousseau had an axe to grind with Rameau, who had severely criticized his articles on musical subjects in the *Encyclopédie*. Although Rameau's position was essentially unshaken, he (whose principal collaborators had been Cahusac in the forties and Marmontel in the fifties) practically ceased to compose for the operatic stage. It was only in the twentieth century that Rameau's music, along with that of Lully and Couperin, was resurrected from near-oblivion, and even today performances of his operas are rare.

P.-M. Masson, *L'opéra de Rameau* (Paris: Laurens, 1930); J. Tiersot, "Rameau," *Musical Quarterly*, XIV (1928), 77-107; E. Kisch, "Rameau and Rousseau," *Music & Letters*, XXII (1941), 97-114.

1. Name given to the famous controversy between the friends and foes of *opera buffa* in Paris (1752-1754). Originating in Naples, the *opera buffa*, a typically Italian form of comic opera, grew out of the interludes *(intermezzi)* performed between the acts of *opera seria*. Perhaps the most famous *intermezzo* is Pergolesi's *La serva padrona* of 1733, a revival of which resulted in the *guerre des bouffons*. The *opera buffa*, with its elaborate finale, was further developed by Baldassare Galuppi and Piccinni and brought to perfection by Paisiello, Cimarosa and Rossini. One of the finest examples of *opera buffa* after Donizetti is Verdi's *Falstaff*.

Letter to Houdart de la Motte
of the Académie Française,
Containing the Request for a Libretto (1727)
JEAN-PHILIPPE RAMEAU

WHATEVER your reasons, Sir, for not expecting from my music for the theater as great a success as from that of composers outwardly more experienced in that musical genre, allow me both to combat them and to defend my own bias. Let it be understood, however, that I do not want to derive other advantages from my art than those which you and I regard as legitimate. Those who speak of learned musicians usually mean men who know everything about the various tone combinations; but in doing so they imply that these men are so preoccupied with them that they sacrifice everything (common sense, feeling, wit, and meaning) for their sake. These composers are the ones trained in the schools, where one speaks of nothing but notes, to the extent that one has good reason for preferring composers who care less about technique than taste. However, he whose taste was formed solely in relation to his own feelings can at best excel in certain genres, namely in those which are suited to his temperament. If he has a gentle nature, he will succeed in expressing tenderness; and if he is lively, jovial, and playful, his music will be correspondingly so. But if he departs from the genres which are natural to him, you won't recognize him any longer. And since he draws everything from his own imagination, without the help of art and its relation to the expressions, he will soon exhaust his talent. In the first fire of enthusiasm he was quite brilliant; but this fire subsides all the more quickly the more he wants to kindle it; and in his works one finds nothing but clichés and platitudes. It seems desirable, therefore, to find an operatic composer who has studied nature before painting it, and whose art enables him to choose exactly those shades and colors which his wit and his taste suggest as being suited to the required expressions. I am far from believing that I am that composer; but at least I have the advantage over the others of knowing the shades and colors of which they have but a confused notion, and which they use only haphazardly. They possess taste and imagination, but both are confined within the limits of their feelings, where the various objects concentrate in a small range of colors, beyond which they see nothing. Nature has not altogether deprived me of its gifts, and I have not experimented with tone combinations to the point of forgetting their intimate relation with "natural beauty" *(le beau naturel)* which pleases by itself but which is not easily found in soil that lacks fertility and which, moreover, has been exhausted. Find out what people think of my two Cantatas, which were taken from me a dozen years ago, and copies of which are so scattered throughout France that I have found it useless to publish them, since in doing so I would lose both time and money; unless I should add some additional pieces, which I cannot do for the lack of suitable texts. One is called *The Abduction of Orithia* and contains airs and recitatives full of character; the other *Thetis.*[2] In the latter you will mark the degrees of anger I apportioned to Zeus and Neptune, according to the need of giving more presence of mind or rage to the one than to the other, and with regard to the manner in which their orders are to be carried out. It is up to you to find out how I have characterized the songs and dances of the savages who appeared one or two years ago, at the *Théâtre Italien*, and how I have treated such subjects as "The Sighs," "The Gentle Complaints," "The Cyclopes," "The Whirlwinds" . . . , "The Conversation of the Muses," a Musette, a Tambourin, etc.[3] They will tell you that I am no novice in the art and that, above all, I do not parade my knowledge in my works, where I try to hide art by art itself. For I write only for the people of taste, and not for the experts, since there are so many of the former and so few of the latter.

Translated by Ulrich Weisstein from *Ecrits de musiciens, xv*-xviii* siècles*, edited by J.-G. Prud'homme (Paris: Mercure de France, 1912).

2. *Aquilon et Arithie* and *Thétis* are two of Rameau's cantatas for baritone and continuo.

3. "Les soupirs," "Les tendres plaintes," "Les Cyclopes," "Les tourbillons," "L'entretien des Muses," "Musette en rondeau," and "Tambourin" belong to the *Pièces de clavecin* of 1724.

FRANCESCO ALGAROTTI (1712-64)

A NATIVE OF VENICE, Algarotti left Italy in 1735 and became a true cosmopolite, moving from Paris (where Voltaire befriended him) to London, St. Petersburg, Berlin, and Dresden. From 1740 to 1742 and, again, from 1746 to 1749 he lived at the court of Frederick the Great, whom he assisted in the execution of many cultural projects, especially in connection with the designing of opera librettos for Carl Heinrich Graun. At Dresden he was patronized by August III, who commissioned him to acquire pictures for the Dresden Gallery. In 1753 Algarotti re-established himself in Italy and aided in the construction of an opera house in Parma. He died at the age of fifty-one in Pisa.

Algarotti's knowledge was encyclopedic. A champion of the Enlightenment, he was one of the leaders of the anti-Arcadian faction which sought to rid Italy of the Baroque. His correspondence with Metastasio was extensive, especially between 1745 and 1747.

Following is an excerpt from Algarotti's *Saggio sopra l'opera in musica*, written around 1754 but widely known only since the 1763 edition. The work, which Grout calls "the most popular manifesto of operatic reform" in the eighteenth century, was quickly translated into the major European languages: an English version appeared in 1768, a German one in the following year, and the French translation of François-Jean Chastellux (*vide* our selections from Metastasio and Diderot) in 1773. The *Saggio* is divided into five chapters, dealing with the libretto, the instrumental and vocal music, the dance, and the structure of operatic theaters respectively, and followed by the sketch of an opera on the subject of *Aeneas in Troy* and a full-length libretto, *Iphigenia in Aulis*.

Algarotti principally aimed at checking operatic abuses and urged the poet to "resume the reins of power, which have been so unjustly wrested from his hands." Even though some of the improvements suggested by him may have had a direct influence on Gluck (as exemplified by the latter's preface to *Alceste* of

1768), his preference for subjects capable of much embellishment hardly conforms to the Gluckian spirit. Wieland, whose "Versuch über das deutsche Singspiel" is, in part, a rejoinder to the *Saggio*, strongly rejected some of Algarotti's criteria while sharing his predilection for pastoral subjects.

~

Essay on Opera (1754)
FRANCESCO ALGAROTTI

THE NECESSARY DISCIPLINE having been established in the theater, attention should be focused on the various ingredients of opera with a view toward making the improvements of which each of these stands in need. The first thing to be carefully considered is the nature of the subject or choice of the libretto, which is more important than is commonly assumed. For the success or failure of an opera depends in large measure on the success or failure of its plot, which is the architect's drawing and the painter's sketch to be colored by the composer's music. The poet directs the dancers, the stagehands, the scenic designers, and those in charge of the costumes. And those parts which he himself does not execute are, nevertheless, to be determined by him.

At the beginning of operatic history, the poets regarded pagan mythology as the best source for their librettos. Hence the *Dafne, Euridice,* and *Arianna* of Ottavio Rinuccini,[1] the first operas produced at the beginning of the last century if we except Poliziano's *Orfeo* (also performed with instrumental accompaniment),[2] that medley of dance and music which Bergonzo Botta produced for a duke of Milan at Tortona,[3] the work of

---

1. Rinuccini's librettos *Euridice* and *Dafne* were set to music by Peri as well as Caccini. *Arianna* is the almost completely lost opera which Monteverdi composed in 1608.

2. Angelo Poliziano's drama *Orfeo* (with music "consisting of at least three solo songs and one chorus") was performed in 1471 or 1472 at Mantua.

3. In 1488, Bergonzo Botta of Tortona prepared a spectacle for the marriage of Galeazzo Sforza and Isabella of Aragon. An account of this production is quoted by Stefano Arteaga in his book *Le rivoluzioni del teatro musicale italiano della sua origine fino al presente* (Venice, 1785).

the famous Zarlino staged before Henry the Third in Venice,[4] and other such productions as may be considered preludes to, or sketches for, opera proper.

The aim of our poets was to revive Greek tragedy on the modern stage and to introduce Melpomene accompanied by music, dancing, and all that pomp which adorned her in the age of Sophocles and Euripides. And in order that this pomp might seem to be natural to tragedy, they derived the plots of their operas from the heroic times, i.e., from the age of mythology. At the poet's behest, mythology brought to the theater all the pagan gods, taking the audience now to Olympus and the Elysian fields and then to Tartarus as well as Thebes and Argos. With the appearance of these gods, the strangest and most marvelous happenings became verisimilar. And by raising, to a certain extent, everything above the human level, mythology made the singing in opera seem to be the natural language of the characters.

For the same reason, elaborate machinery was used in the first operas, performed on the occasion of royal nuptials or in the palaces of the nobility. In this way effects were produced nothing more marvelous than which was ever seen on earth or in heaven. Numerous choruses, various kinds of dances, and combinations of the two were used, for the introduction of all of which the action furnished an excuse. No doubt, then, can remain as to the great pleasure engendered by these productions, since the unity of the plot was not destroyed by the infinite variety of embellishments.

A faithful image of all this still exists in the French theater, where opera was introduced by Cardinal Mazarin in strict adherence to the Italian practice.[5] These representations, however, must later have suffered greatly from the use of buffo characters

---

4. Henry III of France passed through Venice in 1574 on his return from Poland. There is some question as to whether the work mentioned by Algarotti was composed by Claudio Merulo, the first organist, or Gioseffe Zarlino, the *Kapellmeister* at St. Mark's.

5. Mazarin patronized the Barberini, who had left Italy upon the election of Pope Innocent X in 1644. Three years later, Luigi Rossi's *Orfeo* was staged in Paris—one of the first operas to be given there.

ill-suited to the gods and heroes. By causing the audience to laugh at inappropriate moments, these figures disturbed the gravity of the action. Some traces of this abuse are still to be found in French opera.

Opera did not long remain confined to palaces and courts but gained a foothold in the public theaters, where the beauty and novelty of the thing attracted large audiences. But, as can be imagined, it was impossible to retain the pomp and splendor of the spectacle under these circumstances. The difficulties were enhanced by the exorbitant fees demanded by the singers, whose salaries, modest in the beginning—as witnessed by the nickname *"Centoventi"* given to a singer performing during an entire season for that amount—soon began to exceed all limits.

Since the managers could not afford such great expenses, it became necessary for them to use new measures and devices, so that they could save money on the one side while wasting it on the other. Abandoning the mythological subjects, all of which, in a manner of speaking, embrace the entire universe and are by their very nature extremely costly, they turned to historical plots, which are circumscribed in much narrower limits. In this way, opera may be said to have descended from heaven to earth and to have exchanged the company of gods for that of human beings. The great pomp and variety of the settings, to which the audience was accustomed, was now replaced by a greater regularity of the plot, the artifices of poetry, and the charms of a more refined music. And such a practice took root all the more easily since while one of the arts turned to the imitation of ancient authors the other was bent on enriching itself with new ornaments, which led to the belief that the genre had nearly reached perfection. But in order that the performance might not remain too bald and monotonous, intermezzos and ballets were introduced for the entertainment of the audience. Thus opera gradually took the form that is familiar to us.

It is true that the subjects derived from both mythology and history have certain drawbacks attached to them. In view of the large number of machines and props which they require, the mythological plots tend to place too many restrictions on the poet for him to be able to unravel the action as it ought to be, since he has neither the time nor the space to fully portray the passions and the characters afflicted by them. This, however, is essential in opera, which, substantially, is nothing but tragedy recited to music. This explains why so many French operas—not to mention the first Italian ones—are mostly a feast for the eyes and seem to be masquerades rather than plays, the principal action in them having been smothered by the embellishments, and the poetical part being so weak and wretched that these works were, with some justification, labeled strings of madrigals.

The historical subjects, on the other hand, are not as well suited to music, which seems less verisimilar in them. This can be observed every day on our operatic stages, since it is obvious that the trills of an aria are less natural in the mouth of Caesar or Cato than in that of Venus or Apollo. Also, historical subjects fail to furnish as much variety as their mythological counterparts. They tend to suffer from austerity and monotony. The stage seems to be invariably empty, unless one wants to count the rabble of extras who, in our operas, accompany the kings even to their private chambers. In addition, it is much more difficult to find dances and other embellishments that are suited for such historical subjects. For these embellishments should be properly fused with the drama by becoming integral parts of it, just as the embroidery in good materials helps sustain, rather than merely decorates, the fabric. Such, for example, is the dance of the shepherds at the wedding of Medoro and Angelica, on which occasion Orlando is made aware of his wretchedness.[6] But this fusion is rarely achieved by the embellishments of our Italian operas where, although the subject be Roman and the dancers be dressed as Roman soldiers, the ballet in no way contributes to the action but merely interrupts and inconveniences it like a Scotch dance or the *furlana*. This explains why historical subjects often remain bald or wear ill-fitting clothes that hang limply on them.

The poet can conquer these difficulties only by choosing the subject of his libretto with the greatest care. And in order to

6. In Lully's opera *Roland* of 1685.

carry out his intention, namely to move the heart, delight the eye, and charm the ear, without offending reason, he should take his plot from events remote in time, or at least in place, that furnish occasion for marvelous happenings while at the same time being extremely simple and well-known. The remoteness of the action will make the musical setting less improbable. The marvelousness will permit the poet to introduce ballets, choruses, and all sorts of other embellishments. The simplicity and notoriety, finally, will save him the trouble of having to give lengthy introductions concerning the characters and circumstances. Thus he is free to concentrate on the passions, which are the mainspring and soul of drama.

The two operas *Dido* and *Achille in Sciros,* written by the celebrated Metastasio, come close to the mark.[7] Their plots are simple and are drawn from remotest antiquity, without being too far-fetched. In the midst of splendid feasts, magnificent embassies, embarkations, choruses, battles, and fires take place, and it seems that here the realm of opera is ampler and, in a manner of speaking, more legitimate than is usually the case. The same would apply to an opera about Montezuma,[8] as much on account of the strangeness and novelty of the action as on that of the pleasure derived from the Spanish and Mexican costumes seen together for the first time. And the strange magnificence of America would form a striking contrast with Europe.

Similarly well-suited subjects could be drawn from Ariosto and Tasso, especially since here, in addition to the familiar stories and strong passions, the charms of magic are apparent. This is true also of the stories of Aeneas in Troy and Iphigenia in Aulis, where to the great variety of settings and machines is superadded the charm of Virgil's and Euripides' poetry.[9] Nor are other

---

7. *Didone abbandonata,* often considered the paragon of librettos, formed the basis of more than twenty operas, the first musical setting being that of Domenico Sarro in 1724. *Achille in Sciros* was composed by Caldara (in 1736) and several other musicians.

8. Graun's opera *Montezuma,* based on a plot outline by Frederick the Great himself, was performed in Berlin in January, 1755.

9. Glucks *Iphigénie en Aulide,* based on a libretto by Roullet, was staged in 1774. Diderot mentions the same subject in his *Entretiens sur "Le fils naturel."*

suitable subjects lacking. The poet who knows how to use with discretion the favorable aspects of the mythological as well as the historical subjects will be in a position to do with opera what has to be done with states which, in order to keep alive, have to go back to their roots from time to time.

Translated by Ulrich Weisstein from Algarotti's *Opere scelte*, edited by G. Gherardini (Milan, 1823).

VOLTAIRE (*1694-1778*)

VOLTAIRE, the towering figure in eighteenth-century French literature and thought, had a divided attitude toward opera. In a letter of 1732 to his friend Cideville he scornfully decried the Opéra as a "public gathering place where one meets on certain days without quite knowing why" and as a "house frequented by everybody although its master is poorly regarded and boredom reigns supreme." But in the very same year he was writing the first of several librettos for Jean-Philippe Rameau, with whom he collaborated for a decade. The "*opéra tragi-lyrique*" *Samson* was never performed, however. Nor did *Pandore* (1740) meet with a kinder fate. It was only with the production of the "*comédie-ballet*" *La Princesse de Navarre*, commissioned on the occasion of the Dauphin's marriage in 1745, that the team Voltaire/Rameau became successful on the lyrical stage.

In the late forties Voltaire swung his support to the great master of French music in the preceding century, Jean-Baptiste Lully, several of whose works he singles out for praise in his preface to *Sémiramis*[1] (1748), from which we quote a relevant excerpt. In this preface Voltaire tries to show that modern opera, to a certain extent, "gives us some idea of Greek tragedy." In the fifties and sixties Voltaire seems to have lost interest in opera as an art form. Those were the years of his sojourn at the Prus-

---

1. *Sémiramis* itself is a drama, although it was later set to music by several composers, Rossini among them.

sian court and his settling down at Ferney, the years also which saw the composition of his literary masterpiece, *Candide*. He took no active part in either the *guerre des bouffons* or the feud between Gluckists and Piccinnists in the early seventies. Yet subsequently he came to like the music of the German master, whose operas he never saw performed but only knew in bits and snatches. Voltaire, who despised the opéra comique, nevertheless aided the young Grétry (composer of some fifty works in that vein) to establish himself in the profession. He even wrote two librettos—neither of which was used by his protégé. In his *Dictionnaire philosophique* he more or less accurately predicted that the opéra comique would soon surpass serious opera in popular esteem.

E. Vander Straeten, *Voltaire Musicien* (Paris: Baur, 1878).

Preface to *Sémiramis* (1748)
VOLTAIRE

A FAMOUS [Italian] author has stated that after the grand days of Athens, tragedy, erring and forsaken, has searched in one country after another for somebody who would help restore its former glory, without having as yet been able to find him anywhere. If by this he means that no [modern] nation has dramas in which the chorus is almost constantly in evidence to sing strophes, antistrophes, and epodes accompanied by solemn dances; that no [modern] nation makes its actors appear on some sort of buskin, their faces covered by masks whose one side expresses joy while the other shows pain; that the declamation common to our tragedies has no fixed note values and is not accompanied by flutes he is undoubtedly right. I am not sure however, that this works to our disadvantage. I am not sure whether the form of our tragedies, which is closer to nature, does not equal that of the Greeks, which was grander.

If that author merely wanted to say, however, that, all things considered, that great genre has not been as highly esteemed since the renaissance of letters as it was beforehand; that there are European nations which on occasion have treated the successors of Sophocles and Euripides with ingratitude; that our theaters are not those splendid edifices of which the Athenians were so proud; that we do not take the same pains with those spectacles which have become so necessary in our vast cities, one can wholly share his opinion. . . .

Where can one [presently] find a spectacle that furnishes an idea of the Greek stage? Perhaps it is in your [Italian] tragedies, called operas, that its image persists. "What," I am told, "an Italian opera resembles in any way the Athenian drama?" Yes, indeed. The Italian recitative is precisely the *melopoeia* of the ancients. It is that declamation with fixed note values that is accompanied by musical instruments. That *melopoeia*, which is boring only in your worst tragedy-operas, is admirable in your best lyrical dramas. The choruses which you have added in recent years, and which are so tightly linked to the plot, resemble the ancient choruses all the more closely in that their music is different from that of the recitatives, just as the strophe, epode, and antistrophe were sung by the Greeks in a manner totally different from the *melopoeia* of the scenes. Add to these similarities the fact that in many of the tragedy-operas authored by the famous Abbé Metastasio the unities of place, action, and time are observed. These pieces, moreover, abound in that expressive poetry and continuous elegance [of diction] which embellish nature without doing violence to it—signs of a talent which, in the modern age, our own Racine and England's Addison were the only ones to possess.

I know that these tragedies, so agreeable through the charm exuded by their music and the magnificence of the spectacle, have a flaw which the Greeks always managed to avoid. I also know that this flaw has made monsters out of the most beautiful and regularly constructed plays. It consists in the introduction of short little airs, those detached ariettas which interrupt the action and stress the trills of an effeminate though brilliant voice at the expense of interest and common sense. The abovementioned author, who derives many of his librettos from our tragedies, has, by dint of his genius, amended that fault which is now *de rigueur.* The words of his detached airs often embellish the principal subject [of the opera]. They are passionate and sometimes compete with the most beautiful odes of Horace. . . . There are many airs of this kind; but what are beauties out of place? What would the Athenians have said if Oedipus and Orestes, at the moment of recognition, had sung little airs with grace notes and recited similes to Jocasta and Electra? One must admit that in enchanting the Italians by the charm of its music, opera has destroyed true Greek tragedy in one respect while reviving it in another.

Our French opera ought to cause us even greater headaches. Our *melopoeia* differs much more than yours from normal diction. It is more languid and does not permit the scenes to attain their proper length. It requires brief dialogues in the form of an exchange of terse maxims, each of which branches out into a kind of song.

May the connoisseurs of foreign literatures, whose knowledge is not confined to the airs of our ballets, remember the admirable scene in *La Clemenza di Tito*[2] between Titus and his favorite, who has conspired against him. . . . Let them reread [Titus'] subsequent monologue. . . , which should serve as an eternal lesson for kings and enchant all human beings. . . . These two scenes, compatible with, if not superior to, anything to be found in Greek tragedy; these two scenes worthy of Corneille when he isn't rhetorical and Racine when he doesn't falter; these two scenes which are not based on operatic love but on the noblest sentiments of the human heart are at least three times as long as those found in [French] musical tragedies. Pieces of that kind would not be tolerated on our lyrical stage, which maintains itself only with the help of amorous commonplaces and abortive passions—with the exception of *Armide* and the finest scenes in *Iphigénie,*[3] works which are more admired than imitated.

As for our native products, we have, like you, numerous de-

---

2. Metastasio's drama of 1734, which Antonio Caldara (1670-1736) was the first to set to music.

3. *Armide et Renaud* is by Quinault and Lully (1686); Voltaire is referring to *Iphigénie en Aulide* by either Caldara (1718) or Graun (1748).

tached airs in our most tragic operas. These are more faulty than yours, however, since they are less closely linked with the central theme. Their lyrics are nearly always brought under the subjection of the composers, who, unable to express the virile and energetic accents of our language in their little airs, ask for effeminate, vague, and soft words that are alien to the plot and lend themselves as well as possible to the writing of tunes similar to those which they call barcaroles in Venice. . . . In spite of these flaws I still think that our best tragedy-operas, such as *Atis, Armide*, and *Thésée*,[4] can still supply us with some idea of the Greek drama, because they are sung like the ancient tragedies and because the chorus, even though defective, since it utters tedious panegyrics on love morals, resembles that of the Greeks in being frequently on stage. [However,] it neither says what it ought to say nor teaches virtue.

But all things considered, one has to admit that the form of our tragedy-operas gives us some idea of Greek tragedy. The experts in ancient literature, whom I have consulted, seem to share my view that the tragedy-operas are both a copy and the ruin of Athenian drama. They are a copy insofar as they use *melopoeia*, choruses, machines, and deities. They are destructive to the extent to which they accustom young people to being more concerned with sound than with sense, to preferring their ears to their souls and trills to sublime thoughts, and to liking, at times, the most insipid and poorly constructed works on account of the enchanting airs which they contain. But in spite of all these flaws, the pleasure we derive from this happy mixture of scenes, choruses, dances, orchestral music, as well as from the variety of settings, subjugates even the critic himself. And the best comedies and tragedies are never as assiduously frequented by the same people as are mediocre operas. The regular, noble, and stern beauties are not the ones most eagerly sought out by the masses . . . , and in all genres the little charms triumph over the real merits.

Translated by Ulrich Weisstein from Voltaire's *Oeuvres complètes* (Paris: Garnier, 1877).

4. *Atys* (1676) and *Thésée* (1675) are by Quinault and Lully.

Knowledge of the Beauties and Flaws of Poesy
and Eloquence in the French Tongue
*(Connaissance des beautés et des défauts de la poésie
et d'eloquence dans la langue française)* (1749)

VOLTAIRE

SINCE YOU INTEND to frequent our spectacles while you are in Paris, I shall say something about opera, although in the present work I do not expressly deal with tragedy and comedy; my reason being that so many excellent treatises on the tragic and comic theater have been written, especially in the form of prefaces to our most outstanding plays, whereas very little has been said about opera.

Saint-Evremond has exhausted himself in cold railleries against that kind of spectacle. He finds it ridiculous to set passions and dialogues to music. He does not know that the Greek and Roman tragedies were chanted; that the scenes had melodies which resembled our recitatives and were written by composers; and that their choruses were treated very much like ours. Who does not know that music expresses the passions? In praising *Sophonisbe*[5] and scorning the opera based on it, Saint-Evremond proved that he lacks taste and is hard of hearing.

The great vice of our opera derives from the fact that a tragedy cannot throughout be passionate, that reasoning, details, and prepared actions are also needed, and that music cannot too well render that which is not animated and that which does not penetrate to the heart. . . . In our country, therefore, we are reduced to suppressing in opera all those details which do not interest on their own account but help to render a play interesting. One speaks only of love; and in opera even that passion is never given the scope needed to make it touch us and exert its full force. . . .

Theseus,[6] in the opera by that name, tells his mistress without any preparation: "I am the king's son." She replies: "You, Sire?"

5. An opera by Caldara based on Metastasio's libretto of 1734.
6. Quinault/Lully's opera?

The secret of his birth is not otherwise explained. This is a basic flaw. And if this recognition had been well prepared and handled, if all the details which would render it both probable and surprising had been used, the flaw would have been even greater, since the music would have made all these details boring.

Here, then, we have a poem that is intrinsically defective. Add to these imperfections that which derives from its subjugation to the sterility of the composers, who cannot express all the words of our native tongue in the same way in which the Italian composers can render theirs. They are forced to write little airs, for which the poet has to supply a certain number of dull and uninspiring words, which often have no direct bearing on the action. . . .

That puerile constraint is further enhanced by the paucity of words in French that are suitable to be set to music. Ask a composer to set the words "*Que vouliez-vous qu'il fît contre trois?—Qu'il mourût,*" or the lines "*Si j'avais mis ta vie à cet indigne prix./ Parle, aurais-tu quitté les dieux de ton pays?*"[7] The composer requires instead of these beautiful verses amorous discourses, love affairs, brooks, birds, charms, and alarms.

This, then, is the reason why since the days of Quinault we have had almost no tragedies that are tolerable when set to music. The authors have sensed the extreme difficulties involved in interspersing social gatherings with grand and pathetic actions, omitting necessary details, and keeping up the interest. They have almost invariably turned to an even more mediocre genre, namely the ballet. . . . A single love scene, nicely set to music and sung by a popular actor, attracts the attention of all Paris and renders the true beauties insipid. The members of the court feel unable to support [Corneille's] *Polyeucte* after attending a ballet containing easily remembered snatches of song. Thus the lack of taste increases, and what has made the glory of the nation is gradually forgotten. I repeat it once more: opera must be raised to a higher level before it will cease to deserve the derision by which it is met all over Europe.

Translated by Ulrich Weisstein from Voltaire's *Oeuvres complètes* (Paris: Garnier, 1871).

7. From Act Five, Scene Five, of Voltaire's *Alzire.*

JEAN-JACQUES ROUSSEAU (1712-78)

ACCORDING to Grove's *Dictionary*, Jean-Jacques Rousseau, who engaged in the formal study of music between 1727 and 1730, "remained to the end a poor reader and an indifferent harmonist, though he exercised a great influence on French music." In 1743 the future author of *The New Heloïse* and the *Confessions*, who, for a time at least, had earned his livelihood as a copyist of music, published a *Dissertation sur la musique moderne*. And in 1747 he composed an opera, *Les muses galantes*, whose musical soundness and effectiveness Rameau, the leading French composer of the time, put in question. This marked the beginning of a lifelong tug-of-war between the two artists. In 1749 Rousseau was asked to write the articles on music for the *Encyclopédie*, which its chief editor, Diderot, had originally commissioned from Rameau. (Rameau had declined the offer but shown his willingness to check material written by other contributors.) The content of Rousseau's articles, which were not submitted to Rameau, aroused the latter's ire; and a prolonged exchange of pamphlets ensued. The year 1752 witnessed the beginning of the *guerre des bouffons*, fought between the adherents of French and Italian opera. Along with the other Encyclopedists, Rousseau sided with the Italian faction and actively interfered in its behalf with his *Lettre sur la musique française* of 1753. In the preceding year he had composed *Le devin du village* as a practical demonstration of *opera buffa*. It had an enormous success when performed before the French king in October, 1752. In 1767 Rousseau completed his *Dictionnaire de musique*, from which our selection is taken; parts of it were incorporated into the supplement of the *Encyclopédie* which saw print in 1777. In October, 1775, Rousseau, who had recently been converted into admiration of Gluck, produced his lyrical drama *Pygmalion*, the music of which is kept purely instrumental. He also left a fragment of an opera, *Daphnis et Chloë*.

M. Josephson, *Jean-Jacques Rousseau* (London, 1932); A. R. Oliver, *The Encyclopedists as Critics of Music* (New York, 1947); H. V. Somerset, "Jean-Jacques Rousseau as a Musician," *Music and Letters*, XVII (1936), 37-46, 218-224; E. Kisch, "Rameau and Rousseau," *Music and Letters*, XXII (1941), 97-114.

Dictionary of Music (1764)

JEAN-JACQUES ROUSSEAU

COUNTER-SENSE: A vice of the composer who renders a thought other than that which he ought to render. Since music, according to M. d'Alembert, is merely a translation of words into song, it is obvious that counter-senses may exist. And they are as difficult to avoid in music as they are in literature.

Counter-sense in expression: when the music is sad where it should be gay, and gay where it should be sad; when it is light where it should be serious, and serious where it should be light; etc.

Counter-sense in prosody: when long notes appear on short syllables, and short notes on long syllables; when the accent of the language is not observed; etc.

Counter-sense in declamation: when contrasting or different feelings are expressed by the same modulations; when the words rather than the feelings are rendered; when the music dwells on details over which it ought to pass quickly; when repetitions are unduly prolonged.

Counter-sense in punctuation: when the musical phrase concludes with a perfect cadence at a place where the meaning is still suspended, or when it is inconclusive in a passage whose meaning is established.

I speak here of counter-senses in the strict sense of the word; but the lack of expression is perhaps the most serious flaw of all. I prefer the music which says something it is not supposed to say to that which expresses nothing at all.

Opera: A dramatic and lyrical spectacle in which one endeavors to combine all the graces of the fine arts in the representation of a passionate action, with the intention of arousing interest and creating illusion by means of pleasant sensations.

The constituent parts of opera are the libretto, the music, and the scenery. The poetry speaks to the mind, the music to the ears, and the painting to the eyes. Together these arts should conspire to move the heart and convey to it the same impression simultaneously through different organs. Of these three ingredients I shall discuss the first and third only insofar as they are related to the second. Thus I immediately pass on to the latter.

The art of pleasurably combining [musical] sounds may be considered from two entirely different points of view. Regarded as a natural phenomenon, music limits its effect to the sensation and the physical pleasure we derive from melody, harmony, and rhythm. This is generally true of church music, songs, and dance tunes. But as an essential ingredient of the lyrical drama, whose main object is imitation, music becomes one of the fine arts, and as such is able to portray all situations, arouse all emotions, struggle with the poetry, infuse it with new strength, add new charms to it, and triumph over it by crowning it.

The sounds of the spoken language, being neither sustained nor harmonious, are negligible and, accordingly, cannot form a pleasant alliance with vocal or instrumental music, at least in our languages, which are so far from being musical. For one cannot read the Greeks' own explanation of their manner of reciting without concluding that their language was so well accentuated that the inflections of speech in sustained declamation formed musical and appreciable intervals among themselves. Thus one can say that their drama was a kind of opera; and it is for this reason that no actual operas did exist among them.

Judging by the difficulty of joining song to speech in our language, it is easy to see why the intervention of music as an essential ingredient must give to the lyrical drama a character different from that of either tragedy or comedy, thus producing a third type of drama with its own special rules. But these differences cannot be determined without perfect knowledge of the added part, of the means employed in joining it to speech, and of its natural relations with the human heart. These details are better understood by the philosopher than by the artist; and the pen that is made to elucidate all the arts is best suited to explain to the artist the principles of his craft, and to the connoisseurs the sources of their pleasure.

Limiting myself thus to a few historical rather than critical observations on my subject, I begin by stating that the Greeks had no theatrical genre comparable to our lyrical drama, and that the genre to which they gave that name did not in the least resemble ours. Since there are plenty of accents in their language, and little din in their music, all their poetry was musical, and all their music declamatory; to the extent that their song was little more than sustained speech and that they actually sang their verses, as they announce at the beginning of their poems. Which practice, by way of imitation, has led the Romans (and later ourselves) to the silly habit of saying "I sing" when there actually is no singing. As for that genre which they specifically called the lyrical, it was a type of heroic poetry whose style was pompous and measured, and which was mostly accompanied by the *kithara* or the *lyra*. It is certain that the Greek tragedies were recited in a song-like fashion with instrumental accompaniment, and that the action was relieved by choruses.

But if, for these reasons alone, one wants to call them operas in the modern sense, one has to think of operas without arias; for it is virtually certain that Greek music (including the instrumental) was no more than a veritable recitative. It is true that this recitative, which combined the grace of musical sounds with the harmony of poetry and the full strength of declamation, must have had considerably more force than its modern counterpart, which has to use one of these advantages at the expense of the others. In our living languages, most of which reflect the rough climate in which they originated, the application of music to words is much less natural. An uncertain prosody agrees badly with regular measures; mute and deaf syllables, harsh articulations, and sounds which are neither striking nor varied do not easily lend themselves to melody. A poetry that is scanned solely according to the number of syllables will not agree with the musical rhythm and will constantly obstruct the diversity of values and movements. These are the difficulties to be overcome or skirted in the process of creating a lyrical drama. And yet the attempt was made to fashion a suitable language by choosing the proper words, lines, and phrases; and that language, called lyrical, was rich or poor in proportion to the sweetness or roughness of the tongue from which it was derived.

Having somehow shaped the words for the music, the composers were faced with the task of applying music to speech, and of rendering it so proper on the lyrical stage that the whole could be taken for a single idiom. Thus arose the need for continuous singing (to imitate continuous speaking), a need which increases to the extent to which the language is less musical. For the less sweet and accentuated a language, the harder and more shocking to the ear will be the transition from speech to song, and from song to speech. Hence the need for replacing the spoken dialogue by a sung dialogue that could imitate it so closely that it was distinguished from speech only by its more perfect harmony. (See *Recitative.*)

This manner of joining music to poetry in the theater, which stimulated interest and created illusion among the Greeks because it was natural, for the opposite reason could not suffice us for the same purpose. Listening to a constrained and artificial language, we find it hard to grasp the meaning of what is said. With much noise one conveys little emotion. Hence the need for buttressing the moral pleasure with the physical, and for supplementing the power of expression with the allure of harmony. And the less one is able to touch the heart, the more one must seek to flatter the ear. Thus we are compelled to find in mere sensation the pleasure which feeling refuses to yield. This is the origin of arias, choruses, overtures, and that enchanting melody with which modern music is often decked out at the expense of the poetry, but which the connoisseur despises if it flatters instead of moving him.

At the birth of opera, its creators, wishing to avoid what might seem unnatural in the union of music and language in the imitation of human life, decided to transplant the scene to heaven or hell. And since they did not know how to make human beings speak, they made gods and devils rather than heroes and shepherds sing. Soon magic and the marvelous became the props of the lyrical stage; and, content with having a new genre, nobody thought of inquiring whether it was the one that ought to have been invented. To sustain such a strong illusion one had to exhaust the most seductive charms to be imagined by a people among whom the love of pleasure and the fine arts was tantamount. That famous nation, of whose ancient virtues only the artistic ones remain, squandered its taste and wit to endow the new spectacle with all the pomp it needed. All over Italy theaters, equal in size to royal palaces and in elegance to the ancient monuments which abound in that country, were erected. To decorate them they perfected the arts of perspective and scenery. The artists of each genre let their talents shine. The most ingenious machines, daring flights, storms, thunder and lightning were employed to stun the eyes, while a multitude of instruments and voices astounded the ears.

In spite of all this, the action remained always cold, and the situations lacked interest. Since there was no intrigue that could not be solved easily by the intervention of some god, the spectator, aware of the poet's power, wholly relied on him for rescuing his heroes from the most dangerous situations. Thus the machinery was immense without producing much effect, since the imitation was always imperfect and crude, the action unnatural and without human interest, and the senses ill disposed toward illusion which did not involve the heart. All told, it would have been difficult to bore an audience at a greater expense.

This spectacle, imperfect as it was, was long admired by the contemporaries, who knew nothing better. They even congratulated themselves for having invented such a beautiful genre. We have added a new principle to those established by Aristotle, they said, by adding admiration to pity and terror. They did not see that this apparent wealth was only a sign of sterility, like the flowers which cover the fields before mowing time. They wished to stun because they could not move the audience; and the alleged admiration was actually a puerile amazement of which they should have been ashamed. A false air of magnificence, magic, and enchantment impressed the people to such an extent that they spoke with enthusiasm and respect of a genre that deserved to be hissed from the stage. With the greatest credulity they venerated both the stage and the phantasms which were represented on it. As if it were better to assign a dull speech to the king of gods than to the last of men, and as if Molière's servants were not preferable to the heroes of Pradon.

Although the authors of these first operas aimed simply at dazzling the eyes and deafening the ears, it would have been strange if the composers had never been tempted to render by means of their art the feelings scattered in the poems. The songs of nymphs, the priests' hymns, the warriors' cries, the infernal curses did not fill these rude dramas so completely that no moment of interest was left and no situation in which the spectator was not inclined to be moved. Soon one began to feel that independent of the musical declamation, which was often hampered by the language, the choice of tempo, harmony, and song had something to do with the feelings to be expressed and that, consequently, the effect of the music itself, which was hitherto limited to the senses, could also be extended to the heart. Melody, which hitherto had only reluctantly deviated from the poetry, took advantage of this independence to give itself absolute and purely musical beauties. The newly discovered or perfected harmony opened new ways of pleasing and moving an audience; and the meter, freed of the embarrassment of the poetic rhythm, thus acquired a kind of cadence peculiar to it.

Having thus become a third art of imitation, music soon had its own language and expression, and its own situations—all independent of the poetry. Even the overture learned to speak without the aid of words; and often the orchestra rendered emotions that were no less vivid than those conveyed by the actors. It was in this manner that, tired of the glitter of magic, the puerile noise of machines, and the fantastic images of things that had never been seen, one attempted, by imitating nature, to create truer and more interesting situations. Until that time, opera was only what it could be under the circumstances; for what better usage could be made in the theater of a music that was unable to portray anything except by representing objects that do not exist and with regard to which nobody is in a position to compare the real thing with its image? It is impossible to know whether one is as affected by the image of something marvelous as one would be by its actual presence, whereas everybody can judge for himself whether an artist has succeeded in making passion speak in its true language, and whether natural objects are well imitated. But as soon as music had learned to paint and speak, the charms of the feelings soon caused those of the fairy wand to be forgotten. The theater was purged of the mythological jargon. Interest replaced the marvelous, the machines of the poets and carpenters were destroyed, and the lyrical drama took on a nobler and less unwieldy shape. Whatever moves the heart was successfully used, and there was no need for imposing upon it by introducing creatures shaped by the intellect, or rather, by folly. And the gods were driven from the stage as soon as the representation of human beings on it became possible. That wiser and more regular form was found to be much better suited for creating illusion. One felt that it was the greatest virtue of the music to make itself inconspicuous; that by causing confusion and disorder in the soul of the spectator, the latter could be kept from distinguishing the tender and pathetic songs of a lamenting heroine from the true accents of pain; and that the infuriated Achilles could frighten us to the bone in a language that would have shocked us in his mouth at any other time.

These observations gave rise to a second, equally significant operatic reform. It was felt that there should be nothing cold and rational in opera, nothing that the audience could hear so calmly as to be able to reflect on the absurdity of what was presented to it. And this is the main difference between the lyrical drama and tragedy proper. All political deliberations, all conspiracies, expositions, narrations, sententious maxims, in short: whatever speaks to the reason alone was banished from the language of the heart, together with all sorts of witticisms, madrigals, and intellectual pastimes. Even the tone of simple flattery, which ill accords with the great passions, was reluctantly admitted at the height of tragic situations, whose effect it almost always spoils; for it is never more obvious that an actor sings than when he sings a ditty.

The force of all the emotions and the violence of all the passions are, then, the principal object of the lyrical drama; and the illusion which constitutes its charm is destroyed as soon as the author and the actor leave the spectator for a single moment to himself. Such are the principles on which modern opera is based. Apostolo Zeno, the Italian Corneille, and his young disciple, Italy's Racine, have introduced and perfected the new method. They ventured to place great historical figures on a stage that seemed to be made for fairy-tale phantasms. Cyrus,

Caesar, and even Cato strutted the stage successfully; and the spectators, most appalled by hearing such men sing, soon forgot that they were singing, stunned and enraptured as they were by the magnificence of a music that was as full of nobility and dignity as it was of fire and enthusiasm. One began to see why feelings so radically different from ours must be expressed in such a different manner.

These new poems, which genius had created and genius only could support, easily routed the mediocre composers who possessed merely the mechanical skill of their art and who, lacking the fire of invention and the gift of genuine imitation, made operas just as they would have fabricated boots. No sooner were the shouts of the Bacchantes, the conjurings of the sorcerers, and all empty noises banished from the stage; no sooner had the attempt been made to replace the barbarous din by the true accents of wrath, pain, lament, weeping, and all the other motions of an agitated soul than, forced to endow their heroes with feelings and invent a language of the heart, the Vinci, Leo, and Pergolesi,[1] shunning the servile imitation of their predecessors and branching out in a new direction, bridged the gap on wings of genius and reached their goal after having taken only a few steps. But one cannot march long on the road of good taste without ascending or descending, and perfection is a point to which it is difficult to cling. Having tried and felt its strength, music, ready to march by itself, began to despise the poetry it was supposed to accompany and to increase its own importance by seeking to draw from within itself the beauties it used to share with poetry. It still pretends to render the meaning and the emotions provided by the poet; but in some way it uses a different language. And although the object is still the same, the poet and the composer, divided in their work, produce simultaneously two similar but different images that harm each other. The mind, forced to divide itself, decides to attach itself to one image rather than the other. Thus the composer, if he is the greater artist, effaces the poet; and the actor, noticing that the

---

1. Leonardo Vinci (1690-1730), a composer of the Neapolitan school, wrote several comic and serious operas. Leonardo Leo (1694-1744), another member of the Neapolitan school, composed many comic operas. Giovanni Battista Pergolesi (1710-36) is best known for his intermezzo *La serva padrona* (1733), which still continues to be performed.

spectator sacrifices the words to the music, himself sacrifices the theatrical actions and gestures to the song and the display of his voice. This causes the drama to be altogether forgotten and the spectacle to be transformed into a veritable concert. If, on the other hand, the advantage is with the poet, the music becomes nearly indifferent, and the spectator, deceived by the noise, is misled to the point of attributing the merit of an excellent poet to a mediocre musician, and of believing that he admires harmonic masterpieces when responding to well-written poems.

These are the flaws which the absolute perfection of music and its lack of application to language may cause in an opera to the extent in which the two causes conspire. It is only fair to state that the languages best suited to adjust to the law of [musical] meter and melody are those in which the duplicity I mentioned is least apparent, since, when the music solely lends itself to the poetic ideas, the latter follow the inflections of the melody, and because when music ceases to observe the rhythm, accent, and harmony of the verse, the verse subserves and yields to the cadence of [musical] meter and accent. When a language is neither sweet nor flexible, however, the harshness of its poetry keeps it from lending itself to song—just as the very sweetness of the melody prevents it from making the recitation of the poetry more effective—and one feels in the unnatural union of the two arts a perpetual constraint that offends the ear and destroys the charm of the melody as well as the effect of the declamation. This flaw cannot be removed; and to wish to force music upon an unmusical language means to make it coarser than it would be by itself.

Translated by Ulrich Weisstein from *Oeuvres complètes,* edited by G. Petitain (Paris: Lefevre, 1939).

DENIS DIDEROT (1713-84)

DENIS DIDEROT, the editor-in-chief of the *Encyclopédie* (to which he contributed articles on various subjects, especially on the construction of musical instruments), took an interest in the scientific aspect of music—notably in its mathematical bases—long before he began to practice the art. According to his own testimony, he embarked on a systematic study of music in 1751, and subsequently had such eminent composers as Rameau and Philidor as masters.

In the third of the so-called *Entretiens avec Dorval* (1757) as well as in his *Discours sur la poésie dramatique* (1758) he pointed out the operatic element inherent in Racine's drama *Iphigénie*, the very subject which François du Roullet was to propose to Gluck in 1772. Romain Rolland and other historians of music go so far as to claim that Diderot had, in fact, "prepared, announced, and expected" Gluck's operatic revolution. But although it is true that both the writer and the composer sought to do away with the stifling rules of propriety embraced by the classicists, this claim would seem to be exaggerated for two reasons. In the first place, Diderot sought to push the expression of passion in the lyrical drama to its limits ("the cry of passion" being one of the most frequently recurring themes in his writings on opera), whereas Gluck believed in self-imposed limitations. Secondly, and more significantly, he maintained in his "Letter Concerning the Observations of the Chevalier de Chastellux on the *Treatise on Melodrama*" that Marmontel had not succeeded in writing librettos "until he read and imitated Metastasio, convinced that the poet exists only for the sake of the composer." Gluck, however, in his dedication of *Orfeo ed Euridice* to Grand-Duke Leopold of Tuscany expressly stated that it was his aim to "restrict music to its true function, namely to serve the poetry by means of the expression." Diderot's view of opera is thus obviously more Romantic than Gluck's, although it is a historical fact that the Encyclopedists vigorously supported the German master.

Diderot, by the way, is known to have sketched the libretto of a comic opera.

A. R. Oliver, *The Encyclopedists as Critics of Music* (New York: Columbia University Press, 1947); A. M. Wilson, *Diderot: The Testing Years 1713-1759* (New York: Oxford University Press, 1957); J. R. Loy, "Diderot's Unedited *Plan d'un opéra-comique*," *Romanic Review*, XLVI (1955), 3-24.

Rameau's Nephew
DENIS DIDEROT

He: . . . Lyrical poetry is yet to be born; but they will get there. By listening to the music of Pergolesi, le Saxon, Terradeglias, Traetta, and the others; by reading Metastasio; they will bring it about.

I: Could it be possible that Quinault, La Motte, and Fontenelle have heard nothing?

He: Not as far as the new style is concerned. In all their charming works there are no six consecutive lines which can be set to music. They write clever aperçus or tender, delicate, and nimble madrigals. But if you want to know how unsuited these are as a basis for our art—the most passionate of all, not excepting that which was practiced by Demosthenes—let somebody recite these pieces. How cold, languid, and monotonous they will appear, because there is nothing in them that can serve as a model for song. I had just as well write music for La Rochefoucauld's *Maximes* or Pascal's *Pensées*. It is the animal cry of passion which ought to determine our course. These expressions must press hard upon each other; the phrase must be short, its meaning broken, suspended. The composer must be able freely to dispose of the whole of every part, omitting or repeating a word, adding one that is lacking, turning it in all directions, like an octopus, without destroying it. All this is much harder to accomplish in French poetry than in the languages naturally capable of inversion. . . . The passions must be strong, and the tenderness of both poet and composer extreme. The aria is almost always the peroration of a scene. We need exclamations, interjections, suspensions, interruptions, affirmations, and negations; we call, invoke, shout, weep, cry, and laugh copiously. No wit, no epigrams, no subtle phrases—these are too far removed from simple nature. And don't think that the gestures or the declamation of our actors can serve us as a model. We need something more forceful, less mannered, and truer to life. The simple expressions and common voices of passion grow increasingly important as the speech becomes more monotonous and less expressive. They are furnished by the animal cry of the impassioned individual. . . .

Translated by Ulrich Weisstein from Diderot, *Oeuvres,* edited by André Billy (Paris: Éditions de la Pleïade, 1951).

Conversations about *The Natural Son* (1757)
DENIS DIDEROT

(Dorval considers the embodiment of genuine tragedy in the lyrical theater as one of the goals still to be accomplished.)

I: What kind of tragedy do you want to see used for opera?

D: The ancient one.

I: Why not the domestic one?

D: Because tragedy, like all works intended for the operatic stage, must be in verse, and the domestic tragedy seems to preclude the use of metrical language.

I: But do you believe that this genre will provide all the resources the composer requires for his art? Each art has its own merits. It is with the arts as with the senses. All sensory perception is a kind of touch, just as every art is a form of imitation. But each sense touches, and each art imitates, in a specific manner.

D: There are two different musical modes, one simple and the other stylized. What would you say if I showed you, in the works of our playwrights, pieces to which the composer can apply, at his discretion, the force of the one or the wealth of the other? When I say composer, I mean a man of genius and not a person adept in threading up modulations and putting notes together.

I: Quote me such a piece, Dorval!

D: Gladly. Lully himself is said to have noticed the passage I am about to cite, which may go to prove that all he lacked were poems of a different kind, and that he felt capable of greater things.

Clytemnestra, whose daughter is about to be taken away from her in order to be immolated, envisages the priest's knife raised over her heart, the blood flow, and the priest consult the gods in her trembling heart. Troubled by these images, she exclaims:

.   .   .   .   *O mère infortunée!*
De festons odieux ma fille couronnée,
Tend la gorge aux couteaux par son père apprêtés.
Calchas va dans son sang . . . Barbares! arrêtez!
C'est le pur sang du dieu qui lance le tonnerre . . .
J'entends gronder la foudre et sens trembler la terre.
Un dieu vengeur, un dieu fait retentir ces coups.
[Racine, *Iphigénie*, V, iv]

I know of no verses, either in Quinault or in any other poet, that are more lyrical, nor of situations that are better suited to imitation by music. Clytemnestra's state of mind must wrest from her inmost heart the cry of nature; and the composer will convey it to my ear in its most subtle shades.

If he composes the piece in the simple style, he will fill himself with the pain and despair of Clytemnestra. He will not start to compose until he himself is haunted by the ghastly images that obsess her. How well the first lines lend themselves to a recitative *obbligato!* How perfectly the various phrases suit the plaintive *ritournelle! O ciel! . . . O mère infortunée! . . .* How many different moods could be expressed in that symphony! I can hear it render lament, pain, consternation, horror, and fury.

The aria proper begins with *"Barbares, arrêtez."* Let the composer express the words *"barbares"* and *"arrêtez"* in as many ways as possible; he would be unusually sterile if these words did not suggest to him an inexhaustible wealth of melodies. . . .

Let these lines be sung by Mlle Dumesnil: and, unless I am greatly mistaken, she will render the confusion in Clytemnestra's mind, the feelings which succeed each other in her soul. Her genius will provide her with the proper clues, and it is with her declamation in mind that the composer ought to approach his task. Let us try it out, and you shall see how nature furnishes the same ideas to the singer and the musician.

But what if the composer prefers the stylized manner? A different declamation, a different melody and other ideas will be required. He will put into the voice what the other reserved for the orchestra. He will let the lightning strike and the thunder roll. He will show me Clytemnestra terrifying her daughter's murderers with the image of the god whose blood they are about to shed. With the utmost veracity he will fire my imagination, which has been affected by the pathos of the verses and the situation, with this image. The former was preoccupied with the accents of Clytemnestra's grief; the latter will pay some attention to its expression. I no longer hear Iphigenia's mother; I hear the thunder roll, the earth tremble, and the air resound with frightful noises.

A third composer will try to combine the advantages of the two styles; he will fasten on the cry of nature in its most violent and inarticulate stage, making it the basis of his melody. It is on the strings of this melody that he will let the thunder roll and rumble. Perhaps he will try to invoke the revenging god; but he will let the various traits of this painting be pierced by the cries of a disconsolate mother.

But no matter how prodigious the talent of that composer, he will never achieve one end without jeopardizing the other. Whatever he spends on description will be lost to pathos. The whole will affect the ears rather than the soul. That composer will be more admired by artists than by connoisseurs.

But don't believe that it is these parasitic words of the lyrical style, "*lancer . . . gronder . . . trembler*," which constitute the pathos of the piece, which is engendered by passion. And if the composer, neglecting the cry of passion, takes pleasure in finding sounds exactly suited to these words, the poet has set a cruel trap for him. Is it on the ideas suggested by "*lance*," "*gronde*," "*tremble*" or on those elicited by "*barbares . . . arrêtez . . . c'est le sang . . . c'est le pur sang d'un dieu . . . d'un dieu vengeur*" that the true declamation is to rest?

Translated by Ulrich Weisstein from Diderot, *Oeuvres*, edited by André Billy (Paris: Éditions de la Pléiade, 1951).

Letter Concerning the Observations
of the Chevalier de Chastellux
on the *Treatise on Melodrama* (1771)
DENIS DIDEROT

THE *Treatise on Melodrama* was written against the Chevalier. The latter replies to his critic in a charming manner, but without humor or satire, and with the simple weapons of common sense and experience.

The main bone of contention between the Chevalier and his antagonist concerns the question of whether the poem ought to be made for the music or whether the poet can give rein to his fantasy with the composer being fated to follow him servilely as his train-bearer. The latter is the opinion cherished by the author of the *Treatise* who, accordingly, is unable to make a real distinction between the *Comédie Française* and the *Opéra*. Since he feels that a lyrical drama and an ordinary tragedy are equally suited for music, let him have somebody make a good opera out of one of Racine's tragedies. I don't see why the argument of the author of the *Treatise* was not quickly demolished by the simple fact that Quinault's plays make exquisite reading while Lully's music is insipid. But this insipid music having been written for the plays, and the plays for this insipid music, all of those who have tried to compose an *Armide* after Lully have written even more insipid music.

I feel that, as a natural consequence, it would be absurd to abandon the old types of music while retaining the old forms of poetry, since the poet's style must conform to that of the composer.

The ridiculous contrast between our poetry and the increasingly popular Italian music, the discordance of these two arts, set the Chevalier to thinking; and he found that if music is essentially a kind of song, that song has to be rigidly constructed. He expanded this idea and came to a conclusion which, heretofore, seemed revolting to Marmontel, namely that verses intended to be set to music must be subjugated—as far as their movement is concerned—to the form of the song. I don't think one can say anything more to the point. Here, then, is an author who, regarding this matter, complains loudly that everything is ruined, that we offend against good taste and return to the barbaric age by subordinating the content to the form, and the poet to the orator.

My goodness, how that frightens me! You good fellow who climbs upon the roof and shouts at the top of your lungs that we are drowning, tell us what we can do to save ourselves. What we can do? Your reply: be at the beck and call of theatrical expression, neglecting structure, method, and coherence.

O the clever fellow who does not see that he curtails music, that powerful art, to a mere nothing, a meaningless distraction, an annoyance likely to undercut the work of both comedian and tragedian.

I know what has led him astray; it is the ancient flutes whose only function it was to accompany the actor. But 1) we don't know anything about that accompaniment; 2) Cicero's eulogy of a contemporary playwright shows clearly that it was considered to be a stroke of genius for a playwright to be able to write his verses so that they suited the instruments. "Who knows," he says, "better than this poet how to adjust his verses to the flute?"; 3) is it certain that, in whatever field it may be, we are unable to surpass the ancients?

The author of the *Treatise* states: "Let us be satisfied with reinforcing the expression with all the power of which music is capable." But, arrant prater, if the poet does not communicate this power, if he has done nothing to assert it, the composer has no choice but to cut the strings of his instrument.

The Chevalier, in his reply, has somewhat restricted the scope of the fine arts, which are commonly said to aim at the imitation of nature. His reflections are very subtle; he claims that there is something inexplicable, because purely organic, in the pleasures derived from sense perception. And he is right. Beautiful harmonies, well placed and enlaced, flatter my ear—an abstract of all the feelings inherent in my soul and all the ideas attached to my intellect; although, to tell the truth, I won't listen very long to music that has no other merits. I never listen to a fine symphony, especially an *adagio* or *andante*, without interpreting it —and often so happily that I correctly identify the subject envisaged by the composer. Nor do I ever scorn the advice I once gave to a skilled harpsichordist: "Do you want to write excellent instrumental music," I told him, "so that your instrument always speaks to me? Put Metastasio on your desk; read one of his arias, and let your imagination roam!"

The Chevalier names six different principles of the effect produced by the fine arts: the immediate sensation (which counts little with me), our awareness of the difficulties that have been overcome (which I scorn if nothing else has been accomplished); variety; interest or the passions; surprise; and imagination.

Of these diverse sources of pleasure one should think that

the Chevalier esteems most highly those from which springs the sublime art, the divine magic that is capable of exciting and tormenting us, of conveying all sorts of accents to our ears, of arousing in us all sorts of phantoms, of causing us to cry or laugh—qualities which the author of the *Treatise* ascribes to Italian music. The Chevalier, too, embraces it firmly. What else can you want? What shall we do with that music whose whole charm you have acknowledged? Use it in the concert hall, says the author of the *Treatise*, but not in the theater! And why?— Because it will kill the poet.—Yes, if his play is poorly written. —Can one improve upon the poetry of Metastasio?—Why not? There is music in *Sylvain*, in *Lucile*.[1] Does that music harm the plays, or do you believe that they can do without it? And if Philidor had found a prophet other than Poinsinet, wouldn't we know, by the success of *Ernelinde*,[2] that there are lyrical tragedies to which one can listen with the greatest interest from beginning to end? I swear that the man who embraces the principles expressed in the *Treatise* is either wrong or a disguised follower of Lully.

And then the Chevalier, having berated his critic, asks him to ponder the following little story: A highly sensual Pasha had commissioned a eunuch to buy him the most beautiful women. The eunuch did his best for more than ten years without fully satisfying his master. A man from Marseille met the eunuch in Smyrna, where he found him surrounded by a group of excessively beautiful Circassian women. "Osmin," said the man from Marseille, "do you notice the one with brown hair and blue eyes whom you seem to disdain? Take her, and upon my word your Pasha will be grateful." Osmin followed the advice and fared well. Six months later, he met his friend in Aleppo, walked up to him, thanked him, told him how enamored the Pasha was of the brown-haired girl, and said he would be much obliged if he told him how he arrived at so apt a choice. "I saw her disembark," said the man from Marseille, "and from that moment on I never stopped dreaming of her and desiring her. I was

---

1. *Sylvain* (1770) and *Lucile* (1769) are comic operas by Grétry (1741-1813) with librettos by Marmontel.

2. *Ernelinde, princesse de Norvège* (1767) is an opera by François André Philidor (1726-95) to a libretto by Poinsinet.

unable to sleep, and be sure that if I had possessed 500 sequins, I would have taken her from you and your Pasha. That's the whole secret." "Ah," said the eunuch, departing sadly, "I see that I myself shall never be able to tell."

The Chevalier de Chastellux is a knowledgeable man; he has wit and discrimination; he thinks well, but his style is ambiguous, twisted, diffuse. There is something abstract about it which exasperates one, and his reply will cause little sensation, even though it is solid and profound.

The author of the *Treatise* reminds me of an observation I have made more than once, namely that there is no absurdity on which people do not expatiate at length.

I forgot to add that for a long time Marmontel held the same notions as the author of the *Treatise,* and that he did not succeed until he read and imitated Metastasio, convinced that the poet exists only for the sake of the composer, and that if the poet pulls the whole blanket over to his side, both will spend a miserable night.

And what follows from all this? That a great poet who is also a great musician will fare better than he who is neither the one nor the other.

Translated by Ulrich Weisstein from Diderot, *Oeuvres complètes,* edited by J. Assezat (Paris: Garnier, 1875).

PIETRO METASTASIO (1698-1782)

PIETRO METASTASIO, the author of twenty-seven *drammi per musica,* must be regarded as the most influential of all librettists, with the possible exception of Eugène Scribe. A student of Porpora and protégé of the singer Marianna Benti-Bulgarelli, he wrote his first operatic text (the famous *Didone abbandonata,* to which both Wieland and Algarotti refer as a model) in 1723. In 1730 he became Apostolo Zeno's successor in the post of Imperial Court Poet at Vienna, a position he occupied until his death, which occasioned Da Ponte's appointment. Metastasio furnished a considerable number of librettos for Caldara, Vinci, and Hasse, many of these librettos being subsequently employed by composers like Handel, Gluck, and Mozart. Next to *Didone abbandonata*, the most widely used of his plays were *Alessandro nell' Indie* (1729), *Artaserse* (1730), *La clemenza di Tito* (1734), *Demoofonte* (1733), and *L'olimpiade* (1733).

Metastasio conducted an extensive correspondence with the members of the European cultural elite. In fact he regarded his plays primarily as dramas and proudly stated that in Italy they were more popular with actors than with singers. His knowledge of literary history and aesthetic theory was so vast as to be almost unparalleled in his time. He boldly denounced the operatic abuses committed by composers who "treat singers as if they were violins" and insisted on the supremacy of poetry in the musical theater. The Marquis de Chastellux, to whom the following letter is addressed, had just published an *Essai sur l'union de la poésie et de la musique*. Diderot's "Lettre au sujet des *Observations* du chevalier de Chastellux sur le *Traité du melodrame*" scrutinizes the same author's reply to an attack directed against his views as expressed in the *Essai*.

L. Russo, *Metastasio* (Bari: Laterza, 1921); R. Rolland, "Metastasio, the Forerunner of Gluck" in *A Musical Tour through the Land of the Past* (London: Paul, Trench & Trubner, 1922); S. Towneley, "Metastasio as a Librettist," in *Arts and Ideas in Eighteenth-Century Italy* (Rome: Edizione di Storia e Letteratura, 1960).

Letter to Francesco Giovanni di Chastellux (1766)

PIETRO METASTASIO

IF I WERE A LITTLE YOUNGER, the vigor, erudition, eloquence, and elegance with which Your Honor sang the praises of music in your last letter would have caused me to abandon all other occupations in order to study that art. But in our day it would not be considered praiseworthy, especially for people like myself, to dabble at such an age with the lyre, whereas among the ancient Greeks even emperors and philosophers were encouraged to do so. However, this fault is amended, among other things, by the realization that we are in such perfect agreement that your judgment forms the most solid support of my own opinions.

We are, then, unanimous in believing that music is an ingenious, marvelous, delectable, and enchanting art which, by itself, is capable of working miracles. But when it allies itself with poetry, and makes good use of its enormous wealth, it is able not only to confirm and express all the changes of the human art but also to illumine and increase them with its imitations. But at the same time we are forced to acknowledge the grave abuses which today, for the most part, the artists perpetrate on this beautiful art by applying its seductive charms haphazardly, out of place and time, and against all common sense, and by imitating at their discretion the rumbling of a storm instead of a heavenly calm or the unbridled joy of the *Bassaridi* rather than the profound sadness of the *Captive Trojans* or the *Argive Suppliants*.[1] Whence arises great confusion in the listener, who, torn between the contradictory passions which the music and the poetry express—passions that instead of enhancing, destroy each other—cannot settle on either mood and finds himself reduced to enjoying the mechanical pleasure resulting from the harmonic progression of the sounds or the marvelous range or agility of a voice. I would gladly put up with such an intolerable abuse on the part of the composers if the faculties of their art were limited. Nor would it then seem strange to me if their impatience to display this severely restricted wealth would render them less scrupulous in using it. But since there is no human passion that this beautiful art cannot vividly express and marvelously adorn in a hundred different ways, why should one tolerate the deliberate insult which these artists perpetrate without rhyme or reason? You will notice that, like yourself, I am partial to music and that, if I detest our contemporary music for the theater I mean only those of our composers who disgrace it.

The other, even more weighty, circumstance that consoles me is the familiarity with Greek drama which your last letter betrays and which assures the unanimity of our opinions.

You have made the learned observation that the founders of tragedy, in accordance with the changing passions, frequently changed the usual iambs into anapests and trochees, in order to enable the music to display its beauties. Nor is it a secret that the same characters sang singly, together, and with the chorus

---

1. The reference is to Aeschylus' *The Suppliants* and Euripides' *The Trojan Women*.

strophes, antistrophes, and epodes, meters which by their very nature require that kind of music which we use in arias and which you so aptly call periodic. Whence it follows with absolute necessity that in flattering the tender ears of the audience we follow illustrious, ancient, and established models, to which we doubtlessly owe arias and recitatives, just as the Latins owed to them their *cantici* and *diverbi*. Another significant proof of the ancient origin of our arias is provided by the Greek word *strophe*, which professional writers as well as the common people still use to refer to the various parts of our arias and songs.

Don't believe, Your Honor, that I have forgotten your exhortations. You would like one to recognize a Republic of the Arts just as one speaks of the Republic of Letters. And according to your view, poetry, music, and their sister arts should coexist amicably but totally independent of each other. I, to tell the truth, am not a Republican. I do not think that it, in preference to all other forms of government, can pride itself on making virtue its principle. It seems to me that all forms of government are equally subject to grave infirmities. I am swayed by the venerable example of supreme paternal authority. I dare not refute the axiom which states that the simplest and least complicated machines are the most durable and least imperfect ones. Nevertheless there is nothing I would not do to be at one with you. I am, then, since you so desire, a Republican. But you know that even the most ardent Republicans (namely the Romans), convinced of the advantage offered by the concentration of authority in one hand, chose a dictator in times of stress; and when they made the mistake of dividing that absolute authority between Fabius and Minucius, they ran the risk of perishing altogether. The execution of a play is an extremely difficult undertaking in which all the arts participate; and they, in order to assure the best possible success of their venture, appoint a dictator. Does the music perhaps aspire to this high office? It will occupy it on occasion, but in that case it will slight the subject and the economy of the plot; will determine the moments of the individuals' entrances as well as their characters and the situations; will imagine the decorations, invent the songs, and commission [the] poetry to furnish suitable verses. And if it refuses to do all this, because of the many qualities necessary for the creation of a play, it possesses only the science of sounds, it leaves the rule to that art which has them all and, imitating the repentant Minucius in admitting that it cannot command, obeys. In other words, if by the grace of its venerable patron it did not carry the name of *fugitive slave*, it could not avoid being called a Republican rebel.

I know that the French have a theater they call "lyrical" which, because there they make use of music, leads Your Honor to believe that the latter should be the mistress, as being in its own house. But among the ancients that circumstance never led to the creation of a separate theater. Among the six necessary qualitative ingredients of tragedy—that is to say, among the parts which do not occur from time to time but prevail throughout the entire action—namely plot, character, thought, diction, decoration, and music, Aristotle includes music but mentions it last. In fact, one cannot speak to an audience and make oneself clearly understood without notably elevating, stretching, and sustaining the voice beyond the degree common in ordinary speech. Such decisive changes in the voice require an art capable of establishing the right proportions, since otherwise they would produce poorly modulated, disagreeable, and often ridiculous sounds. The art predestined for this task is none other than music; and he who speaks to an audience is so much in need of it that if the actors cannot find a professional composer they are compelled to provide their own music, which goes under the name of declamation. But if one still wanted to distinguish it from the theater, the difference would be that, although dramatic —if one cares to use the distinctive qualities of Pindar, Homer and their followers—this art uses music with restraint. If in such a lyrical theater one represents an action, creates complications of plot, unravels a story, and if there are persons and characters, then the music is in somebody else's house and cannot act the mistress.

But, my dear Sir, it is time for me to conclude my letter. I would be unable to bring myself to do so (such is the benefit and the pleasure I derive from freely conversing with so learned, so intelligent, and so benevolent a person as you have shown yourself to be) if my indispensable duties did not call me to other work. But if they left me enough leisure to put in order some extracts from Aristotle's *Poetics*, as I have wanted to do for a long time already, I would by this means communicate to you the various observations I have privately made about the Greek playwrights, as well as those [observations] which the practice of our own, already half-elapsed, century has—without too much perspicacity on my part being required—suggested to me; but under the condition that what happened with my first letter to you (which was published without my consent) is not repeated. The opinions which conflict with those now prevalent, even though they are lucid and irrefutable, cannot triumph without a fight; and fighting, my dear Sir, is a business I am temperamentally disinclined to, untrained for, and incapable of conducting because of my age. Nor am I as spiteful as in this case I would have to be. It is a business in which, as you will have noticed, the loudest voices and the most erudite syllogisms count as valid arguments and in which, since one usually ends up by exchanging insults, one needs either great forbearance in order to endure them or great moral indifference in striking counterblows. I seem unable to part from you, but my adored sovereign, who, thanks to the excessive grace he bestows on me, is not yet tired of my chattering song, urges me boldly on toward Parnassus; and I must leave everything in order to obey him, even in defiance of Horace who shouts in my ear:

> *Solve senescentem mature sanus equum, ne*
> *Peccet ad extremum ridendus, et ilia ducat.*

Translated by Ulrich Weisstein from *Metastasio: tutte le opere* (Milan: Mondadori, 1954).

CHRISTOPH WILLIBALD GLUCK
(*1714-87*)

ACTIVE ALMOST EXCLUSIVELY as a composer for the lyrical stage, Christoph Willibald Gluck is a key figure in eighteenth-century opera history. As a reformer he had an even greater impact on the evolution of the genre than the author of *Don Giovanni* and *Die Zauberflöte*.

Relatively little is known about Gluck's early musical training. The years between 1737 and 1745, at any rate, were spent in Italy, where his first half-dozen operas (mostly on texts by Metastasio) originated. After conducting in London, Denmark, and numerous German cities, the composer took up residence in Vienna, which remained his principal abode for approximately twenty years. In the fifties he was largely absorbed with writing music for the then fashionable comic operas in the French manner.

His reform work proper was initiated with *Orfeo ed Euridice* (1762), the first of three operas for which Raniero Calsabigi was his librettist, the other two being *Alceste* (1767) and *Paride ed Elena* (1770). As Gluck put it in the dedicatory letter to Grand-Duke Leopold, his principal aim was to "restrict music to its true function, namely to serve the poetry by means of the expression." Early in 1773 Gluck went to Paris, the scene of his operatic triumphs for the next six years, to help prepare the production of *Iphigénie en Aulide,* for which François du Roullet, an attaché at the French embassy in Vienna, had furnished the libretto on the basis of Racine's and Euripides' dramas. The work was successfully staged in April, 1774. It was followed by French adaptations of *Orfeo* (1775) and *Alceste* (1776). With the arrival in Paris in the latter year of the Italian composer Piccinni, a feud between the champions of French and Italian opera erupted. Gluck had to battle such formidable enemies as Marmontel and de la Harpe, but emerged triumphant when the famous musicologist Padre Martini decreed that he was superior in the tragic genre, Piccinni in the comic. Of Gluck's two operas performed in 1779, only one, *Iphigénie en Tauride* (again after Euripides), won approval. The failure of the other, *Echo et Narcisse,* caused the master to return to Vienna, where he spent the remainder of his life in semi-retirement.

A. Einstein, *Gluck* (New York: Dutton, 1954); H. Berlioz, *Gluck and his Operas* (London: Reeves, 1915); E. Istel, "Gluck's Dramaturgy," *Musical Quarterly*, XVII (1931), 227-233; J. Tiersot, "Gluck and the Encyclopedists," *Musical Quarterly*, XVI (1930), 336-357; Kerman, *Opera as Drama* pp. 38-47.

Four Letters (1769-77)

CHRISTOPH WILLIBALD GLUCK

Dedication of *Alceste*—Letter to Grand-Duke Leopold of Tuscany (1769):

When I undertook to write the music for *Alceste*, I decided to rid it altogether of those abuses which, introduced either by the inappropriate vanity of the singers or an exaggerated complaisance on the part of the composers, have long disgraced the Italian opera, and which have transformed the most stately and most beautiful of all spectacles into the most foolish and boring one. I sought to restrict music to its true function, namely to serve the poetry by means of the expression—and the situations which make up the plot—without interrupting the action or diminishing its interest by useless and superfluous ornament. I thought that it should do for the poem what the vivid colors and the skillfully contrived contrasts of light and shade, which serve to animate the figures without changing their outline, do for a correct and well-proportioned drawing. Accordingly, I did not wish to stop an actor in the greatest heat of dialogue in order to let him wait for a dull ritournelle; nor did I want to interrupt a word on a suitable vowel to let him display, in an extended passage, the agility of his fine voice; or let him wait for the orchestra to indicate, by a cadence, the resumption of the melody. I refused to let the singers glide rapidly over the second part of an aria, which may be the most passionate and important one, to have them repeat four times the words of the first part; or to end an aria when its full meaning has perhaps not yet been conveyed, in order to give the singer a chance to show how capriciously he can vary a passage in diverse manners. In short: I have done my best to banish all those abuses against which common sense and reason have vainly protested for such a long time.

I wanted the overture to give an idea of the action which was to follow, and to furnish, so to speak, its argument. The orchestral part was to be gauged to the interest and intensity of the action, and I wanted to avoid an undue break in the dialogue between recitative and aria as well as the intrusion of counter-sense through an undue interruption of the heat and force of the action.

I finally had the notion that the composer's greatest effort should be expended in the search for simple beauty; and I have avoided all manifestations of difficulty at the expense of clarity. I have not cherished the invention of novel devices except when they were demanded by the situation and the expression. There was, finally, no rule which I did not gladly violate for the sake of the intended effect.

These, then, are my principles. By a stroke of luck the libretto was admirably suited to my intentions, its famous author having constructed it according to a new dramatic plan. He has replaced the flowery descriptions, superfluous similes, and cold and sententious maxims by the language of the heart, by strong passions, interesting situations, and a constantly changing spectacle. The success has warranted my principles, and the general approbation in such an enlightened city has clearly shown that simplicity and naturalness are the highest principles of beauty in all artistic creations.

Dedication of *Paride ed Elena*—Letter to the Duc de Bragance (1770):

The sole reason which induced me to publish the score of *Alceste* was the hope of finding imitators willing to abolish, on the path already opened to them and encouraged by the unanimous approval of an enlightened public, the abuses introduced into Italian opera, and to bring that genre as close as possible to perfection. I regret that so far I have not succeeded.

The connoisseurs and purists, whose number is legion and who are the greatest obstacle to the progress of the fine arts, have reviled a method which, if it takes root, will with one blow destroy all their pretensions to the caprices of judgment and the creative faculty. People thought they could judge *Alceste* after crude, badly staged, and even more poorly executed performances. One has calculated in a room the effect it would have in the theater. . . . A delicate ear has perhaps found this phrase too harsh and that passage too rude or poorly organized, without considering that in the proper surroundings it may produce the maximum effect and the most beautiful contrast. A purist has profited from a judicious oversight, or perhaps a wrong impression, by condemning it as an unpardonable desecration of the mysteries of harmony; and then people unanimously denounced this barbarous and extravagant music. It is true that its other parts are judged by the same criterion, and that one judges them almost with the assurance of not deceiving oneself. But Your Highness will soon see the reason for this. The more one strives for truth and perfection, the more necessary are precision and exactitude. The difference between Raphael and the common run of painters is imperceptible, and a slight change in the outline, which does not spoil the likeness of an ugly face, completely disfigures the portrait of a beautiful woman. It requires very little for my aria "Che farò senz' Euridice" to turn into a *saltarello* by Burattani—no more, in fact, than a slight change of expression. A note more or less sustained, a change of tempo or rhythm in the vocal part, an untimely appoggiatura, a trill, a coloratura can ruin an entire scene in an opera of that type while doing little harm—or even embellishing—an ordinary opera. Thus the composer's presence at the performance of such music is as necessary as the presence of the sun in the works of nature. He is its very life and soul, and without him everything is confusion and darkness.

But one must be prepared for such obstacles, since there are so many people in the world who think they are entitled to decide questions of taste because they have the privilege of owning a pair of eyes and ears, no matter of what kind. The desire to talk about things one does not understand is common enough among people, and I have recently seen one of the greatest philosophers of our century get involved in writing about music and proclaim, like an oracle, "dreams of the blind and romantic follies."

Your Highness is certainly familiar with the drama *Paride* and may have observed that it does not furnish the composer's imagination with those strong passions, grand images, and tragic situations which, in *Alceste*, stir the audience and produce such great harmonic effects. Thus one cannot expect to find in this opera the same force and energy of music, just as one cannot extract from a subject painted in broad daylight the chiaroscuro effects and contrasts contrived by a painter whose subject derives from a scene observed in semi-darkness. Here we do not encounter a wife about to lose her husband who, in order to save him, has the courage to invoke the infernal deities among the somber shadows of the night and in a wild forest; a woman who, in the agony of death, must still tremble for the fate of her children and be separated from the husband she adores. Here we have to do with a young lover contrasted with an honest but jealous woman, who finally triumphs over her with all the art of a cunning passion. I had to invent the needed variety of color by seeking it in the different characters of the Phrygian and Spartan peoples, by contrasting the rudeness and wildness of the one with the delicacy and softness of the other. I thought that since song, in opera, merely substitutes for declamation, it ought to imitate in Helen the innate rudeness of her nation. I also feel that one ought not to reproach me for having, at times, stooped to the trivial in order to preserve that aspect in my music. If one seeks the truth, one must change style according to the subject, the greatest beauties of melody and harmony turning into faults and imperfections when they are out of context. I don't expect *Paride ed Elena* to be as successful as *Alceste*. As for my intention to induce the other composers to change the style of their compositions, I foresee ever greater obstacles; but I will never cease to renew my efforts in that direction.

Letter to the *Mercure de France* (1773):

One could justly reproach me, and so would I myself, if, after having read the letter written from here to one of the directors of the Royal Academy of Music, which you published in your October issue, and which concerns itself with my opera *Iphigénie;* if, I say, after having shown my gratitude to the author of that letter for having deigned to lavish praises on my work, I did not hasten to declare that, undoubtedly, his friendship and a bias in my favor has carried him away, and that I am far from flattering myself that I deserve the praise he has bestowed upon me. I would deserve even greater censure if I consented to let the invention of the new genre of Italian opera, whose success has justified the venture, be ascribed to me. It is M. Calsabigi to whom belongs most of the credit. And if the music is in the least striking, I must own that it is to him that I am indebted for it, since it was he who enabled me to draw on the resources of my art. That author, full of genius and talent, has followed, in the librettos for *Orfeo*, *Alceste*, and *Paride*, a path little known to the Italians.

These works contain many well-contrived situations as well as those terrible and pathetic traits which furnish the composer the means of expressing great passions and writing music that is both strong and touching. Whatever the composer's talent, he will compose nothing but mediocre music unless the poet inspires him with that enthusiasm without which all works of art remain weak and dull. The imitation of nature is the acknowledged goal which all artists must set themselves: it is that which I, too, try to attain. Always as simple and natural as I can make it, my music strives toward the utmost expressiveness and seeks to reinforce the meaning of the underlying poetry. It is for this reason that I do not use those trills, coloraturas, and cadences the Italians employ so abundantly.

Letter to M. de la Harpe[1] (published in the *Journal de Paris*, 1777):

It is impossible for me, Sir, not to agree with your most judicious observations about my operas, which appeared in the October 5 issue of your *Journal de littérature*. I have absolutely nothing to say by way of reply. Heretofore I have been foolish enough to believe that it was with music as with the other arts, namely that all the passions form its subject, and that it should please no less by expressing the outbursts of a furious man and the cry of pain than by painting the sighs of love.

> There is no snake, no odious monster
> Which, imitated by art, cannot please the eyes.

I took this rule to be as valid in music as it is in poetry. I was persuaded that the song, completely filled, as it were, with the

---

1. Jean François de la Harpe (1739-1803), like Marmontel and d'Alembert, took Piccinni's side in the Gluck-Piccinni quarrel.

tint of the feelings which it aims at expressing, ought to change along with them, and use as many different accents as they have different nuances. Finally, I believed that the voices, the instruments, all the sounds, and even the silences, ought to have only one aim, namely that of expression, and that the union of music and words ought to be so intimate that the poem would seem to be no less closely patterned after the music than the music after the poem.

Those were not my only errors, however. I thought I had observed that the French language was relatively little accented, and did not have the fixed quantities characteristic of the Italian tongue. I was struck also by another difference between the singers of the two nations. For while I found the voices of the Italian singers to be softer and more flexible, the French singers appeared to put more force and energy into their action. From that I concluded that the Italian manner of singing cannot suit the French. Leafing through the scores of your ancient operas, I found, in spite of the trills, cadences, and other faults with which their arias seem to abound, sufficient beautiful passages to make me believe that the French, too, have their native resources.

This, Sir, was my notion when I chanced upon your observations. Immediately light pierced the darkness. I was stunned to see, that, in a few hours devoted to reflection, you have learned more about my art than I after having practiced it for over forty years. You show me, Sir, that it is sufficient to be a man of letters in order to be able to discuss everything. I am quite convinced now that the music of the Italian masters is music *par excellence*, that the singing, in order to please, must be regular and periodic, and that even in those moments of confusion when the singer, driven by several passions, passes successively from one to the other, the composer ought to stick to one melody.

I agree with you that of all my compositions *Orphée* is the only acceptable one. I ask forgiveness of the god of taste for having deafened my audience with my other operas. The number of performances they have received, and the applause accorded to them, do not keep me from seeing that they are pitiful.

I am so convinced of this that I want to rewrite them. And since I notice that you like gentle music, I shall make the furious Achilles utter a song so touching and sweet that the spectators will be moved to tears by it.

As for *Armide*, I shall beware of letting the libretto stand as it is; for, as you have rightly observed, "the operas of Quinault, although full of beautiful things, are tailored in a fashion unsuitable to music; they make very fine poems but exceedingly poor operas." If, then, they have to be transformed into bad poems, as they must in order to become operas that you would consider beautiful, I beg you to procure me the acquaintance of some versifier who can refashion *Armide* according to your formula and who can squeeze two arias into every scene. Together we shall set the length and meter of the verse and, provided the number of syllables is correct, I shall not worry about the rest. I, for my part, shall compose music from which, as befits the work, I shall banish all noisy instruments such as the kettledrum and the trumpet. In my orchestra I want no instruments to be heard except oboes, flutes, French horns, and violins —muted ones, to be sure. There won't be any difficulty in making the words fit the music, since we have taken our measure beforehand.

Thus the role of Armide will no longer be "a monotonous and dull brawling"; Armide will no longer be a "Medea," a "sorceress," but an "enchantress." In her despair I want her to sing an aria so "regular" and "symmetrical," and yet so tender, that even the most timid housewife can listen to it without having her nerves upset.

If some mocking spirit should dare tell me: Sir, beware, lest the furious Armide speak like Armide swayed by love, I shall reply that I do not want to "offend the ears" of M. de la Harpe, or "contradict nature," but that I want to "beautify" it and make Armide "enchant you" rather than "shout" at you. If he persists in his argument by telling me that Sophocles, in his finest tragedy, dared to exhibit before the Athenians the bloodstained eyes of Oedipus, and that the recitative or measured declamation by which the eloquent plaints of that unfortunate king are expressed was certainly intended to convey the most vivid pain, I shall simply reply that M. de la Harpe does not want to hear "the cry of a man who suffers."

Translated by Ulrich Weisstein from *Ecrits de musiciens, xvᵉ-xviiiᵉ siècles*, edited by J.-G. Prud'homme (Paris: Mercure de France, 1912).

CHRISTOPH MARTIN WIELAND
(1733-1813)

CHRISTOPH MARTIN WIELAND was one of the most prolific and influential writers of the eighteenth century. He wrote several outstanding novels *(Agathon* and the satirical *Geschichte der Abderiten* among them) as well as the Romantic epic *Oberon*, on which Weber's opera is based; translated twenty-two of Shakespeare's plays into German prose; and edited the important literary magazine *Der teutsche Merkur* from 1773 to 1789. He was Goethe's co-resident at Weimar, where he had gone in 1772 to tutor the future Grand Duke Karl August.

His interest in opera was greatly stimulated by the success of Gluck's *Alceste*. He subsequently wrote a libretto on the same subject and defended his choice in two critical essays published in 1773: *Briefe an einen Freund über das Singspiel Alceste* and *Über einige ältere Singspiele, die den Namen Alceste führen*. By "Singspiel" Wieland meant opera "in Metastasio's manner," not the genre represented by Mozart's *Entführung aus dem Serail*. (The first serious opera performed in Germany was Rinuccini's *Dafne* in a translation by Martin Opitz and with music by Heinrich Schütz. This work was given at Torgau in 1627. The beginnings of German opera proper, however, were made in Hamburg in the last quarter of the seventeenth century. The leading composer was Reinhard Keiser, who wrote well over one hundred works for the musical stage. Georg Philipp Telemann also composed numerous German operas.) Two years later he wrote a third essay on the subject of opera, in which he developed his aesthetic of the genre. It is from this *Versuch über das deutsche Singspiel und einige dahin einschlagende Gegenstände* that the following excerpts are taken. In this work Wieland does not show himself to be too original a thinker, since many of his ideas are derived from the writings on opera by Francesco Algarotti and the Frenchman Rémond de Saint-Mard. However, he strongly rejects certain of their theories. As a typical representative of the Rococo, Wieland, naturally, felt disinclined to subscribe to the more radical aspects of Gluck's melo-dramaturgy. For him it was a "fundamental law that music ceases to be music when it ceases to give pleasure." At the end of his *Versuch* he outlines his ideal of a pastoral opera based on the idyls of Salomon Gessner and embellished with music by Pergolesi. How strange that Wieland himself should have preferred a Euripidean plot!

Alceste, for which Anton Schweitzer supplied the music, was performed in 1773 in both Weimar and Mannheim. Seven years later the same team produced a second German opera, *Rosamund*. Neither of these works, however, was as well received as Ignaz Holzbauer's *Günther von Schwarzburg* (premiered at Mannheim in 1777), which draws considerably closer to the goal that was finally attained by Mozart's *Zauberflöte* of 1791.

A. Fuchs, "Wieland et l'esthétique de l'opéra," *Revue de Littérature Comparée*, X (1930), 608-633.

Essay Concerning German Opera
and a Few Related Subjects (1775)
CHRISTOPH MARTIN WIELAND

OPERA, insofar as it is a form of drama, shares all the essential qualities of the latter with all the other types of drama; and insofar as it approaches ancient, and especially Euripidean, tragedy more closely than any modern type, it also shares that genre's artistic aims and modes of expression. However, it is distinguished —if not from Greek tragedy, which, in all likelihood, was in itself a kind of opera—from all the other kinds of drama presently in vogue by the important circumstance that everything which in the latter is merely speech or pantomime, in opera is song or instrumental music. In other words: music must be considered the true language of opera.

People whom nature seems to have endowed with more cold reason than feeling and musical taste have called unnatural the feature that makes opera what it is, and that solely because they reject the whole genre as something altogether absurd and incapable of being truly imitative. If they had attended a performance of [Metastasio's] *Didone abbandonata* in an Italian opera house, the irrefutable testimony of their senses would have convinced them that one can be moved by a heroine who sings with orchestral accompaniment. But even without such tangible evidence a little reflection would have shown them that their proof was fatuous since, as proof, it proves too much and works against them. For the very critics who wanted to banish opera as a monstrous creation, since nobody sings in everyday life or reveals his passions, needs, and decisions in full-scale arias, should, for the same reason, have denounced not only all the ancient dramas but modern French and English tragedy in rhymed or unrhymed verses, and all plays in general, as well, because people are not in the habit of discussing their most secret and important affairs aloud with themselves or their trusted friends in the presence of several hundred spectators under the assumption that they are unobserved.

Every kind of play presupposes an unwritten agreement between the poet and the actor on one hand and the listener on the other. The latter concedes to the former that as long as a certain verisimilitude of character, passions, customs, language, action, and logic is preserved, he will not let himself be disturbed in the deception which the theatrical performance produces by any device that is either a necessary prerequisite of the art or is introduced for the sake of increasing the pleasure of the audience. In opera, the poet, the composer, and the singers step forward and say: "Let us see how well our combined efforts will succeed in placing before you an interesting dramatic plot that has been perfected to the utmost degree of deception. We are not foolish enough to wish to make you believe that Iphigenia, Dido, or Alcestis have actually died singing harmoniously and accompanied by basses, violins, flutes, and oboes. We don't ask you to regard poetic, musical, and dramatic imitation, and the ideal which they engender, as nature itself. . . . If in certain crucial moments we succeed in deceiving your imagination, move your hearts and fill your eyes with tears, we have reached our goal and ask for nothing else. And why should you want more?" I think this is a fair enough proposition that leaves no room for objections. . . .

Music is the language of passion. No matter how significant and capable of inspiring the poet to the creation of great moral characters, lofty feelings, and noble conflicts between virtue and passion—i.e. so many occasions for filling our hearts with beautiful moral ideals and admirable maxims—the plot of an opera may be, as soon as the subject becomes political and the hero turns into a statesman . . . or even a stoic . . . , neither the composer nor the singers and spectators will be content. For in order to please the latter to some extent, the poet will be obliged to render these plays (which are rather tragic than lyrical) more musical— in a manner of speaking—by adding episodic love affairs. By doing so, however, he is bound to decrease their value and produce a work to which one could justly apply the Horatian image of the beautiful monster. Plays whose action requires a lot of political arguments, or in which the characters are forced to deliver lengthy speeches in order to convince one another by the strength of their reasons or the flow of their rhetoric, should, accordingly, be altogether excluded from the lyrical stage.

But not all the passions are equally well suited to be rendered and properly expressed through vocal or instrumental music. Dido's beautiful speech from Metastasio's *Didone abbandonata*, which ends with the moving words

> *-e puoi lasciarmi?*
> *Ah non lasciarmi, no*
> *Bel Idol mio!*
> *Di chi mi fideró*
> *Se tu m'inganni?*

can only gain by being sung. But could one believe that the speech of Augustus in which he reproaches and pardons [Corneille's] Cinna for his crime would in any way be improved by its being treated as an accompanied or unaccompanied recitative? The farewell of the dying Alcestis:

O mütterliches Land, o Schwester, o Gemahl,
Zum letzten Mal, zum letzten Mal
Sieht euch Alceste . . . .

is very effective when set to music; for one can well die singing, if one dies as gently and as beautifully as Alcestis does. But the ravings and the despair of the dying Cleopatra in Corneille's *Rodogune* would either be so ennobled by the musical rendition that, contrary to the poet's intentions, the audience would be moved to tears; or the composer, if he tried to compete with the poet, would torment our ears with glaring dissonances, and the singer would be compelled to howl instead of singing.

It seems to be a fundamental law that music ceases to be music when it ceases to give pleasure. It lies in its nature to beautify everything it imitates. The wrath it depicts is the wrath of an angel who pushes rebellious Satan into the abyss; its fury is the fury of the goddess of love directed at jealous Mars, who has killed her Adonis. Music must refrain from painting the fury of an Oedipus who, in his despair, gouges his eyes and curses the day of his birth. All those subjects which do not allow for broken colors, all the wild and unruly passions that are unmitigated by hope, fear, or tenderness, are beyond its reach.

I say this not without fear of having said too much and of having set unduly narrow limits to this divine art. For who can tell how much a Michelangelo of music—a Gluck or Haydn—could successfully widen the scope of the expression and imitation of nature? It is certain, however, that nature itself has set definite limits to each art, which it should never try to exceed. Those who boldly venture beyond it are bound to come to grief. . . . The composer should never forget that . . . when he makes us cry, the tears we shed must not be painful but voluptuous ones, tears expressing joy, love, and the emotions of an overflowing heart.

This consideration would seem to exclude Oedipus . . . and perhaps the majority of tragic heroes from the lyrical stage. Should not, for different but equally compelling reasons, a play that is overburdened with action, or whose action is too complicated, also be unsuited for musical treatment? I admit that too little action will make even the lyrical drama too weak and soporific if poet and composer have failed to do their duty. But one such case does in no way invalidate the theory, which is based on the nature of things, not on accidental circumstances. The greatest possible simplicity of plot is proper to and necessary for opera. Action, after all, cannot be sung but has to be demonstrated; and the more action, the less singing. To be sure, unforeseen happenings, a lot of turmoil, many episodic scenes, etc., render a play more variegated and may endear it to a public fond of noises and too impatient to dwell with any—even the most important—subject. But the music itself derives little advantage from such things, and a sensitive audience even less. Of what nature are the scenes in which the composer is able to give free rein to his genius, where music can manifest its power by compelling our souls and warming our hearts to the melting-point? They are those in which the poet and the composer, with united strength, lead us from one emotion to another, never resting until they have put us into the same frame of mind as the characters they have created. Under such circumstances, a few words—and often a single one—, a sound, a glance, a gesture suffice to affect us deeply. And how does it happen that so small a cause can have so large an effect? Simply because our souls have been slowly prepared, softened, and undermined. Often a chain of preparatory ideas and feelings is needed to give full force to a single blow which the poet wants to aim at our hearts. If in a musical drama the poet or the composer has failed to make these secret preparations, he must not be surprised if we remain indifferent toward a passage that was meant to be extraordinarily effective.

An elaborate treatment and development of the emotions thus seems to be very essential in opera. But the poet can never or rarely achieve it in a subject that is complex, complicated, and full of intrigues. For in such plots he has no time to reveal the innermost feelings of his characters. He cannot put us in such close touch with them that our interest grows to the point where we are more sympathetic toward them than we could be toward characters who lack this appeal and remain strangers to us even though we see and hear them all the time. But is it the composer's fault if such a work remains ineffective? What can he do but try to please at least the ears of his audience by means of the resources provided by harmony and melody, by skillfully executed passages, sparkling arias, unexpected phrases, instrumental solos, etc., if he sees no way of touching our hearts?

I find as little favor with the opinion that the subject of opera ought to be taken from the realm of the marvelous, because in opera everything is music, as I would with the attempt to restrict the engraver to the use of the marvelous on the grounds that engravings are executed in black and white. It is no more marvelous to portray emotions and passions by means of a limited number of related or contrasting sounds than it is to do the same with a little black ink on a white sheet of paper. Nature and truth are no more violated in one case than they are in the other. As has been noted above, opera presupposes a silent agreement between the work of art and the listener; but that is what the listener desires. The work of art does not want to be mistaken for nature; but it exults if with the help of its magic wand it creates effects even greater and more beautiful than those which nature produces.

Algarotti's objection to the use of historical subjects in opera seems to me unfounded. I agree with him when he says that "one strongly feels that trills and coloraturas are not as fitting in the mouth of a Julius Caesar or a Cato as in that of Venus or Apollo." But this merely proves the foolishness of the poet who chooses a hero whose character is unsuited for operatic treatment, and of the composer who portrays a great man like an effeminate Atys. No true connoisseur of music who grasps the nature of opera will be annoyed by hearing Alexander or Porus sing in a musical drama. But he will be vexed by the poor judgment of a composer, the stubbornness of a singer, and the tyranny of fashion, to which even the greatest composers have yielded, if Alexander and Porus do not sing in a way becoming the greatness of their characters.

Algarotti's other objections to historical opera are even less weighty, since they are rooted in the conventional definition of the genre. According to our definition of opera, it matters little "that most historical events are unspectacular" (for an opera is no kaleidoscope) and "that it is difficult to invent dances and instrumental interludes that suit them" (for dances and interludes are in no way essential to the lyrical drama). The only thing that matters is whether the historical subject is simple as well as interesting and capable of being set to music. If these conditions are met, it has all the qualities needed for opera. The rest depends on the talent and skill of the poet, the composer, and the singers. The genre is not to blame if a subject falls into the wrong hands.

However, it cannot be denied that since, in opera, music and song constitute a kind of ideal language (which is far superior to the real one), there is something in its nature which we cannot help but associate with the idea of the marvelous. If one wanted to imagine a language of the gods, one would inevitably be led to think of music. Accordingly, there must be an intrinsic reason for our intuitively considering the Greek gods and heroes as being at home on the lyrical stage, whereas they would be out of place—and even offensive—in the spoken theater, including Greek tragedy. In this respect, all mythological subjects—all other things being equal—are indeed better suited for operatic treatment than historical ones.

The same applies to subjects derived from the heroic age of the Greeks or any other people. For if I prefer operatic subjects taken from Greek mythology, it is mainly because our upbringing, luckily, has made them more familiar and hence more interesting to us than Hyperborean, Indian, Mexican, or any other subjects. But the fact that we associate the idea of a people especially favored by the Muses with the Greeks may also play a part in this. Subjects derived from the heroic age are particularly apt in opera, since everything that distinguishes such an age from ours arouses in us a feeling of the marvelous, which increases in proportion with the growing distance placed between us and the life of a people still unsubdued, hardy, and in full possession of its natural powers. It seems quite natural to us that the people of such an age should use a language infinitely richer, stronger, and more emotional than ours, e.g. that they should sing instead of speaking, just as one can expect them to have more violent feelings, to make nobler decisions, and perform more courageous deeds. So it comes about that we regard Alcestis, Ariadne, Medea, and Iphigenia as being as much at home on the lyrical stage as the goddesses and nymphs, which we commonly take to be creatures of a higher order but still related to us.

Properly speaking, the age of the knight errants . . . does not constitute a distinct era in the history of man, since in all essential points it is identical with the heroic age of the Greeks. . . . The same applies also to the pastoral world . . . which, for us, is equally marvelous but much more attractive than the heroic age. For what could be more pleasant, especially at a time or in a mood when we are tired of the tumult, the fetters, follies, and troubles of life in the city and at court, than these joyous pictures of peace, innocence, love, and happiness, and this carefree life at nature's bosom, where one occupies oneself only for pleasure's sake and not because necessity dictates? This blissful equality, this beautiful simplicity, these perfect manners, which are equally removed from savagery and sophistication, and of which our heart tells us that without them we can never be really happy. How natural, then, that we like to be transported into this Arcadia, that we love its appearance in the lyrical drama, and that we might prefer the latter to all other genres if a poet like Gessner were to collaborate with a composer like Pergolesi in the creation of pastoral operas.

I hope to have successfully proved "that the librettist of an opera has at his disposal not only the world of gods, heroes, and shepherds and the Middle Ages," but actual history as well; but that not every subject taken from one of these sources is suitable, so that he should select those which lend themselves to musical treatment. Firt of all, he should discard all those subjects which, because of the nature of their plots or on account of their complexity and the number of incidents connected with them, are better suited for drama than for opera. Secondly, he should select those characters, passions, and episodes whose truthfulness is not impaired by the musical embellishment. Thirdly, he should devise a plot as simple and limited in the number of *dramatis personae* as possible. And even though he does not eliminate all the episodes, he should eradicate those which weaken the interest in the central action. He should, finally, aim at presenting his characters more in view of their feelings and emotions than with regard to their external actions.

In these obvious principles, it seems to me, everything which

—in addition to the rules that apply to all types of theatrical presentations—the librettist of an opera ought to know, both with regard to the choice and the treatment of subject matter, is contained. These same principles determine what an audience can justly expect of and demand from the poet, insofar as it cannot release him from these obligations without diminishing its own pleasure.

Translated by Ulrich Weisstein from Wieland's *Sämmtliche Werke* (Leipzig: Goeschen, 1857).

JOHANN WOLFGANG VON GOETHE
(1749-1832)

GOETHE, whose musical taste in no way matched his knowledge and appreciation of the plastic arts, was nevertheless genuinely interested in music, especially in the ways in which it can be made to join with language. In judging compositions that were submitted to him by aspiring artists he relied heavily on the opinions of his friends Reichardt and Zelter. He did not see eye to eye with Beethoven, whose personal acquaintance he made in 1812, and remained untouched by Schubert's *Lieder* and Berlioz' setting of scenes from *Faust*.

His favorite operatic composers were Cherubini and Mozart, whose operas he frequently staged at the Weimar theater, of which he was the general manager. He thought exceedingly well of *Don Giovanni* and *Die Zauberflöte*, to which latter he wrote a sequel. For many years he regarded Mozart as the only composer who could have done justice to his *Faust*, but later he maintained in a conversation with Eckermann (January 25, 1827) that Meyerbeer, too, was equipped to furnish the music for that portion of the third act of *Faust II* which had been conceived along operatic lines. At no point in his career, however, would Goethe have shared Schiller's opinion (as expressed in a letter to him of December 29, 1797) that a regeneration of the drama might well be effected by way of opera since opera, by abstaining from servile imitation of nature, was able to insure the return of the ideal to the theater. (Schiller's thoughts, by the way, which found application in his choral play *Die Braut von Messina* [1802], are distinctly echoed by Hugo von Hofmannsthal.)

Goethe's contribution to opera proper consists in the creation of a number of librettos for *Singspiele*, for some of which he enlisted Philipp Christoph Kayser's help. Kayser, a Frankfurt acquaintance, became his collaborator, and a lively correspondence ensued after the composer had moved to Zurich in 1775. Of Kayser's settings only four songs for *Erwin and Elmire* and his music for *Scherz, List und Rache* are extant, and the score of *Jerry und Bätely* is lost.

C. A. H. Burckhardt, *Goethe und der Komponist Philipp Christoph Kayser* (Leipzig, 1879); H. J. Moser, *Goethe und die Musik* (Leipzig: Peters, 1949); O. Janowitz, "Goethe as Librettist," *German Life and Letters*, n. s., IX (1956), 265-276; O. Seidlin, "Goethe's *Magic Flute*" in *Essays in German and Comparative Literature* (Chapel Hill, 1961).

Letters to Philipp Christoph Kayser (1779-86)
JOHANN WOLFGANG VON GOETHE

December 29, 1779:

Herewith enclosed, my dear Kayser, I am sending you an operetta I have written for you on the way. It constitutes no more than a simple contour, which it will be up to you to fill with light, shadows, and colors if you want to please and impress your audience. . . . You will see for yourself that I have aimed at presenting a large variety of lively emotions in a quickly progressing action, letting them succeed each other in such a way as to permit the composer to show his mastery by furnishing transitions and suitable contrasts. I shall discuss this matter further once I have received your reply. Only one other thing I should like to point out to you for the time being: kindly observe that the work provides for three different types of vocal music:

First there are the songs, of which it is assumed that the singer has learned them somewhere by heart and is now applying them to one or the other situation. These songs can and should have peculiar, distinct, and rounded melodies that please the ear and are easily memorized. Secondly, there are the arias in which the characters express their momentary feelings and where, being entirely wrapped up in them, they sing from the bottom of their hearts. These arias should be sung in a simple, pure, and sincere fashion, and all the shades from the most gentle to the most violent feelings should be rendered. Both the vocal melody and the orchestral accompaniment should be treated very conscientiously.

Thirdly there is the rhythmic dialogue, which sets the pace for the entire play. By means of it the composer can either accelerate or retard the action, treating it now as declamation in broken rhythms, and then causing it to move swiftly in a bouncing melody. This dialogue must fit the position and motion of the actor, whom the composer must constantly keep in mind lest he impede the progress of his gestures and movements. You will notice that throughout my play the dialogue is kept in an almost uniform meter; and if you are lucky enough to find a principal theme that suits it, you will do well to use it repeatedly and add the necessary variety through modulation from major to minor and through the acceleration or deceleration of tempo. Since toward the end of the play the singing is to be continuous, you will know what I mean; for in that case one must beware of bringing about confusion. The dialogue should be like a smooth golden ring on which arias and songs are mounted like gems. Naturally, this does not apply to the prose dialogue, which I wish to be spoken, although it is up to you whether you want, here and there, to add some orchestral accompaniment.

January 20, 1780:

You cannot fail to grasp the character of the whole. Light, simple, and pleasing is the element in which so many passions, from heartfelt emotion to the most excessive ire, alternate. Noble characters have been dressed as peasants, and the pure and simple nobility of human nature should always remain the same in its true and adequate expression. As I am writing this, you have probably learned more from reading the play than my description could teach you. Let me urge you once more, however, to acquaint yourself thoroughly with the work before composing it. Arrange your melodies, accompaniments, etc., in such a way that everything relates to the whole and can be explained by the whole. I advise you to be sparing with the accompaniment; for the greatest virtue lies in moderation. Those who know their job can do more with two violins, a viola, and a bass than others can accomplish with a full-sized orchestra. Use the wind instruments individually and like spices: now the flute, now the bassoon, and then the oboe. Thus you set a mood and everybody knows what he is enjoying. Most of our modern composers are like cooks who mix all sorts of things into a stew where fish and meat, baked and broiled things taste alike.

My plan does not call for any recitative whatsoever. If you want to retard the action and slow down the motion at any particular place, it is up to you whether you want to effect this change through pauses or through a change of tempo. But you are free to do as your inner ear bids you. I am eager to have your comments on the work.

I should like to call one other thing to your attention. Beginning with the moment at which Thomas starts to sing his *quodlibet*, the music continues uninterruptedly to the end of the piece. In technical terms: it turns into a finale. I am sure I would run into trouble with any musician except you, because quite a few melodies and moods are pressing upon each other, the action leaving no room for long preparations, executions, or transitions. But with you I feel entirely safe. What I like most in your compositions is their chastity and the ease with which you accomplish much with small means. You do more with a single stroke than others with their most effusive outpourings. . . . But surely I am telling you a lot of things which you know much better than I myself do. Still, it is good for you that even at a distance we know that we are in full agreement. Study the little piece carefully and show the wealth of your talent by putting no more into it than is fitting.

January 23, 1786:
Your reply amply compensates me for my letter, which was longer than any I have written in recent years and causes me once more to write at length to you. Your remarks prove anew your genuine interest in the matter, your conscientiousness, and your artistic taste. And here is how I counter your arguments:

I propose that we leave the first act as it is until you have read the rest and can judge the work as a whole. We'll talk about it afterwards, and you'll intuitively do the right thing.

You are quite right in saying that in a manner of speaking my play is like a musical composition. One could also call it a pantomime. To use a familiar comparison: the contour is firm, but it is left to the composer to add the colors and the chiaroscuro, insofar as it is not implied in the contour. It is true that he cannot increase its scope, but he can compensate for this by reaching up into the third heaven. How far you yourself have transcended the commonplaces of melody and melancholy, of waterfalls and nightingales! I have written the piece with you in mind. You understand me and exceed my expectations. My next play will also be for you, if you want it. We'll come to terms more easily then; and in the meantime, I won't deal with anybody else.

Your other observation, unfortunately, also hits the mark. The piece is too condensed and strained for a musical drama. The three characters are kept too busy. All I can say by way of apology is that I won't write another one like it (although I have one in my drawer, a most charming plot for three characters, even more complex and turbulent than this one).

Every artistic invention has something arbitrary about it. My highest conception of drama is continuous action. I conceived the plot, set to work, and realized too late that it was too dense for a musical drama. I tried to remedy this and let the matter rest for half a year. At last I finished the play, and there it is. It is a *tour de force*, for which we have no actors. Let those we have use it to train themselves.

It is true that the singers want to be physically more at rest. Running, jumping, gesticulating, fighting, and singing are all right in a finale. But one can't have them throughout. My next piece will, accordingly, be more sedate.

Your remarks about rhythm came at the proper time. Let me tell you my own story concerning it:

I know the rules, and you'll find them generally observed in the pleasing arias and the duets where people are of one mind or have only slightly different opinions. I also know that the Italians never stop the flowing rhythm once they have introduced it, and that this is probably the reason why their melodies are so beautifully rounded. But as a poet I am so fed up with the limitations of the iambs, trochees, and dactyls that I have deliberately done away with them. Gluck's compositions in particular have inspired me to do so. For if I wanted to substitute a German text for the original French one which underlies his melodies, I would have to break the rhythm which the French librettist thought to have rendered so very smoothly. In view of the doubtful length of the French words, Gluck actually changed at will the long and short syllables and thus used a different meter from that which the text suggested. I was also intrigued by his setting of Klopstock's[1] poems, which he had charmed into a musical rhythm. Accordingly, I began to interrupt the flow of an aria at the onset of passion; or rather, I thought to enhance and intensify it, as would be the case if I were only reading or reciting. Likewise, in duets where opinions differ, people quarrel, or transitory actions occur, I neglected the parallelism or rather deliberately destroyed it. And as often happens when one sets out in a new direction, one easily oversteps one's goal.

My point of view was further strengthened by the observation that the composer himself is often inspired to beautiful melodies in the way in which a brook runs in beautiful curves when its path is obstructed by a rock.

Translated by Ulrich Weisstein from Goethe, *Gedenkausgabe der Werke, Briefe und Gespräche*, edited by E. Beutler (Zürich: Artemis-Verlag, 1951).

WOLFGANG AMADEUS MOZART
(1756-91)

BOTH AS A HISTORICAL FIGURE and an operatic composer Mozart is too well known to the general public to require a special introduction. His major operas are firmly anchored in the repertory,

1. Friedrich Gottlieb Klopstock (1724-1803), author of the religious epic *Der Messias*, several of whose odes and songs Gluck had set to music between 1773 and 1785. Gluck had also planned to compose an opera, *Die Hermanns-Schlacht*, based on a libretto by the same author.

and even such less universally praised works as *Idomeneo* and *La clemenza di Tito* are intermittently revived in Salzburg and other places. Mozart the correspondent, however, is much less familiar, and that in spite of Emily Anderson's authoritative translation of his letters. Unlike Gluck or Wagner, Mozart was not a theorizer, and we do not possess a single document from his hand that furnishes a convenient summary of his views on musical drama. Even the letters make no extended reference to the works planned or in the process of being executed. This is regrettable, especially in the case of the masterpieces *(Figaro, Don Giovanni, Così,* and *Die Zauberflöte*). About the genesis of the former two we learn more from Da Ponte than from their composer. Although it is generally assumed that Mozart had an unfailing sense of dramatic values, there is relatively little evidence to prove that he actively participated in shaping the librettos of his operas.

The following letters are concerned with *Die Entführung aus dem Serail* (1782) and the unfinished *Oca del Cairo,* an *opera buffa* Mozart wanted to write for the Italian *stagione* of 1783 and for which he asked the Salzburg Abbate Varesco to provide the text. Given Mozart's dramaturgical skills, it seems strange that he should have asserted the absolute priority of his art by stating that "in an opera the poetry must be altogether the obedient daughter of the music."

A. Einstein, *Mozart: His Character and His Work* (London: Oxford University Press, 1945); W. J. Turner, *Mozart: The Man and His Works* (New York: Doubleday, 1954); E. J. Dent, *Mozart's Operas* (London: Oxford University Press, 1960); H. Redlich, "*L'oca del Cairo,*" *Musical Review,* II (1941), 122-131; Kerman, *Opera as Drama,* pp. 77-128.

Letters to His Father (1781-83)
WOLFGANG AMADEUS MOZART

September 26, 1781:

Forgive me for having made you pay an extra heavy postage fee the other day. But I happened to have nothing important to tell you and thought that it would afford you pleasure if I gave you some idea of my opera. As the original text began with a

monologue, I asked Herr Stephanie[1] to make a little arietta out
of it—and then to put in a duet instead of making the two chatter together after Osmin's short song. As we have given the part
of Osmin to Herr Fischer, who certainly has an excellent bass
voice (in spite of the fact that the Archbishop told me that he
sang too low for a bass and that I assured him that he would
sing higher next time), we must take advantage of it, particularly
as he has the whole Viennese public on his side. But in the
original libretto Osmin has only this short song and nothing else
to sing, except in the trio and the finale; so he has been given
an aria in Act I, and he is to have another in Act II. I have
explained to Stephanie the words I require for this aria—indeed
I had finished composing most of the music for it before Stephanie knew anything whatever about it. I am enclosing only
the beginning and the end, which is bound to have a good effect.
Osmin's rage is rendered comical by the accompaniment of the
Turkish music. In working out the aria I have given full scope
now and then to Fischer's beautiful deep notes (in spite of our
Salzburg Midas). The passage "Drum beim Barte des Propheten"
is indeed in the same tempo, but with quick notes; but as Osmin's
rage gradually increases, there comes (just when the aria seems
to be at an end) the allegro assai, which is in a totally different
measure and in a different key; this is bound to be very effective.
For just as a man in such a towering rage oversteps all the bounds
of order, moderation, and propriety and completely forgets himself, so must the music too forget itself. But as passions, whether
violent or not, must never be expressed in such a way as to excite
disgust, and as music, even in the most terrible situations, must
never offend the ear, but must please the hearer, or, in other
words, must never cease to be *music*, I have gone from F (the
key in which the aria is written), not into a remote key, but
into a related one, not, however, into its nearest relative D minor,
but into the more remote A minor. Let me now turn to Belmonte's aria in A major, "O wie ängstlich, o wie feurig." Would
you like to know how I have expressed it—and even indicated

1. Gottlieb Stephanie, Jr., based the libretto of *Die Entführung aus dem
Serail* on a similar text by Bretzner. He also provided Mozart with the
book for *Der Schauspieldirektor* (1786) and Carl Ditter von Dittersdorf
with that for the Singspiel *Doctor und Apotheker* (1786).

his throbbing heart? By the two violins playing octaves. This is the favorite aria of all those who have heard it, and it is mine also. I wrote it expressly to suit Adamberger's voice. You feel the trembling—the faltering—you see how his throbbing breast begins to swell; this I have expressed by a crescendo. You hear the whispering and the sighing—which I have indicated by the first violins with mutes and a flute playing in unison.

The Janissary chorus is, as such, all that can be desired, that is, short, lively, written to please the Viennese. I have sacrificed Constanze's aria a little to the flexible throat of Mlle. Cavalieri, "Trennung war mein banges Los und nun schwimmt mein Aug' in Tränen." I have tried to express her feelings, as far as an Italian bravura aria will allow it. I had exchanged the "Hui" to "schnell," so it now runs thus—"Doch wie schnell schwand meine Freude." I really don't know what our German poets are thinking of. Even if they do not understand the theater, or at all events operas, yet they should not make their characters talk as if they were addressing a herd of swine. Hui, sow!

Now for the trio at the close of Act I. Pedrillo has passed off his master as an architect—to give him an opportunity of meeting his Constanze in the garden. Bassa Selim has taken him into his service. Osmin, the steward, knows nothing of this, and being a rude churl and a sworn foe to all strangers, is impertinent and refuses to let them into the garden. It opens quite abruptly—and because the words lend themselves to it. I have made it a fairly respectable piece of real three-part writing. Then the major key begins at once pianissimo—it must go very quickly—and winds up with a great deal of noise, which is always appropriate at the end of an act. The more noise the better, and the shorter the better, so that the audience may not have time to cool down with their applause.

I have sent you only fourteen bars of the overture, which is very short with alternate fortes and pianos, the Turkish music always coming in at the fortes. The overture modulates through different keys; and I doubt whether anyone, even if his previous night has been a sleepless one, could go to sleep over it. Now comes the rub! The first act was finished more than three weeks ago, as was also one aria in Act II and the drunken duet *(per i signori viennesi*) which consists entirely of my Turkish tattoo. But I cannot compose any more, because the whole story is being altered—and, to tell the truth, at my own request. At the beginning of Act III there is a charming quintet or rather finale, but I should prefer to have it at the end of Act II. In order to make this practicable, great changes must be made, in fact an entirely new plot must be introduced—and Stephanie is up to the eyes in other work. So we must have a little patience. Everyone abuses Stephanie. It may be that in my case he is only very friendly to my face. But after all he is arranging the libretto for me—and, what is more, as I want it—exactly—and, by Heaven, I do not ask anything more of him.

October 13, 1781:

Now as to the libretto of the opera. You are quite right so far as Stephanie's work is concerned. Still, the poetry is perfectly in keeping with the character of stupid, surly, malicious Osmin. I am well aware that the verse is not of the best, but it fitted in and it agreed so well with the musical ideas which already were buzzing in my head, that it could not fail to please me; and I would like to wager that when it is performed, no deficiencies will be found. As for the poetry which was there originally, I really have nothing to say against it. Belmonte's aria "O wie ängstlich" could hardly be better written for music. Except for "Hui" and "Kummer ruht in meinem Schoss" (for sorrow cannot rest), the aria is not bad, particularly the first part. Besides, I should say that in an opera the poetry must be altogether the obedient daughter of the music. Why do Italian comic operas please everywhere—in spite of their miserable libretti—even in Paris, where I myself witnessed their success? Just because there the music reigns supreme and when one listens to it all else is forgotten. Why, an opera is sure of success when the plot is well worked out, the words written solely for the music and not shoved in here and there to suit some miserable rhyme (which, God knows, never enhances the value of any theatrical performance, be it what it may, but rather detracts from it)—I mean, words or even entire verses which ruin the composer's whole idea. Verses are indeed the most indispensable element for music—but rhymes—solely for the sake of rhyming—the most detrimental. Those high and mighty people who set to work in this pedantic fashion will always come to grief, both they and their music. The best thing of all is when a good composer, who understands the stage and is talented enough to make sound suggestions, meets an able poet, that true phoenix; in that case no fears need be entertained as to the applause even of the ignorant. Poets almost remind me of trumpeters with their professional tricks. If we composers were always to stick so faithfully to our rules (which were very good at a time when no one knew better), we should be concocting music as unpalatable as their libretti.

December 6, 1783:

Now let us talk of something else. I have only three more arias to compose and then the first act of my opera will be finished. I can really say that I am quite satisfied with the aria buffa, the quartet, and the finale and am looking forward to their performance. I should therefore be sorry to have written this music to no purpose, I mean, if we do not secure what is absolutely necessary. Neither you nor Abbate Varesco[2] nor I have noticed that it will have a very bad effect and even cause the entire failure of the opera if neither of the two principal female singers appear on the stage until the very last moment, but keep on walking about on the bastions or on the ramparts of the fortress. The patience of the audience might hold out for one act, but certainly not for a second one—that is quite out of the question. This first occurred to me at Linz, and it seems to me that the only solution is to contrive that some of the scenes in the second act shall take place in the fortress—*camera della fortezza*. The scene could be so arranged that when Don Pippo gives orders for the goose to be brought into the fortress, the stage should represent a room where Celidora and Lavina are. Pantea comes in with the goose and Biondello slips out. They hear Don Pippo coming and Biondello again becomes a goose. At this point a good quintet would be very suitable, which would

2. The Abbate Giambattista Varesco also wrote the libretto for *Idomeneo* (1781), after the play of one Danchet.

be the more comic as the goose would be singing along with the others. I must tell you, however, that my only reason for not objecting to this goose story altogether was because two people of greater insight and judgment than myself have not disapproved of it, I mean yourself and Varesco. But there is still time to think of other arrangements. Biondello has vowed to make his way into the tower; how he manages to do so, whether in the form of a goose or by some other ruse, does not really matter. I should have thought that effects far more natural and amusing might be produced, if he were to remain in human form. For example, the news that in despair at not being able to make his way into the fortress he has thrown himself into the sea, could be brought in at the very beginning of Act II. He might then disguise himself as a Turk or anyone he chose and bring Pantea with him as a slave (a Moorish girl, of course). Don Pippo is willing to purchase the slave for his bride. Therefore the slave-dealer and the Moorish girl must enter the fortress in order to be inspected. In this way Pantea has an opportunity of bullying her husband and addressing all sorts of impertinent remarks to him, which would greatly improve her part, for the more comic an Italian opera is the better. Well, I entreat you to expound my views very clearly to Abbate Varesco and to tell him that I implore him to go ahead. I have worked hard enough in this short time. Why, I should have finished the whole of Act I, if I did not require some alterations in the words of some of the arias.

December 24, 1783:

I have received your last letter of the 19th enclosing a portion of the opera. Well, let me deal with this, which is the most urgent matter. Abbate Varesco has written in the margin beside Lavina's cavatina: "a cui servira la musica della cavatina antecedente" [for which the music of the preceding cavatina will do], that is, Celidora's cavatina. But that is out of the question, for in Celidora's cavatina the words are very disconsolate and despairing, whereas in Lavina's they are most comforting and hopeful. Besides, for one singer to echo the song of another is a practice which is quite out of date and is hardly ever made use of. It can only be tolerated in the case of a soubrette and her amant, that is, in the *ultime parti* [secondary characters]. My opinion is that the scene should start with a fine duet, which might very well begin with the same words and with a short *aggiunta* addition for the coda. After the duet the conversation can be resumed. *E quando s'ode il campanello della custode* [and when the duenna's bell is heard] Mlle. Lavina, not Celidora, will be so good as to remove herself, so that the latter, as a prima donna, may have an opportunity of singing a fine bravura aria. Some arrangement of this kind would suit much better the composer, the singer, the spectators, and the audience, and the whole scene would undoubtedly become far more interesting. Further, the audience would hardly be able to tolerate *the same aria* from the second singer, after having heard it sung by the first. In the next place, I do not know what you are both driving at by the following arrangement. At the end of the newly inserted scene between the two women in Act I, the Abbate writes: *Segue la scena VIII che prima era la VII e cosi cangiansi di mano in mano i numeri* [Scene VIII, formerly Scene VII, then follows, and thus the numbers are correspondingly altered]. From this description I am to suppose that, contrary to my wish, the scene after the quartet in which both women sing their little tunes in turn at the window, is to remain; but that is impossible. For not only would the act be very much lengthened, and to no purpose, but it would become very tedious. It always seemed to me very ridiculous to read:

Celidora: *Tu qui m'attendi, amica. Alla custode*
            farmi veder vogl'io; ci andrai tu poi.
            [Wait for me here, my friend, I wish
            to show myself to the duenna. You may
            go later.]

Lavina: *Si, dolce amica, addio.* (Celidora parte.)
            [Yes, sweet friend, good-bye. (Exit Celidora.)]

Lavina sings her aria. Celidora comes in again and says: *Eccomi*, or *vanne*, etc. [Here I am, now you may go, etc.]. Now it is Lavina's turn to go and Celidora sings her aria. They relieve each other like soldiers on guard. Moreover, as in the quartet, they all agree to carry out their proposed scheme, it is far more natural that the men should go off and beat up the people required for this purpose and that the two women should betake themselves quietly to their apartments. The most they could still be allowed is a few lines of recitative. Indeed, I have not the smallest doubt that it was never intended that the scene should be retained, and that Varesco simply forgot to indicate that it was to be omitted. I am very curious to see how you carry out your capital idea of bringing Biondello into the tower. Provided it is diverting, I shall raise no objection, even if it is a little unnatural. I am not at all alarmed at the notion of a few fireworks, for the arrangements of the Viennese fire brigade are so excellent that there is no cause for uneasiness about having fireworks on the stage.

Reprinted from *The Letters of Mozart and His Family*, edited and translated by Emily Anderson (London: Macmillan, 1938), by permission of the author and of Macmillan & Co., Ltd., The Macmillan Company of Canada Limited, and St. Martin's Press, Inc.

LORENZO DA PONTE *(1749-1838)*

LORENZO DA PONTE, a Venetian by birth, was the legitimate successor of Apostolo Zeno (1668-1750) and Metastasio (1698-1782) as librettist of the principal composers of opera in the Italian style. Having studied for the priesthood and taught rhetoric at the University of Treviso, he came to Vienna in 1786. He remained attached to the Imperial Theater until the death, in 1790, of Joseph II, his patron. He then made London his European headquarters and, in 1805, emigrated to America, where he became the first holder of a chair in Italian at Columbia University.

Da Ponte is chiefly known as the librettist of Mozart's finest Italian operas: *Le nozze di Figaro* (1786), *Don Giovanni* (1787), and *Così fan tutte* (1790). It is now generally assumed that Casanova, Da Ponte's friend, had a hand in refashioning the libretto of *Don Giovanni* for its premiere in Prague. Da Ponte also furnished librettos for a host of other composers, among them

Salieri (whose *Tarare* he adapted for Vienna) and Vicente Martin y Soler (Martini), from whose opera *La cosa rara* Mozart quotes in the banquet scene of his *Don Giovanni*.

J. L. Russo, *Lorenzo Da Ponte* (New York: Columbia University Press, 1922); E. J. Dent, *Mozart's Operas* (London: Oxford University Press, 1913); P. Nettl, "Casanova and Music," *Musical Quarterly*, XV (1929), 212-232.

Memoirs (1830)
LORENZO DA PONTE

THERE were only two [composers] in Vienna deserving of my esteem: Martini, at the time the composer most favored by Joseph II, and Wolfgang Mozart, whom I had the opportunity of meeting in just those days at the house of Baron Wetzlar, his great admirer and friend. Though gifted with talents superior perhaps to those of any other composer in the world, past, present or future, Mozart had, thanks to the intrigues of his rivals, never been able to exercise his divine genius in Vienna, and was living there unknown and obscure, like a priceless jewel buried in the bowels of the earth and hiding the refulgent excellence of its splendors. I can never remember without exultation and complacency that it was to my perseverance and firmness alone that Europe and the world in great part owe the exquisite vocal compositions of that admirable genius. The unfairness and envy of journalists, gazetteers, and, especially, of biographers of Mozart, have never permitted them to concede such glory to an Italian; but all Vienna, all those who knew him and me in Germany, Bohemia, and Saxony, all his family and more than anyone else, Baron Wetzlar, under whose roof the first scintillation of that noble flame was allowed to glow, must bear me witness to the truth which I now reveal. . . .

Soon after the success of the *Burbero*[1] I went to Mozart and recounted my experiences with Casti[2] and Rosenberg[3] on the

1. *Il burbero di buon core* (1786) is an opera by Martin y Soler for which Da Ponte had written the libretto (after Goldoni's French comedy *Le bourru bienfaisant*).

2. Giovanni Battista Casti was one of Salieri's three principal librettists. He provided the text for *Prima la musica e poi le parole*, an opera about opera first performed at Schönbrunn in 1786.

3. Franz Xavier Count von Rosenberg-Orsini was the Director of Spectacles under Emperor Joseph II of Austria.

one hand, and with the Sovereign on the other; and asked him whether he would care to set to music a drama I should write for him. "I would do so most willingly," he replied at once. "But I am certain that I should never get permission." "That," I added, "will be my affair." I began, accordingly, to consider the choice of two subjects best suitable to two composers each of highest genius, but almost diametrically opposed to each other in the manner of their composing. . . .

I returned in all peace of mind to my search for subjects to be written for my two dear friends, Mozart and Martini. As for the former, I could easily see that the sweep of his genius demanded a subject of great scope, something multiform, sublime. In conversation with me one day in this connection, he asked me whether I could easily make an opera from a comedy by Beaumarchais—*Le mariage de Figaro.* I liked the suggestion very much, and promised him to write one. But there was a very great difficulty to overcome. A few days previous, the Emperor had forbidden the company at the German theater to perform that comedy, which was too licentiously written, he thought, for a self-respecting audience: how then propose it to him for an opera? Baron Wetzlar offered, with noble generosity, to pay me a handsome price for the words, and then, should we fail of production in Vienna, to have the opera presented in London, or in France. But I refused this offer and proposed writing the words and the music secretly and awaiting then a favorable opportunity to show them to the Directors, or to the Emperor himself, for which step I confidently volunteered to assume the responsibility. Martini was the only one who learned of the beautiful secret from me, and he, with laudable highmindedness, and because of his esteem for Mozart, agreed that I should delay working for him until I should have finished the libretto for *Figaro.*

I set to work, accordingly, and as fast as I wrote the words, Mozart set them to music. In six weeks everything was in order. Mozart's lucky star ordained that the Opera should fail of scores at just that moment. Seizing that opportunity, I went, without saying a word to a living person, to offer *Figaro* to the Emperor. "What?" he said, "Don't you know that Mozart, though a wonder at instrumental music, has written only one opera, and nothing remarkable at that?" "Yes, Sire," I replied quietly, "but without Your Majesty's clemency I would have written but one drama in Vienna!" "That may be true," he answered, "but this *Mariage de Figaro*—I have just forbidden the German troupe to use it."

"Yes, Sire," I rejoined, "but I was writing an opera, and not a comedy. I had to omit many scenes and to cut others quite considerably. I have omitted or cut anything that might offend good taste or public decency at a performance over which the Sovereign Majesty might preside. The music, I may add, as far as I may judge of it, seems to me marvelously beautiful." "Good! If that be the case, I will rely on your good taste as to the music and on your wisdom as to the morality. Send the score to the copyist.". . .

I thought that it was time to refresh my poetical vein, which had seemed to me utterly dried out when I was writing for Reghini[4] and Piticchio.[5] The opportunity was offered me by *maestri* Martini, Mozart, and Salieri who came all three at the same time to ask me for books. I loved and esteemed all three of them, and hoped to find in each compensation for past failures and some increment to my glory in opera. I wonder whether it might not be possible to satisfy them all, and write three operas at one spurt. Salieri was not asking me for an original theme. While in Paris he had written the music for *Tarare*, and wished now to see it Italian in manner as regards both words and music. What he wanted, therefore, was a free adaptation. Mozart and Martini were leaving everything to me.

For Mozart I chose the *Don Giovanni*, a subject that pleased him mightily; and for Martini the *Arbore di Diana*.[6] For him I wanted an attractive theme, adaptable to those sweet melodies of his, which one feels deep in the spirit, but which few know how to imitate. The three subjects fixed on, I went to the

4. Vincenzo Righini, an Italian composer from Bologna, lived in Vienna from 1777 to 1788. In his opera *Il convitato di pietra* he anticipated Mozart's *Don Giovanni* by a decade. Da Ponte had written the libretto of a comic opera *(Il filosofo punito)* for him; it was a theatrical failure.

5. Da Ponte had furnished the text for Francesco Piticchio's opera *Bertoldo* (1787).

6. This was an original libretto by Da Ponte. The opera was performed in October, 1787.

Emperor, laid my idea before him, and explained that my intention was to write the three operas contemporaneously. "You will not succeed," he replied. "Perhaps not," said I, "but I am going to try. I shall write evenings for Mozart, imagining I am reading the *Inferno;* mornings I shall work for Martini and pretend I am studying Petrarch; my afternoons will be for Salieri. He is my Tasso." He found my parallels very apt.

I returned home and went to work. I sat down at my table and did not leave it for twelve hours continuous. . . . The first day, between the Tokay, the snuff, the coffee, the bell, and my young muse, I wrote the two first scenes of *Don Giovanni*, two more for the *Arbore di Diana*, and more than half of the first act of *Tarare*, a title I changed to *Assur*. I presented those scenes to the three composers the next morning. They could scarcely be brought to believe that what they were reading with their own eyes was possible. In sixty-three days the first two operas were entirely finished and about two thirds of the last.

From *The Memoirs of Lorenzo da Ponte* translated by Elisabeth Abbott. Copyright 1929 by Elisabeth Abbott; copyright renewed 1957 by Elisabeth Abbott. Published by J. B. Lippincott Company.

BEAUMARCHAIS (1732-99)

PIERRE AUGUSTIN CARON DE BEAUMARCHAIS, the well-known French playwright and pamphleteer of the prerevolutionary period, was himself a fairly accomplished musician. He enjoyed a fine reputation as a harpist and instructed the daughters of Louis XV in that instrument. The first of his two most famous plays, *Le barbier de Seville*, was originally intended as a comic opera, the early editions containing five songs composed, or more likely adapted from the Spanish, by the author. When the Italian comedians to whom Beaumarchais had offered the work rejected it, he rewrote it as a comedy. As such it was successfully staged in February, 1775. Paisiello set it to music in 1782 and Rossini did so thirty-four years later. Its sequel, *La folle journée*, is said to have contained music by Antoine Baudron, a member of the orchestra at the Comédie Française, but the concluding vaudeville was written by Beaumarchais himself. Due to the king's objections (which were later echoed by Joseph II) the work could not be performed until 1784. Da Ponte adapted *La folle journée* for Mozart, whose *Nozze di Figaro* had its premiere in May, 1786. The libretto of *Tarare* was originally offered to Gluck, who recommended his pupil Salieri, Mozart's chief rival in Vienna. Salieri carried out his assignment, and the opera was successfully staged in June, 1787. It was subsequently adapted by Da Ponte for Vienna, where *Axur, re d'Ormus* was so enthusiastically welcomed in January, 1788, that it helped to crowd Mozart's *Don Giovanni* out of the repertory. In his dedication of *Tarare* to the composer, Beaumarchais, curiously enough, credits Salieri with "having helped him to give the French an idea of the Greek plays such as I have always imagined them to be." The preface, which is addressed to the holders of season tickets at the Opéra, appeared in the second edition of the libretto, published in 1790.

G. Lemaître, *Beaumarchais* (New York: Knopf, 1949); H. Kling, "Caron de Beaumarchais et la musique," *Rivista Musicale Italiana,* VII (1900), 673-697, E. Newman, "Beaumarchais and the Opera," *The Monthly Musical Record,* May 1, 1902, pp. 82-84.

Preface to *Tarare* (1790)
BEAUMARCHAIS

I DO NOT WISH to discuss the art of singing, that of modulating well, or the various tonal combinations. Nor do I want to entertain you by talking about music as such. Rather, I wish to examine the effect of poetry on music, and the latter's reaction to dramatic poetry, with a view toward those works in which the two arts are united. I am less concerned with creating a novel type of opera than with finding a new way of arousing interest in opera.

To make you more favorably inclined to my words, my dear contemporaries, let me tell you that there is no century in which I would rather have been born, and no nation to which I would rather belong. Apart from all the things I like in French society, I have noticed among ourselves, in the last twenty or thirty years, a vigorous upsurge, a general desire to expand our ideas by useful researches and increase the general welfare through the application of reason.

One speaks of the last century as one that has produced great literature. But what is literature compared with the mass of useful objects? A noble intellectual pastime. Our century will be called a profoundly scientific and philosophical one, rich in discoveries and full of strength and reason. The spirit of our nation seems to undergo a fortunate crisis, as a vivid and widely diffused light makes everybody feel that everything could improve. People are restless and active; they invent and improve, and from the profound science which regulates the acts of government to the lighter talent of writing popular songs, from that elevation of genius which makes us admire Voltaire and Buffon to the easy and lucrative profession of pointing out what still remains to be done, I observe in all social classes a desire to excel, to be superior, to expand one's ideas, one's knowledge, and one's pleasures, which can only turn to universal advantage. It is thus that everything grows, prospers, and improves. Let us try, if possible, to improve upon a grand spectacle.

You know that not everybody is equally well predisposed to the execution of great designs. We are that as which we were born, and later develop according to our talents. Not every moment in the life of an individual, no matter how patriotic, is equally suited to produce works of merit. But if few people can choose the kind of work they do, everybody can at least select his own pleasures; and it is perhaps in that choice that an observer should look for the true secret of the human character. The mind has to relax from time to time. After the strenuous hours of business everybody follows his inclination when amusing himself. Some hunt, some drink, some play cards, and some busy themselves with intrigues. And I, who do not care for any of these things, write a modest opera.

I naïvely admit—in order to avoid quarrels—that of all literary trifles a work of that genre is perhaps the most trifling. I further grant that, if the author of such a work were to take offense at how little attention is paid to these products, he would be

the greatest of his enemies, being unhappy because of this neglect and ridiculous because of this unhappiness.

But whence arises this disdain for the libretto of an opera?
For, after all, it is not easy to construct one. Could it be that
the French, fonder of popular songs than of serious music,
prefer epigrams and ballads to operatic arias? Somebody has
remarked that the French, while genuinely fond of popular
songs, merely pretend to like serious music. Let us not press
the point, however, for fear of confirming that opinion.

Does not the cold disdain in which opera is held result,
rather, from the fact that this spectacle, poorly concocted of
the many arts required for its formation, has ended by throwing
us into confusion as to the rank each should occupy and the
peculiar pleasure it should afford?

The true hierarchy of these arts, it seems to me, ought to
proceed as follows in the esteem of the spectators: first comes
the action or plot, which commands the greatest interest, next
the beauty of the poem or the easy manner of relating the
events, then the charm of the music, which is but a novel
expression added to the charm of the poetry, and finally the
ballet, whose grace and gaiety help to warm some frigid situations. Such, in the order of the pleasure they afford, is the rank
occupied by all these arts.

By a bizarre inversion which is peculiar to opera, however,
the drama seems to be little more than a banal means, a pretext
for making the other ingredients scintillate. Here the accidents
have become the substance, while the substance of the plot is
treated as an accident, as the cloth which everyone embroiders
as he wishes.

But what caused us to be thus deceived? How is it that we
Frenchmen, known for our vivid interest in everything that pertains to pleasure, have proved so indifferent toward this one?

Let us try to explain why even the most enthusiastic opera
lovers (I first of all) are always bored at the Opéra. Let us
find out why, in opera, the drama is counted for nothing, and
why the music, insignificant as it is without this buttress, en-
gages us more than the words—and the ballet still more than

the music. This problem has needed explanation for a long time; let me try to give it, as best I can, in my own way.

First of all, I have convinced myself that the public is never mistaken in its judgment of a spectacle, and that it cannot possibly be. Drawn toward pleasure, it seeks it out and follows it everywhere. If it misses it in one spot, it tries to seize it in another. Since in opera it cannot understand the words, it turns to the music. Devoid of the interest which the drama arouses, the latter, barely amusing the ears, gives way to the dance, which pleases the eyes in addition. In that doleful submission to the theatrical effect it is always pleasure that is sought after; the rest is of no avail. If the opera, instead of arousing a powerful interest, offers me but a puerile amusement, what claim does it have to my esteem? The spectator is right, then, and the spectacle wrong. Boileau wrote to Racine: "No good opera will ever be written; for music cannot tell a story." He was right, in his time, and could have added: "Music cannot speak in dialogue." There was then no doubt that it would never be able to do so.

In a letter written by the man who has thought and said everything, in a letter sent by Voltaire to Cideville in 1732, one reads the following remarkable words: "The Opéra is only a public meeting-place, where one gets together on certain days without quite knowing why. It is a house that everybody frequents, although one does not think highly of its master, and although boredom reigns supreme."

Before him, La Bruyère had said: "It is obvious that opera is the design of a grand spectacle of which it gives an idea. But I do not know why, with such splendid music and such a royal expenditure, it invariably bores me."

They said openly what everybody knew to be true, but which a certain national vanity kept us from admitting. Alas! Vanity even to the point of boredom in a spectacle. I am tempted to say like Abbé Bazile: "Whom are they cheating here? Everybody's in on the secret."

As for me, who was born highly susceptible to the charms of music, I have long sought to discover why opera bores me in spite of all the efforts made and moneys spent to the opposite effect; and why a detached piece that charms me when played on the harpsichord nearly tires me out, if not actually boring me, when transferred from the drawing room to the operatic stage. And here is what I seem to have noticed:

There is too much music in our music for the theater; it is always supercharged with it. And to use the naïve remark of a justly famous man, the illustrious Chevalier Gluck, "our opera stinks of music" *(puzza di musica).*

It is my personal opinion that the music of an opera, like its poetry, is merely a new way of embellishing the words and must, therefore, never be abused.

Our playwrights have long felt that the magnificence of words and all the poetic finery which comes handy in poetry was a little too exalted for the stage. They all realized that if one desires to hold the interest of a theatrical audience, one must tone down that dazzling splendor of words by bringing them closer to nature, the best interest of the spectacle requiring such plain and simple truth as is incompatible with that luxury.

That reform, accomplished, luckily for us, in drama, still remains to be carried out in opera. For if it is true (as it doubtless is) that music is in the opera what the verses are in the drama—a more stately expression, a stronger means of presenting thoughts and emotions—let us beware of abusing that kind of affectation and of using that manner of painting too lavishly. A faulty overabundance stifles and smothers the truth; the ear is sated but the heart remains empty. On this point I appeal to everybody's experience.

But what happens when the ambitious composer, lacking both taste and talent, tries to lord it over the poet or fashion his music into a work by itself? The subject goes to the winds, and all one finds is incoherence of thoughts, division of effects, and lack of unity; for these two distinct and separate effects cannot produce the desired unity without which one cannot enjoy a spectacle.

Just as a French author says to his translator: "Sir, you are from Italy? Translate this work of mine into Italian, but do not make the slightest change in it," so I, a librettist, could say to my collaborator: "My friend, you are a composer? Translate my play into music; but do not, like Pindar, get lost in your images by speaking of Castor and Pollux in connection with an Olympic victory; for they don't concern me here."

And if my composer has a true talent, if he reflects before writing, he will feel that his duty and his success lie in rendering my thoughts in a language which is simply more harmonious, in making them more expressive, and not in creating a work apart. The imprudent composer who wants to shine by himself is, at best, a cold light, a will-o'-the wisp. If he tries to live without me, he will merely vegetate: his excessive ambition threatens my existence as well as his own. He dies with the last sound of the violins, and together we plunge noisily from the stage to the bottom of Erebus.

I can't repeat it too often, and beg you to think it over carefully: our grand operas fail by having too much music in their music.

Here is why everybody is bored by them. While the actor sings, the action rests (that is, if he sings merely for the sake of singing); and where the action rests, we lose our interest. But, you will object, must he not sing, since this is his only idiom? True; but let me try to forget it—that, at least, is what the composer should aim at.. Let him sing his piece as one versifies it, simply in order to adorn it; let me find an added charm in it and not a source of distraction.

"I, who have always faithfully and unfalteringly loved music, often, when listening to my favorite pieces, find myself shrugging my shoulder and whispering disgruntled: 'Shame on you, music! Why repeat so much? Instead of telling a story rapidly, you dawdle; instead of painting a passion, you sluggishly cling to the words.' "[1]

And what results from all this? If, while the poet, sparing of words, strives hard to tighten his style and condense his thought, the composer, contradicting him, delays, draws out the syllables, and drowns them in trills, thereby depriving them of their force or meaning, the one moves right as the other

[1] From Beaumarchais' preface to *Le barbier de Seville*.

moves left, and one doesn't know whom to follow. Then I start yawning, and boredom drives me from the theater.

What do we ask of the theater? That it should entertain us. The union of all the charming arts ought surely to provide the most vivid pleasure at the Opéra. Is it not from the union itself that the spectacle derives its name? Their displacement, their abuse have made the Opéra an abode of boredom.

Let us restore the pleasure by re-establishing their natural order without robbing that great entertainment of any of the advantages which it offers. That is a task well worth while undertaking. Let us add some observations regarding the libretto and its mixture to the efforts that have been made since *Iphigénie*, *Alcestis*, and the Chevalier Gluck, in order to improve the quality of the spectacle. Let us devise a sound doctrine and let us add an example to the precept. Finally, let us try to gain approval for the happy union of both.

First of all let us remember that an opera is neither a tragedy nor a comedy but participates in both and can embrace all the genres.

Accordingly, I shall not choose a subject that is altogether tragic, since the general mood would be so sinister that the festive occasions would seem to drop out of nowhere, thereby killing the interest. Let us also refrain from using purely comic intrigues, from which the passions and grand effects are excluded, so that the music lacks nobility, since the passions as well as all grand effects are excluded.

It seems to me that in opera historical subjects cannot be as effective as imaginary ones.

Are we then restricted to pure fantasy, to those subjects where the marvelous, always in the guise of the impossible, shocks us by its absurdity? But experience shows that those actions that are resolved by a fairy's wand or the intervention of the gods leave our hearts cold; and all mythological subjects suffer from that defect. But in my operatic system I cannot minimize music except by greatly increasing the [dramatic] interest.

Above all, we must not forget that, the slow progression of music being a hindrance to the action, special emphasis must be placed on the clarity and impact of the parts executed simultaneously. For if the greatest appeal of a play derives from its action, how much more important will the latter be in opera, by dint of the necessity of compensating for the other ingredient [language], which one is so often forced to renounce.

I shall propose, then, to take a subject halfway between the marvelous and the historical. I also have observed that our overly civilized manners are too methodical to be theatrically effective. Oriental manners, less familiar and more outlandish, leave more room for the imagination and appear to be better suited for our purpose.

Where despotism prevails, salient customs easily develop. There slavery approaches greatness, love ferocity, and the passions of the great surpass all limits. There one can see, united in the same individual, the most abysmal ignorance joined to unrestrained power, and despicable weakness to the most disdainful haughtiness. There I see the abuse of power toy with the lives of men and the pudicity of women, revolt march side by side with cruelest tyranny, and the despot making everybody tremble until he himself trembles—and often both at the same time. This disorder befits our subject; it stimulates the poet's imagination; it excites the mind that inclines toward the exotic.

These, then, are the manners we need for our opera. They permit the use of all the moods; and the harem, too, gives rise to all sorts of happenings. I can show myself lively, imposing, gay, serious, playful, terrible, and sprightly in turn. The oriental customs even have something magical about them, something marvelous that helps to entrance our minds and enliven our interest in the action.

If I could crown the work with a great philosophical idea— even in giving birth to the plot—I am sure that such a spectacle would bear its fruits, and that intelligent people would be grateful for my work. While partisan spirit, ignorance, and the desire to harm inspire the barking pack, the public feels no less that such an enterprise is not to be despised. Perhaps it will even go so far as to encourage more gifted men to continue my work and develop a new form of entertainment worthy of the greatest nation on earth.

. . . The music, that stubborn obstacle to the development of the characters, preventing me from presenting fully rounded individuals in an action so far removed from our own circumstances (a certain familiarity with the characters being required to arouse any interest in a plot), I have fashioned a novel prologue, in which everything one needs to know concerning my plot and my characters is presented in such a way as to make the audience enter with ease into the spirit of the action, the necessary information also being provided. This prologue is the exposition. Enacted by airy creatures, illusions, and nimble shadows, it constitutes the marvelous portion of the libretto; and I have taken pains not to deprive our opera of any of the advantages it offers. The marvelous, too, has its merits, as long, that is, as one does not abuse it.

I have arranged it so that my work offers the variety which renders it palatable, that one act brings respite from the other, and that each has a character of its own. Thus, the elevated tone, the gay mood, the tragic or comic style, festive occasions, simple and noble music, a grand spectacle, and forceful situations will, I hope, each in turn, sustain the people's interest and curiosity. The constant danger to which my protagonist is exposed, his virtue, his touching belief in the native deities, contrasted with the despot's ferocity and the politics of a Brahmine will, I hope, furnish ample contrast and edification. . . .

When the play was finished, I found in an Arabian tale certain situations resembling those of *Tarare*.[2] They reminded me of the fact that a while ago I heard somebody read that tale out in the country. How lucky, I said, turning over the pages anew, I was to have such a poor memory. I took over from the tale what I could use; the rest was unsuited to my purpose. If the reader wants to follow suit, if he is patient enough to read volume III of the *Djinnies*, he will see what belongs to me, what I owe to the Arabian story, and how the confused memory of an object that has struck our fancy is fertilized by the imagination and ripens in the memory without our being aware of it.

But that which belongs even less to me is the fine music of my friend Salieri. This great composer, the *lumen* of the Gluck

2. The source has been identified as the Persian story of "Sadak and Kalasrade" from *Le cabinet des fées*, t. xxx (Amsterdam, 1786).

school, possessing the style of that great master, is naturally endowed with an exquisite taste, a just mind, and a dramatic talent combined with an almost unique inventiveness. He has had the good sense to renounce for my sake a host of musical beauties that embellished his opera, solely because they unduly prolonged the action. But the masculinity, pace, and boldness of the work will amply recompense him for all these sacrifices.

That talented man, so disregarded, so disdained for his fine opera *Les Horaces*,[3] has anticipated in *Tarare* the one objection that will be raised against it, namely that my play is not sufficiently lyrical. After all, this was not our aim, since we were merely concerned with creating a musical drama. My friend, I said to him, to soften one's ideas, to effeminate one's phrases in order to make them more musical is the main source of the abuses which have spoiled our pleasure in opera. Let us raise music to the height of a vigorous and well-constructed drama. Let us restore its ancient nobility, and perhaps we will achieve the grand effects which are so highly praised in Greek tragedy. These, then, are the labors we have undertaken during the past year. And I frankly admit: under no circumstances could I have been induced to leave my study in order to create, in collaboration with an undistinguished individual, the work which, thanks to M. Salieri, has become the chief diversion of my evenings and often a delectable pleasure.

I think that our discussions would have formed a rather nice poetics of opera; for M. Salieri is a born poet, and I am a bit of a musician. Never perhaps will one succeed without this coincidence.

If the part usually called the recitative, if, in one word, the action of *Tarare* is not as simple as my system requires, the reasons adduced by him in explanation of this circumstance are so just that I should like to transmit them to you.

To be sure, Salieri said, one cannot simplify the action too much. But the human voice, when speaking, progresses by tone graduations almost impossible to catch, by quarter tones, sixth tones, or eighth tones. And in the harmonic system one does not write for the voice except at the intervals, strictly observed, of

---

3. Salieri's opera *Les Horaces* was premiered in September, 1786.

whole tones and semitones. The rest depends on the singers; get them to assist you. The music I compose conforms to the austere rules of the art. But you tell me all along that in comedy the greatest feat of the actor consists in making one forget the poetry while preserving its meter. All right, then, once our singers have learned this trick, they will be true actors.

To simplify the recitative without disturbing the harmony, to bring it closer to the spoken language, is the real task we tackled in our rehearsals. And I must openly praise the efforts made by all our singers. Short of using the spoken language the composer could hardly have done better; but to use the spoken language would have robbed the action of the strong support which our skilled composer has taken care to furnish as often as possible through the orchestra.

Orchestra of our Opéra! Noble protagonist in Gluck's, Salieri's and my own system! If you stifle the words, you are a mere noise-maker; your true merit lies in expressing their emotional content.

You know it as well as I do. But if my composer has agreed to divide our work in half through constant variety, that is, by relieving the music through the action, and vice versa, the orchestra and the singers ought to reach a similar agreement rather than boring the audience. If the composer's soul entered into that of the poet and has, in a sense, espoused it, all the contributing arts ought to listen to, and wait for, each other rather than impeding and stifling one another. From their union results pleasure, from their vanity boredom.

The best orchestra imaginable, were it to produce the grandest effects, would kill the pleasure if it covered up the voices. It is the same with a theatrical spectacle as with a beautiful face outshone by a cluster of diamonds: they overshadow its beauty rather than enhancing it. Which shows that the project which has constantly occupied us is an attempt to add to the finest spectacle in the world the only beauties it lacked: a rapid action, a lively and pressing interest, and, most of all, the honor of being listened to.

Two brief maxims have, during our rehearsals, served to summarize my theory of opera. To our cooperative actors I gave but one advice: ENUNCIATE CLEARLY! To the best orchestra in the world I addressed only the words: PLAY MORE SOFTLY! If this is well understood, I added, it will render us worthy of the public's attention. "But," somebody will say, "if we don't understand a thing, what are we supposed to listen for?" Gentlemen, in the spoken drama one understands every single word; but hitherto one has not understood a thing in opera. Do you forget that, in the latter, to sing means simply to speak more forcefully and harmoniously? What is it that deafens your ears? Is it the intermingling of voices or the noise produced by the orchestra? ENUNCIATE CLEARLY! PLAY MORE SOFTLY! These are the best remedies which the singers and the orchestra possess against this malady.

But I have discovered a secret I should like to reveal to you. I have found the principal reason why we don't hear the words of an opera. Shall I name it, gentlemen? It is our inability to listen. The lack of interest in opera has caused this inattention. But in several recent works, which are full of excellent things, I have observed that certain felicitous passages captivated the audience. And I, whether worthy or not, ask for your whole-hearted attention on the opening night of *Tarare*. And may an infernal noise revenge the audience afterward if I have shown myself unworthy of it.

You want to judge me without listening to me? Leave that privilege to the posters of tomorrow which are often printed today.

Is it asking too much from you to concentrate for three hours on a work created in as many years? I beg everybody, especially my enemies, to grant me that favor. It is mainly for their sake that I speak of this. If they give me the slightest excuse at the first performance, they can count on my taking advantage of this circumstance in the subsequent ones. It is better for them if I fall rather than being pushed.

They say that the newspapers are enjoined to treat the Opéra kindly in their pages. I should think little of their reputation if they did not receive permission to make an exception with *Tarare*.

There remains, at any rate, the certain means of anonymous

letters, epigrams, broadsheets, printed invectives dispersed by the thousands in our salons. Who knows whether an eloquent orator may not arise in the temple of the Muses of literature and good taste who, disliking *Tarare*, will find some way of discrediting the author and his work for all time? This happened to the unfortunate *Figaro* who, having been placed under such an anathema, has fallen upon evil days and a languishing old age.

All these means of doing harm to a work are good, effective, customary; famished hatred thrives on them; malice claims them; our urbanity tolerates them; the author mocks them or is grieved by them; the piece continues to be performed or is dropped from the repertory; and in the end everything returns to the old order of indifference: that is the worst of evils.

May public taste and the obstinacy of hatred preserve us from such a fate for a little while. May the leading authors embrace my principles and improve upon them. My friends can tell whether I will envy or embrace them. Indeed, I shall do the latter joyfully, happy, o my contemporaries, to have made a tiny furrow, which others will cultivate, in the field of your pleasures.

Translated by Ulrich Weisstein from Beaumarchais, *Oeuvres choisies* (Paris: Didot, 1822).

ANDRE ERNEST GRETRY (1741-1817)

GRETRY was the principal composer of opéra comique in eighteenth-century France and, as such, cultivated a genre that owed its popularity partly to Charles Simon Favart, the playwright and director of the Comédie-Italienne from 1758 to 1769, and partly to the composer Pierre Monsigny (1729-1817). Of Walloon descent (he was born in Liège), Grétry began his musical training at the age of nine as a choir boy and in 1758 wrote his first orchestral compositions, a group of miniature symphonies. Between 1759 and 1766 he studied in Rome but was pronounced unable to master the science of harmony. His musical talent, indeed, was largely melodic. He visited Voltaire at Ferney on returning from Italy and asked him in vain to supply a libretto.

He arrived in Paris in the fall of 1767 and in the following year enjoyed his first operatic success with *Le Huron*, performed at Favart's theater. This marks the beginning of an operatic career that extended until 1803.

Grétry wrote approximately seventy operas, few if any of which are performed in our day, perhaps the only work of his now in the repertory being the suite from *Cephalus and Procris* that is occasionally heard in the concert hall. The success of Grétry's more ambitious operas on historical, legendary, and mythological subjects was small, although *Richard Coeur-de-Lion* is widely praised as one of his finest works. (For Grétry's suggestions concerning the revision of the final scene of that work see his letter of October 23, 1784, as reprinted in Julien Tiersot's *Lettres de musiciens écrites en français du xv*e *au xx*e *siècles* [Turin: Bocca, 1924]). His chief librettists were Marmontel and Michel Jean Sedaine, Diderot's emulator in the writing of *comédies larmoyantes*. In 1791 Grétry expressed a desire to set Beaumarchais' play *La mère coupable* to music, but nothing came of the proposal. His letter to the playwright is found in L. de Loménie's study *Beaumarchais et son temps* (Paris: Levy, 1873), II, 456.

Reflections on Music (1789)
ANDRE ERNEST GRETRY

I MUST NOT QUIT the beautiful country that has been the cradle of my meager talents without throwing a glance at the present state of Italian opera. Although it would seem ungrateful of me to reproach, at times, the art that is closest to my heart, my love emerges all the more fervently afterward.

The Italian school is the best now in existence, as far as both instrumental and vocal music are concerned. The melody of the Italians is simple and beautiful; and it is not permitted to render it harsh and bizarre. The melodic line of a song isn't beautiful unless it comes naturally and without effort. In the serious as well as the comic genre their *obbligato* recitatives, their expressive or *cantabile* arias, their duets, their cavatinas (which bring timely relief from the recitatives), their *bravura* arias, and their finales have served all Europe as a model.

There is no use praising the efficacy of their verse, for it is nearly impossible to miss, their language being accentuated and free because of the frequent elision of vowels. The Italian public actually never criticizes a composer on that point. I have listened to the aria of a master beginning with the word "*amor*," and although the "a" is short, it was sustained throughout several bars in 4/4 without anybody's taking exception. The Italian loves music too much to give it fetters other than those which are self-imposed. He willingly sacrifices the beauty of his language to that of the song.

The Italian language itself is so fond of melody that it lends itself to everything, even to the extravagances of the composer, without the slightest objection on the part of its grammarians.

"What does it matter," the nation seems to say, "that in order to create a new melody in song one has to strangle the prosody and even the meaning of the words? The song retains its beauty, and other words are easily found to suit it." The French may feel the same way one day; but then they will love music passionately, and feeling will have replaced the mania for analyzing and dissecting their pleasures.

What, then, do the Italians lack in order to have a good serious opera? For during the nine or ten years which I spent in Rome I didn't see a single *opera seria* succeed. If, at times, large audiences gathered, it was with the intention of hearing this or that singer. But as soon as he left the scene, everybody retired into his box in order to play cards or eat ices. And the parterre yawned.

Old teachers have assured me, however, that formerly the librettos of Zeno and Metastasio were truly successful. And having questioned them about the manner in which these were treated by the composers of their time, I realized that their arias were shorter than ours, that there were fewer ritornellos and almost no coloraturas and repetitions. One need not look further for the cause of the boredom and indifference with which the contemporary operas are greeted. For if one took the trouble to cut out the repetitions, coloraturas, and ritornellos, I am certain that the scores would be shorter by two thirds and that the action, having been contracted in this manner, would create a genuine interest. Comic operas are much less subject to this flaw, since boredom is almost exclusively generated by the poor construction of the plot. The Italian composers will yet learn how to be dramatic. For I know that our French scores circulate in the conservatories of Naples and are studied with this in mind.

I have noticed another shortcoming in the Italian opera, which might be called their dramatic counter-sense. The best singers are not always charged with the principal parts, because often the mixed arias,[1] which are found in the parts of the secondary characters, suit them best. But either on account of their talent or because the composer has stressed their parts, they invest everything they sing with so much charm that their roles, in spite of the poem's intentions, become the principal ones. It is only too obvious that this shift in dramatic interest will tend to confuse the hearer, and that the best singer ceases to be an actor at the moment he begins to please at the expense of the dramaturgically important role.

Tragedy certainly offers less variety to the composer than comedy, because in it all the characters are noble. But it is by no means necessary that the composer restrict himself to the use of three types of arias with which to render the passions in an *opera seria*. There are many shades capable of differentiating the characters, and one does not have to be satisfied with producing arias *di bravura*, pathetic arias, and those of the mixed variety. But look at the number of *bravura* arias found in most Italian operas, most of them identical in character and even with identical coloraturas, no matter how different the situation. How should one not be bored by such monotony, and how can one keep the public from focusing attention on an excellent singer who possesses the gift of making them forget the opera?

There is general agreement that the instrumental music of the Italians is weak. How can it attain to equal rank among good compositions? It almost invariably lacks melody for, in that

---

1. As Grétry explains in the chapter "De l'imitation" of the seventh book of his *Mémoires*, there are three types of music: the pathetic, the gay, and "a third that participates in both of these and is called mixed or *demi-caractère*."

case, the composers seem to be mainly concerned with harmony. But one finds little harmony, since they do not know how to modulate. However, if harmony and melody are lacking, all that remains is noise. As far as their effect is concerned, the choruses also are nonexistent. Perhaps one should not blame the composers too strongly for this fault, since the Italians are prejudiced against the use, on the stage, of fugues and anything that resembles them. But there is no other means except a more or less strictly constructed fugue for rendering convincingly the choruses of priests, conspiracies, and all that pertains to magic. This unwarranted prejudice must be blamed for the unpardonable harmonic poverty. The Italian dance tunes are usually pitiable, for they are neither dance tunes, nor singing tunes, nor harmonious. The simple recitative is derived from the accent of their language; but the length of the scenes and the relative lack of energy on the part of the enervated creatures who sing it makes it extremely soporific.

We are also agreed that the Italian compositions are dry and fairly monotonous. This is partly due to their harmonic deficiency. That queen of music is much neglected even by the pupils of Durante, who possessed it in such large measure.[2] . . .

But where the technique is lacking, the sensibility that is natural to the inhabitants of the warmer countries is the true source of melodic song. And it is here that the Italians excel.

What, then, is needed in order to perfect the Italian opera? The excessively long scenes will have to be cut, the action tightened by pruning the ritornellos, coloraturas, and repetitions, which are especially dull when the action moves quickly. The choruses will have to be rendered more dramatic, with more variety in harmony and modulation. The Italian composers will have to follow their French and German colleagues in the instrumental parts, i.e. overtures, marches, and dances. Only then will the interest arise from the very heart of the drama, and the singer will turn actor in spite of himself. He will no longer be permitted to leave the stage in order to suck an orange while his partner continues to talk to him as if he were still present.

---

2. Francesco Durante (1684-1755) was a prolific composer and a famous teacher of music at various Naples conservatories.

An opera made in accordance with my suggestions will be successful even if performed by mediocre artists. If the singers know their business, the success will be overwhelming. But I venture to say, without fear of uttering a paradox, that a famous singer to whose talents everything is sacrificed ruins the total effect, especially if he is surrounded by middling colleagues whom he eclipses.

Translated by Ulrich Weisstein from Grétry's *Mémoires ou Essais sur la musique* (Paris: Verdière, 1812).

Of the Need for Comic Opera (1812)
ANDRE ERNEST GRETRY

IN MUSIC there are several types of comedy: the comedy of manners, the comedy of situation, verbal comedy, the decently, sweetly, and tenderly humorous, the subtly humorous, and the coarsely humorous. The comedy of manners should be treated austerely by the composer. It is not the comedy he should see but the underlying moral. The tunes ought to be just as austere. Unwittingly I seem to have observed this rule when I composed the aria "Pour tromper un pauvre vieillard" for *Le tableau parlant*.[3] The piece is written in a minor key and frequently uses syncopation and counter-movements, almost in the style of the ancient counterpoint. The music is only intermittently humorous, for instance in the passage: "Tantôt c'est une main friponne/ Qu'on lui passe sous le menton." But the austere style returns in the following line, "Le bon homme enchanté s'écrie."

It is not the fool I have musically depicted but the dupe. When the situation is humorous, when the parterre laughs before the actors have spoken, the composer should use restraint in his intonation as well as in his use of comic devices. He needs to do very little. In such cases, as in many others, I advise him to write a simple tune. If he also seeks to be funny, superfluity will ensue, since the situation speaks for itself. Enhance it but do not spoil it, and you will have done enough!

The verbally humorous should be more nimble and genuinely

3. *Le tableau parlant*, with a libretto by Louis Anseaume, was first performed at the Comédie-Italienne on September 20, 1769.

felt, since the composer has often but a single moment in which to strike home. Should the poet change tone in order to express a humorous sentiment? If so, the composer should follow suit. The decently, sweetly, and tenderly humorous is hard to achieve, since neither too much nor too little is wanted. In this case I prefer too little to too much. The aria of little Lucette in *Silvain*,[4] "Je ne sais pas si ma soeur aime," exemplifies the decently and naïvely humorous. When that air is sung—and, strangely enough, everybody sings it well—the audience barely smiles, but it smiles.

The subtly humorous is very hard to express in music. If the composer fails to display good taste, it falls flat. That genre of the comic scares me the most when I tackle it. A lot of composers are less squeamish, and I know why: they aren't aware of the danger. There are a few pieces in *L'ami de la maison*[5] with which I am almost satisfied, like the little duet "Vous avez deviné cela!" But, as Montaigne says, "one doesn't know everything of anything." I tremble when such pieces are sung lest I have colored the truth or forced the expression. I fear that the actress will exaggerate her playing and that the orchestra, remembering but one single note of the accompaniment, will try to say everything and usurp the full expression. That comic genre, then, is extremely hazardous. The poet, the composer, the singer, and the orchestra have to share one feeling, and so much sensitivity is not given to that many individuals. If one single performer gives the show away, everything is lost.

The coarsely humorous is the easiest of them all, so much so that it ought to be banished from the arts. By the coarsely humorous I do not mean the humor of Molière, even where it seems trivial. When I see a procession of enemas arrive in the *Malade imaginaire*, when I see druggists multiply everywhere, I laugh because there's a moral attached. I imagine that in those times Parisian doctors had the mania of purging all mankind.

Translated by Ulrich Weisstein from Grétry's *Memoires ou Essais sur la musique* (Paris: Verdière, 1812).

4. *Silvain*, with a libretto by Marmontel after Gessner, received its première on February 19, 1770 at the Comédie-Italienne.

5. *L'ami de la maison*, with a libretto by Marmontel, was premiered on October 26, 1771 at Fontainebleau.

LUDWIG VAN BEETHOVEN
(1770-1827)

OF THE MANY operatic projects pondered by Beethoven over the years, only one, *Fidelio*, came to fruition; and it appeared only after a prolonged period of gestation, composition, and often agonizing revision. What a pity that the admirer of Goethe (whom he had met in Teplitz in 1812) never carried out his plan to set *Faust* to music, an undertaking that might have been the epitome of his career. In addition to *Fidelio*, Beethoven's contribution to opera consists of a fragment from *Vestas Feuer* based on a libretto by Schikaneder, the author of *Die Zauberflöte* and director of the Theater an der Wien, with whom Beethoven had entered into contract in 1803. The opera was subsequently composed by Weigl. However, Beethoven wrote several *Schauspielmusiken*, of which that to Goethe's *Egmont* is by far the most elaborate and familiar, as well as music for ballets (such as *Die Geschöpfe des Prometheus*), *Festspiele*, etc.

The plot of *Fidelio* is based on an actual experience undergone by Jean Nicolas Bouilly, the librettist of Cherubini's opera *Les deux journées*, in the aftermath of the French Revolution. The book was first set to music by Pierre Gaveaux (1798), and an Italian version with music by Paer was performed in Vienna in 1809. Beethoven seems to have started work on Joseph Sonnleitner's German translation in 1803 or 1804. The première of the first version of *Fidelio*, at any rate, took place on November 20, 1805, a few days after the occupation of Austria's capital by the French. The need for cuts and revisions was widely felt, and Röckel, the Florestan of the version premiered on March 29, 1806, gives a plastic account of how Beethoven's friends persuaded him to follow their suggestions. It was only in 1814 that *Fidelio* was given its final shape. Friedrich Treitschke, whose report on Florestan's "starvation" aria is included here, helped in the revisions. *Fidelio* as we now know it was first performed on May 23, 1814.

Beethoven, unfortunately, never explained his poetics of opera, if he had conceived one at all. If we want to find out what he thought about musical dramaturgy, we must, therefore, rely on fragmentary statements and second-hand reports and recollections like those reproduced on the following pages.

Willy Hess, *Beethovens Oper "Fidelio" und ihre drei Fassungen* (Zürich: Atlantis-Verlag, 1953); id., *Beethovens Bühnenwerke* (Göttingen: Vandenhoeck und Rupprecht, 1962).

Revising *Fidelio* (1861)

J. A. Röckel's Report As Given to A. W. Thayer

It was in December, 1805—the opera house An-der-Wien and both the Court theaters of Vienna having been at that time under the direction of Baron Braun, the court banker—when Mr. Meyer, brother-in-law to Mozart and stage director at the opera An-der-Wien, came to fetch me to an evening meeting in the palace of Prince Karl Lichnowsky, the great patron of Beethoven. *Fidelio* had been performed a month ago, unhappily just after the arrival of the French, when the city was shut off from the suburbs. The whole theater was occupied by the French, and only a few friends of Beethoven ventured to hear the opera. These friends were now at the soiree intending to make Beethoven consent to the changes they wanted to make in the opera in order to remove the heaviness of the first act. The necessity of these improvements was already acknowledged and settled among themselves. Meyer had prepared me for the coming storm, when Beethoven should hear of leaving out three whole numbers of the first act.

At the soiree were present Prince Lichnowsky and the Princess, his lady, Beethoven and his brother Kaspar, Stephan von Breuning, Heinrich von Collin, the poet, the actor Lange (another brother-in-law to Mozart), Treitschke, Clement, the conductor of the orchestra, Meyer and myself. Whether Kapellmeister von Seyfried was there, I am not certain, though I believe he was. I had arrived in Vienna only a short time before and met Beethoven for the first time on this occasion.

As the whole opera was to be gone through, we went directly to work. Princess Lichnowsky played on the grand piano the great score of the opera, and Clement, sitting in a corner, accompanied with his violin the whole opera by heart, playing all the solos of the different instruments. The extraordinary memory of Clement being universally known, nobody was astonished except myself. Meyer and I made ourselves useful by singing as well as we could, he (basso) the lower, I the higher parts of the opera. Though Beethoven's friends were fully prepared for the battle, they had never seen him in such excitement, and without the entreaties of the very sensitive Princess, who, as he himself acknowledged, was a second mother to Beethoven, his friends were not likely to have succeeded in this, even to themselves, very doubtful enterprise.

But when, after their united endeavors from seven till after one o'clock, the sacrifice of the three numbers had been accepted, and when we, exhausted, hungry and thirsty, went to restore ourselves with a splendid supper, none was happier and gayer than Beethoven himself. Had I seen him before in his fury, I saw him now in his best mood. When he saw me, who was sitting opposite him at the table, intently occupied with a French dish, he asked me what I was eating. And when I answered: "I don't know," he roared: "He eats like a wolf, without knowing what! Ha, ha, ha!"

The condemned numbers were: 1) a great aria with chorus of Pizarro; 2) a comic duet between Leonore (Fidelio) and Marcelline, with violin and cello solo; and 3) a comic tercet between Marcelline, Jacquino and Rocco. Many years after, Mr. Schindler found the scores of these three pieces amongst a pile of music discarded by Beethoven and got them as a present from the composer.

A question has been raised concerning the accuracy of Röckel's memory in his statement of the numbers canceled on this occasion; to which it may be remarked that the particulars of this first and extraordinary meeting with Beethoven would naturally impress themselves very deeply upon the memory of the young singer; that the numbers to be condemned had been previously agreed upon by the parties opposed to the composer in the transaction, and doubtless made known to Röckel; that Röckel's relations to Meyer were such as to render it in the highest degree improbable that he should confound Rocco's gold aria with either of the Pizarro airs with chorus belonging to Meyer's part; that both of these belong to the first and second original acts—i.e. to the first act of the opera as Röckel knew it; that he (Röckel) in his letter to the writer is not reporting upon the pieces actually omitted in the subsequent performance three or four months later, but upon those which, at this meeting, Beethoven was with great difficulty persuaded to omit; that the objections made to them were not to the music, but because they retarded the action; and, therefore, that the decision now reached was by no means final, provided the end desired could be attained in some other way. Perhaps it may yet appear that Beethoven, now cunningly giving way, succeeded in winning the game and retaining all three of the pieces condemned.

Reprinted from Alexander Wheelock Thayer, *The Life of Ludwig van Beethoven*, edited by H. E. Krehbiel, by permission of Princeton University Press.

Changing Florestan's "Starvation" Aria
FRIEDRICH TREITSCHKE

I VOICED MY OBJECTION to having a man nearly dead of starvation sing a *bravura* aria. We considered several alternatives until at last, according to Beethoven's opinion, I hit the nail on the head. I wrote words which describe the last upsurge of life before its fading ("Und spür' ich nicht linde, sanft säuselnde Luft . . ."). What I now relate will forever live in my memory. He came to my house at about seven o'clock in the evening. After we had talked about other things, he asked how the aria was progressing. I had just finished it and handed it to him. He read it, paced up and down in the room, mumbled and hummed, as he usually does instead of singing, and opened the piano. My wife had often asked him in vain to play; but on this day he placed the words in front of him and set out on the most striking improvisations, of which, unfortunately, no magic could preserve a record. Out of these he seemed to conjure up the motive of the aria. The hours passed, but Beethoven continued to improvise. The dinner he wanted to share with us was served, but he did not let himself be interrupted. He embraced me only in the late evening and rushed home without having eaten. On the following day he completed the excellent piece of music.

Translated by Ulrich Weisstein from Paul Bekker, *Beethoven* (Berlin/Leipzig: Schuster & Loeffler, 1911) by permission of Mrs. Maximiliane Kraft-Bekker.

FRANZ GRILLPARZER (1791-1872)

FRANZ GRILLPARZER, the eminent Austrian dramatist (adequate English translations of whose plays are only now becoming available), throughout his life took exceptional interest in music.

He studied harmony, loved to improvise on the piano, tried his hand at composition, and was active as a music critic and aesthetician. Especially in the early stages of his career he conceived plans for a number of librettos. In 1823 Beethoven asked him to suggest revisions in the text of Kotzebue's *Die Ruinen von Athen*, for which he had written incidental music. Shortly afterward, Grillparzer submitted to Beethoven the libretto of the Romantic opera *Melusina*. Beethoven liked the work and repeatedly discussed it with its author. Although at one point he claimed to have already composed it (in his head?), no traces of a score were found after his death. He probably abandoned the idea in 1826 when the director of the Berlin opera, Count Brühl, rejected the subject on the grounds that it was too similar to that of E. T. A. Hoffmann's *Undine*, which had been successfully performed a decade earlier. Another idea broached by Grillparzer—that of an opera entitled *Drahomira*—also failed to materialize. *Melusina* was finally set to music by Konradin Kreutzer (1833). Although Beethoven encouraged several prominent playwrights of the time to write librettos for him, *Fidelio* (1805, revised 1814) remains his only contribution to the operatic genre.

D. W. McArdle, "Beethoven and Grillparzer," *Music & Letters*, XL (1959), 44-55; P. Gordon, "Franz Grillparzer: Critic of Music," *Musical Quarterly*, II (1916), 552-567; P. Nettl, "Beethoven's Unwritten Operas," *Opera News*, XV/22 (1950/51), 29-31.

Der Freischütz, Opera by Carl Maria Weber (1821)
FRANZ GRILLPARZER

THIS COMPOSER [Weber] apparently belongs to some extent to the class of individuals who do not understand the difference between poetry and music, and between words and sounds. Music has no words, i.e. arbitrary signs that acquire meaning only from that which they designate. Sound, on the other hand, in addition to being—on occasion—a sign, is also a thing. Like combinations of plastic forms, combinations of sounds please long before any idea has been associated with them. Like ugly forms in sculpture, a discord revolts us physically without the intervention of reason. Whereas words affect first the reason and then, through it, the feelings (the senses playing a very subordinate part), music and the plastic arts primarily affect the senses and subsequently, through their agency, the feelings; the reason being the last faculty to share in the overall impression. In the plastic arts, this consideration has led the greatest experts (Mengs, Lessing, and Goethe among them) to postulate the beauty of form as an indispensable, even the supreme, law.

What is true of the plastic arts applies even more strongly to music. Its first, immediate effect lies in the stimulation of nerves and senses, which explains why Kant—correctly, within his frame of reference—assigns to it a much lower place than to any other art. He regards its effects as being so overwhelmingly physical that the reason, whose regulative participation Kant takes to be the criterion most important in the evaluation of any art, has, in this case, only a minor influence on the feeling of pleasure or displeasure generated by the work of art. Although Kant has gone a little too far, the facts on which his opinion is based are incontrovertible. The auditory sense, which subserves the reason when we listen to words, in the case of music partly seems to escape its rule and, in view of the immediacy of the effects produced upon it, begins to resemble the lower senses— a similarity strikingly illustrated, among other things, by our reaction to the indistinct sounds of a French horn played at a distance. However, it is generally known and taken for granted that no free, no fine art can be based on the lower senses, no matter how sweet and how easily invested with meaning these sense impressions may be.

Musical sounds, in their original and primary meaning, are sense impressions that please or displease by themselves, i.e., without the intervention of reason. Even in the most skillful combination of intervals, the judgment relating to them is a sensuous one, since even the most ingenious theory of intervals relates to the pleasant or unpleasant effect of the sounds, which is determined by the natural disposition of our organs of hearing.

If one proceeds further in the consideration of sounds and sound combinations, a new aspect, which establishes the connection with reason that is required by every art, is soon discovered and thus music as an art made possible. For in addition to the fact that musical sounds are inherently pleasant or unpleasant, experience teaches us that they evoke certain states of mind which, accordingly, they can be used to designate. Joy and sadness, desire and love have their corresponding sounds; and even pain, terror, and wrath have theirs, which it is not impossible to raise to the level of music. Even though the ability of music to designate is thus restored, two things must be kept in mind. First of all, musical designations are not as precise as those furnished by ideas and by the words conveying them. Secondly, the original, purely sensuous nature of music cannot be altogether suppressed by a subsequent broadening of its meaning. Even the most refined music, that is to say, initially affects the senses, the first impression being so exceedingly strong that often it is almost irresistible. In view of the relative vagueness of the designations music is able to provide, reason, which operates only remotely, is not in a position to neutralize, by its approval, any unpleasant sensations that may have overwhelmed the listener.

As for the ability of music to designate specific things, I am willing completely to alter the words—or even the mode of the feelings—in any of the arias of Mozart, who is certainly the greatest of all composers, without arousing the suspicion, or lessening the admiration, of anyone who hears it for the first time. Since people will object by saying that such an experiment cannot be conducted, I will adduce even stronger proof by suggesting that ten individuals who are thoroughly versed in music and poetry be asked to furnish a suitable text to Beethoven's most characteristic symphony. One will be surprised to see how different their versions will turn out to be. Music differs from all the other arts to the extent to which symphonies, sonatas, and concertos are possible—works, that is to say, which, without designating anything in particular, please on account of their inner structure and the accompanying indistinct feelings. These indistinct feelings are the very essence of music. In this respect poetry is inferior to it. Where words are insufficient, music takes their place. A musical sound expresses that which words cannot render: speechless longing, mute desire, love's hidden wishes, sadness looking for an object and afraid of finding it in itself; belief that soars upward; prayer that mumbles and stammers. Whatever exceeds the power of words in depth or height belongs to music. There it has no peer, while in all other respects it is inferior to its sister arts.

"What conclusions can one draw from these observations?" people will inquire. Should music desist from wanting to designate? Should it cease to stick closely to the words of the libretto? Should it stop trying to satisfy the reason? I conclude that music should, first of all, endeavor to accomplish what it can. It should continue to do that in which it excels language rather than compete with the spoken word on its own grounds. It should not attempt to make words out of sounds; for like every art it ceases to be art as soon as it passes beyond its appointed limits. Music ought, accordingly, to aim at creating beautiful sounds, as the plastic arts aim at creating beautiful shapes. Just as the poet who tries to imitate the composer by means of sound effects is a fool, so the composer who wants to render music as precise as language is crazy. This is why Mozart is the greatest composer—and Weber not the greatest.

Translated by Ulrich Weisstein from Grillparzer's *Sämtliche Werke*, edited by M. Necker (Leipzig: Hesse, n. d.)

E. T. A. HOFFMANN (1776-1822)

TRAINED IN THE LAW, E. T. A. Hoffmann spent the larger part of his mature life in the service of the Prussian government, first, from 1800 to 1806, in Poland—this period ended with the French occupation of Warsaw in the latter year—and then from 1814 to his death in Berlin, where he advanced to the position of *Kammergerichtsrat*. His musical interests, stimulated by his studies with Goethe's friend Reichardt, resulted in the composition of a first, unperformed opera, *Die Maske*, in 1799, which was followed by a setting of Goethe's *Scherz, List und Rache* (1801) and a musical version of Clemens Brentano's *Die lustigen Musikanten* (1805). Between 1804 and 1814 Hoffmann made music his profession, first as musical director and advisor at the Bamberg theater and subsequently as operatic conductor of the

Sekonda company in Leipzig and Dresden. An opera *(Aurora)* he composed in 1811 was resurrected in the twentieth century. Hoffmann's operatic masterpiece, *Undine*, was successfully performed in Berlin in 1816 (see Weber's review in the present anthology). This was a setting of the fairy tale by La Motte-Fouqué which was so dear to the Romantics—of whom Hoffmann was one of the most typical.

In addition to writing a number of instrumental compositions (among them a Mass, a symphony, and several pieces of chamber music), Hoffmann was active as a music critic, in which capacity he contributed both reviews and musical fantasies to the Leipzig *Allgemeine Musikalische Zeitung*. He is far more important as a writer than as a composer, and many of his literary creations (especially the so-called *Kreisleriana*) are concerned with musical subjects. Offenbach made use of a number of Hoffmann's stories in his opera *The Tales of Hoffmann*. "Der Dichter und der Komponist" (The Poet and the Composer), which forms part of the sequence *Die Serapionsbrüder*, originally appeared in the *Allgemeine Musikalische Zeitung*.

H. W. Hewett-Thayer, *Hoffmann, Author of the Tales* (Princeton University Press, 1948); G. Abraham, "Hoffmann as Composer," *Musical Times*, August, 1942, 233-235; A. R. Neumann, "Musician or Author? E. T. A. Hoffmann's Decision," *Journal of English and Germanic Philology*, LII (1943), 174-181.

The Poet and the Composer (1816)

E. T. A. Hoffmann

FERDINAND inquired solicitously what Ludwig had composed in the meantime and was amazed when the latter confessed that he still had not gotten around to writing and producing an opera, since, so far, no libretto had been able to inspire him by its form or subject matter.

I don't see, Ferdinand replied, why you yourself haven't written a libretto, since, considering your vivid imagination, you should have little trouble inventing a plot and putting its action into words.

Ludwig: I admit that my imagination is lively enough to give birth to many a successful operatic plot. Especially at night, when a slight headache puts me into a dreamlike state that marks the struggle between sleep and waking, I not only invent fairly good and truly Romantic operas but actually see them performed with my own music. As far as the ability to remember them distinctly and write them down is concerned, however, I am afraid that I do not possess it. And how can you expect us composers to acquire, in order to versify our librettos, the mechanical skill needed in every art and presupposing constant endeavor and continuous practice? But even if I had acquired the skill demanded for the versification and construction of a drama, I would still feel disinclined to write my own libretto.

Ferdinand: But nobody could possibly have a better understanding of your intentions than you yourself do.

L.: That is certainly true. And yet it seems to me that the composer who sits down to write his own libretto must feel like a painter who, before being permitted to work on the painting itself, is compelled to make an engraving of the subject his imagination has conceived.

F.: Do you think, then, that the creative fire needed in the act of composition would fizzle out and disappear in the act of versification?

L.: Precisely that. And in the end my own verses would seem to me to be as wretched as the paper cartouches of the firecrackers that only yesterday rose with dazzling splendor into the sky. But seriously: in no other art does it seem so necessary for the success of a work that its creator grasp the whole with all its parts, down to the smallest detail, in his first enthusiasm. For nowhere is it more harmful and useless to polish and to improve. I know from experience that the melody which spontaneously suggests itself in the course of reading a poem is always the best and, as far as the composer is concerned, the only true one. While writing the libretto, the composer simply could not help but think of the music which the situations demand. Carried away and enraptured by the melodies that suggest themselves to him, he would vainly endeavor to find the appropriate words; and if he could force himself to concentrate on the language, the stream of musical invention, no matter how strong its current, would soon dry out as if in barren sand. To express my innermost conviction even more strongly: in the moment of musical inspiration every word or phrase would seem inadequate and weak, and the composer would have to descend from his height in order to beg for the bare means of existence in the lower realm of words. Would he not, like the captive eagle, soon find his wings paralyzed as he vainly strove to soar upward?

F.: This sounds fairly reasonable. But do you know, my dear friend, that you apologize for your unwillingness to struggle through the necessary scenes, arias, duets, etc., rather than convincing me of the truth of your contention?

L.: That may well be so. But let me renew an old reproach. Why did you refuse, at the time when we shared the same artistic ideals, to write the libretto I so ardently desired?

F.: Because I consider it to be the least rewarding of all tasks. You must admit that nobody is more stubborn in his demands than you composers. And if you claim that one cannot impose upon the musician to acquire the mechanical skill required for versification, I maintain that the poet is greatly handicapped by having to consider your needs, the structure of your tercets, quartets, finales, etc., in order not to sin every moment—as is frequently the case—against the forms cherished by you with goodness knows what justification. When we have striven ever so hard to give the proper poetic expression to every portion of our work, and paint each situation in glowing words and charming, smoothly running verses, it is frightful to see how mercilessly you obliterate our finest lines and mangle our best verses by twisting, inverting, or drowning them in music. This much about the vain attempt to carefully work out details. And how many admirable subjects which we have conceived in a state of poetic frenzy and offered to you in the hope that they will fully satisfy your demands, you reject as being unsuited to and unworthy of musical treatment. Often this is sheer obstinacy or goodness knows what else on your part. For frequently you settle on texts that are of the poorest caliber.

L.: Slowly, my dear friend. There are indeed composers to whom music is as uncongenial as poetry is to many a poetaster. It is they who use texts that are pitiful from every point of view.

But the genuine composers, who live in and for the sublime and holy art of music, solely choose truly poetical subjects.

F.: But Mozart?

L.: Selected for his classic operas only such poems as were suited for music, although this may seem paradoxical to many a person. Apart from this, I think that one could closely define what subjects are fit for opera, so that the poet would run no risk of making the wrong choice.

F.: I confess that I have never thought of this and that, given my scanty musical knowledge, I certainly would have lacked a firm basis of judgment in this matter.

L.: If by musical knowledge you mean the so-called musical training acquired in the schools, one does not need to have that in order to be able to judge the needs of the composer. For without it one can understand the nature of music so well that, in this respect, one is a much better musician than one who, having formally studied the subject and having imbibed a great many errors, worships the rules (like a fetish made with one's own hands) as the living spirit, and whom this idolatry deprives of the bliss which emanates from the higher realm.

F.: Do you really think that a poet can grasp the true essence of music without having been initiated by the schools?

L.: Assuredly, Yes, from that remote realm which we often envisage in strange forebodings, beautiful voices emanate that awaken the music imprisoned in our breasts. Thus liberated, the music rises so joyously, happily, and with such a fire that we begin to share the bliss of that Paradise where the poet and the composer are members of one church. For the secret of word and sound, which this consecration reveals, is one and the same.

F.: I hear you, my dear Ludwig, strive to explain in lofty maxims the mysterious nature of art. And indeed, I begin to see the abyss that, in my opinion, separated the poet from the musician, vanish from before my eyes.

L.: Let me try to give you an idea of what I consider to be the true nature of opera. Briefly put: only that work can be a true opera in which music is a necessary and direct outgrowth of the poetry.

F.: I admit that I don't quite follow you as yet.

L.: Is not music the mysterious language of a distant realm of spirits, whose lovely sounds re-echo in our soul and awaken a higher, because more intensive, life? All the passions, arrayed in shining and resplendent armor, vie with each other, and ultimately merge in an indescribable longing that fills our breasts. This is the heavenly effect of instrumental music. But now music is to enter into life, take hold of its phenomena, and, embellishing both words and deeds, delineate specific actions and emotions. Can one speak of common things in lofty language? Is music able to express anything but the marvels of that land whence it issues? Let the poet prepare for the bold flight into the distant realm of Romanticism. There he will encounter the marvelous, which he is to transport into life, glowing with such vivid colors that one willingly believes in its existence and wanders, as in a blissful dream that is far removed from the meager everyday reality, along the flowery paths of the Romantic life, wary only of its language, which is the word transfigured by music.

F.: Then you approve solely of the Romantic opera, with its fairies, spirits, miracles, and metamorphoses?

L.: I actually regard the Romantic opera as the only true one. For music is at home only in the realm of Romanticism. You can believe me, however, when I tell you how utterly I despise those pitiful creations in which silly, stupid spirits appear and marvels are piled on top of each other without rhyme or reason, merely for the entertainment of the idle crowd. Only the inspired poet is capable of writing a truly Romantic opera. For he alone can infuse life into the strange apparitions from the spirit realm. On his wings we traverse the chasm that separates us from it. Once having accustomed ourselves to the unfamiliar country, we believe in the marvels which abound in it as visible, necessary manifestations of the influence of higher beings upon our existence. These latter are responsible for all those forceful and gripping scenes which now fill us with fear and trembling and then with indescribable bliss. It is, in one word, the magic power of poetic truth which the poet who depicts the marvelous must have at his disposal. It alone can overwhelm us, while a whimsical succession of idle tricks . . . will always leave us cold and unmoved. In opera, my dear friend, the intervention of supernatural powers must be made visible. Thus a romantic realm is to be created in which language, too, acquires a new meaning (or rather: where, issuing from that distant realm, it has itself been transformed into song and music) and where the dramatic actions and situations, suffused with forceful sounds and melodies, affect us all the more strongly. In this way music, as I have previously indicated, becomes a direct and necessary outgrowth of poetry.

F.: Now I fully comprehend your meaning and am reminded of Ariosto and Tasso. Yet I think it would be difficult to write a musical drama according to your specifications.

L.: It is the work of the truly Romantic poet of genius. Think of the superb Gozzi.[1] In his dramatic fairy tales he has met all the conditions I have set for the librettist. And it is incomprehensible to me why this rich treasure of operatic subjects has not been used more frequently.

F.: I admit that when I read Gozzi's works several years ago they strongly affected me, although naturally I did not look at them from your point of view.

L: One of his finest fairy tales is undoubtedly *The Raven* . . . .

F.: I distinctly recall this wonderful and fantastic play and can still feel the deep impression it made on me. You are right in saying that here the marvelous appears as necessary and is so poetically true that one willingly believes in it. It is Millo's deed, the murder of the raven, which seems to knock at the brazen door of the somber realm of spirits. Now the latter opens musically, the spirits invade the human realm and enmesh the characters in that marvelous and mysterious fate which rules over them.

L.: Very true. And now consider the powerful and magnificent scenes the poet has managed to draw from this conflict with the realm of spirits. Jennaro's imposing self-sacrifice, Armilla's heroic deed—there is a greatness in these which is quite unknown to our moralizing playwrights, who wallow in the

---

1. Carlo Gozzi (1720-86), a contemporary and rival of Goldoni, is best known for his dramatic fairy tales. Although he himself was not active as a librettist (except perhaps once for Galuppi), several of his plays have found favor through the operatic medium: *Turandot* was set to music by Puccini, *The Love of the Three Oranges* by Prokofieff, and *King Stag* by Hans Werner Henze.

inanities of everyday life as if in the remains of a feast that have been thrown into the garbage can. And how beautifully the humorous parts of the masks are blended with the rest.

F.: Indeed. Only in truly Romantic works does one find that perfect fusion of tragic and comic elements which touches the audience in a unique and marvelous way.

L.: Even our contemporary mass producers of opera have dimly felt this. Hence the so-called mock-heroic operas, in which the heroic parts are often really humorous, while the humorous ones are heroic only insofar as they heroically defy the basic rules prescribed by taste, decency, and good manners.

F.: How few operas there are that conform to your theory of the genre!

L.: Indeed. Most of the so-called operas are meaningless plays with music superimposed upon them. And the total lack of dramatic impact results only from the haphazard sequence of scenes that are devoid of poetic interest and incapable of putting the spark of life into music. Often the composer, without intending it, works only for himself, and the miserable poem runs alongside the music without ever catching up with it. The music itself may well be adequate, i. e. it may evoke the same feeling which is engendered by a sparkling symphony of colors, without profoundly affecting the audience. Where this happens, opera turns into a theatrical concert with costumes and stage-settings.

F.: Since you seem to approve solely of operas that are properly Romantic, what do you make of the musical tragedies and especially our comic operas in modern dress? Do you reject them *in toto?*

L.: Not at all. In most of the older tragic operas, of the kind which is, unfortunately, no longer written and composed, it is the truly heroic aspect of the action and the inner strength of both the characters and the situations which strongly affects an audience. The mysterious, unknown power that rules over gods and men alike struts visibly before its eyes; and it hears the eternal and unalterable decrees of fate, by which the gods, too, are bound, uttered in strange and foreboding tones. The fantastic element proper is excluded from these purely tragical subjects; but in conjunction with the gods, who inspire a more exalted life and perhaps even divine actions in the individual, a sublimer language will be heard in the marvelous strains of the music. Were not the ancient Greek tragedies, too, performed with musical declamation? And was this not a symptom of the need for a loftier form of expression than that which the spoken language offers?

Our music dramas have inspired the composers of genius in a very special way to a lofty, I should almost say a holy, style. It seems as if the individual were marching solemnly, to the accompaniment of tunes issuing from the golden harps of cherubim and seraphim, into the realm of light, where the mystery of his own being is revealed to him. My dear Ferdinand, I wanted to suggest no less than the intimate relation which exists between religious and operatic music, and from which the older composers derived the magnificent style, no vestige of which remains in the works of their successors, not even in the luxuriant melodies of Spontini.[2] I dare not mention the great Gluck and his heroic stature. Just in order to show you how even minor talents have occasionally grasped the nature of the grand style, consider the chorus of the priests of the night in Piccinni's *Dido*.[3]

F.: I feel exactly as I did in the former, golden days of our friendship. In talking so enthusiastically about your art you furnish me with new insights into the nature of music. And, believe me, at this point I imagine that I know a great deal about music. I even believe that I could not invent a good line of poetry without seeing it already clothed in music.

L.: Is this not the true enthusiasm of the librettist? I maintain that like the musician, the librettist must immediately compose everything he conceives, and that it is only the distinct awareness of particular melodies and notes as distributed among the various

2. Gasparo Spontini (1774-1851), who belongs to the generation between Cherubini and Meyerbeer, began his operatic career in Naples. He lived in Paris from 1803 to 1819 and spent the following two decades as conductor at the Court Opera in Berlin, where E. T. A. Hoffmann must have met him. Spontini's most famous operas are *La Vestale* (1805) and *Olympie* (1819), whose German version was prepared by Hoffmann.

3. Niccolo Piccinni (1728-1800) became Gluck's chief competitor after his arrival in Paris in 1776. His Italian operas (such as the *Didone abbandonata* mentioned by Hoffmann) are largely based on texts by Metastasio, his French operas on librettos by Marmontel.

voices and instruments and the complete mastery over the inner realm of sounds which distinguish the former from him. But I still owe you my opinion of the *opera buffa*.

F.: You will surely disapprove of it in its present form?

L.: I, on my part, dear Ferdinand, must confess that I do not only prefer it in the modern dress but consider the form and character which the agitated and mobile Italians have given to it the only adequate one. I mean especially the fantastic element that derives partly from the adventurous nature of the various characters and partly from the grotesque pranks of chance which boldly interfere with everyday life and turn everything upside down. Admittedly, this is one's neighbor in his familiar, cinnamon-colored Sunday best with gilded buttons. But what has gotten into the man that he should act so crazily? Imagine a reputable party of male and female cousins in the company of a lovelorn girl; add to these a number of students serenading the latter and playing the guitar in front of her window. Let the spirit Puck have his fun with them, so that everybody hatches out crazy ideas and is afflicted with strange jerks and weird grimaces. A peculiar star has risen, and everywhere chance lays its traps, in which even the soberest people are caught if they stick out their noses, be it ever so little. In my opinion, the very essence of *opera buffa* lies in this intrusion of the spirit of adventure and freakishness into everyday life, and in the confusion which results therefrom. It is precisely this concretization of the fantastic, which is usually remote, that makes the acting of the Italian comedians so inimitable. They understand the poet's hints and with their play clothe the skeleton he furnished with flesh and blood.

F.: I think I know exactly what you mean. In the *opera buffa*, as you see it, it is the fantastic element which takes the place of the Romantic traits you consider so essential to opera. And it is the poet's task to create characters who are not only fully rounded and verisimilar but so lifelike and individual that everybody immediately says: this is my neighbor such-and-such, and this the student who goes to school in the morning and sighs heavily when passing by his cousin's window. And now you demand that the adventures they embark on as if in a crisis, and everything that happens to them, should affect us so strongly as to make us believe that life is full of mad apparitions which irresistibly draw us into the circle of their practical jokes.

L.: You express my innermost thoughts. But I may add that according to my theory the music must suit the *opera buffa* and that, once again, a peculiar style must result that is capable of touching the heart of each listener.

F.: But can music express the many subtle shades of humor?

L.: I am convinced it can, and composers of genius have a hundred times proved this to be true. Music, for instance, is capable of expressing the delightful irony that prevails in Mozart's superb opera *Così fan tutte*.

F.: It occurs to me that according to your theory the often scolded libretto of this opera is a truly operatic one.

L.: That's exactly what I was thinking of when, a moment ago, I said that for his classic operas Mozart selected only such texts as were perfectly suited, although *The Marriage of Figaro* is a musical comedy rather than an opera. The attempt to transform sentimental comedies into operas, however, is bound to fail.

F.: These operas, if well performed, have always greatly entertained me; and I have been impressed by what the poet in Tieck's *Der gestiefelte Kater*[4] says to the audience: that if they really wanted to enjoy the play they would have to forget whatever education they possessed and turn once more into children, so as to be able to enjoy it as such.

L.: Unfortunately, these, like many other admonitions of a similar kind, fell on barren soil, where they could not take root. But the people's voice, which in theatrical matters comes very close to being the voice of God, drowns the scattered sighs uttered by the connoisseurs faced with the silly and artificial devices used in what they consider to be foolish works. There are even people who, carried away by the wild enthusiasm of the crowd, suddenly burst into a tremendous laughter while at the same time confessing their inability to explain this behavior.

---

4. Ludwig Tieck (1773-1853) was one of the principal German writers of the Romantic period as well as a pioneer of literary realism. His comedy *Der gestiefelte Kater* (Puss in Boots) of 1797 offers many striking examples of Romantic irony.

F.: Should not Tieck be the poet who could write Romantic operas according to your specifications?

L.: Definitely, since he is a truly Romantic poet. I actually remember having seen an opera of his which, though genuinely Romantic in design, was too rich in subject matter and too extended for the purpose. If I am not mistaken, its title was *The Monster and the Enchanted Forest.*

F.: Your remarks remind me of a difficulty with which you face the librettist. It is the incredible brevity you prescribe. All our attempts to conceive and adequately portray this or that situation, or the genesis of this or that passion, are in vain. For everything must be settled in a few lines which, in addition, have to submit to the ruthless treatment you inflict upon them.

L.: I should say that, like the stage designer, the librettist ought, on the basis of a clear outline, to paint his subject with large and forceful strokes. For it is up to the music to add the light and the perspective which bring everything to life and create a pattern out of the apparently fortuitous individual brush-strokes.

F.: Is it a sketch, then, which we should furnish instead of a finished poem?

L.: Not at all. It is obvious that the librettist has to follow the appropriate dramatic rules concerning the arrangement and economy of the whole. But he must be doubly careful to arrange the scenes in such a way that the action unfolds clearly and distinctly before the eyes of the audience. For even while barely able to comprehend the text, the spectator must be in a position to reconstruct the action from what happens on stage. No other dramatic poem is so much in need of lucidity, since apart from the fact that even with the clearest enunciation the words are difficult to understand, the music itself tends to distract the listener's attention, so that it must be constantly directed toward the points of the greatest dramatic effect and concentration. As far as the words are concerned, the composer likes them best when they strongly and succinctly express the passions and situations to be represented. There is no room for adornments, and especially not for poetic images.

F.: But how about Metastasio, who is so fond of metaphors?

L.: He actually had the quaint notion that, particularly in an aria, the composer needed the inspiration furnished by a poetic image. Hence the endless repetitions in the opening stanzas of his lyrics: like a turtle, like foam in the storm, etc. And often the cooing of doves and the roaring of waves can actually be heard in the orchestra.

F.: But should we refrain not only from employing poetic images but also from elaborating interesting situations? For example: a youthful hero going to war and taking leave of his dejected father; the old king, whose empire a victorious tyrant has shaken in its very foundations; or the cruel fate that separates a lover from his beloved. Should these two utter nothing but a scant farewell?

L.: Let the former briefly assert his courage and his belief in the just cause; and let the latter tell his beloved that without her life is but a slow death. But a simple farewell in itself will suffice for the composer, who must be inspired by actions and situations rather than words, as a stimulus for his eloquent portrayal of the feelings of the youthful hero and the parting lover. How often have the Italians sung the word *addio* in a most moving way! Musical expression, after all, is capable of innumerable nuances. It is the special privilege of music that where language fails it opens an inexhaustible source of expression.

F.: Thus the librettist ought to strive for the utmost simplicity of language; and it would be sufficient for him to suggest a situation nobly and forcefully.

L.: Indeed; for, as I mentioned before, it is the subject, the action, and not the luxuriant word, that goes to inspire the composer. And except for the so-called poetic images all reflections are mortifying to the musician.

F.: Don't you see how difficult it is to write an opera according to your prescription? Especially that simplicity of language....

L.: Will come hard to those who love to indulge in words. But just as, in my opinion, Metastasio in his operas has shown how librettos should not be written, many Italian poems can be regarded as models of the operatic lyric. There could hardly be anything simpler than the following well-known stanza:

Almen se non poss'io
Seguir l'amato bene
Affetti del cor mio
Seguite lo per me!

How well these few, simple words indicate the feelings of love mixed with pain! Grasping the nature of this mixed emotion, the composer should be able to express the appropriate state of mind with all the required efficacy. The particular situation out of which these words arise will work on his imagination in such a way as to allow him to give each line its distinct musical profile. This explains why most poetic composers write beautiful music based on the dullest poetry when a truly Romantic and operatic subject has inspired them. Mozart's *Magic Flute* is a case in point.

Translated by Ulrich Weisstein from Hoffmann's *Sämtliche Werke*, edited by E. Grisebach (Leipzig: Hesse, n. d.).

CARL MARIA VON WEBER (1786-1826)

BORN AT EUTIN near Lübeck in northern Germany, the son of a musician, one of whose nieces had recently become Mozart's wife, Carl Maria von Weber as a youth studied composition with Joseph Haydn's brother Michael in Salzburg and the famous Abbé Vogler in Vienna. The principal stages of his career as an operatic conductor are marked by periods in Breslau (1804-06), Prague (1814-16), and Dresden, where he held a lifetime appointment in a post later occupied by Richard Wagner. Enormously active as a composer, he wrote his first opera when still in his teens, but was not too successful in this capacity until approximately 1820. Only one of his three operatic masterpieces —*Der Freischütz*, of 1821—is currently in the repertory of opera houses in the German-speaking countries, the other two—*Euryanthe* (1823) and *Oberon* (1826)—having fallen out of favor on account of their clumsily executed librettos.

Although E. T. A. Hoffmann's *Undine* and Ludwig Spohr's *Faust* were both performed in 1816, the breakthrough of German

Romantic opera did not occur until Weber's *Freischütz* which, in the words of Donald Grout, "dealt the deathblow to the century-long Italian reign in the German theatres." Weber established a native operatic tradition characterized by the use of local or national history or legend (in Wagner: Nordic mythology), as well as folk motifs and melodies. This tradition was subsequently upheld by composers like Heinrich Marschner (*Hans Heiling*, 1833), Konradin Kreutzer (*Melusine*, 1833), Albert Lortzing (*Undine*, 1845), and Wagner, who was Weber's successor as *Kapellmeister* in Dresden. More recently, Hans Pfitzner and Paul Hindemith have produced works in a similar vein.

Euryanthe, commissioned for the Vienna *Theater am Kärntnertor*, is said to have been rewritten twelve times by Helmine von Chézy, whose correspondence with Weber has, unfortunately, not as yet been published. Although Weber advocated the greatest possible fusion and cohesion of dramatic elements in opera, his method of composing was hardly conducive to the creation of a true *Gesamtkunstwerk*. (Weber is reported to have worked on the scores of his operas not systematically from beginning to end but as his inspiration moved him.) He was extraordinarily active as a writer on musical subjects and left behind fragments of an autobiographical novel entitled *Tonkünstlers Leben*.

Max Maria von Weber, *Carl Maria von Weber* (London, 1865/68); L. C. and R. P. Stebbins, *Enchanted Wanderer: The Life of Carl Maria von Weber* (New York: Putnam, 1940); A. Coeuroy, "Weber as a Writer," *Musical Quarterly*, XI (1925), 482-505.

On E. T. A. Hoffmann's Opera *Undine* (1817)
CARL MARIA VON WEBER

A FAIR JUDGMENT of a work of art that unfolds in time requires that quiet and unprejudiced mood which, receptive to every kind of impression, should remain aloof from any definite aim or predisposition of feeling, except for a certain opening of the soul toward the subject matter in question. Only in this way is the artist in a position to gain ascendancy over the soul and the power to draw it, through his emotions and characters, into the world he has created and in which he, a mighty ruler over strong passions, allows us to feel, with and through him, pain and pleasure as well as love, joy, terror, and hope. Quickly and clearly it will then be shown whether he has succeeded in creating a grand work that profoundly and permanently affects us or whether, his artistry resulting from strokes of undisciplined genius, he has made us admire certain individual traits at the expense of the total effect.

In opera, this kind of effect is harder to avoid, and hence more common, than in any other art form. By opera I naturally mean that type of musical drama which is dear to the Germans: a fully rounded and self-contained work of art in which all the ingredients furnished by the contributing arts disappear in the process of fusion and, in thus perishing, help to form an entirely new universe. . . .

The nature and essence of opera, consisting, as it does, of wholes within a whole, causes this enormous difficulty, which only the masters have managed to overcome. Each musical number, on account of the structure that is peculiar to it, appears to be a self-contained, organic unit. Yet as part of a larger unit it is supposed to vanish as we contemplate the latter. Nevertheless, the operatic ensemble, revealing several external aspects at one and the same time, can and should be a Janus head to be taken in at one single glance.

This is the inmost secret of music, which can be felt but cannot be explicitly stated: the undulation and the contrasting natures of wrath and love, of blissful pain, in which salamander and sylph embrace and merge, are here united. In other words: what love is to man, music is to man as well as to the arts; for it is love itself, the purest, most ethereal language of the passions, containing their innumerable and constantly changing colors, yet expressing only one truth that is immediately understood by a thousand people endowed with the most widely divergent feelings.

Translated by Ulrich Weisstein from Weber's *Sämtliche Schriften,* edited by G. Kaiser (Berlin/Leipzig: Schuster & Loeffler, 1908).

ARTHUR SCHOPENHAUER
(1788-1860)

UNLIKE KANT, the great worshiper of reason, who ranked music lowest among the arts, Arthur Schopenhauer ranked it highest, since he took it to be an objectification of the will, a direct copy of the world (in which the will is embodied), a universal language intuitively understood by all men, and a *universale ante rem*. He finds its effect to be "stronger, quicker, more necessary and infallible" than that created by literature or the plastic arts. Among the ingredients of music, melody is the one which comes closest to mirroring the will, that irrational force which lies at the bottom of all things. Melody, according to Schopenhauer, "expresses the multifarious efforts of will, but always its satisfaction also by the final return to an harmonious interval and, still more, to the key-note." Language, which reintroduces the *principium individuationis*, must naturally be inferior to music, which deals with universals. The operatic composer who seeks to stress situations and words at the expense of music thus fails to realize the true nature of their relationship.

Schopenhauer's theory of opera as a form of absolute music is directly opposed to the classicist one which postulates, in Gluck's words, that music "must serve the poetry by means of the expression." It is closer to Wagner's, in which music is made to represent the *Urgrund* (deepest source) of being. But it is Rossini upon whose compositions Schopenhauer bestows the highest praise: "His music speaks its own language so distinctly and purely that it requires no words, and produces its full effect when rendered by instruments alone."

L. D. Green, "Schopenhauer and Music," *Musical Quarterly*, XVI (1930), 199-206; I. Knox, *The Aesthetic Theories of Kant, Hegel and Schopenhauer* (New York: Columbia University Press, 1936).

The World as Will and Idea (1818)
ARTHUR SCHOPENHAUER

THE (Platonic) Ideas are the adequate objectification of will. To excite or suggest the knowledge of these by means of the representation of particular things (for works of art themselves are always representations of particular things) is the end of all the other arts, which can only be attained by a corresponding change in the knowing subject. Thus all these arts objectify the will indirectly only by means of the Ideas; and since our world is nothing but the manifestation of the Ideas in multiplicity, through their entrance into the *principium individuationis* (the form of the knowledge possible for the individual as such), music also, since it passes over the Ideas, is entirely independent of the phenomenal world, ignores it altogether, could to a certain extent exist if there was no world at all, which cannot be said of the other arts. Music is as direct an objectification and copy of the whole will as the world itself, nay, even as the Ideas, whose multiplied manifestation constitutes the world of individual things. Music is thus by no means like the other arts, the copy of the Ideas, but the copy of the will itself, whose objectivity the Ideas are. This is why the effect of music is so much more powerful and penetrating than that of the other arts, for they speak only of shadows, but it speaks of the thing itself. Since, however, it is the same will which objectifies itself both in the Ideas and in music, though in quite different ways, there must be, not indeed a direct likeness, but yet a parallel, an analogy, between music and the Ideas, whose manifestation in multiplicity and incompleteness is the visible world. The establishing of this analogy will facilitate . . . the understanding of this exposition, which is so difficult on account of the obscurity of the subject.

It must never be forgotten . . . that music never expresses the phenomenon, but only the inner nature, the in-itself of all phenomena, the will itself. It does not therefore express this or that particular and definite joy, this or that sorrow, or pain, or horror, or delight, or merriment, or peace of mind; but joy, sorrow, horror, delight, merriment, peace of mind themselves, to a certain extent in the abstract, their essential nature, without accessories, and therefore without their motives. Yet we completely understand them in this extracted quintessence. Hence it arises that our imagination is so easily excited by music, and now seeks to give form to that invisible yet actively moved spirit-world which speaks to us directly, and clothe it with flesh and blood, i. e., to embody it in an analogous example. This is the origin of the song with words, and finally of the opera, the text of which should therefore never forsake that subordinate position in order to make itself the chief thing and the music a mere means of expressing it, which is a great misconception and a piece of utter perversity; for music always expresses only the quintessence of life and its events, never these themselves, and therefore their differences do not always affect it. It is precisely this universality, which belongs exclusively to it, together with the greatest determinateness, that gives music the high worth which it has as the panacea for all our woes. Thus, if music is too closely united to the words, and tries to form itself according to the events, it is striving to speak a language which is not its own. No one has kept so free from this mistake as Rossini; therefore his music speaks its own language so distinctly and purely that it requires no words, and produces its full effect when rendered by instruments alone.

According to all this, we may regard the phenomenal world, or nature, and music, as two different expressions of the same thing, which is therefore itself the only medium of their analogy, so that a knowledge of it is demanded in order to understand the analogy. Music, therefore, if regarded as an expression of the world, is in the highest degree a universal language, which is related indeed to the universality of concepts, much as they are related to the particular things. Its universality, however, is by no means that empty universality of abstraction, but quite of a different kind, and is united with thorough and distinct definiteness. In this respect it resembles geometrical figures and numbers, which are the universal forms of all possible objects or experience and applicable to them all *a priori*, and yet are not abstract but perceptible and thoroughly determined. All possible efforts, excitements, and manifestations of will, all that goes on in the heart of man and that reason includes in the wide, negative concept of feeling, may be expressed by the infinite number of possible melodies, but always in the universal, in the mere form, without the material, always according to the thing-in-itself, not the phenomenon, the inmost soul, as it were, of the phenomenon, without the body. This deep relation which music has to the true nature of all things also explains the fact that suitable music played to any scene, action, event, or surrounding seems to disclose to us its most secret meaning, and appears as the most accurate and distinct commentary upon it. This is so truly the case, that whoever gives himself up entirely to the impression of a symphony seems to see all the possible events of life and the world take place in himself, yet if he reflects, he can find no likeness between the music and the things that passed before his mind. For, as we have said, music is distinguished from all the other arts by the fact that it is not a copy of the phenomenon, or, more accurately, the adequate objectivity of will, but is the direct copy of the will itself, and therefore exhibits itself as the metaphysical to everything physical in the world, and as the thing-in-itself to every phenomenon. We might, therefore, just as well call the world embodied music as embodied will; and this is the reason why music makes every picture, and indeed every scene of real life and of the world, at once appear with higher significance, certainly all the more in proportion as its melody is analogous to the inner spirit of the given phenomenon. It rests upon this that we are able to set a poem to music as a song, or a perceptible representation as a pantomime, or both as an opera. Such particular pictures of human life, set to the universal language of music, are never bound to it or correspond to it with stringent necessity; but they stand to it only in the relation of an example chosen at will to a general concept. In the determinateness of the real, they represent that which music expresses in the universality of mere form. For melodies are to a certain extent, like general concepts, an abstraction from the actual. This actual world, then, the world of particular things, affords the object of perception, the special and individual, the particular case, both to the universality of the concepts and to the universality of the melodies. But these two universalities are in a certain respect opposed to each other; for the concepts contain particulars only as the first forms abstracted from perception, as it were, the separated shell of things; thus they are, strictly speaking, *abstracta;* music, on the other hand, gives the inmost kernel which precedes all forms, or the heart of things. This relation may be very well expressed in the language of the schoolmen by saying the concepts are the *universalia post rem*, but music gives the *universalia ante rem*, and the real world the *universalia in re*. To the universal significance of a melody to which a poem has been set, it is quite possible to set other equally arbitrarily selected examples of the universal expressed in this poem corresponding to the significance of the melody in the same degree. This is why the same composition is suitable to many verses; and this is also what makes the vaudeville possible. But that in general a relation is possible between a composition and a perceptible representation rests, as we have said, upon the fact that both are simply different expressions of the same inner being of the world. When now, in the particular case, such a relation is actually given, that is to say, when the composer has been able to express in the universal language of music the emotions of will which constitute the heart of an event, then the melody of the song, the music of the opera, is expressive. But the analogy discovered by the composer between the two must have proceeded from the direct knowledge of the nature of the world unknown to his reason, and must not be an imitation produced with conscious intention by means of conceptions, otherwise the music does not express the inner nature of the will itself, but merely gives an inadequate imitation of its phenomenon. All specially imitative music does this; for example, *The Seasons* by Haydn; also many passages of his *Creation*, in which phenomena of the external world are directly imitated; also all battle-pieces. Such music is entirely to be rejected.

The unutterable depth of all music by virtue of which it floats through our consciousness as the vision of a paradise firmly believed in yet ever distant from us, and by which also it is so fully understood and yet so inexplicable, rests on the fact that it restores to us all the emotions of our inmost nature, but entirely without reality and far removed from their pain. So also the seriousness which is essential to it, which excludes the absurd from its direct and peculiar province, is to be explained by the fact that its object is not the idea, with reference to which alone deception and absurdity are possible; but its object is directly the will, and this is essentially the most serious of all things, for it is that on which all depends. How rich in content and full of significance the language of music is, we see from the repetitions, as well as the *Da capo*, the like of which would be unbearable in works composed in a language of words, but in music are very appropriate and beneficial, for, in order to comprehend it fully, we must hear it twice.

Reprinted from Schopenhauer, *The World as Will and Idea*, translated by R. B. Haldane and J. Kemp (London: Kegan Paul, Trench, Trubner & Co., 1896), by permission of Routledge & Kegan Paul Ltd. and Humanities Press.

GIOACCHINO ROSSINI (1792-1868)

GIOACCHINO ROSSINI, both of whose parents were practicing musicians, made a very early start as an operatic composer. His first work for the musical stage dates from his fourteenth year, the first stage performance from his eighteenth. In the decade between 1810 and 1820 Rossini created no less than thirty operas, among them *La scala di seta* (1812), *L'Italiana in Algeri* (1813), *Otello*—before Verdi—and *Il barbiere di Seviglia* (both in 1816), and *La cenerentola* (1817). In 1824 the composer went to live in Paris, where he was to spend much of the remainder of his life. It was in that year that Stendhal, who had taken up Rossini's cause upon his return from Milan in 1821, published his *Life* of the artist. During the first years of his sojourn in the French capital Rossini wrote approximately one opera per year, the last one in the series being *Guillaume Tell*, based on Schiller's play. In 1829 the government of Charles X had pledged to pay him 7500 francs per annum in return for the biennial delivery of one new opera. However, when the government fell in 1830, Rossini's hopes were shattered. He never composed another opera, but restricted himself to writing religious music (such as the *Stabat Mater*). It was only in the mid-thirties, however, that he formally vowed to abandon his profession. Among the factors involved in this decision, the enormous success of Meyerbeer's *Les Huguenots* in 1836 was surely not the least important one. In the final years of his life, Rossini devoted himself increasingly to the fine art of cooking.

Stendhal thought of Rossini as being not too much inferior to Mozart; and Schopenhauer lavished praise on him for writing music "that requires no words and produces its full effect when rendered by instruments alone," even though Rossini himself asserted that "music produces marvelous effects when it is joined to dramatic art."

F. Toye, *Rossini: A Study in Tragi-Comedy* (New York: Knopf, 1934); H. Prunières, "Stendhal and Rossini," *Musical Quarterly*, VII (1921), 133-155; E. Istel, "Rossini: A Study," *Musical Quarterly*, IX (1923), 401-422.

Conversations
GIOACCHINO ROSSINI

A COMMON ERROR prevails even among those who make music their profession. As an art, music is not imitative. It is ideal as far as its principles, stimulative and expressive as far as its aims, are concerned. Painting and sculpture are essentially imitative, since they imitate reality; and the ideal of these arts consists in fashioning a perfect whole out of various selected parts. By imitating they reproduce what is seen, and speak to the eyes as well as the mind with the mute language of gesture. Music cannot, and does not, intend to convey to the ears a likeness of everything we hear; rather it arouses and animates us amidst the dangers of the battle, comforts and cheers us in the loneliness of the fields, and with a new language, all its own, talks to the heart, describes the feelings more vividly, gladdens, saddens, frightens, and moves. There are four kinds or genres of music: the martial and the pastoral, the severe and the gracious. The war-like and the pastoral music, originating in olden times, are the invention of man, whose nature it is to seek out pleasure, and who is in need of excitement and comfort. The other two genres—they, too, ideal—are more directly expressive. . . .

Music can produce imperfect imitations only of those aspects of reality which generate sounds: rain, thunder, storms, lamentable chatter, and festive noise. The song, yes, the song, expressive by nature, in a certain way imitates declamation; but such a limited faculty cannot be regarded as the essential attribute of imitation. Music is a sublime art precisely because, unable to imitate reality, it rises above ordinary nature into an ideal world, and with celestial harmony moves the earthly passions....

Don't forget that musical expression is not identical with that of painting and does not consist in the accurate rendering of the external signs of the emotions, but in arousing such emotions in the listener. This is also the power of language, which expresses and does not imitate; with the difference that whereas the force of language is more extensive, that of music is more intensive. Words are able to transmit feelings to the mind and arouse them in the heart; music solely arouses them, but all the more strongly so. Music is a kind of harmonious language. Musical expression is not as clear and explicit as the meaning of words; nor is it as apparent and vivid as are pictorial images. But it is more convincing and more poetic than any poetry. Words would be empty sounds without the meaning assigned to them by convention. This is not true of music, a language expressive in itself which, without the aid of the listener's mind, penetrates deeply into the soul and moves it strongly. The language of music is common to all generations and nations; it is understood by everybody, since it is understood with the heart. Add to this the fact that it is capable of infinite variety and modulation while gaining strength and grace from the concourse of voices and sounds, whereas words follow upon each other and, if many of them occur at one and the same time, produce a confused noise and lose all their efficacy. Music produces marvelous effects when it is joined to dramatic art, when the ideal expression of music allies itself with the expression of poetry and the imitative art of painting. Thus, while words and actions express the most detailed and concrete elements of feeling, music has a much higher, wider, and more abstract goal. Music becomes, in a way, the moral atmosphere which fills the space in which the characters of the drama portray the action. It expresses the fate that pursues them, the hope which animates them, the gaiety which surrounds them, the felicity which is in store for them, the abyss into which they are to fall; and all that in an indefinite way, but as movingly and penetratingly as neither words nor deeds can do. There are many things within us which, not by means of imitation or through conventional signs, but by their own nature express and arouse our feelings. A serene sky does not imitate a smile, and only because it makes us gay do we call it "smiling." The night is called "sad" solely because it engenders melancholy thoughts. Dramatic music often takes the place of things (mark well: takes their place, and does not imitate them) which, without being the actual cause of the feelings, arouse them in us by their very existence, because they precede the cause, accompany it, or are correlated with it. . . .

Musical expression lies in the rhythm; and in the rhythm lies all the power of music. The sounds do not subserve the expression except as component parts of the rhythm. The mastery of a composer consists in the ability to prearrange in his mind the scenes, or principal situations, of the musical drama he wants to write, and to select the most suitable characters, passions, the moral intentions, and the catastrophe of the drama. He must then skillfully adapt the character of the music to the subject of the drama, and find, if he can, a thoroughly new rhythm with novel effects, which helps to express the essence of the drama and reveals, step by step, its most relevant situations, characters, and passions. He should not bother about the words, except to see to it that the music suits them without, however, deviating from its general character. He will operate in such a way that the words are subordinate to the music rather than the music to the words. In a pathetic or terrible scene the words will be gay or sad, hopeful or fearful, imploring or threatening, according to the movement which, by degrees, the poet wants to give to the scene. If the composer sets out to follow the meaning of the words with equal steps, he will write music that is not expressive by itself, but is poor, vulgar, mosaic-like, and incongruous or ridiculous.

Translated by Ulrich Weisstein from Antonio Zanolini, *Biografia di Gioachino Rossini* (Bologna: Zanichelli, 1875).

STENDHAL (1783-1842)

HENRI BEYLE (Stendhal), author of *The Red and the Black* and *The Charterhouse of Parma* and hero-worshipper of Napoleon, with whose armies he served north and south of the Alps, was a lover of Italian painting (Correggio, Raphael) and operatic music. He was especially charmed by the works of Paisiello and Cimarosa but also admired Mozart and Rossini. "If I were to desire melody," he said, "I should turn to [Cimarosa's] *Il matrimonio segreto* or [Paisiello's] *Il re Teodoro*. If I wanted to enjoy both [melody and harmony] simultaneously . . . I should pay a visit to La Scala for a performance of *Don Giovanni* or [Rossini's] *Tancredi*. But . . . if I were to plunge any deeper than this into the black night of harmony, music would soon lose the overwhelming charm which it holds for me." During his sojourn in Milan, Stendhal was an ardent frequenter of opera who, writer though he was, advised his fellow opera enthusiasts never to be "so imprudent as to read the entire libretto" but to content themselves with inquiring what specific emotion a given aria or ensemble was supposed to express. What an excellent librettist Stendhal would have made, could he have been persuaded to indulge in such drudgery!

In 1814, this highly sensitive critic wrote—or rather, compiled —a book about Haydn, Mozart, and Metastasio. Ten years later he published his *Life of Rossini,* a veritable manifesto of Romantic aesthetics, from which the following excerpts are taken. No greater contrast could be conceived than that which exists between Gluck's and Stendhal's approach to melo-dramaturgy.

H. Prunières, "Stendhal and Rossini," *Musical Quarterly,* VII (1921), 133-155; J. W. Klein, "Stendhal as Music Critic," *Musical Quarterly,* XXIX (1943), 18-31; J. Harthan, "Stendhal and Mozart," *Music and Letters,* XVII (1946), 174-179.

Life of Rossini (1824)
STENDHAL

UPON TANCRED'S ENTRY [in the opera *Tancredi*], the orchestration reaches a superb climax of *dramatic harmonization*. This is not (as is foolishly believed in Germany) the art of employing clarinets, 'cellos and oboes to reecho the emotions of the characters on the stage; it is the much rarer art of using the instruments to voice nuances and overtones of emotion which the characters themselves would never dare put into words. When Tancred lands on his deserted beach, he needs no more than a phrase or two of speech to portray his emotions; voice and gestures express something; but completeness requires an instant or two of silence while he contemplates, with mingled sensations of pleasure and sadness, the ungrateful country to which he has returned. If he should speak in this instant, Tancred would dissipate our interest in him, and shatter, in our entranced imagination, the perception which we have of the thoughts deeply stirring in him, as he looks again upon the land which is the home of Amenaida. Tancred *must* not speak; but while he is contained in a silence so perfectly expressive of the feelings raging within him, the sighing horns of the orchestra conjure up a new portrait of his spirit, and echo emotions which, perhaps, he hardly dare acknowledge to himself, and which certainly will never find form in words.

An achievement of this character is something new in music; it was unknown in the times of Pergolese and Sacchini,[1] and it is still unknown to our worthy Teutonic friends. They use *their* instruments to furnish us, as crudely as possible, with certain necessary information which the singer on the stage should, properly speaking, convey to us in words. Their vocal passages, on the other hand, being either wholly expressionless, or else hopelessly overburdened with expression, just as reproductions of paintings by Raphael are normally overburdened with exaggerated color, serve largely to give the imagination a rest from the ideas suggested by the orchestra. Thus their operatic heroes act very much like those Sovereigns who, filled brim-full with the finest intentions in the world, yet find themselves unable, with their own tongue, to utter anything but commonplaces of the worst order, and so are constantly referring the petitioner to

1. Antonio Sacchini (1730-86), whose early operas were performed in Rome, Naples, and Venice, spent the last fifteen years of his life in London and Paris, where his most popular opera, *Oedipe à Colone*, was premiered in the year of his death.

their Minister-of-State whenever some question arises which requires an important answer.

Every instrument in the orchestra, like every individual human voice, has its own distinctive characteristics; for example, in Tancred's aria and recitative, Rossini scores for the flute; the particular virtue of the flute lies in its ability to portray joy mingled with sadness; and this complex mixture of emotions is precisely that which Tancred experiences when his eye lights once more on that ungrateful land to which he can no longer return save in disguise.

If this conception of the relationship between orchestral and vocal music can be made any clearer by an analogy, I would suggest that Rossini successfully employs a device invented by Walter Scott—that same technical device which, perhaps, was responsible for all the most astounding triumphs of the immortal author of *Old Mortality*.[2] Just as Rossini uses his *orchestral harmony* to prepare the way for, and to reinforce, his passages of vocal music, so Walter Scott prepares the way for, and reinforces, his passages of dialogue and narrative by means of *description*. Consider, for instance, the very first page of *Ivanhoe*, with its magnificent description of the setting sun; how its rays, already losing strength and falling almost horizontal, struggle through the lowest and thickest branches of the trees which conceal the dwelling of Cedric the Saxon. And then how, in the center of a woodland glade, this dying-diminishing light picks out the curious garments worn by Wamba the Jester and Gurth the Swineherd. Before the great Scottish writer has even completed his description of this forest lit with the departing beams of a sun already lying on the tree-tops, and of the curious garments worn by these two characters . . . already we find ourselves disposed, prophetically as it were, to be affected by the words which they have yet to utter. And when at last they do speak, their least syllables are rich with infinite significance. Imagine the opening of this chapter, which itself opens the novel, rewritten,

2. Sir Walter Scott (1771-1832) was a prolific English novelist whose works profoundly affected the members of the French Romantic school. *Old Mortality* appeared in 1816, *Ivanhoe* in 1820, and *Peveril of the Peak* in 1827.

with the dialogue *un*prepared by the description: the whole effect would be ruined.

Composers of genius, then, relate orchestral harmony to vocal melody in precisely the same manner as Walter Scott relates *description* to *dialogue* in *Ivanhoe;* the rest . . . tumble their harmony in pell-mell. . . . Walter Scott is forever interrupting and reinforcing his dialogue with description, at times even in a manner which is decidedly irritating, as, for instance, when the entrancing little dumb girl, Fenella, in *Peveril of the Peak*, is trying to stop Julian leaving the castle of Holm-Peel in the Isle of Man. Here we have a clear case where the mind of the reader is exasperated by the descriptions, just as the ear of the average Italian listener is exhausted and irritated by German-style orchestration: nevertheless, when description is properly employed, it works on the mind, creating an emotional state in which it is admirably susceptible to the impact of the simplest dialogue; and it is indeed thanks to the art of such wonderful descriptive passages that Walter Scott found the courage to be *simple*, to abandon the rhetoric which Jean-Jacques [Rousseau] and so many others had made fashionable in the novel, and, finally, to risk a kind of dialogue which was, in very truth, *borrowed from nature.*

Observe that here [in a discussion of Rossini's opera *L'Italiana in Algeri*], as indeed everywhere, I am concerned with the music, never with the words, which, to tell the truth, I do not know. It is my invariable habit to rewrite the words of any opera for my own satisfaction. I take the plot which the librettist has invented, and I require further from him one word, and *one only*, to give me the key to the mood of the scene. For example, I take Mustafa to be a man who is bored with his mistress and his own greatness, and yet, being a sovereign, not devoid of vanity. Now, it is not improbable that, if I were to follow the dialogue as a whole, this general impression would be ruined. So what is the remedy? Ideally, of course, the answer would be to have had Voltaire or Beaumarchais compose the libretto; in which case it would be as delightful as the music, and never a breath of disenchantment in the reading of it! But happily (since Voltaires are rare in our imperfect world), the delightful art which is our present study can well continue without the services of a great poet . . . provided always that one avoids the sinful indiscretion of reading the libretto. At Vicenza, I observed that, on the first night, it was customary to skim through it just sufficiently to gain some notion of the plot, glancing, as each new episode opened, at the first line, just so as to appreciate the emotion or the shade of emotion, which the music was supposed to suggest. But not once, during all the forty performances which came after, did it occur to one single member of the audience to open that slim little volume with its gilt-paper binding.

Still more apprehensive of the disagreeable impression which might be gleaned from the libretto, Signora B., in Venice, used to refuse to allow anybody at all to bring it into her box, even at the premiere. She used to get someone to prepare her a summary of the plot, some forty lines in all; and then, during the performance, she would be informed, in four or five words, of the theme of each aria, duet, or ensemble, which had previously been numbered 1, 2, 3, 4 . . . etc., as each item was introduced in the performance; for instance, simply: Ser Taddeo is jealous; Lindoro is passionately in love; Isabella is flirting with the Bey, etc.—this condensed summary being followed by the first line of the aria or duet which happened to be in question. I observed that everyone approved of this procedure, and thought it most suitable. In such a fashion should all libretti be printed for those—to tell the truth, I hardly know how to find an epithet which does not merely appear conceited!—for those who appreciate music as music is appreciated in Venice.

The whole art of operatic music, in fact, has likewise made immense progress since Paisiello's[3] day; it has rid the stage of the intolerable, interminable recititatives which burdened the style of the earlier epoch; and it has learned the essential secret of mastering the ensemble. "It is absurd," maintain certain poor,

---

3. Giovanni Paisiello (1740-1816), a composer of the Neapolitan school, wrote both comic and serious operas. He spent eight years in St. Petersburg and four years in the service of Napoleon in Paris. His best known work is the pre-Rossinian version of *Il Barbiere di Siviglia* (1782).

passionless, *blunt-minded* creatures, "for five or six people to sing all at once." Agreed. It is supremely absurd for even *two* people to sing at once; for when does it ever occur that two people, even supposing them to be dominated by the most violent of passions, should go on speaking simultaneously for any length of time? Rather the opposite, if anything; the more extreme the passion, the greater the attention we should normally pay to the protest of that antagonist, whose conversion to our own point of view appears to be a matter of such dire consequence. This observation holds good, for instance, even of the poor Indian savages, or of the heathen Turks; yet nothing is further from their minds than any longing to be thought intelligent or sophisticated. Is not this an admirably logical argument? Could anything be more reasonable? And yet experience proves it false from top to bottom. In practice, there is nothing more delightful than a duet. . . . It is precisely the mounting excitement, the crescendo, of these ensembles, which dissipates the boredom of those poor, unfortunate, *right-thinking* people, whom fashion, pitiless and implacable as ever, has hounded into the *Théâtre Louvois,* and prods them into some semblance of wakefulness.

A hunting-horn, echoing over the hills of the Scottish highlands, can be heard at a considerably greater distance than the human voice. In this respect, *but in this respect only,* art has outdistanced nature: art has succeeded in increasing the *volume* of sound produced. But in respect of something infinitely more important, namely inflection and ornamentation, the human voice maintains its superiority over any instrument yet invented, and it might even be claimed that no instrument is satisfactory except in so far as it approximates to the sound of the human voice.

I would suggest that, if, in some moment of pensive stillness and brooding melancholy, we were to peer into the very depth of our soul, we would discover that the fascination of the human voice springs from two distinct causes:

(1) The suggestion of passion, which, to a greater or lesser degree, inevitably colors anything which is sung by living man

or woman. Even the least impassioned of *prime donne* . . . whose voices express no positive emotion, still radiate a kind of indeterminate *joy*. (I make a half-exception only in favor of Signora Catalani, whose prodigiously beautiful voice fills the soul with a kind of astonished wonder, as though it beheld a miracle; and the very confusion of our hearts blinds us at first to the noble and goddess-like impassivity of this unique artist.) Sometimes, in an idle moment, I like to imagine a creature who combines the voice of Signora Catalani with the impassioned soul and dramatic instinct of La Pasta—a fond, sweet chimaera, whose dream-quality leads only to sadness and regret for a thing which is not; and yet, whose very possibility leaves one convinced that music sways a greater power over the soul than any other art.

(2) The second advantage which the human voice possesses by comparison with the instrument lies in its command of *language*, which can, as it were, storm the imagination, and fill it directly with the kind of imagery which the music is to embroider and develop.

If the human voice is weak in tone, compared with certain instruments, it can claim the power of *graduating* sounds to a degree of perfection inconceivable in any mechanical device.

The human voice commands an infinite variety of inflections (which is the same thing as saying that a *totally passionless* voice is a practical impossibility); and, to my mind, this particular quality is of far greater significance than its other distinguishing characteristic, the power to express itself in language.

To start with, the excruciating doggerel which forms the verbal skeleton of the average Italian aria is hardly ever recognizable as verse of any description, owing to the multiplicity of repeats; the language which greets the listener's patient ear is pure prose. Furthermore, the beauty of poetry does not lie in its bold and melodramatic exclamations . . . but in its shades and subtleties, in the skilled ordering or selection of words; and it is these nuances which convince the reader of the poet's sincerity, and which ultimately awaken his sympathy and understanding. But there is no room for nuances among the haphazard jumble of 50-60 words which go to form the text of the average Italian aria; and so language, *as such*, can never be anything more than a *bare canvas;* the task of decorating this canvas with all the glint and glitter of a thousand tints and colors lies with the *music.*

Would you like a further proof that words are fundamentally unimportant in relation to music, and that, in practice, they are nothing but *labels to stick on emotions?* Consider any aria you like, sung with all the deep and impassioned sincerity of a Madame Belloc or of a Signorina Pisaroni; and then consider the same aria sung an instant later by one or other of our book-learned, half-frozen tailor's dummies from the North. The latter worthy, if frigid, songstress will undoubtedly utter the very same words . . . as the great artist who has just preceded her; but what can *words* do to shatter the creeping rim of ice which has fastened on to our hearts?

Two words, three words . . . just enough to tell us that the hero is sunk into depths of despair, or else that he is winging across the infinite spaces of happiness—this is all we need to grasp; if we then catch, or fail to catch completely, the words of the rest of the aria, either way is utterly indifferent; all that really matters is that they should be *sung* with passionate sincerity. This is what makes it possible to listen with appreciable delight to a good performance of an opera in a foreign language, even though, in this case, the words may be entirely incomprehensible; so long as some kind neighbor gives one the key to the more important arias, nothing else is needed. The same principle holds good in the spoken theater: it is quite conceivable to derive considerable pleasure from watching a great tragic actor playing in a language with which one has but the sketchiest acquaintance. The conclusion to be drawn from all these observations would seem to be, that the inflection of the words is of far greater importance in opera than the words themselves. No quality is more essential in a singer than his power of *dramatic expression.*

> *Se tu più mormori*
> *Solo una sillaba,*
> *Un cimiterio*
> *Qui si farà.*

(If you murmur one single syllable more, this very spot will become a graveyard!)

If such notions seem ridiculous to us in Paris, it must be remembered all the same that in Italy they represent a model example of the librettist's art. The meaning is clear; the emotion is intense; there is comedy in the style of the expression; and last, but not least, there is no trace of that super-refined, elaborate preciosity which we associate with Marivaux.[4] Every instant spent in appreciating such finesse, in admiring and applauding it, is just so much time lost for the appreciation of the *music*, and worse still, would continue to distract the attention for a long time to come. To enjoy the finesse of verbal wit requires *critical penetration* at an intellectual level; but critical penetration is the very faculty which must be jettisoned for good and all if we are to allow music to weave its elusive web of dreams about our soul; the two pleasures of sense and intellect are distinct, and the belief that both can be enjoyed at once, a dangerous hallucination. Nobody, save a *French literary critic*, could stubbornly persist in this illusion, which can be dispelled by one single comment: In music, the same word or phrase is subject to constant repetition, each successive restatement infusing the spoken material with new meaning. Yet somehow it still passes the understanding of our venerable literary gentlemen that, in poetry proper, a single repetition of this character can murder the verse, the rhythm, and the rhyme, and that the most brilliant shaft of wit, repeated, or even *pronounced slowly*, would normally disintegrate into complete inanity.

In opera, *verse* is confined to the published libretto, and exists only by the good graces of the type-setter, who disposes his words in an artificial order on the printed page; in the theater, once the music escapes from the narrow bonds of recitative into the impassioned flights of song, the ear hears nothing but prose; a man who was blind would never for one single instant recognize the succession of sounds which came to his awareness as verse.

Music is incapable of sustaining rapid dialogue; it can portray the subtlest shades of the most ephemeral emotions, shades so

4. Pierre Marivaux (1688-1763), though much less accomplished than Molière, is one of the classic writers of comedy in French. He is especially known for *Les fausses confidences* (1737).

fine and delicate that they may elude even the greatest of writers; it might even be suggested that the real domain of music begins only where the domain of the spoken word finishes; but music has one vital limitation: it cannot *sketch* an idea. In this respect, music shares the disadvantages of sculpture, as compared with sculpture's rival among the visual arts, painting; the majority of objects which strike us as remarkable in real life are valueless as subjects for the sculptor, for the simple reason that the chisel cannot leave anything half-said. The brush of a Veronese or of a Rubens can create a magnificent portrait out of some famous warrior in full armor; but nothing is heavier, or more absurd, than the same subject under the sculptor's chisel. If you want an example, take the statue of Henri IV in the courtyard of the Louvre.

Imagine some idiotic braggart retailing gaudy and totally unfounded anecdotes of battles, wherein he, the hero of heroes, has won immortal crowns of glory; in musical terms, the *melodic line* would give us, in all sincerity, his own estimate of himself; but the *accompaniment*, all the while, would be full of mockery and disbelief. Cimarosa[5] has created a score of little masterpieces founded upon some principle of this sort.

Melody can do nothing with emotional half-tones and suggestions; these qualities are found only in the under-currents of orchestral harmony. Yet note that even *harmony* cannot convey any but the most fleeting, the most ephemeral of images, for, as soon as harmony starts to claim too much attention in its own right, it threatens to kill the melody, as indeed does happen in certain passages of Mozart; in which case, harmony, having now usurped the dominating role in the partnership of composition, becomes itself incapable of suggesting the half-expressed and the half-perceived. I ask pardon for this brief excursion into metaphysics, which I could certainly contrive to make less obscure if only I could play a few illustrations on a piano.

Reprinted from Stendhal's *Life of Rossini*, translated by Richard N. Coe (New York: Criterion Books, 1957), by permission of John Calder Ltd.

5. Domenico Cimarosa (1749-1801), another composer in the Neapolitan *opera buffa* tradition, spent several years in St. Petersburg and at the court of Vienna. His masterpiece, *Il matrimonio segreto*, was first performed at the *Burgtheater* in February, 1792, only a few months after Mozart's death.

SØREN KIERKEGAARD (1813-55)

LIKE SCHOPENHAUER in his *The World as Will and Idea*, Soren Kierkegaard, in his *Either/Or*, acknowledges the superiority of music over the other arts. He, too, emphasizes its immediacy. However, for him music is not a copy of the world as such or a direct embodiment of the will, but rather the most adequate expression of sensuousness—in other words, a feeling and not an idea. In Kierkegaard's opinion, Mozart's *Don Giovanni*, whose subject is love in the abstract, is ideally suited for opera, its hero being not a character in the strict sense of the word but a symbolic expression of the erotic: "Faust represents the demonic intellectually, which thought must unfold; and so Faust has received frequent dialectical treatment. Don Juan represents the demonic sensuously, which music alone can unfold." To call Mozart's opera immoral means, for Kierkegaard, to falsify its spirit of immediacy by allowing reflection to intervene. Music is superior to language precisely because it retains immediacy without ever being devoid of meaning. Unlike drama (action), which exists by dint of its forward thrust, music, which also unfolds in time, transcends time lyrically by evoking a mood. The nature of opera proper is constituted by the fusion and alternation of lyrical and dramatic moments related to such an abstract (i.e., non-individualized) concept as love in its sensuous aspects.

T. H. Croxall, *Kierkegaard Commentary* (New York: Harper, 1956), 47-59; W. J. Turner, *Mozart: The Man and His Works* (New York: Doubleday, 1954), 332-347.

Either/Or (1843)
SOREN KIERKEGAARD

I BELIEVE . . . that the following considerations may open the way for a classification of the arts which will have validity, precisely because it is altogether accidental. The more abstract and hence the more poverty-stricken the medium is, the greater the probability is that a repetition will be impossible; the greater the probability is that when the idea has once obtained its expression, then it has found it once for all. The more concrete and consequently the richer the idea, and similarly the medium, the greater is the probability for a repetition. When I now arrange the classics side by side, and without wishing to rank them relatively, find myself wondering at their lofty equality, it nevertheless easily becomes apparent that there are more works in one section than another, or, if this is not the case, that some unequal representation is easily conceivable.

This point I wish to develop a little more in detail. The more abstract the idea is, the smaller the probability of a numerous representation. But how does the idea become concrete? By being permeated with the historical consciousness. The more concrete the idea, the greater the probability. The more abstract the medium, the smaller the probability; the more concrete, the greater. But what does it mean to say that the medium is concrete, other than to say it is language, or is seen in approximation to language; for language is the most concrete of all media. The idea, for example, which comes to expression in sculpture is wholly abstract, and bears no relation to the historical; the medium through which it is expressed is likewise abstract, consequently there is a great probability that the section of the classic works which includes sculpture will contain only a few. In this I have the testimony of time and experience on my side. If, on the other hand, I take a concrete idea and a concrete medium, then it seems otherwise. Homer is indeed the classic epic poet, but just because the epic idea is a concrete idea, and because the medium is language, it so happens that in the section of the classics which contains the epic, there are many epics conceivable, which are all equally classic, because history constantly furnishes us with new epic material. In this, too, I have the testimony of history and the assent of experience.

Now when I propose to base my subdivision wholly on the accidental, one can hardly deny its accidental character. But if, on the other hand, someone should reproach me, my answer would be that the objection is a mistake, since the principle of classification ought to be accidental. It is accidental that one section numbers, or can number, many more works than another.

But since this is accidental, it is evident that one might just as well place the class highest which has, or can have, the greatest number. Here I might fall back upon the preceding discussion, and calmly answer that this is quite correct, but that I ought for this very reason to be all the more lauded for my consistency in accidentally setting the opposite class highest. However, I shall not do this, but, on the other hand, I shall appeal to a circumstance that speaks in my favor, the circumstance, namely, that those sections which embrace the more concrete ideas are not yet completed, and do not permit of being completed. Therefore it is quite natural to place the others first, and to keep the double doors wide open for the latter. Should someone say that this is an imperfection, a defect, in the former class, then he plows a furrow outside of my field of thought, and I cannot pay attention to his words, however thorough he is otherwise; for it is my fixed point of departure, that everything is essentially equally perfect.

But which idea is the most abstract? Here the question is naturally concerned only with such ideas as lend themselves to artistic representation, not with ideas appropriate only for scientific treatment. And what medium is the most abstract? The latter question I shall answer first. The most abstract medium is the one farthest removed from language.

But before I pass on to reply to this question, I desire to remind the reader of a circumstance which affects the final solution of my problem. The most abstract medium is not always employed to express the most abstract idea. The medium employed by architecture is thus, for example, doubtless the most abstract medium, but the ideas which receive expression in architecture are by no means the most abstract. Architecture stands in a much closer relation to history than sculpture, for example. Here we are again confronted with a new alternative. I may place in the first class in this arrangement either those works of art which have the most abstract medium, or those whose idea is most abstract. In this respect I shall choose the idea, not the medium.

Now the media employed in architecture and sculpture and painting and music are abstract. Here is not the place to investigate this matter farther. The most abstract idea conceivable is sensuous genius. But in what medium is this idea expressible? Solely in music. It cannot be expressed in sculpture, for it is a sort of inner qualification of inwardness; nor in painting, for it cannot be apprehended in precise outlines; it is an energy, a storm, impatience, passion, and so on, in all their lyrical quality, yet so that it does not exist in one moment but in a succession of moments, for if it existed in a single moment, it could be modeled or painted. The fact that it exists in a succession of moments expresses its epic character, but still it is not epic in the stricter sense, for it has not yet advanced to words, but moves always in an immediacy. Hence it cannot be represented in poetry. The only medium which can express it is music. Music has, namely, its moment in time, but it does not take place in time except in an unessential sense. It cannot express the historical in the temporal process.

The perfect unity of this idea and the corresponding form we have in Mozart's *Don Juan*. But precisely because the idea is so tremendously abstract, the medium is also abstract; so it is not probable that Mozart will ever have a rival. It was Mozart's good fortune to have found a subject that is absolutely musical, and if some future composer should try to emulate Mozart, there would be nothing else for him to do than to compose *Don Juan* over again. Homer found a perfect epic subject, but many epic poems are conceivable, because history commands more epic material. This is not the case with *Don Juan*. What I really mean will perhaps be best understood if I show the difference in connection with a related idea. Goethe's *Faust* is a genuinely classical production, but the idea is a historical idea, and hence every notable historical era will have its own *Faust*. *Faust* has language as its medium, and since this is a far more concrete medium, it follows on this ground also, that several works of the same kind are conceivable. *Don Juan*, on the other hand, will always stand alone by itself, in the same sense that the Greek sculptures are classics. But since the idea in *Don Juan* is even more abstract than that underlying Greek sculpture, it is easy to see that while classic sculpture includes several works, in music there can be only one. There can, of course, be a number of classical musical productions, but there will never be more than the one work of which it is possible to say that the idea is absolutely musical, so that the music does not appear as an accompaniment, but reveals its own innermost essence in revealing the idea. It is for this reason that Mozart stands highest among the Immortals, through his *Don Juan*.

In a drama the chief interest quite naturally centers around what one calls the hero of the play; the other characters in relation to him have only a subordinate and relative importance. The more the inward reflection penetrates the drama with its divisive power, however, the more the subordinate characters tend to assume a certain relative absoluteness, if I may say so. This is by no means a fault, but rather a virtue, just as the contemplation of the world which sees only the few eminent individuals and their importance in the world development, but is unaware of the common man, in a certain sense stands higher but is lower than the contemplation which views the lesser man in his equally great validity. The dramatist will succeed only to the degree in which nothing of the incommensurable remains, nothing of the mood from which the drama originates, that is to say, nothing of the mood *qua* mood, but in which everything is converted into the sacred dramatic coin: action and situation. In the same degree as the dramatist is successful in this, to that degree the general impression his work produces will be less that of a mood than of a thought, an idea. The more the general impression of a drama is that of a mood, the more certain one can be that the poet himself has anticipated it in the mood, and continually allowed it to become that, instead of seizing upon an idea, and letting this dramatically unfold itself. Such a drama then suffers from an abnormal excess of the lyric. This is a fault in a drama, but by no means such in an opera. That which preserves the unity in the opera is the keynote which dominates the whole production.

What has been said here about the general dramatic effect also applies to the individual parts of the drama. If I were to characterize in a single word the effect of the drama, insofar as this is different from the effect which every other kind of poetry produces, then I should say: the drama operates in the contemporary. In the drama I see the factors standing outside one another, together in the situation, a unity of action. The more, then, the individual factors are separated, the more profoundly the dramatic situation is self-reflective, the less will the dramatic unity manifest itself as a mood, the more it will become a definite idea. But as the totality of the opera cannot be thus self-reflective, as in the case of drama proper, so this is also the case with the musical situation, which is indeed dramatic, but which still has its unity in the mood. The musical situation has the contemporary quality like every dramatic situation, but the activity of the forces is a concord, a harmony, an agreement, and the impression made by the musical situation is the unity achieved by hearing together what sounds together. The more the drama is self-reflective, the more the mood is explained in the action. The less action, the more the lyrical moment dominates. This is quite proper in the opera. The opera does not have so much character delineation and action for its immanent goal; it is not reflective enough for that. On the other hand, passion, unreflective and substantial, finds its expression in opera. The musical situation depends on maintaining the unity of mood in the plurality of voices. This is exactly the characteristic of music that it can preserve the diversity in the unity of the mood. When in ordinary conversation one uses the word majority, one commonly means by that a unity which is the final result; this is not the case in music.

The dramatic interest requires a swift forward movement, what one might call the inherent, increasing tempo of the denouement. The more the drama is interpenetrated by reflection, the more impetuously it hurries forward. On the other hand, if the lyric or the epic moment is one-sidedly predominant, this expresses itself in a kind of lethargy which allows the situation to fall asleep, and makes the dramatic process and progress slow and laborious. This haste is not inherent in the nature of the opera, for this is characterized by a certain lingering movement, a certain diffusion in time and space. The action has not the swiftness of the denouement, or its direction, but it moves more horizontally. The mood is not sublimated in character and action.

As a result, the action in an opera can only be immediate action.

If we apply this explanation to the opera *Don Juan*, we shall have an opportunity to see it in its true classic validity. Don Juan is the hero of the opera, the chief interest centers about him; not only so, but he lends interest to all the other characters. This must not be understood, however, in a merely superficial sense, for this constitutes the mysterious in this opera, that the hero is also the animating force in the other characters. Don Juan's life is the life-principle within them. His passion sets the passion of all the others in motion; his passion resounds everywhere; it sounds in and sustains the earnestness of the Commandant, Elvira's anger, and Anna's hate, Ottavio's conceit, Zerlina's anxiety, Masetto's exasperation, and Leporello's confusion. As hero in the play, he gives it his name, as is generally true in the case of the hero, but he is more than a name, he is, so to speak, the common denominator. The existence of all the others is, compared with his, only a derived existence. If we now require of an opera that its unity provide the keynote, then we shall easily see that one could not imagine a more perfect subject for an opera than Don Juan. The keynote can really be, in relation to the forces of the play, a third force which sustains these. As an illustration of such an opera, I might mention *The White Lady*,[1] but such a unity is, with relation to the opera, a more external determination of the lyric. In *Don Juan* the keynote is nothing other than the primitive power in the opera itself; this is Don Juan, but again—just because he is not character but essentially life—he is absolutely musical. Nor are the other persons in the opera characters, but essentially passions, who are posited with Don Juan, and insofar again become musical. That is, as Don Juan; they are the external consequences his life constantly posits. It is this musical life of Don Juan, absolutely centralized in the opera, which enables it to create a power of illusion such as no other is able to do, so that its life transports one into the life of the play. Because the musical is omnipresent in this music, one may enjoy any snatch of it, and immediately

---

1. *La dame blanche*, François Adrien Boieldieu's (1775-1834) most famous opera, has a libretto by Scribe (after Walter Scott). The work was premiered at the Opéra-Comique in 1825.

be transported by it. One may enter in the middle of the play and instantly be in the center of it, because this center, which is Don Juan's life, is everywhere.

We know from experience that it is not pleasant to strain two senses at the same time, and it is often very confusing if we have to use our eyes hard when our ears are already occupied. Therefore we have a tendency to close our eyes when hearing music. This is true of all music more or less, about *Don Juan in sensu eminentiori:* As soon as the eyes are engaged, the impression becomes confused; for the dramatic unity which is seen is always subordinate and diffuse in comparison with the musical unity which is heard at the same time. This, at least, has been my own experience. I have sat close up, I have sat farther and farther away, I have tried a corner in the theater where I could completely lose myself in the music. The better I understood it, or believed that I understood it, the farther I was away from it, not from coldness, but from love, for it is better understood at a distance. This has had for my life something strangely mysterious in it. There have been times when I would have given anything for a ticket. Now I need no longer spend a single penny for one, I stand outside in the corridor; I lean up against the partition which divides me from the auditorium, and then the impression is most powerful; it is a world by itself, separated from me; I can see nothing, but I am near enough to hear, and yet so infinitely far away.

Since the characters appearing in the opera do not need to be so self-reflective that as characters they become transparent, it also follows from this, as I earlier emphasized, that the situation cannot be perfectly developed or expanded, but to a certain extent is carried by mood. The same applies to the action of an opera. What one in a stricter sense calls action, a deed undertaken with consciousness of purpose, cannot find its expression in music, but only in what we might call immediate action. Both are the case in *Don Juan.*

Reprinted from Kierkegaard, *Either/Or,* translated by D. F. and L. M. Swanson (Princeton: Princeton University Press, 1944), by permission of the publisher.

HECTOR BERLIOZ (1803-69)

HECTOR BERLIOZ, the giant among Romantic composers in the generation after Beethoven (whom he adored), was constitutionally unable to conceive music without some sort of literary background. Once this source of inspiration was established, however, he proceeded on the basis of purely musical considerations. Hence the important role which this composer plays in the development of program music, the tone poem, and the *leitmotif (idée fixe)*. The same attitude also explains his peculiar views concerning the musical drama and his failure to create enduring operas. What could be more unashamedly Romantic than the explanation he gives for his use of a Hungarian scene in the first part of his *"opéra à concert" La damnation de Faust* (1846): "People have asked why the author made his hero go into Hungary. He did so because he wished to compose a piece of instrumental music whose theme is Hungarian [the Rakoczy March]. . . . He would have sent him anywhere else if he had found the slightest musical reason for doing so." *La damnation de Faust*, by the way—whose dramatic effect is also spoiled by the ineptness with which the Goethean text is handled or, at times, "improved upon"—grew out of *Huit scènes de Faust* (1829), a cantata based on the translation by Gérard de Nerval. Berlioz had sent the score to Goethe, who, having received a negative report from his friend Zelter, did not deign to acknowledge receipt of either the music or the accompanying letter.

Of Berlioz' operas in the strict sense of the word, *Les Troyens* (1856-59) is by far the most accomplished one. But even in this bipartite work, which is rarely to be heard in the environment for which it was originally intended, he succumbs to the temptation of making music "free and wild and sovereign." *Les Troyens* is a true *grand opera*, i. e., a work of the kind best represented in Meyerbeer's *oeuvre*. Essentials of *grand opera* as given in *Grove's Musical Dictionary*, 5th ed., (New York: St. Martin's Press, 1959), III, 757, are "a serious, often tragic subject of an epic or historical nature, the use of the chorus in action, the inclusion of a ballet, at least one spectacular scene with elaborate writing for the solo and choral voices in concert and (normally) division into five acts, with or without subdivision into a larger number of scenes." Berlioz' other works for the lyrical stage include *Benvenuto Cellini* (1838) and the comic opera *Béatrice et Benedict* (1862), one of numerous works for which Shakespeare provided the initial impulse.

H. Berlioz, *Memoirs*, translated by R. & E. Holmes (New York: Knopf, 1932); H. Berlioz, *Evenings in the Orchestra*, translated by J. Barzun (New York: Knopf, 1956); J. Barzun, *Berlioz and His Century* (Boston: Little, Brown, 1950).

Preface to the Opera *Faust's Damnation* (1846)
HECTOR BERLIOZ

THE VERY TITLE of this work suggests that it is not based on the principal theme of Goethe's *Faust*, since Faust is saved in that illustrious poem. The author of *Faust's Damnation* has merely borrowed from Goethe a certain number of scenes whose attraction upon his mind proved irresistible, and which suited the plan he had devised. But granted he had been faithful to Goethe's idea, he would still have incurred the reproach of having disfigured a monument which already has been leveled at him (and partly with bitterness) by several individuals.

Actually it is common knowledge that it is impracticable to set to music a poem of some length, not written for the express purpose of being sung, without subjecting it to numerous changes. And of all the dramatic poems in existence *Faust* is certainly the least suited to be sung integrally from beginning to end. But if, in preserving the theme of Goethe's *Faust*, one must change that masterpiece in a hundred different ways in order to render it suitable for composition, the capital crime against genius is just as apparent in this case as in the other and, accordingly, merits equal reprobation.

It follows, then, that composers should be forbidden to choose famous poems as subjects for composition. We would thus be deprived of Mozart's *Don Giovanni*, whose libretto is Da Ponte's adaptation of Molière's *Don Juan*. Nor would we possess *The*

Marriage of Figaro, whose librettist has hardly respected Beaumarchais' comedy *The Barber of Seville* (for the same reason), or Gluck's *Alceste,* which is a somewhat crude paraphrase of Euripides' tragedy. The same applies to Gluck's *Iphigenia at Aulis,* in making which one has uselessly marred certain of Racine's verses which, with their spotless beauty, would have perfectly suited the recitatives. The numerous operas based on Shakespeare's plays would have remained unwritten, and M. Spohr would be blameworthy for having produced a *Faust*[1] which contains a witches' sabbath in addition to the figures of Faust, Mephisto, and Gretchen, and which bears no other resemblance to Goethe's poem.

It will be just as easy to answer the detailed views which have been uttered with regard to the libretto of *Faust's Damnation.*

People have asked why the author made his hero go into Hungary. He did so because he wished to compose a piece of instrumental music whose theme is Hungarian. This he freely confesses. He would have sent him anywhere else if he had found the slightest musical reason for doing so. Goethe himself sends his hero to Sparta, and into the palace of Menelaus.

The legend of Dr. Faust can be treated in all sorts of ways; it is public property. It was dramatized before Goethe and had circulated for a long time, and under various guises, in the literary world of northern Europe when Goethe took hold of it. Marlowe's *Faust* had even enjoyed a kind of celebrity in England, a real fame which Goethe caused to fade and disappear.

As for those German verses in *Faust's Damnation* which differ from Goethe's original, they are bound to shock German ears, just as Racine's lines, adapted to Gluck's *Iphigenia,* offend the ears of the French. But one should not forget that the score of the work was written to a French text certain portions of which constitute a translation from the German, and that, in order to gratify the composer's desire to submit his opera to the judgment of the most musical public in Europe, a translation of that translation had to be prepared.

These observations may seem childish to the refined spirits

---

1. Louis Spohr (1784-1859) was Germany's leading Romantic composer of grand opera. His *Faust,* based on the legend rather than on Goethe's drama, was first performed in Prague in September, 1816.

who immediately grasp the essence of things, and who do not like to see one go to the trouble of proving that one cannot dry the Caspian Sea or move Mont Blanc. Yet M. Hector Berlioz thought it necessary to offer them, it having pained him to see himself accused of having betrayed the religion of his whole life and of having, even indirectly, failed to pay due respect to genius.

Translated by Ulrich Weisstein from Hector Berlioz, *La Damnation de Faust*, partition de piano avec le texte français et allemand (Paris: S. Richault, n. d.).

Letter to the Princess Sayn-Wittgenstein (1856)

HECTOR BERLIOZ

How MUCH I thank you, Princess, for the exquisite kindness which made you write me such a precious letter. That's what I call an analysis! This is what is meant by entering into the spirit of things!

You wished to encourage me. . . . You even go so far as to credit me with the beauties of Virgil's poetry and to praise me for my pilferings from Shakespeare. Rest assured that I shall have the courage to see matters through. There was no need to try to snare me with undeserved praises. It is beautiful because it is Virgil; it is captivating because it is Shakespeare. I know well that I am merely a marauder. I have foraged in the garden of two geniuses and have cut a sheaf of flowers in order to use them as a bed for my music, in which God may grant that it won't be asphyxiated by their perfume. . . .

Thank you ever so much for everything your kindness has made you tell me by way of encouragement. Upon my return to Paris I shall try to free myself from all other occupations in order to concentrate on my musical task. It will be a hard one, and I shall be lost unless all the Virgilian gods come to my aid. The difficulty lies in discovering the musical *form*, that form without which the music does not exist or exists only as the humble slave of the word. That precisely is Wagner's crime; he wants to dethrone it, to reduce it to *expressive accents* by exaggerating Gluck's system—which the latter fortunately did not succeed in translating from theory into practice. I am for the music which you yourself call *free*. Yes, free and wild and sovereign; I want it to conquer everything, to assimilate everything to itself. I don't want any Alps or Pyrenees to exist for it. In order to conquer, however, it must fight in person and not through its lieutenants. I'll gladly have it make use of fine verses arrayed in battle formation; but it must brave the fire like Napoleon and march at the head of the phalanx like Alexander. It is so powerful that in certain cases it conquers *all by itself* and that a thousand times it has had the right to say, like Medea, "Myself, that is enough." To want to reduce it to the declamation of the ancient chorus is the most incredible and, luckily, most insensate folly in the entire history of art.

The real problem lies in finding the means of being *expressive* and *true* without ceasing to be a musician, and to find new ways of making the music dramatic. . . . There is still another stumbling block ahead of me in my attempt to write the music for this drama. The emotions which I have to express affect me too much. This is unfortunate; for one must endeavor to do the passionate things coldly. It is that which hampered me so much when composing the adagio and the final scene of *Roméo et Juliette*. I thought that I would never be able to complete them.

Translated by Ulrich Weisstein from Berlioz' *Briefe an die Fürstin Carolyne Sayn-Wittgenstein*, edited by La Mara (Leipzig: Breitkopf & Haertel, 1903).

From *Alkestis* of Euripides and those of Quinault and Calzabigi; the scores of Gluck, Schweitzer,[2] Guglielmi,[3] and Handel[4] on this subject
HECTOR BERLIOZ

When Gluck says that the music of a lyrical drama has no other aim but to add to the poetry that which the color adds to the design of a painting, I think that he is greatly mistaken. It

2. Anton Schweitzer's *Alceste* had a libretto by Wieland.
3. Pierre Guglielmi's *Alceste* was first performed at Milan in 1769. Stendhal repeatedly mentions Guglielmi in his *Life of Rossini*.
4. Handel wrote incidental music for Tobias Smollett's play *Alceste* (1750, unperformed).

seems to me that the task of an operatic composer is of considerably greater importance. His work constitutes the design as well as the coloring and, to continue Gluck's comparison, the words are little more than the subject of the picture. Expression is by no means the only goal of dramatic music. It would be as stupid as it is pedantic to disdain the purely sensual pleasure which is derived from certain effects of melody, harmony, rhythm, and instrumentation, independent of their relation to the portrayal of the feelings and passions of the drama.

Moreover, even if one wanted to deprive the listener of that source of pleasure rather than permitting him to revive his interest by turning it temporarily away from its principal object, there would still be cases where the composer is called upon to sustain by himself the interest in the lyrical drama. Of what importance is the poet in the character dances, in the pantomimes, the marches, and all those pieces in which the orchestra bears the entire burden? . . . The music must, then, forcibly contain both the design and the coloring.

RICHARD WAGNER (1813-83)

RICHARD WAGNER, who together with Giuseppe Verdi dominated the operatic scene in the latter part of the nineteenth century, was born in Leipzig only a few months prior to the battle which sealed the fate of the first Napoleon. He was schooled in Dresden as well as Leipzig. Wagner spent the years 1839-42 in Paris, where Meyerbeer—to whose art Wagner's first grand opera, *Rienzi*, pays tribute—gave him a helping hand. In 1842 the German composer was appointed *Kapellmeister* at Dresden, where for the next years he walked in the footsteps of Carl Maria von Weber. *Rienzi*, *Der fliegende Holländer*, and *Tannhäuser* were all performed in the Saxon metropolis.

Having become embroiled in revolutionary activities, Wagner was forced, in 1849, to go into exile. Under the patronage of Otto Wesendonk he resided in Switzerland, where he became acquainted with Schopenhauer's philosophy. In 1864 King Ludwig II of Bavaria called him to Munich, but in the following year he was once again forced into exile, although the king remained his loyal supporter. Wagner returned to Switzerland and soon began to develop his plans for a theater solely devoted to the performance of his music dramas. In August, 1876, the Bayreuth Festspielhaus was opened with the first production of the entire *Ring*. The premiere of *Parsifal* in 1882, one year before Wagner's death in Venice, completed his break with Nietzsche, whose anti-Wagnerian manifestos—together with Eduard Hanslick's scathing critiques—set the stage for the rebellion against the *Gesamtkunstwerk* on the part of the leading composers and schools of the twentieth century. To be a Wagnerian after Busoni, Cocteau, Stravinsky, and Brecht means to be, like Pfitzner, a reactionary.

Wagner was also enormously active as a writer on aesthetic and political subjects. His speculations on the art of the future are too well known to require recapitulation. Let it merely be noted that the Wagnerian operas, whose composer doubled as librettist (a term he heartily despised), form the backbone of the modern repertory in conjunction with those of Mozart, Verdi, Puccini, and Strauss.

E. Newman, *The Life of Richard Wagner* (New York: Knopf, 1943-46), 4 vols.; E. A. Lippmann, "The Esthetic Theories of Richard Wagner," *Musical Quarterly*, XLIV (1958), 209-220; J. M. Stein, *Richard Wagner and the Synthesis of the Arts* (Wayne State University Press, 1960); Kerman, *Opera As Drama*, pp. 194-216.

Opera and Drama (1851)
RICHARD WAGNER

LET US NOW clearly bring into focus the form of the drama with which we are here concerned, in order that we may hold it up to recognition, with all its necessary and constantly renewed changes, as being by its very nature the only complete and unified one. But we also have to consider what makes this unity possible.

The unified artistic form can only be conceived as a manifestation of a unified content. A unified content can only be recognized by its being given an artistic expression that directly communicates with our feelings. A content which makes a two-fold expression necessary—an expression, that is, which forces the author to turn alternately to reason and feeling—must likewise be divided and ambiguous.

Every artistic intention originally craves for a unified form; for only in the degree that it approaches this form can any manifestation become an artistic one. Division inevitably commences at the point where the intention can no longer be fully conveyed by the means of expression at one's disposal. As it is the instinctive desire of every artistic intention to speak to the feelings, a divisive expression will be one that is incapable of doing so. But an expression must speak to our feelings if it is to convey its full meaning.

The poet proper finds this total involvement of the feelings impossible in his medium of expression; and what he cannot convey to the feelings he is obliged to communicate to reason, so as to be able to fully clarify his aims. He is thus forced to let the mind think what he is unable to make the heart feel; and when the decisive moment is reached, he can only realize his intentions by means of sententious utterances, or as intention in its naked form. Thus he shifts, of sheer necessity, the content of that intention to an unartistic level.

While the work of the poet thus appears as an unrealized poetic intention, the work of the composer of absolute music must be regarded as one altogether lacking in poetic intent; for although feelings may well be aroused by purely musical means, they cannot by such means be fixed as to their actual nature.

The limited range of expression at the poet's disposal forces him to divide his contents into those related to feeling and those related to reason, which causes the feeling to be restless and dissatisfied and the reason to reflect vainly on the restlessness of the feeling. The musician faces the same dilemma as the poet, since he compels the reason to assign a meaning to the expression which strongly arouses the feelings, without leading from this extreme commotion to a resting point. The poet furnishes this content in the form of sententious statements, while the musician, in order to create the semblance of some intention not actually present, prefaces his composition by a title. Both are thus compelled to turn from feeling to reason: the poet in order to define an incompletely determined emotion, the musician in order to apologize for having aroused a feeling to no purpose.

Should we, accordingly, wish to name the kind of expression whose unity renders a unity of content possible, we must define it as that which is able to convey the most comprehensive intention of the poetic mind most suitably to the feelings. Now an expression of this kind is one in which the poetic intention inheres in each situation but, at the same time, is concealed in each from the feeling by being realized.

This complete realization of the poetic intention would not be possible even in the case of vocal music were it not for the presence of a second musical medium that coexists with it. Thus wherever vocal music, as the most direct refuge of the poetic intention, is forced to lower its own expression so deeply—for the sake of the unbreakable tie between this intention and ordinary life—as barely to cover it with a musical veil that is nearly transparent, the equilibrium of the unified emotional expression can be successfully sustained.

We have seen that the orchestra is the agent which constantly completes the unity of expression and which, wherever the vocal expression of the dramatic characters lowers itself in order to define the dramatic situation more clearly—and that to the extent of demonstrating its relation to the expression of ordinary life in a rational manner—balances the abated expression of the dramatic character. It does so by means of its ability to evoke past and future in such a way that the feelings that have been aroused continue on their level of elevation and are not forced also to descend to the level of purely rational activity. The same height of feeling, from which no descent, but only ascent, is possible, is determined by the same height of expression and, through it, by the sameness, i. e., the unity of content.

We must also bear in mind that the orchestral passages in which this levelling of the elements of expression occurs are never to be determined by the arbitrary will of the musician as a sort of decorative embellishment, but solely by the poetic intention. If these passages express anything that is either inconsistent with, or superfluous to, the dramatic situation, the unity of expression is disturbed by a deviation from content. The purely musical embellishment of abated or foreshadowed situations (such as those which have found favor in opera in the form of the so-called *ritornello*, in interludes, and even in orchestral accompaniments) radically destroys all unity of expression and affects our sense of hearing no longer as a means of expression but rather as expression itself.

These situations, too, must be strictly guided by the poetic intention, and that in such a way as to focus our feelings, by way of anticipation or remembrance, always and exclusively upon the characters and their dramatic context. These anticipatory or reminiscent orchestral passages should be felt as the completion of a message which the character now before our eyes is either unable or unwilling to transmit.

Through the orchestra these melodic passages, which are in themselves suited to maintain the emotion on the same level of intensity, become, in a way, so many sign-posts for the feelings throughout the drama's complex structure. Through them we gain access to the innermost secrets of the poetic intention and participate in its realization. Between them (as the vehicles of anticipation and retrospection) there stands verse melody, the active and passive individuality, which is conditioned by the emotional context consisting of the moments in which the character's own feelings or those of others, whether previously felt or still to be experienced, are manifested. These passages, which meaningfully complete the emotional expression, are relegated to the background as soon as the character proceeds to the full expression of the verse melody. Then it is that the orchestra merely continues to support the verse melody by exercising its explanatory power, so as to be able, whenever the glowing tints of the verse melody's expression fade away into melodious prose phrases, to complement the general expression of feeling once more by anticipatory reminiscences, as well as to effect, as it were, the necessary transitions of feeling, by means of our own interest that has been kept alive throughout.

These melodic passages—in which presentiment is remembered while remembrance turns into presentiment—have sprung naturally from the principal dramatic motives which constitute the condensed and intensified *leitmotifs* of an action that is equally condensed and intensified. The poet uses these motives as pillars of his dramatic structure, using them not in helter-skelter profusion but so sparingly as to enable him to arrange them plastically and conspicuously.

In these *leitmotifs*, which are no sententious utterances but plastically developed emotional situations, the poetic intention becomes most clearly intelligible, since it is realized in the receptivity of feeling. The musician who realizes the poet's intentions has to arrange these motives (condensed into melodic passages) in such perfect agreement with these intentions that the most unified musical form results as a natural consequence of the perfectly natural mutual repetition—a form hitherto arbitrarily invented by the composer, but which can only be properly unified, i.e., made intelligible, when corresponding with the design of the poet.

In opera, up to now, the composer did not even try to achieve unity of form for his entire work, each single number having its independently filled-out form and being related to the other closed numbers of the opera only in point of external structure, but possessing no actual affinity based on subject matter. Incoherence was thus peculiar to operatic music. Only the single number, within its self-appointed limits, possessed any formal coherence, which, having been brought about by the requirements of absolute music, was upheld by custom and foisted upon the poet as a burden. What was coherent in this form was a theme composed beforehand and alternating with a second theme, the repetitions being introduced arbitrarily and for purely musical reasons.

Change, repetition, shortening or lengthening of the theme constituted the only motion of the instrumental compositions on a larger scale (the symphonic movement) conditioned by them and striving to acquire unity of form by means of the fusion and repetition of themes justified, as far as possible, before the feeling. The justification of this return, however, always rests on the mere assumption of an underlying content, and only the poetic intention is able to render the justification possible, because it urgently demands this justification as a necessary condition of intelligibility.

In their return, which is so naturally guided by relationships similar to those observed in the use of rhyme, the principal motives of the dramatic action, having now attained to the condition of a distinct melodic phrase that fully realizes the underlying intentions, are gathered into a unified artistic form extending, as a binding medium, not merely over individual parts but over the drama as a whole. In this way not only these melodic passages, which elucidate each other and thus create a unity, but also the emotional and phenomenal motives to which they refer are transmitted to the feeling. In this context, the perfectly unified form has been accomplished, and, through it, a unified content is manifested or, better still, rendered possible.

In summarizing once again everything that is relevant to the problem in question, we designate as the most perfect unified form of art that in which the widest range of human experiences —as content—is conveyed to the feelings in so completely intelligible a manner that the manifestation of this content at every point of the action first arouses and then satisfies the emotions. The content must, accordingly, be closely linked to the expression, while the expression must continuously evoke the content in its full scope. For that which is not present to the senses is grasped by thought alone, while feeling comprehends only that which is brought before it.

In this unity, which results from an expression that renders everything present and embraces the content according to the structural correlation of its parts, the problem of the unity of time and place is also solved in the most conclusive manner.

Space and time, as abstractions of the real and corporeal qualities of action, only attracted the attention of our playwrights because a unified expression capable of completely realizing the desired poetic content was not within their reach. Space and time are imaginary qualities ascribed to real, corporeal phenomena which, being isolated, immediately lose their impact. The body of these abstractions is the real and sensuous element of action manifested in a definite spatial environment and in a progression of movement dependent therefrom.

To base the unity of the drama upon unity of time and space is to base it upon nothing: for space and time in themselves are nothing. They turn into something only when negated by something real, a human action and the context out of which it grows. This human action must constitute that which is unified, i.e., coherent, in itself. Its temporal extension depends on the possibility of rendering its context intelligible, its spatial extension on the possibility of an appropriate setting. For its sole desire is to communicate with the feeling. The greatest condensation of space and time may result in the unfolding of an action that is utterly disunited and incoherent, as may easily be gauged from contemporary plays in which the unities are observed.

Unity of action, on the other hand, depends on the intelligibility of the context itself, which can be obtained by one means only: neither by space nor time, but by expression. If, in the foregoing, we have shown this expression to be a unified one, i.e., one whose parts are interconnected and constantly evoke the total context, we have also re-entered into the possession of that which had been separated by time and space but which is now again reunited and ever present there where intelligibility requires it. Its necessary presence lies not in time and space but in the impression which time and space make upon us. The conditions which resulted from the lack of this expression (connected, as they were, with time and space) have been annulled by the acquisition of this expression; and time and space have been annihilated by the reality of the drama.

Thus the real drama is no longer subject to any external influences but is something organically being and becoming which, prompted by its own internal conditions, develops and forms itself by the one required contact with the external world, namely the necessity of making its manifestation (a manifestation of its being and becoming) understood. This intelligible formation, however, benefits from the fact that from a deep-seated urge it gives rise to the expression of its content that renders everything possible.

Translated by Ulrich Weisstein from Wagner's *Gesammelte Schriften und Dichtungen* (Leipzig: Fritzsch, 1897).

GEORGES BIZET (1838-75)

THE CHILD of extremely musical parents, Bizet entered the Paris Conservatory at the age of ten, and after distinguishing himself in several departments, won the Prix de Rome in 1857. He spent the following three years in Italy, and upon his return to France embarked on his only partly successful career as an operatic composer—the best known of his nonoperatic works being the Symphony in C Major which he wrote at the age of seventeen. Among the ten works for the musical stage which Bizet created, only four have gained some measure of popularity: *Les Pêcheurs de perles* (1863), *La jolie fille de Perth* (1867), *Djamileh* (1872), and, naturally, *Carmen* (1875). To these the frequently performed incidental music for Daudet's play *L'Arlesienne* (1872) must be added.

A radical change in Bizet's attitude toward music in general and opera in particular took place while he was working on *La jolie fille de Perth*. Having been censured by the music critic of *Le Temps*, Johannes Weber, he candidly admitted in a letter: "This time, I still have made concessions, which I regret. Like you I do not believe in the false gods. The school of frills, trills, and lies is dead, gone forever. Let us bury it without tears, without regrets, and without emotion, and let us march on." Bizet's quest for dramatic realism culminated in *Carmen*, a work which, with one blow, transformed the genre of the *opéra comique* into something far more serious than had hitherto seemed possible. (The original version of *Carmen* retains the spoken dialogue.) But even now the composer did not altogether scorn concessions.

The difficulties he and his librettists encountered on the part of
the two directors of the Opéra-Comique are recalled by Halévy
in his commemorative article, a corrective to which is supplied
by Paul Landormy, whose discovery of Bizet's version of the
text for the *Habanera* led him to believe that the composer substantially aided in fashioning the libretto of his opera. With Mina
Curtiss[1] "One can only regret that because of Bizet's proximity
to Halévy and Meilhac in Paris most of the collaboration on
Carmen was carried on orally and therefore remains unrecorded."
Bizet's only written statement about his operatic masterpiece is
contained in a letter to his friend Edmond Galabert of June 17,
1872. It reads: "I have been asked to compose three acts for the
Opéra-Comique. Meilhac and Halévy are writing the libretto.
The work will be gay, but of a kind of gaiety that allows for
style."

R. Northcott, *Bizet and "Carmen"* (London, 1916); E. Istel, *Bizet und
"Carmen"* (Stuttgart: Engelhorn, 1927); W. Dean, *Bizet* (London: Dent,
1948, and New York: Collier Books, 1962); M. Curtiss, *Bizet* (New York:
Knopf, 1958).

The One Thousandth Performance of *Carmen* (1905)
LUDOVIC HALEVY

IT WAS BIZET who, in 1873, had the idea of extracting an opera
libretto from the admirable novella of Merimée.[2] Meilhac[3] and
I immediately shared his feelings, and so did Du Locle[4] when
I talked to him about it. But at the same time he was worried.
"There is Leuven,"[5] he told me, "whom such a subject will scare.
But go see him. He loves you dearly, and perhaps you'll manage
to persuade him." . . . I went to see Leuven; and he actually inter-

1. In *Bizet* (New York: 1958), p. 352.
2. Prosper Merimée's novella *Carmen* was first published in the *Revue
des deux mondes* of October 1, 1845.
3. Henri Meilhac and Ludovic Halévy, the nephew of the composer of
La juive, collaborated on the libretto of *Carmen*. Both are among Offenbach's chief librettists.
4. Camille du Locle was one of the directors of the Opéra-Comique.
5. De Leuven was Du Locle's co-administrator but resigned, perhaps in
consequence of his aversion to *Carmen*.

rupted me after the first sentence. "*Carmen!* Merimée's *Carmen!* Isn't she killed by her lover? And these bandits, gypsies, and girls working in a cigar factory! At the Opéra-Comique! The family theater, the theater of wedding parties, seven or eight of which rent boxes for each performance. You'll frighten our audience away. That's impossible."

I insisted and explained to Mr. Leuven that ours was a *Carmen*, to be sure, but a toned-down, softened *Carmen*, and that we had actually introduced some characters perfectly in keeping with the style of the *opéra comique*, especially a young girl of great chastity and innocence [Micaëla]. There were indeed gypsies, but of the humorous variety (they really weren't). And Carmen's death, the inevitable catastrophe at the end, would be sneaked in somehow at the conclusion of a lively and brilliant act, in broad daylight, on a holiday filled with processions, dances, and gay fanfares. Mr. de Leuven acquiesced, but after a prolonged struggle. And when I left his office, he said: "Please try not to let her die. Death at the Opéra-Comique. That's never happened before, do you hear, never. Don't let her die, I implore you, my dear child." . . .

But Bizet still felt the need for making concessions. Three pieces of his score fit into the customary form of the *opéra comique:* the duet between Micaëla and Don José in the first act ["Ma mère, je la vois, je revois mon village"], the entrance of the Torero in the second ["Votre toast, je peux vous le rendre"], and Micaëla's aria, written for the virtuoso voice of Mlle. Chapuy, in the third ["Je dis rien ne m'épouvante"]. Here Bizet obviously sought to achieve effects in the familiar style, and quite successfully so. I have already noted that these were the only pieces to attract attention and to be applauded, although indifferently. In the rest of the score, he has tried only to impart the greatest possible degree of truth and passion to his work. He has scorned all cheap effects and kept in mind only the overall effect. His music sticks closely to the action and never stops in order to force the audience to applaud.

Translated by Ulrich Weisstein from Halévy, "La millième représentation de *Carmen*," *Le théâtre*, January, 1905.

Bizet's Contribution to the *Carmen* Libretto (1924)
PAUL LANDORMY

FOR THE MUSIC of the *Habanera* in the first act Ludovic Halévy had originally written the following verses:

> *Hasard et fantaisie*
> *Ainsi commencent les amours*
> *En voilà pour la vie*
> *Ou pour dix mois ou pour trois jours.*
> *Un matin sur sa route*
> *On trouve l'amour, il est là.*
> *Il vient sans qu'on s'en doute*
> *Et sans qu'on s'en doute il s'en va.*
> *Il vous prend, vous enlève,*
> *Il fait de vous tout ce qu'il veut.*
> *C'est un délice, un rêve*
> *Et ça dure ce que ça peut.*

[Chance or fantasy, this is how love begins, either to last a lifetime or ten months or three days. One morning, one finds love in one's path, and there it is. It comes without one's suspecting it, and without one's suspecting it it goes. It takes hold of you, carries you away, and does with you what it wants. It is a delight, a dream, and lasts as long as it can.]

Halévy accompanied his missive to Bizet with the remark: "Here are the twelve lines you demanded. Are they fitting? I would have written more tender ones, but I think that in the beginning, Carmen should not appear too melancholic, and that some banter wouldn't do any harm."

Here one gets a first-hand view of the bad habits of a typically Parisian librettist who merely seeks to entertain his audience, even at the expense of the truth of character and situation. Meilhac and Halévy have sufficiently watered down the roles of Carmen and Don José. What would *Carmen* have turned into in their hands if Bizet had let them proceed as they wanted, if he had let them use at every turn the kind of banter that assures the success of their operettas? One begins to wonder how much Bizet really contributed to the drama and whether his contribution did not often exceed the musical limits. It is certain, at any rate, that the text offered by Halévy failed to please the composer and that the lines finally adapted to the music of the *Habanera* are, except for a few corrections, Bizet's own. Perhaps Bizet also furnished other texts to his collaborators, or at least caused them to make changes without our being able to tell. If *Carmen* still retains some of the violent passion and the crude color of Merimée's novella, this is, perhaps, due to Bizet's intervention.

Bizet appears here, at any rate, if compared with Meilhac and Halévy, as the one collaborator with the soundest intuition and the deepest understanding of the subject under consideration. The words he wrote are among the best in the entire libretto and may be regarded as the only ones that really enable one to fully understand Carmen's character.

Translated by Ulrich Weisstein from Paul Landormy, *Bizet* (Paris. Alcan, 1924), by permission of Presses Universitaires de France.

FRIEDRICH NIETZSCHE (1844-1900)

FRIEDRICH NIETZSCHE, in his youth a great admirer of Chopin, was appointed Professor of Classical Philology at the University of Basle at the age of twenty-four. He curtailed the scope of a treatise on Greek culture in order to humor Richard Wagner, whom he had first met in Leipzig, where he was a student, and the acquaintance with whom he had renewed after his arrival in Switzerland. The torso *Die Geburt der Tragödie aus dem Geiste der Musik* (The Birth of Tragedy), completed during the Franco-German war, is climaxed by an apotheosis of *Tristan und Isolde,* which is described in glowing terms as the most striking instance of the near-perfect fusion of the Apollonian and Dionysian principles. Wagner, then, is presented as the only artist capable of bringing about the rebirth of Greek tragedy in the German spirit.

The philosopher's admiration for the composer did not flag until the opening of the Bayreuth *Festspielhaus* in 1876. In spite of the disillusionment resulting from this occasion (a disillusionment later shared by a whole generation of composers), he continued to praise the master in his *Richard Wagner in Bayreuth* (1876). A complete break between the two was not effected until the publication, in the *Bayreuther Blätter* of 1878, of an essay entitled "Public and Popularity," in which Nietzsche was indirectly attacked. The parting of ways was completed when Nietzsche came to realize that in *Parsifal* Wagner had betrayed their common, "pagan" ideal to the spirit of Christianity. In the early eighties, the philosopher, who was also an amateur composer, came under the influence of his pupil Peter Gast, who awakened in him a constantly growing interest in "Mediterranean" music; and shortly afterward Bizet became his idol. But not until five years after Wagner's death (which coincided with the completion of Part I of *Zarathustra*) did Nietzsche openly repudiate his former idol. *Der Fall Wagner* (The Case of Wagner), *Götzendämmerung,* and *Nietzsche contra Wagner* followed closely upon each other. They were to furnish ammunition for the anti-theatrical and anti-Romantic campaigns of *Les Six* and those who shared their neoclassical views in the early decades of our century.

P. Lasserre, *Les idées de Nietzsche sur la musique* (Paris, 1907); J. W. Klein, "Nietzsche and Bizet," *Musical Quarterly,* XI (1925), 482-505; E. Foerster-Nietzsche, "Wagner and Nietzsche: The Beginning and End of Their Friendship," *Musical Quarterly,* IV (1918), 466-489; G. Abraham, "Nietzsche's Attitude to Wagner: A Fresh View," *Music & Letters,* XIII (1932), 64-74.

The Birth of Tragedy (1872)
FRIEDRICH NIETZSCHE

TRAGEDY ABSORBS the highest musical orgasm into itself, so that it absolutely brings music to perfection among the Greeks, as among ourselves; but it then places alongside thereof tragic myth and the tragic hero, who, like a mighty Titan, takes the entire Dionysian world on his shoulders and disburdens us thereof; while, on the other hand, it is able by means of this same tragic myth, in the person of the tragic hero, to deliver us from the intense longing for this existence, and remind us with warning hand of another existence and a higher joy, for which the struggling hero prepares himself presentiently by his destruction, not by his victories. Tragedy sets a sublime symbol, namely the myth, between the universal authority of its music and the receptive Dionysian hearer, and produces in him the illusion that music is only the most effective means for the animation of the plastic world of myth. Relying upon this noble illusion, she can now move her limbs for the dithyrambic dance, and abandon herself unhesitatingly to an orgiastic feeling of freedom, in which she could not venture to indulge as music itself, without this illusion. The myth protects us from the music, while, on the other hand, it alone gives the highest freedom thereto. By way of return for this service, music imparts to tragic myth such an impressive and convincing metaphysical significance as could never be attained by word and image, without this unique aid; and the tragic spectator in particular experiences thereby the sure presentiment of supreme joy to which the path through destruction and negation leads; so that he thinks he hears, as it were, the innermost abyss of things speaking audibly to him.

If in these last propositions I have succeeded in giving perhaps only a preliminary expression . . . to this difficult representation, I must not here desist from stimulating my friends to a further attempt . . . for the perception of the universal proposition. . . . I have only to address myself to those who, being immediately allied to music, have it as it were for their mother's lap, and are connected with things almost exclusively by unconscious musical relations. I ask the question of these genuine musicians: whether they can imagine a man capable of hearing the third act of *Tristan and Isolde* without any aid of word or scenery, purely as a vast symphonic period, without expiring by a spasmodic distention of all the wings of the soul? A man who has thus, so to speak, put his ear to the heart chamber of the cosmic will, who feels the furious desire for existence issuing therefrom as a thundering stream or most gently dispersed brook, into all the veins of the world, would he not collapse all at once? Could he endure, in the wretched fragile tenement of the human individual, to hear the re-echo of countless cries of joy and sorrow from the "vast void of cosmic night" without flying irresistibly toward his primitive home at the sound of this pastoral dance-song of metaphysics? But if, nevertheless, such a work can be heard as a whole, without a renunciation of individual existence, if such a creation could be created without demolishing its creator—where are we to get the solution of this contradiction?

Here there interpose between our highest musical excitement and the music in question the tragic myth and the tragic hero—in reality only as symbols of the most universal facts, of which music alone can speak directly. If, however, we felt as purely Dionysian beings, myth as a symbol would stand by us absolutely ineffective and unnoticed, and would never for a moment prevent us from giving ear to the re-echo of the *universalia ante rem.* Here, however, the Apollonian power, with a view to the restoration of the well-nigh shattered individual, bursts forth with the healing balm of a blissful illusion: all of a sudden we imagine we see only Tristan, motionless with hushed voice saying to himself: "the old tune, why does it wake me?" And what formerly interested us like a hollow sigh from the heart of being, seems now only to tell us how "waste and void is the sea." And when, breathless, we thought to expire by a convulsive distention of all our feelings, and only a slender tie bound us to our present existence, we now hear and see only the hero wounded to death and still not dying, with his despairing cry: "Longing! Longing! In dying still longing! For longing not dying!" . . . However powerfully fellow-suffering encroaches upon us, it nevertheless delivers us in a manner from the primordial suffering of the world, just as the symbol image of the myth delivers us from the immediate perception of the highest cosmic idea, just as the thought and word delivers us from the unchecked effusion of the unconscious will. The glorious Apollonian illusion makes it appear as if the very realm of tones presented itself to us as a plastic cosmos, as if even the fate of Tristan and Isolde had been merely formed and molded therein as out of some most delicate and impressible material.

Thus does the Apollonian wrest us from Dionysian universality and fill us with rapture for individuals; to these it rivets our sympathetic emotion, through these it satisfies the sense of beauty which longs for great and sublime forms; it brings before us biographical portraits, and incites us to a thoughtful apprehension of the essence of life contained therein. With the immense potency of the image, the concept, the ethical teaching and the sympathetic emotion—the Apollonian influence uplifts man from his orgiastic self-annihilation, and beguiles him concerning the universality of the Dionysian process into the belief that he is seeing a detached picture of the world, for instance, Tristan and Isolde, and that, through music, he will be enabled to see it still more clearly and intrinsically. What can the healing magic of Apollo not accomplish when it can even excite in us the illusion that the Dionysian is actually in the service of the Apollonian, the effects of which it is capable of enhancing; yea, that music is essentially the representative art for an Apollonian substance?

With the pre-established harmony which obtains between perfect drama and its music, the drama attains the highest degree of conspicuousness, such as is usually unattainable in mere spoken drama. As all the animated figures of the scene in the independently evolved lines of melody simplify themselves before us to the distinctness of the catenary curve, the coexistence of these lines is also audible in the harmonic change which sympathizes in a most delicate manner with the evolved process: through which change the relations of things became immediately perceptible to us in a sensible and not at all abstract manner, as we likewise perceive thereby that it is only in these relations that the essence of a character and of a line of melody manifests itself clearly. And while music thus compels us to see more extensively and more intrinsically than usual, and makes us spread out the curtain of the scene before ourselves like some delicate texture, the world of the stage is as infinitely expanded for our spiritualized, introspective eye as it is illumined outwardly from within. How can the word-poet furnish anything analogous, who strives to attain this internal expansion and illumination of the visible stage-world by a much more imperfect mechanism and an indirect path, proceeding as he does from word and concept? Albeit musical tragedy likewise avails itself of the word, it is at the same time able to place alongside thereof its basis and source, and can make the unfolding of the word, from within outward, obvious to us.

Of the process just set forth, however, it could still be said as decidedly that it is only a glorious appearance, namely the aforementioned Apollonian illusion, through the influence of which we are to be delivered from the Dionysian obtrusion and excess. In point of fact, the relation of music to drama is precisely the reverse; music is the adequate idea of the world, drama is but the reflex of this idea, a detached umbrage thereof. The identity between the line of melody and the living form, between the harmony and the character relations of this form, is true in a sense antithetical to what one would suppose on the contemplation of musical tragedy. We may agitate and enliven the form in the most conspicuous manner, and enlighten it from within, but it still continues merely phenomenon, from which there is no bridge to lead us into the true reality, into the heart of the world. Music, however, speaks out of this heart; and though countless phenomena of the kind might be passing manifestations of music, they could never exhaust its essence, but would always be merely its externalized copies.

Reprinted from *The Complete Works of Nietzsche*, edited by Oscar Levy, in the translation of W. A. Haussmann (New York: Macmillan, 1924), by permission of George Allen & Unwin Ltd.

The Case of Wagner (1888)
FRIEDRICH NIETZSCHE

YESTERDAY—would you believe it?—I heard Bizet's masterpiece for the twentieth time. Once more I attended with the same gentle reverence; once again I did not run away. This triumph over my impatience surprises me. How such a work completes one! Through it one almost becomes a "masterpiece" oneself. And, as a matter of fact, each time I heard *Carmen* it seemed to me that I was more of a philosopher, a better philosopher than at other times: I became so forbearing, so happy, so Indian, so settled. To sit for five hours: the first step to holiness! May I be allowed to say that Bizet's orchestration is the only one that I can endure now? That other orchestration which is all the rage at present—the Wagnerian—is brutal, artificial, and "unsophisticated" withal, hence its appeal to all the three senses of the modern soul at once. How terribly Wagnerian orchestration affects me! I call it the Sirocco. A disagreeable sweat breaks out all over me. All my fine weather vanishes.

Bizet's music seems to me perfect. It comes forward lightly, gracefully, stylishly. It is lovable, it does not sweat. "All that is good is easy, everything divine runs with light feet": this is the first principle of my aesthetics. This music is wicked, refined, fatalistic: and withal remains popular—it possesses the refinement of a race, not of an individual. It is rich. It is definite. It builds, organizes, completes: and in this sense it stands as a contrast to the octopus in music, to "endless melody." Have more painful, more tragic accents ever been heard on the stage before? And how are they obtained? Without grimaces! Without counterfeiting of any kind! Free from the lie of the grand style! In short: this music assumes that the listener is intelligent even as a musician—thereby it is the opposite of Wagner, who, apart from everything else, was in any case the most ill-mannered genius on earth (Wagner takes us *as if* . . . , he repeats a thing so often that we become desperate, that we ultimately believe it).

And once more: I become a better man when Bizet speaks to me. Also a better musician, a better listener. Is it in any way possible to listen better? I even burrow behind this music with my ears. I hear its very cause. I seem to assist at its birth. I tremble before the dangers which this daring music runs, I am enraptured over those happy accidents for which even Bizet himself may not be responsible. And, strange to say, at bottom I do not give it a thought, or am not aware how much thought I really do give it. For quite other ideas are running through my head the while. Has any one ever observed that music emancipates the spirit? gives wings to thought? and that the more one becomes a musician the more one is also a philosopher? The grey sky of abstraction seems thrilled by flashes of lightning; the light is strong enough to reveal all the details of things; to enable one to grapple with problems; and the world is surveyed as if from a mountain top. With this I have defined philosophical pathos. And unexpectedly answers drop into my lap, a small hailstorm of ice and wisdom, of problems solved. Where am I? Bizet makes me productive. Everything that is good makes me productive. I have gratitude for nothing else, nor have I any other touchstone for testing what is good.

Bizet's work also saves; Wagner is not the only "Saviour." With it one bids farewell to the damp north and to all the fog of the Wagnerian ideal. Even the action in itself delivers us from these things. From Merimée it has this logic, even in passion, from him it has the direct line, inexorable necessity; but what it has above all else is that which belongs to sub-tropical zones—that dryness of atmosphere, that *limpidezza* of the air. Here in every respect the climate is altered. Here another kind of sensuality, another kind of sensitiveness, and another kind of cheerfulness make their appeal. This music is gay, but not in a French or German way. Its gaiety is African; fate hangs over it, its happiness is short, sudden, without reprieve. I envy Bizet for having had the courage of this sensitiveness, which hitherto in the cultured music of Europe has found no means of expression—of this southern, tawny, sunburnt sensitiveness. . . . What a joy the golden afternoon of its happiness is to us! When we look out, with this music in our minds, we wonder whether we have ever seen the sea so calm. And how soothing is this Moorish dancing! How, for once, even our insatiability gets sated by its lascivious melancholy! And finally love, love translated back into Nature! Not the love of a "cultured girl"—no Senta-sentimentality.[1] But love as fate, as a fatality, cynical, innocent, cruel—and precisely in this way Nature! The love whose means is war, whose very essence is the mortal hatred between the sexes! I know no case in which the tragic irony, which constitutes the kernel of love, is expressed with such severity, or in so terrible a formula, as in the last cry of Don José with which the work ends: "Yes, it is I who have killed her,/ I—my adored Carmen!"

Such a conception of love (the only one worthy of a philosopher) is rare: it distinguishes one work of art from among a thousand others. For, as a rule, artists are no better than the rest of the world, they are even worse—they misunderstand love. Even Wagner misunderstood it. They imagine that they are self-

---

1. Senta is the heroine of Wagner's *Flying Dutchman.*

less in it because they appear to be seeking the advantage of another creature often to their own disadvantage. But in return they want to possess the other creature. . . . "*L'amour*"—and with this principle one carries one's point against Gods and men— "*est de tous les sentiments le plus égoïste, et par conséquent, lorsqu'il est blessé, le moins généreux*" [Benjamin Constant].[2]

Perhaps you are beginning to perceive how very much this music improves me? *Il faut méditerraniser la musique:* and I have reasons for this principle. The return to Nature, health, good spirits, youth, virtue. And yet I was one of the most corrupted Wagnerites. I was able to take Wagner seriously. Oh, this old magician! what tricks has he not played upon us! The first thing his art places in our hands is a magnifying glass: we look through it, and we no longer trust our own eyes. Everything grows bigger, even Wagner grows bigger. What a clever rattlesnake! Throughout his life he rattled "resignation," "loyalty," and "purity" about our ears, and he retired from the corrupt world with a song of praise to chastity! And we believed it all.

In Wagner's case the first thing we notice is a hallucination, not of tones, but of attitudes. Only after he has the latter does he begin to seek the semeiotics of tone for them. If we wish to admire him, we should observe him at work here: how he separates and distinguishes, how he arrives at small unities, and how he galvanizes them, accentuates them, and brings them into preeminence. But in this way he exhausts his strength: the rest is worthless. How paltry, awkward, and amateurish is his manner of "developing," his attempt at combining incompatible parts. His manner in this respect reminds one of two people who even in other ways are not unlike him in style—the brothers Goncourt;[3] one almost feels compassion for so much impotence. That Wagner disguised his inability to create organic forms, under the cloak of a principle, that he should have constructed

2. Benjamin Constant (1767-1830), the French writer and politician, is the author of the novel *Adolphe*.

3. The brothers Goncourt (Edmond, 1822-96, and Jules, 1830-70), cultural historians, are best known for their diary. They also wrote one of the first naturalistic novels, *Germinie Lacerteux*.

a "dramatic style" out of what we should call the total inability to create any style whatsoever, is quite in keeping with that daring habit, which stuck to him throughout his life, of setting up a principle wherever capacity failed him. . . . Once more let it be said that Wagner is really only worthy of admiration and love by virtue of his inventiveness in small things, in his elaboration of details—here one is quite justified in proclaiming him a master of the first rank, as our greatest musical miniaturist, who compresses an infinity of meaning and sweetness into the smallest space. His wealth of color, chiaroscuro, of the mystery of a dying light, so pampers our senses that afterward almost every other musician strikes us as being too robust. If people would believe me, they would not form the highest idea of Wagner from that which pleases them in him today. All that was only devised for convincing the masses, and people like ourselves recoil from it just as one would recoil from too garish a fresco. What concern have we with the irritating brutality of the overture to *Tannhäuser?* Or with the Walkyrie circus? Whatever has become popular in Wagner's art, including that which has become so outside the theater, is in bad taste and spoils taste. The *Tannhäuser* March seems to me to savor of the Philistine; the overture to the *Flying Dutchman* is much to do about nothing; the prelude to *Lohengrin* was the first, only too insidious, only too successful example of how one can hypnotize with music (I dislike all music which aspires to nothing higher than to convince the nerves). But apart from the Wagner who paints frescoes and practices magnetism, there is yet another Wagner who hoards small treasures: our greatest melancholic in music, full of side glances, loving speeches, and words of comfort, in which no one ever forestalled him—the tonemaster of melancholy and drowsy happiness. . . . A lexicon of Wagner's most intimate phrases—a host of short fragments of from five to fifteen bars each, of music which nobody knows. . . . Wagner had the virtue of *decadents*—pity.

Even in his general sketch of the action, Wagner is above all an actor. The first thing that occurs to him is a scene which is certain to produce a strong effect, a real *actio*, with a basso-relievo of attitudes; in an overwhelming scene, this he now proceeds to elaborate more deeply, and out of it he draws his characters. The whole of what remains to be done follows of itself, fully in keeping with a technical economy which has no reason to be subtle. It is not Corneille's public that Wagner has to consider, it is merely the nineteenth century. Concerning the "actual requirements of the stage" Wagner would have about the same opinion as any other actor of today: a series of powerful scenes, each stronger than the one that preceded it, and, in between, all kinds of clever nonsense. His first concern is to guarantee the effect of his work; he begins with the third act, he approves his work according to the quality of its final effect. Guided by this sort of understanding of the stage, there is not much danger of one's creating a drama unawares. Drama demands inexorable logic: but what did Wagner care about logic? Again, I say it was not Corneille's public that he had to consider; but merely Germans. Everybody knows the technical difficulties before which the dramatist often has to summon all his strength and frequently to sweat his blood: the difficulty of making the plot seem necessary and the unravelment as well, so that both are conceivable only in a certain way, and so that each may give the impression of freedom (the principle of the smallest expenditure of energy). Now the very last thing that Wagner does is to sweat blood over the plot; and on this and the unravelment he certainly spends the smallest possible amount of energy. Let anybody put one of Wagner's plots under the microscope, and I wager that he will be forced to laugh. Nothing is more enlivening than the dilemma in *Tristan*, unless it be that in the *Mastersingers*. Wagner is no dramatist; let nobody be deceived on this point. All he did was to love the word *drama*— he always loved fine words. Nevertheless, in his writings the word *drama* is merely a misunderstanding (and a piece of shrewdness: Wagner always affected superiority in regard to the word opera). . . .

He was not enough of a psychologist for drama; he instinctively avoided a psychological plot—but how? By always putting idiosyncrasy in its place. Very modern—eh? Very Parisian! Very decadent! . . . Incidentally, the plots that Wagner knows how to unravel with the help of dramatic inventions are of quite another kind. For example, let us suppose that Wagner requires a female voice. A whole act without a woman's voice would be impossible. But in this particular instance not one of the heroines happens to be free. What does Wagner do? He emancipates the oldest woman on earth, Erda: "Step up, aged grandmamma! You have got to sing!" And Erda sings. Wagner's end has been achieved. Thereupon he immediately dismisses the old lady: "Why on earth did you come? Off with you! Kindly go to sleep again!" In short, a scene full of mythological awe, before which the Wagnerite wonders all kinds of things.

"But the substance of Wagner's texts! Their mythical substance, their eternal substance!" Question: How is this substance, this eternal substance tested? The chemical analyst replies: Translate Wagner into the real, into the modern—let us be even more cruel, and say: into the bourgeois! And what will then become of him? Between ourselves, I have tried the experiment. Nothing is more entertaining, nothing more worthy of being recommended to a picnic party, than to discuss Wagner dressed in a more modern garb: for instance Parsifal as a candidate in divinity, with a public-school education (the latter quite indispensable for pure foolishness). What surprises await one! Would you believe it that Wagner's heroines one and all, once they have been divested of the heroic husks, are almost indistinguishable from Madame Bovary!—just as one can conceive conversely of Flaubert's being well able to transform all his heroines into Scandinavian or Carthaginian women, and then to offer them to Wagner in this mythologized form as a libretto. Indeed, generally speaking, Wagner does not seem to have become interested in any other problems than those which engross the little Parisian decadents of today.

Always five paces away from the hospital! All very modern problems, all problems which are at home in big cities! Do not doubt it! Have you noticed (it is in keeping with this association of ideas) that Wagner's heroines never have any children? They cannot have them. The despair with which Wagner tackled the problem of arranging in some way for Siegfried's birth betrays how modern his feelings on this point actually were. Siegfried "emancipated woman"—but not with any hope of offspring. And now here is a fact which leaves us speechless: Parsifal is Lohengrin's father! How ever did he do it? Ought one at this juncture to remember that "chastity works miracles"? *Wagnerus dixit princeps in castitate auctoritas.*

Reprinted from *The Complete Works of Friedrich Nietzsche*, edited by Oscar Levy, in A. M. Ludovici's translation (New York: Macmillan, 1924), by permission of George Allen & Unwin Ltd.

GIUSEPPE VERDI (1813-1901)

GIUSEPPE VERDI, Wagner's great compeer south of the Alps, dominated the Italian operatic scene from approximately 1850 until the early nineties, when Verismo had its brief hour of triumph and Puccini began to lay the foundations of his art. The most popular among the thirty lyrical dramas composed by Verdi were all performed within the short space of three years: *Rigoletto* in 1851, *Il trovatore* and *La traviata* in 1853. The next unqualified success came with *Aïda* (1872), which was followed, after a long interval, during which Verdi had abandoned all interest in opera, by the two masterpieces of his old age, *Otello* (1887) and *Falstaff* (1893).

Throughout his life Verdi displayed an eminent sense for dramatic values and greatly suffered from the mediocrity of his librettists, whom he persistently admonished to give him "*la parola scenica*" (the scenic word) and to break, if necessary, with the shopworn operatic conventions of formal recitatives and arias: "I, if the action demanded it, would immediately abandon rhythm, rhyme, and stanza. . . . Especially in the theater it is sometimes necessary for poets and composers to possess the talent of creating neither poetry nor music." It was not until his encounter with Arrigo Boito that he was fully able to realize the "*opera a intenzione*" (in which the music carries out the intentions of the dramatic situation) by breaking up the rigid patterns hitherto imposed upon operatic composers.

Verdi, many of whose works are based on dramas of considerable literary merit (Byron and Victor Hugo furnished the plots for two, Schiller for four of them), felt strongly akin to Shakespeare, whom he regarded as an unsurpassable model: "Shakespeare was a realist, only he did not know it. He was a realist by inspiration; we are realists by intention and calculation." In addition to *Otello* and *Falstaff* (in which latter two Shakespearean plays are fused) he wrote *Macbeth* and gave serious thought to *Lear*.

F. Werfel and P. Stefan, *Verdi: The Man in His Letters* (New York: L. B. Fischer, 1942); F. Toye, *Giuseppe Verdi: His Life and Works* (New York: Knopf, 1931); E. Istel: "A Genetic Study of the *Aida* Libretto," *Musical Quarterly*, III (1917), 94-102; E. T. Cone, "The Old Man's Toys: Verdi's Last Operas," *Perspectives USA*, Winter, 1954.

Letters (1853-80)
GIUSEPPE VERDI

To Cesare De Sanctis (1853):

We are fully agreed, then, about the second act [of *Il trovatore*], which I shall have printed as I copied it. There is nothing I want more than to find a good libretto and, accordingly, a good poet (we need one so urgently). But I do not hide from you the fact that I read the librettos that are submitted to me with great reluctance. It is impossible, or nearly impossible, that another person should divine my wishes. I want subjects that are new, great, beautiful, varied, and daring (and daring in the extreme), with novel forms, etc., etc., and at the same time capable of being set to music. When people say: "I have done so because Romani, Cammarano, etc., have done so," no understanding is possible. Just because these great men have done things one way, I want to do them in another. At Venice I shall stage *La dame aux camélias*, probably under the title of *La traviata*. It is a contemporary subject. Another composer might not have treated it because of the costumes, the age, and a thousand other silly scruples. I treat it with great pleasure. Everybody cried out when I proposed to put a hunchback on stage. Well, I was happy to write *Rigoletto*. The same with *Macbeth*, etc.

To Antonio Somma (1853):

I have received the rest of the first act [of *Il re Lear*] and have nothing to say about the verses, which are beautiful throughout and worthy of you; but with all due respect, which I have for your talent, I must tell you that the form is not too well suited to music. There is no one who loves novelty of form more than I do, but only such novelties as can be set to music. It is true that everything can be set to music, but not everything can be effective. In order to make music, one needs stanzas for *cantabiles*, stanzas for *largos, allegros*, etc., and all these alternating in such a way that the audience is neither bored nor indifferent.

To Antonio Gallo (1869):

I thank you for your first letter and the other one with the note by Z. . . . He has clearly gone out of his mind. The arias and duets [in *La forza del destino*] between Colini, Stolz, and Fraschini have affected his brain and will finally cause him to be committed to an asylum. Imitating our public, he doesn't speak at all of variegated and more extended scenes that fill half of the work and actually constitute the musical drama. How strange and, at the same time, how discouraging! While everybody shouts "progress" and "reform," the public, on the whole, does not applaud, and the singers care for nothing but arias, romances, and canzonettas. I know that dramatic scenes *(scene di azione)* are also in vogue, but only indirectly as frame for the picture. The order has been inverted. The frame has turned into the picture. To conclude, in spite of the praise which all of you have bestowed upon me in connection with the present work, I believe and am convinced that the solo numbers and those designed for several soloists will be marvelously successful, whereas the work (I mean: Work), i.e., the scenic and musical drama, will be only imperfectly executed. What do you say, Monsieur Toni?

However, good luck to everybody! To me personally it matters very little; but the artist of the future should think it over carefully. One can't proceed in this manner. Either the composers will have to go backward or all other people will have to move forward. Addio!

To Antonio Ghislanzoni (1870):

On returning home I found your verses [for *Aïda*] on my desk. If you want my frank opinion, I will tell you that it seems to me that the consecration scene has not as well succeeded as I had envisaged. The characters do not always say what they ought to say, and the priests are not priestly enough. It also seems to me that the scenic word is missing, or if it is there, that it is buried under the rhyme and the meter and, accordingly, does not emerge as clearly and markedly as it should. I shall write tomorrow when I have reread the scene at greater leisure and will tell you then what I think ought to be done. Certainly, this scene, from a point still to be determined, needs all the emphasis and solemnity possible.

To the same (1870):

There are excellent things at the beginning and at the end of the duet, although it is a little too long and drawn out. It seems to me that the recitative could be slightly shortened. The lines are all right up to "*a te in cor destò.*" But when, subsequently, the action warms up, the scenic word *(parola scenica)* appears to be lacking. I don't know whether the phrase "scenic word" is clear to you. What I mean is the word that puts the situation in the proper relief and renders it clear and obvious. For instance, the words

> *In volto gli occhi affisami*
> *E menti ancor se l'osi:*
> *Radames vive . . . .*

> (Look me straight in the eyes
> And lie if you dare:
> Radames lives . . . .)

are theatrically less effective than the more brutal words:

> *. . . con una parola*
> *strapperò il tuo segreto.*
> *Guardami t'ho ingannata: Radames vive.*

> (. . . with one word
> I shall tear open your secret.
> Look, I have deceived you:
> Radames lives. . . .)

And also the verses:

> *Per Radames d'amore*
> *Ardo e mi sei rivale.*
> *—Che? voi l'amate? Io l'amo*
> *E figlia son d'un re.*

> (For Radames with love
> I burn and know that I have a rival.
> —How? You love him? I love him
> And am the daughter of a king.)

seem to me less theatrical than the words: *"Tu l'ami? ma l'amo anch'io intendi? La figlia dei Faraoni e tua rivale!"* Aïda: *"Mia rivale? E sia: Anch'io son figlia. . . ."* ("You love him? But I love him also, you understand? The daughter of the Pharaohs is your rival!" Aïda: "My rival? Let her be: I, too, am the daughter . . .".)

I know exactly what you will say: And the verse, the rhyme, the stanza? I have no answer. But I, if the action demanded it, would immediately abandon rhythm, rhyme, and stanza. I would use blank verse in order to say clearly and forthrightly all that the action demands. Especially in the theater it is sometimes necessary for poets and composers to possess the talent of creating neither poetry nor music.

To Giulio Ricordi (1880):

The score [of *Simone Boccanegra*], in its present form, is impossible. It is too sad, too disheartening. We don't have to make any changes in the first and last act; and only a few measures in the third one need to be revised. But the entire second act has to be refashioned and must be endowed with more life, variety, and plasticity. Musically speaking, we could retain the cavatina of the lady, the duet with the tenor, and the other duet between father and daughter, although it contains a *cabaletta* ("Open up, earth!"). I am not that much afraid of *cabalettas;* and if tomorrow a young man should be born who were able to write one as good as "Meco tu vieni, o misera" or "Ah, perchè non posso odiarti," I would go to hear it eagerly and renounce all the harmonic tricks and artifices of our learned orchestrations. Ah, progress, science, realism! Be as much of a realist as you wish, but. . . . Shakespeare was a realist, only he did not know it. He was a realist by inspiration; we are realists by intention and calculation. And thus: system for system, I still prefer the *cabalettas*. The curious thing is that in the heat of progress art turns backward. Art which lacks spontaneity, naturalness, and simplicity is no longer art.

Translated by Ulrich Weisstein from *I copialettere di Giuseppe Verdi*, edited by G. Cesari and A. Luzio (Milan, Tip. Stucchi Ceretti et Cie., 1913), by permission of the Municipality of Milan.

ARRIGO BOITO (1842-1918)

ARRIGO BOITO, the son of an Italian miniature painter and a Polish countess, received musical instruction at the Milan Conservatory, where he distinguished himself by collaborating in the writing of two cantatas that led to his being awarded a government fellowship. He went to Paris and there conceived the idea of writing two operas, one on the theme of Faust (Gounod's work by that name had just been performed at the Théâtre Lyrique) and one dealing with the Roman Emperor Nero. Upon his return to Milan Boito was exceedingly active as a journalist, poet, and composer. In 1866 he briefly joined the forces of Garibaldi. His Faust opera, *Mefistofele*, was premiered at La Scala in 1868—and caused a riot. *Nerone* was not completed until 1916. Arturo Toscanini conducted its first performance six years after the composer's death.

A prolific and versatile writer, Boito furnished librettos for numerous operas composed by his contemporaries, Poncielli's *La Gioconda* being the most prominent among them. He came to know Verdi in 1862 when he wrote the words for the latter's Hymn of Nations. In the following decades their friendship did not always remain unruffled. But in the late seventies the son of Verdi's publisher, Giulio Ricordi, managed to persuade the two artists to embark on a joint operatic venture. Boito adapted Shakespeare's *Othello* in a way most congenial to Verdi, who was a very active collaborator. He also assisted Verdi in revamping the libretto of *Simone Boccanegra*. Verdi, who demanded nothing more urgently than the *scenic word*, skilfully skirted the obstacles posed by the over-elaborateness of Boito's poetry. In 1889 Verdi, with some reluctance, set out to write his last opera, for which Boito had drawn material from Shakespeare's *Henry IV* and *The Merry Wives of Windsor*. *Falstaff*, like *Otello*, turned out to be a masterpiece.

F. Torrefranca, "Arrigo Boito," *Musical Quarterly*, VI (1920), 532-552; J. Huneker, "Verdi and Boito" in *Overtones* (New York, 1928); J. W. Klein, "Boito and his Two Operas," *Music & Letters*, VII (1926), 73-80; M. Pagliai, "I libretti di A. Boito" *Rassegna della Letteratura Italiana*, LXVI (1962), 287-309.

Letter to Giuseppe Verdi
Concerning the Opera *Otello* (1881)
ARRIGO BOITO

You BEGAN TO THINK that I had also altogether forgotten about the grand finale of *Otello*.

But this is not the case. I have pondered that finale and, since I am a great fool, have not yet succeeded in assimilating it to the "blood of the form," if that expression is permissible. I have racked my brain not a little to obtain the desired result, which you have previously indicated and which appears to me the logical outcome of all the conversations we had at Sant'Agata.

The ensemble has, as we planned, its lyrical and its dramatic parts fused together. We have, that is to say, a lyrical and melodic piece superimposed upon a dramatic dialogue.

The principal character of the lyrical part is Desdemona; that of the dramatic part Iago.

Thus Iago, having ben stunned for a moment by an event beyond his control (the letter which recalls Othello to Venice), suddenly takes up all the threads of the tragedy with unequaled speed and energy, making the catastrophe his and using the unforeseen event to hasten the course of the final disaster.

All this was in Shakespeare's mind and is clearly expressed in our work. Iago passes from Othello to Rodrigo, the two remaining instruments of his crime. Subsequently, his is the last word and the last gesture of the act.

Judge for yourself whether the two parts, the lyrical and

the dramatic, seem well fused to you. Judge also whether the length of each part is well measured. I have not been sparing with lines, remindful of your admonition: "Say whatever is necessary, and let everything be well explained." Following this advice, I have concluded that the dialogue underlying the lyrical part shoud be extended in order to produce the tragic effect, and have acted accordingly.

And in case the dialogue between Rodrigo and Iago should seem a little too sketchy and obscure to you, here are four lines which will augment and finish it if necessary. . . .

One thing ought to be kept in mind, however. The dialogues between Iago and Othello, and between Rodrigo and Iago, follow directly upon each other. What does Rodrigo do during the conversation between Iago and Othello? Nothing. His voice alone could add another *real part* to the beginning of the ensemble and constitute its fifth ingredient, until the time arrives for his dialogue with Iago. In case this should be agreeable to you, I submit the following four verses which Rodrigo might sing with the others while Othello speaks with Iago and the ensemble begins: . . . .

I also volunteer the following observation: If we have considered Rodrigo's posture during the dialogue between Iago and Othello, why didn't we discuss Othello's pose during that between Iago and Rodrigo? Othello's pose is preformed in and predetermined by the drama. We have seen him leaning weakly against the table after having uttered the words: "Kneel down. And cry!" In this position he ought to remain, without raising himself, as long as the ensemble lasts, even when giving his replies to Iago. There is no need for him to speak or sing while Iago speaks to Rodrigo. Mute he is greater, more frightening and impressive.

He will rise only to shout: "Flee!" Then he will fall to the ground immediately. So far, I hope, we are in perfect agreement. But perhaps you will have noticed that Desdemona—she being, as I mentioned, the principal figure of the lyrical part—should have four additional lines. So much the better that the first four lines assigned to her are not suited to melodic development. . . .

We had agreed that the lyrical portion of the ensemble should have one meter and the dialogue portion (the chorus included) another. This I have arranged. The meter of the dialogue is endecasyllabic. You can break it up at your convenience; broken up, it resolves itself naturally into five-stress lines. You can employ both meters at your discretion. The device was called for, as endecasyllabics, sustained throughout a lyrical movement, would appear too somber, and five-stress lines too gay. I did not want to mix the two meters visibly but have preferred the artifice just now explained to you. I am fully convinced that it will produce the desired effect.

Translated by Ulrich Weisstein from *Carteggi Verdiani*, edited by Alessandro Luzio (Rome: Reale Accademia d'Italia, 1935), by permission of the Accademia dei Lincei in Rome.

MODESTE PETROVICH MUSSORGSKY
(1839-81)

OF THE MANY OPERATIC PROJECTS pondered by Mussorgsky, only one, *Boris Godunov* (first version 1869, second version 1872), grew to completion. But even this music drama became known to the world at large only in the polished form given to it after the composer's death by Nikolai Rimsky-Korsakov. The controversy over the merits of this undertaking is still raging. Of Mussorgsky's other operas, *Khovanshchina* and *The Sorotchintsi Fair* were finished, or nearly finished, in the piano score. Rimsky-Korsakov orchestrated the former and Cesar Cui the latter. *The Sorotchintsi Fair*, like the projected *St. John's Eve* and the unfinished *The Marriage*, is based on a work by Nikolai Gogol (1809-52), whom Mussorgsky greatly admired because he found him congenial. Throughout his operatic career, Mussorgsky, "proceeding from the conviction that human speech is strictly controlled by musical laws," considered it "the task of musical art to be the reproduction in musical sounds not merely of the mood of the feeling but chiefly of the mood of human speech" (from his Autobiographical Notes of June, 1880).

The Marriage, which had been pointed out to him as a subject by his friend Alexander Sergeyevich Dargomizhsky "in earnest" and by his fellow composer Cesar Cui "in jest," occupied him during much of 1868. And his entire poetics of opera can be derived from the letters written during that period. When the rapidly finished first act of the work was privately performed at the home of Rimsky-Korsakov, the reaction on the part of Mussorgsky's colleagues was, on the whole, unfavorable. Borodin called *The Marriage* a "*chose manquée*," and Balakirev and Cui regarded it merely as a "curiosity with interesting declamatory moments." Five years later Mussorgsky presented the score to his intimate Vladimir Stasov, who guarded it closely. It was published only a quarter of a century afterward. Mussorgsky's compatriot Ippolitov-Ivanov completed the work before his death in 1935. However, *The Marriage* has not entered the repertory of Russian or Western European opera houses.

J. Leyda & S. Bertensson, eds., *The Musorgsky Reader* (New York: Norton, 1947); O. von Riesemann, *Moussorgsky*, translated by P. England (New York: Knopf, 1929); M. D. Calvocoressi, *Modest Mussorgsky* (London: Rockliff, 1956).

Letters about *The Marriage* (1868-77)
MODESTE PETROVICH MUSSORGSKY

To Cesar Cui (1868):

The first act will, after all, in my consideration, be able to serve as an experiment in *opera dialogué*. . . . In my *opera dialogué* I am trying to underline as sharply as possible those changes of intonation which occur in the characters during the dialogue, apparently for the most trivial of reasons and in the most insignificant words, in which is concealed, it seems to me, the power of Gogol's humor.

To Ludmila Shestakova (1868):

This is what I would like. For my characters to speak on the stage as living people speak, but besides this, for the character and power of intonation of the characters, supported by the orchestra, which forms a musical pattern of their speech, to achieve their aim directly, that is, my music must be an artistic reproduction of human speech in all its finest shades, that is, *the sounds of human speech*, as the external manifestation of thought and feeling must, without exaggeration or violence, become true, accurate music, but artistic, highly artistic. This is the ideal toward which I strive. So now I work on Gogol's *Marriage*. But the success of Gogol's speech depends on the actor, on his true intonation. Well, I want to fix Gogol to his place and the actor to his place, that is, to say it musically in such a way that one couldn't say it in any other way and would say it as the characters of Gogol wish to speak. That is why in *Marriage* I am crossing the Rubicon. This is living prose in music, this is not a scorning of musician-poets toward common human speech, stripped of all heroic robes—this is reverence toward the language of humanity, this is a reproduction of simple human speech.

To Nikolai Rimsky-Korsakov (1868):

I have looked over my work. In my opinion it is quite interestingly carried out. However, who knows. I worked as well as I was able, and now it's up to all of you to judge its success. I am on trial. I say one thing only: if one completely renounces opera tradition and visualizes musical dialogue on the stage as just ordinary conversation, then *Marriage* is an opera. I want to say that if the expression in sound of human thought and feeling in *simple* speech is truly produced by me in music, and this reproduction is musical and artistic, then the thing is in the bag. This is what you must discuss, and I will stand aside. . . . I have worked briskly, as it happened, but brisk work tells on one: whatever speech I hear, no matter who is speaking (nor what he says) my mind is already working to find the musical statement for such speech.

To Rimsky-Korsakov (1868):

These days I have been bringing order to my country composition, the second, third, and fourth scenes of the first act of *Marriage*, that is, the whole first act. I did not expect to do this. For the first time in my life I *wrote* without the aid of an instrument, that is, without verification of the composed work, and

I thought that in such a thing as musical prose (where the harmonic conditions are terribly capricious) I would not be able to dispense with the instrument. . . . The second act exists only in thought and plan. It cannot be composed yet, too early! Patience, otherwise one would fall into a monotony of intonation, the most horrible of sins in this capricious *Marriage*.

To Vladimir Nikolsky (1868):

The Greeks worshipped nature, meaning man as well. Great poetry and the greatest arts originated in this. I continue: In the scale of nature's creation man constitutes the highest organism (at least on earth) and this highest organism possesses the gift of speech and voice without equal among earthly organisms generally. If one can assume a reproduction, through an artistic medium, of human *speech*, in all its most delicate and capricious shades, a natural reproduction, as natural as is required by the life and character of a man—would this be a deification of the human gift of speech? And if it is possible to tug at the heartstrings by the simplest of methods, merely by obeying an artistic instinct to catch the intonations of the human voice, why not look into this matter? And if, at the same time, one could capture the thinking faculty as well, then wouldn't it be suitable to devote oneself to such an occupation? Without preparation you can't cook a soup. Meaning: preparing oneself for work, even though this may be Gogol's *Marriage*, a most capricious thing for music, wouldn't that be the achievement of a good deed, that is, wouldn't that mean a closer approach to the most cherished aim of life? One can say to that: Why is one always preparing oneself—it's about time to do something. The trifling little pieces were preparations, *Marriage* is a preparation—when will something finally be ready? To this there is only answer: the *power of necessity;* some day it may be ready.

My activity, the activity that I hold under my arm, which I'm not ashamed to show others, if they should question me, started with those trifling little pieces. It's silly to be bashful and put on modest airs when one realizes that those trifling pieces have given me a name, as well, though only among a limited circle, but at least a circle of people who are not narrow-minded.

These trifles have provoked a desire in persons who are rather imposing in music to set me an untouched (in the historical course of music) problem—musically to set forth everyday prose in the form of musical prose. For proof that the solution of such a problem is not easy I offer my humble self. I have composed a whole act of musical prose, I have painted it with four characters—from my point of view the act turned out well, but I don't know what will happen to the other three acts. I know that they must be good, but I don't know whether they can be good. However, one must finish the work one has begun, and then bring in the verdict.

But through the darkness of uncertainty I see a bright spark and this spark is the complete renunciation by the public of the opera-traditions of the past (which, moreover, still exist). Impossible! But why is that spark bright? Because when one opens a new road one feels doubly strong, and when one's strength is doubled (four is exactly twice two) one can work and work joyfully. This situation can end only with the thieves' formula: *la bourse ou la vie—la vie ou le drame musical.* It is needless to say that both life and musical drama are necessary because one without the other is unthinkable.

To Arseni Golenishchev-Kutuzov (1877):

This *[The Fair at Sorochintsi]* is not my first encounter with Gogol, and therefore his capricious prose frightens me no longer; but *Marriage* is only the humble exercise of a musician, or rather a non-musician, who wishes to study and grasp the twistings of human speech in that spontaneous true exposition which is the means used by that greatest genius Gogol. *Marriage* was an etude for a chamber trial. With a large stage it is necessary for the speeches of the characters, each according to his nature, habits, and dramatic inevitability, to be conveyed to the audience in bold relief—it is necessary to construct so that the audience will easily sense all the artless peripeteia of urgent human affairs, at the same time making these artistically interesting. Imagine, my dear friend, that what you read in the speeches of Gogol's characters must be delivered from the stage to us in musical speech by my characters, without any alterations contrary to Gogol's intentions. . . . As only the genuine sensitive nature of an artist can create in the realm of the word, the musician must maintain a very "polite" attitude toward the creation, in order to penetrate into its very substance, into the very essence of that which the musician intends to embody in musical form. The genuine truly artistic cannot be anything but capricious, because independently it cannot easily be embodied in another artistic form, because it is independent and demands profound study and sacred love. But when artistic kinship between workers in different fields of art does work out—it's a fine trip.

Reprinted from *The Musorgsky Reader*, translated and edited by Jay Leyda and Sergei Bertensson, by permission of W. W. Norton & Company, Inc. Copyright 1947 by W. W. Norton & Company, Inc.

PETER ILYCH TCHAIKOVSKY
(1840-93)

ALTHOUGH he wrote a total of ten operas, Peter Ilych Tchaikovsky was eminently more successful as a composer of ballets *(Swan Lake, The Sleeping Beauty,* and *The Nutcracker)* and orchestral music, much of it programmatic. He fully realized that he lacked a "dramatic vein" but nevertheless was unable to resist the temptation: "To refrain from writing operas is the act of a hero, and we have only one such hero in our time—Brahms. Such heroism is not for me. The stage, with all its glitters, attracts me irresistibly" he wrote to Nadezhda von Meck in the early seventies. Tchaikovsky felt a strong aversion to all that smacks of deliberately contrived stage effects, such as abound in Meyerbeer's *L'Africaine* (1865) and Verdi's *Aïda* (1871). He wanted to create characters "whose feelings and experiences [he] shared and understood," and had a great liking for the realism inherent in Bizet's *Carmen.*

The subject of the "lyrical scenes" *Eugen Onegin*—one of three operatic plots he drew from his favorite author, Pushkin—was suggested to him in the spring of 1877 by the wife of the singer Lavrovsky. Tchaikovsky, who had just returned from a

European tour, did not, at first, show great enthusiasm, but when he read the classic verse novella he grew so enchanted that he "produced the sketch of a delicious opera . . . in a sleepless night." The work, a considerable part of which was written in Italy and at the estate of his generous patroness, was premiered in March, 1879, by students of the Moscow Conservatory. The only other Tchaikovsky opera still occasionally performed outside Russia is *The Queen of Spades* (1890).

H. Weinstock, *Tchaikovsky* (New York: Knopf, 1943); G. Abraham, *The Music of Tchaikovsky* (New York: Norton, 1946).

Letter to S. I. Taneiev
Concerning the opera *Eugen Onegin* (1878)
PETER ILYCH TCHAIKOVSKY

VERY PROBABLY you are quite right in saying that my opera is not effective for the stage. I must tell you, however, I do not care a rap for such effectiveness. It has long been an established fact that I have no dramatic vein, and now I do not trouble about it. If it is really not fit for the stage, then it had better not be performed! I composed this opera because I was moved to express in music all that seems to cry out for such expression in *Eugene Onegin*. I did my best, working with indescribable pleasure and enthusiasm, and thought very little of the treatment, the effectiveness, and all the rest. I spit upon "effects"! Besides, what are effects? For instance, if *Aïda* is effective, I can assure you I would not compose an opera on a similar subject for all the wealth of the world; for I want to handle human beings, not puppets. I would gladly compose an opera which was completely lacking in startling effects, but which offered characters resembling my own, whose feelings and experiences I shared and understood. The feelings of an Egyptian princess, a Pharaoh, or some mad Nubian, I cannot enter into, or comprehend. Some instinct, however, tells me that these people must have felt, acted, spoken, and expressed themselves quite differently from ourselves. Therefore my music, which—entirely against my will—is impregnated with Schumannism, Wagnerism, Chopinism, Glinkaism,

Berliozism, and all the other *isms* of our time, would be as out of keeping with the characters of *Aïda* as the elegant speeches of Racine's heroes—couched in the second person plural—are unsuited to the real Orestes or the real Andromache. Such music would be a *falsehood*, and all falsehoods are abhorrent to me. Besides, I am reaping the fruits of my insufficient harvest of book-learning. Had I a wider acquaintance with the literatures of other countries, I should no doubt have discovered a subject which was both suitable for the stage and in harmony with my taste. Unfortunately, I am not able to find such things for myself, nor do I know anyone who could call my attention to such a subject as Bizet's *Carmen*, for example, one of the most perfect operas of our day. You will ask what I actually require. I will tell you. Above all I want no kings, no tumultuous populace, no gods, no pompous marches—in short, none of those things which are the attributes of "grand opera." I am looking for an intimate yet thrilling drama, based upon such a conflict of circumstance as I myself have experienced or witnessed, which is capable of touching me to the quick. I have nothing to say against the fantastic element, because it does not restrict one, but rather offers unlimited freedom. I feel I am not expressing myself very clearly. In a word, Aïda is so remote, her love for Radames touches me so little, since I cannot picture it in my mind's eye, that my music would lack the vital warmth which is essential to good work. Not long since I saw *L'Africaine* in Genoa. This unhappy African, what she endures! Slavery, imprisonment, death under a poisoned tree, in her last moment the sight of her rival's triumph—and yet I never once pitied her! But what effects there were: a ship, a battle, all manner of dodges! When all is said and done, what is the use of these effects? . . .

With regard to your remark that Tatiana does not fall in love with Onegin at first sight, allow me to say—you are mistaken. She falls in love at once. She does not learn to know him first, and then to care for him. Love comes suddenly to her. Even before Onegin comes on the scene she is in love with the hero of her vague romance. The instant she sets eyes on Onegin she invests him with all the qualities of her ideal, and the love she has hitherto bestowed upon the creation of her fancy is now transferred to a human being.

The opera Onegin will never have a success; I feel already assured of that. I shall never find singers capable, even partially, of fulfilling my requirements. The routine which prevails in our theaters, the senseless performances, the system of retaining invalided artists and giving no chance to younger ones: all this stands in the way of my opera being put on the stage. I would much prefer to confide it to the theater of the Conservatoire. Here, at any rate, we escape the commonplace routine of the opera, and those fatal invalids of both sexes. Besides which, the performances at the Conservatoire are private, *en petit comité!* This is more suitable to my modest work, which I shall not describe as an opera, if it is published. I should like to call it "lyrical scenes," or something of that kind. This opera has no future! I was quite aware of this when I wrote it; nevertheless, I completed it and shall give it to the world if Jurgenson[1] is willing to publish it. I shall make no effort to have it performed at the Maryinsky Theater; on the contrary, I should oppose the idea as far as possible. It is the outcome of an invincible inward impulse. I assure you one should compose opera only under such conditions. It is necessary to think of stage effects only to a certain extent. If my enthusiasm for *Eugene Onegin* is evidence of my limitations, my stupidity, and ignorance of the requirements of the stage, I am very sorry; but I can at least affirm that the music *proceeds in the most literal sense from my inmost being.* It is not manufactured and forced. But enough of *Onegin.*

Reprinted from *The Life and Letters of Peter Ilich Tchaikovsky,* edited by Rosa Newmarch (London & New York: John Lane, 1906).

CLAUDE DEBUSSY (*1862-1918*)

CLAUDE DEBUSSY, the leader of the French Impressionist school, was not exactly a born opera composer. His biographer, for instance, quotes him as saying that the theater is a false and in-

1. Tchaikovsky's publisher.

ferior type of art. In 1888 and 1889 Debussy attended the Wagnerian festival at Bayreuth, and in the latter year he witnessed a performance of *Tristan und Isolde*. He immediately realized the danger involved in falling under the spell of the German master, and, becoming suspicious of Teutonic music, with its lack of form, clarity, and nuance, endeavored all the more eagerly to develop a typically French style characterized by greater subtlety and a greater economy of means.

When in 1892 Debussy saw a production of Maurice Maeterlinck's *Pelléas et Mélisande*,[1] he was so entranced by its filigree that he decided to set the play to music, a project which occupied him until 1902, when the opera was first performed. The letter to the Secretary-General of the Opéra-Comique which is here reprinted shows him in the process of formulating his own concept of melo-dramaturgy. Realizing that Wagner had "put the final touches to the music of his time," he wanted "to go beyond Wagner rather than follow in his path." Going beyond Wagner, however, did not mean going against him. *Pelléas* has been called the *Tristan* of Impressionism. According to Grove's *Dictionary*, "much of [Debussy's] vocal writing is essentially the Wagnerian melos in a French dress, and in *Pelléas* there is much of the technique of *Tristan* or the Ring in contrapuntal texture and in the subtle use of leading motives." This explains the open hostility which Cocteau and the other members of the neoclassical faction displayed against Debussy: "The dense fog pierced by the lightnings of Bayreuth turns into a light, snowy mist flecked by the Impressionistic sun. Satie speaks of Ingres; Debussy prepares a Russian version of Claude Monet."

Ten years after the completion of *Pelléas* Debussy allied himself with Gabriele d'Annunzio in the creation of the mystery play *Le martyre de Saint-Sébastien*, which belongs more properly in the concert hall than on the stage.

C. Debussy, *"Monsieur Croche, the Dilettante Hater* (New York: Viking Press, 1928); L. Vallas, *The Theories of Debussy* (London: Oxford University Press, 1929); L. Vallas, *Claude Debussy: His Life and Works* (London: Oxford University Press, 1933); Kerman, *Opera as Drama*, pp. 171-191.

1. Maurice Maeterlinck (1862-1949) was the most important French Symbolist playwright. His *Pelléas et Mélisande* appeared in 1892.

Letter to the Secretary-General
of the Opéra-Comique in Paris (1894)
CLAUDE DEBUSSY

FOR A LONG TIME I have sought to write music for the theater; but the form I wished to employ was so unusual that after a few attempts I almost gave up the idea. Researches I had previously conducted in the field of pure music had led me to despise the kind of development preferred in classical music, whose beauty is nothing but technique and can interest only the Mandarins of our class. I wanted to give music the freedom which, perhaps alone among the arts, it possesses, since it is not bound to a more or less exact reproduction of nature, but alludes to the mysterious correspondences between nature and imagination.

Having been an impassioned pilgrim to Bayreuth for several years, I began to cast doubt on the Wagnerian formula; or rather: it seemed to me that it fitted only the peculiar genius of that composer, who was a great collector of clichés, which he summed up in a formula that seemed universal only because people did not know music well enough. And without denying him genius one can say that he put the final touch to the music of his time, just as Victor Hugo sums up all the poetry written before his age.[2] It was necessary, then, to go beyond Wagner rather than follow in his path.

The drama *Pelléas*, which in spite of its dream-like atmosphere is more human than the so-called documents after life, seemed to be admirably suited to my purpose. Its evocative language expresses a sensibility which can be extended by the music and through the orchestral embellishment. I also endeavored to adhere to a law of beauty that is singularly forgotten in relation to dramatic music. The characters in this drama try to sing like normal human beings, and not in an arbitrary language based on outdated traditions. It is on that account that I am reproached with having used monotonous declamation without the slightest token of melody. . . . But the feelings of a person cannot con-

---

2. Victor Hugo (1802-85) was one of the leaders of the Romantic movement in France. He was active as a playwright, poet, novelist, and critic.

stantly be expressed in melodic fashion, and the dramatic melody ought to be clearly distinguished from melody in general. . . . The people who want to hear music in the theater remind me of the crowd one sees assembled around a group of street singers. There, for two sous on the average, they can buy themselves melodic emotions. . . .

By a singular irony the very public which demands innovations is the one that gets scared and protests every time one tries to change its habits. This may seem to be incomprehensible; but one should not forget that a work of art, or an attempt to create beauty, seems to be regarded by many people *as a personal offense.*

I don't pretend to have solved all the problems in *Pelléas;* but I have tried to beat a path which others can follow by adding their own findings and by ridding dramatic music of the heavy constraint from which it has suffered for such a long time.

Translated by Ulrich Weisstein from Leon Vallas, *Les idées de Claude Debussy, musicien Français* (Paris: Librairie de France, 1927), by permission of Madame de Tinan.

GEORGE BERNARD SHAW
(1856-1950)

GEORGE BERNARD SHAW, who once confessed that "from [his] earliest recorded sign of interest in music when as a small child [he] encored [his] mother's singing of the page's song from the first act of [Meyerbeer's] *Les Huguenots . . .* music had been an indispensable part of [his] life," was fortunate enough to have a professional singer for a mother and to have received a thorough training in harmony and vocal technique. After his early failure as a novelist—of the five novels he wrote between 1879 and 1883 only one, *Cashel Byron's Profession,* was issued in book form —he devoted nearly six years of his life to music criticism. From 1888 to 1889 he wrote for the London *Star* under the pseudonym Corno di Bassetto, and from 1890 to 1894 for the *World,* although in the meantime he had embarked on his career as a dramatist. Grove's *Dictionary* eulogizes Shaw by calling him "one of the most brilliant critics not only of the drama but also of music who ever worked in London, or indeed anywhere." Of his brilliance and competence there can be hardly any question. Shaw was a great admirer of Mozart, especially of *Don Giovanni*, but thought less highly of Verdi's contributions to the repertory. However, nothing matched his enthusiasm for Wagner, whose socio-aesthetic theories he expounded at length in *The Perfect Wagnerite* (1898). In the following essay he makes a case for Wagner the Tone Poet as distinguished from Wagner the composer of operas or symphonist.

G. B. Shaw, *Music in London,* 1890-1894 (London, 1932); G. B. Shaw, *London Music, 1888-1889* (New York: Dodd & Mead, 1937); W. Irvine, "George Bernard Shaw's Musical Criticism," *Musical Quarterly,* XXXII (1946), 319-332; G. S. Barber, "Shaw's Contribution to Music Criticism," *PMLA,* LXXII (1957), 1005-17.

The Tone Poet (1894)
GEORGE BERNARD SHAW

IT IS NOT OFTEN that one comes across a reasonable book about music, much less an entertaining one. Still, I confess to having held out with satisfaction to the end of M. Georges Noufflard's *Richard Wagner d'après lui-même* (Paris, Fischbacher, 2 vols., at 3.50 fr. apiece). Noufflard is so exceedingly French a Frenchman that he writes a preface to explain that though he admires Wagner, still Alsace and Lorraine must be given back; and when he records an experiment of his hero's in teetotalism, he naïvely adds, "What is still more surprising is that this unnatural regime, instead of making Wagner ill, operated exactly as he had expected." More Parisian than this an author can hardly be; and yet Noufflard always understands the Prussian composer's position, and generally agrees with him, though, being racially out of sympathy with him, he never entirely comprehends him. He is remarkably free from the stock vulgarities of French operatic culture: for instance, he washes his hands of Meyerbeer most fastidiously; and he puts Gluck, the hero of French musical classicism, most accurately in his true place.

And here let me give a piece of advice to readers of books about Wagner. Whenever you come to a statement that Wagner was an operatic reformer, and that in this capacity he was merely following in the footsteps of Gluck, who had anticipated some of his most important proposals, you may put your book in the waste-paper basket, as far as Wagner is concerned, with absolute confidence. Gluck was an opera composer who said to his contemporaries: "Gentlemen, let us compose our operas more rationally. An opera is not a stage concert, as most of you seem to think. Let us give up our habit of sacrificing our common sense to the vanity of our singers, and let us compose and orchestrate our airs, our duets, our recitatives, and our sinfonias in such a way that they shall always be appropriate to the dramatic situation given to us by the librettist." And having given this excellent advice, he proceeded to show how it could be followed. How well he did this we can judge, in spite of our scandalous ignorance of Gluck, from *Orfeo*, with which Giulia Ravogli has made us familiar lately.

When Wagner came on the scene, exactly a hundred years later, he found that the reform movement begun by Gluck had been carried to the utmost limits of possibility by Spontini, who told him flatly that after *La Vestale*, etc., there was nothing operatic left to be done. Wagner quite agreed with him, and never had the smallest intention of beginning the reform of opera over again at the very moment when it had just been finished. On the contrary, he took the fully reformed opera, with all its improvements, and asked the nineteenth century to look calmly at it and say whether all this patchwork of stage effects on a purely musical form had really done anything for it but expose the absurd unreality of its pretence to be a form of drama, and whether, in fact, Rossini had not shewn sound common sense in virtually throwing over that pretence and, like Gluck's Italian contemporaries, treating an opera as a stage concert. The nineteenth century took a long time to make up its mind on the question, which it was at first perfectly incapable of understanding. Verdi and Gounod kept on trying to get beyond Spontini on operatic lines, without the least success, except on the purely musical side; and Gounod never gave up the attempt, though Verdi did.

Meanwhile, however, Wagner, to show what he meant, abandoned operatic composition altogether, and took to writing dramatic poems, and using all the resources of orchestral harmony and vocal tone to give them the utmost reality and intensity of expression, thereby producing the new art form which he called "music drama," which is no more "reformed opera" than a cathedral is a reformed stone quarry. The whole secret of the amazing futility of the first attempts at Wagner criticism is the mistaking of this new form for an improved pattern of the old one. Once you conceive Wagner as the patentee of certain novel features in operas and librettos, you can demolish him point by point with impeccable logic, and without the least misgiving that you are publicly making a ludicrous exhibition of yourself.

The process is fatally easy, and consists mainly in shewing that the pretended novelties of reformed opera are no novelties at all. The "leading motives," regarded as operatic melodies recurring in connection with the entry of a certain character, are as old as opera itself; the instrumentation, regarded merely as instrumentation, is no better than Mozart's and much more expensive; whereas of those features that really tax the invention of the operatic composer, the airs, the duos, the quartets, the cabalettas to display the virtuosity of the trained Italian singer, the dances, the marches, the choruses, and so on, there is a deadly dearth, their place being taken by—of all things—an interminable dull recitative.

The plain conclusion follows that Wagner was a barren rascal whose whole reputation rested on a shop-ballad, O star of eve, and a march which he accidentally squeezed out when composing his interminable *Tannhäuser.* And so you go on, wading with fatuous self-satisfaction deeper and deeper into a morass of elaborately reasoned and highly conscientious error. You need fear nothing of this sort from Noufflard. He knows perfectly well the difference between music-drama and opera; and the result is that he not only does not tumble into blind hero-worship of Wagner, but is able to criticize him—a thing the blunderers never could do. Some of his criticisms: for example, his observation that in Wagner's earlier work the melody is by no means so original as Weber's, are indisputable—indeed he might have said Meyerbeer or anybody else; for Wagner's melody was never original at all in that sense, any more than Giotto's figures are picturesque or Shakespeare's lines elegant.

But I entirely—though quite respectfully—dissent from Noufflard's suggestion that in composing *Tristan* Wagner turned his back on the theoretic basis of *Siegfried*, and returned to "absolute music." It is true, as Noufflard points out, that in *Tristan*, and even in *Der Ring* itself, Wagner sometimes got so rapt from the objective drama that he got away from the words too, and in *Tristan* came to writing music without coherent words at all. But wordless music is not absolute music. Absolute music is the purely decorative sound pattern: tone poetry is the musical expression of poetic feeling. When Tristan gives musical expression to an excess of feeling for which he can find no coherent words, he is no more uttering absolute music than the shepherd who carries on the drama at one of its most deeply felt passages by playing on his pipe.

Wagner regarded all Beethoven's important instrumental works as tone poems; and he himself, though he wrote so much for the orchestra alone in the course of his music dramas, never wrote, or could write, a note of absolute music. The fact is, there is a great deal of feeling, highly poetic and highly dramatic, which cannot be expressed by mere words—because words are the counters of thinking, not of feeling—but which can be supremely expressed by music. The poet tries to make words serve his purpose by arranging them musically, but is hampered by the certainty of becoming absurd if he does not make his musically arranged words mean something to the intellect as well as to the feeling.

For example, the unfortunate Shakespeare could not make Juliet say: "O Romeo, Romeo, Romeo, Romeo, Romeo" and so on for twenty lines. He had to make her, in an extremity of unnaturalness, begin to argue the case in a sort of amatory legal fashion, thus:

> O Romeo, Romeo, wherefore art thou Romeo?
> Deny thy father and refuse thy name,
> Or, if thou wilt not, etc., etc., etc.

It is verbally decorative; but it is not love. And again:

> Parting is such sweet sorrow
> That I shall say goodnight till it be morrow;

which is a most ingenious conceit, but one which a woman would no more utter at such a moment than she would prove the rope ladder to be the shortest way out because any two sides of a triangle are together greater than the third.

Now these difficulties do not exist for the tone poet. He can make Isolde say nothing but "Tristan, Tristan, Tristan, Tristan, Tristan," and Tristan nothing but "Isolde, Isolde, Isolde, Isolde, Isolde," to their hearts' content without creating the smallest demand for more definite explanations; and as for the number of times a tenor and soprano can repeat "Addio, addio, addio," there is no limit to it. There is a great deal of this reduction of speech to mere ejaculation in Wagner; and it is a reduction directly pointed to in those very pages of *Opera and Drama* which seem to make the words all-important by putting the poem in the first place as the seed of the whole music drama, and yet make a clean sweep of nine-tenths of the dictionary by insisting that it is only the language of feeling that craves for musical expression, or even is susceptible of it.

Nay, you may not only reduce the words to pure ejaculation, you may substitute mere roulade vocalization, or even balderdash, for them, provided the music sustains the feeling which is the real subject of the drama, as has been proved by many pages of genuinely dramatic music, both in opera and elsewhere, which either have no words at all, or else belie them. It is only when a thought interpenetrated with intense feeling has to be expressed, as in the Ode to Joy in the Ninth Symphony, that coherent words must come with the music. You have such words in *Tristan;* you have also ejaculations void of thought, though full of feeling; and you have plenty of instrumental music with no words at all. But you have no "absolute" music, and no "opera."

Nothing in the world convinces you more of the fact that a dramatic poem cannot possibly take the form of an opera libretto than listening to *Tristan* and comparing it, say, with Gounod's

Romeo and Juliet. I submit, then, to Noufflard (whose two volumes I none the less cordially recommend to all amateurs who can appreciate a thinker) that the contradictions into which Wagner has fallen in this matter are merely such verbal ones as are inevitable from the imperfection of language as an instrument for conveying ideas; and that the progress from *Der flie-gende Holländer* to *Parsifal* takes a perfectly straight line ahead in theory as well as in artistic execution.

Reprinted from *Shaw on Music,* edited by Eric Bentley (New York: Doubleday, 1955), by permission of The Shaw Estate and The Society of Authors.

FERRUCCIO BUSONI (1866-1924)

RADICAL AND CONSERVATIVE IN ONE, Ferruccio Busoni, pianist, composer, and aesthetician, the great admirer of Franz Liszt and teacher at the Berlin conservatory (where Kurt Weill, Philipp Jarnach, and Wladimir Vogel were his pupils), developed the concept of a Young Classicism, which he defined as "the mastery, the sifting and the turning to account of all the gains of previous experiments and their inclusion in strong and beautiful forms" (letter to Paul Bekker of January, 1920). Busoni laid down his views in a number of theoretical writings, the most important of which are the *Entwurf einer neuen Ästhetik der Tonkunst* (A New Esthetic of Music), 1907, and the posthumously published essay *Über die Möglichkeit der Oper und über die Partitur des Doktor Faust.* Hans Pfitzner, composer of *Palestrina* and champion of German opera in the nineteenth-century tradition, poured vitriol on the *New Esthetic* in his pamphlet *Futuristengefahr* (1917). (Busoni, an advocate of experimentation with the diatonic scale, who proposed the division of the octave into thirty-six intervals, had publicly supported the musical views expressed in the Futuristic manifestos.) As for opera, Busoni, the anti-Wagnerian, rejected the empathic mode of creation by postulating that "the artist, if he wants to move others, must not let himself be moved" and by demanding that the audience "if it wants to savor the theatrical effect, must not confuse it with reality." He thus showed himself to be an adherent of Epic Opera *avant la lettre*. Busoni contributed four works to the repertory: *Die Brautwahl* (1910), *Arlecchino* (1916), *Turandot* (1917), and *Doktor Faust*, which latter was not performed until one year after the composer's death.

F. Busoni, *The Essence of Music and Other Papers*, tr. R. Ley (London: Rockliff, 1957); E. J. Dent, *Ferruccio Busoni: A Biography* (London: Oxford University Press, 1933); G. Gatti, "The Stage Works of Ferruccio Busoni," *Musical Quarterly*, XX (1934), 267-277.

A New Esthetic of Music (1907)
FERRUCCIO BUSONI

To MUSIC, INDEED, it is given to set in vibration our human moods: Dread (Leporello), oppression of soul, invigoration, lassitude (Beethoven's last quartets), decision (Wotan), hesitation, despondency, encouragement, harshness, tenderness, excitement, tranquillization, the feeling of surprise or expectancy, and still others; likewise the inner echo of external occurrences which is bound up in these moods of the soul. But not the moving cause of these spiritual affections;—not the joy over an avoided danger, not the danger itself, or the kind of danger which caused the dread; an emotional state, yes, but not the psychic species of this emotion, such as envy, or jealousy; and it is equally futile to attempt the expression, through music, of moral characteristics (vanity, cleverness), or abstract ideas like truth and justice. Is it possible to imagine how a poor, but contented man could be represented by music? The contentment, the soul-state, can be interpreted by music; but where does the poverty appear, or the important ethical problem stated in the words "poor, but contented"? This is due to the fact that "poor" connotes a phase of terrestrial and social conditions not to be found in the eternal harmony, and Music is part of the vibrating universe.

I may be allowed to subjoin a few subsidiary reflections: The greater part of modern theater music suffers from the mistake of seeking to repeat the scenes passing on the stage, instead of fulfilling its own proper mission of interpreting the soul-states of the persons represented. When the scene presents the illusion of a thunderstorm, this is exhaustively apprehended by the eye. Nevertheless, nearly all composers strive to depict the storm in tones—which is not only a needless and feebler repetition, but likewise a failure to perform their true function. The person on the stage is either psychically influenced by the thunderstorm, or his mood, being absorbed in a train of thought of stronger influence, remains unaffected. The storm is visible and audible without aid from music; it is the invisible and inaudible, the spiritual processes of the personage portrayed, which music should render intelligible.

Again, there are "obvious" psychic conditions on the stage, whereof music need take no account. Suppose a theatrical situation in which a convivial company is passing at night and disappears from view, while in the foreground a silent, envenomed duel is in progress. Here the music, by means of continuing song, should keep in mind the jovial company now lost to sight. The acts and feelings of the pair in the foreground may be understood without further commentary, and the music—dramatically speaking—ought not to participate in their action and break the tragic silence.

Measurably justified, in my opinion, is the plan of the old opera, which concentrated and musically rounded out the passions aroused by a moving dramatic scene in a piece of set form (the aria). Word and stage-play conveyed the dramatic progress of the action, followed more or less meagerly by musical recitative; arrived at the point of rest, music resumed the reins. This is less extrinsic than some would now have us believe. On the other hand, it was the ossified form of the aria itself which led to inveracity of expression and decadence.

The sung word on the stage will always remain a convention and an obstacle to the genuine effect of opera. In order to emerge with honor from this conflict, a plot in which characters sing while acting will, from the beginning, have to be gauged to the incredible, the untrue, and the improbable. In thus mutually supporting each other, the two impossibilities become possible and acceptable.

Reprinted from Busoni's *A New Esthetic of Music*, translated by T. Baker (New York: G. Schirmer, Inc., 1911), by permission of the publisher.

I predict a short life for the so-called operatic Verism of Italian vintage, if only for the reason that it ignores this principle.

When viewing the future of opera, one must also consider the following question: On what occasions is the use of music on the stage inevitable? The answer must be: during dances, marches, songs, and when the supernatural intervenes. Accordingly, one possibility for the future development of opera lies in the use of supernatural subjects, another in the pure "game," the entertaining disguise, the stage as make-believe, where humor and fantasy are contrasted with the serious, realistic side of life. Only then is it proper for characters to sing their confessions of love and their avowals of hatred, for actors to die melodically in a duel, and for singers to use grace notes at moments of extreme pathos. Only then are they justified in acting deliberately unrealistically; whereas in our theaters, and especially in opera, the actors do everything wrong inadvertently.

Opera should avail itself of the supernatural and unnatural as the only realm of phenomena and feelings suitable to it. In this way it could create a world of make-believe that reflects life in either a magic or a distorting mirror, and which aims at showing something that is not to be found in real life. The magic mirror for serious opera, the distorting one for its comic counterpart. And let dance, masquerade, and the fantastic be added, so that the audience may constantly be aware of the graceful deception instead of succumbing to it as if it were a real experience.

Just as the artist, if he wants to move others, must not let himself be moved (if he is not to lose control over his means at the crucial moment), the audience, if it wants to savor the theatrical effect, must not confuse it with reality. Otherwise, the aesthetic pleasure deteriorates into human compassion. Let the actor act, and not experience. Let the audience remain incredulous and thus unfettered in its appreciation and *gourmandise*.

Based on such presuppositions, opera might well be expected to have a future. But the first and foremost obstacle, I am afraid, will be offered by the audience itself. I think that with regard to the theater the public acts unforgivably. It seems that most of its members want to see powerful emotions on the stage because, as average individuals, they experience none in real life; but perhaps also because they lack the courage to engage in such conflicts, for which they nevertheless yearn. And the stage presents such conflicts, without the accompanying dangers and evil consequences. Nor does it compromise or, what is more important, tax the strength of the beholder. For the audience neither knows nor wants to know that he who wants to enjoy a work of art must actively contribute to the pleasure.

Translated by Ulrich Weisstein from Busoni's *Entwurf einer neuen Ästhetik der Tonkunst* (Wiesbaden: Insel-Verlag, 1954), by permission of the publisher.

JEAN COCTEAU (1889-1963)

ALTHOUGH NOT HIMSELF a professionally trained musician, Jean Cocteau, perhaps the most Protean of modern writers, is known to possess an uncanny gift for grasping the aesthetic significance of musical phenomena. He was thus ideally suited for becoming the spokesman for a group of French composers—*Les Six*—who were violently opposed to all Romantic modes of creation. Its members were Arthur Honegger, Darius Milhaud, Georges Auric, Francis Poulenc, Germaine Tailleferre, and Georges Durey. Early in 1918 Cocteau, who was a docile pupil of Erik Satie, the ironically inclined prophet of the new classicism, issued their manifesto, *Le coq et l'arlequin* (The Cock and the Harlequin), in which he violently attacked not only the music of Richard Wagner (much in the way in which Nietzsche had done in *The Case of Wagner*) but that of Beethoven, Debussy, and Stravinsky as well. However, Cocteau was subsequently reconciled with Stravinsky to the point of being asked to furnish the original French libretto for the latter's opera-oratorio *Oedipus Rex* (1928).

Cocteau was highly suspicious of the theater, whose corrupting influence he thought to stem from the fact that its audiences were forced to listen "with their faces buried in their hands." The new concept of an anti-theatrical theater, most poignantly exemplified by Stravinsky's *Histoire du soldat* and—with socio-political overtones—in Brecht's *Dreigroschenoper*, was first developed in Cocteau/Satie/Picasso's *Parade* of 1917. In 1921, five of *Les Six* furnished music for Cocteau's farce *Les mariés de la Tour Eiffel*. Cocteau also wrote the libretto for Honegger's opera *Antigone* (1927) and Milhaud's *Le pauvre matelot* (1926) as well as the scenarios for the ballet-comedy *Le boeuf sur le toit* (1919) and the ballet *Le train bleu* (1924), both with music by Milhaud.

N. Oxenhandler, *Scandal and Parade: The Theater of Jean Cocteau* (Rutgers University Press, 1957); V. Rasin, "Les Six and Jean Cocteau," *Music & Letters*, XXXVIII (1957), 164-169; U. Weisstein, "Cocteau, Stravinsky, Brecht, and the Birth of Epic Opera," *Modern Drama*, V (1962), 142-153.

The Cock and the Harlequin (1918)
JEAN COCTEAU

Dedication to Georges Auric:[1]

My dear friend: I admire the harlequins of Cézanne and Picasso, but I do not like Harlequin. He wears a black mask and a costume of many colors. After denying the cock's crow, he goes away to hide. He is a cock of the night.

On the other hand, I like the real cock, who is profoundly variegated. The cock says "Cocteau" twice and lives on his own farm.

Had I not dedicated *Le Cap de Bonne-Espérance* to Garros[2] in captivity, I would dedicate these notes to Garros escaped from Germany. But you are the second friend of mine who has escaped from Germany. I offer them to you because a musician of your age proclaims the richness and grace of a generation which no longer grimaces, or wears a mask, or hides, or shirks, and is not afraid to admire or to stand up for what it admires. It hates paradox and eclecticism. It despises their smile and faded elegance. It also shuns the colossal. That is what I call escaping from Germany.

1. Georges Auric (1899-   ), French composer and member of *Les Six*, is known for his many ballet and film scores.
2. Roland Garros (1888-1918), Cocteau's friend, was a pioneer aviator; a tennis stadium in Paris was named after him.

Long live the cock! Down with Harlequin!

J. C.

March 19, 1918

N. B.—Harlequin also means: "A dish composed of various scraps" (Larousse). . . .

The eyes of the dead are closed gently; we also have to open gently the eyes of the living.

Let us reread Nietzsche's *The Case of Wagner.* Never have shallower and profounder things been said at one and the same time. When Nietzsche praises *Carmen,* he praises the boldness that our generation seeks in the music hall. It is to be regretted that he opposes to Wagner a work of art artistically inferior to Wagner's. Impressionistic music is swept away, for instance, by a certain American dance I saw at the Casino de Paris. . . .

There are certain long works which are short. Wagner's works are long works which are long, and drawn-out, because this old sorcerer looked upon boredom as a drug useful for stupefying the faithful.

It is the same with the mesmerists who hypnotize in public. The genuine "pass" which puts to sleep is usually very short and simple, but they accompany it with twenty sham passes which impress the crowd.

The crowd is won by lies; it is deceived by the truth, which is too simple, too naked, and not sufficiently shocking. . . .

In the midst of the perturbation of French taste and of exoticism, the café-concert remains intact in spite of the Anglo-American influence. It preserves a certain tradition which, however dissolute, has style. It is here, no doubt, that a young musician can pick up the lost thread.

The café-concert is often pure; the theater is always corrupt.

Certain masterpieces of the theater are not theatrical in the proper sense but scenic symphonies, which make no concession to the setting. *Boris Godunov* is a case in point.

Let us discard the theater. I regret to have succumbed to its temptation and to have led two great artists astray.

(It is, naturally, not because of the scandal that I regret it. The full realization of my idea would have caused the same scandal. But we evolve here in an atmosphere where the public, a hundred years behind the times, simply does not count.) "Well, why, then, do you write for the theater?" It is precisely the handicap of the theater to depend upon immediate success for its very existence.

When I say of certain circus or music hall numbers that I prefer them to anything shown in the theater, I do not mean to say that I prefer them to everything that could be presented in the theater.

The music hall, the circus, the American Negro orchestras inspire an artist as much as does life itself. To make use of the feelings which such spectacles arouse does not mean to copy art from art. These spectacles are not art. They stimulate one just as machines, animals, landscapes, and dangers do.

The life force which is expressed in the music hall makes, at first sight, our daring seem outmoded. This is because art is slow and circumspect in its blindest revolutions. In the music hall, one knows no scruples; one skips up the stairs. . . .

In *Parade* I sought to create a good work; but whatever comes into contact with the theater is corrupted. The rich setting, in keeping with the taste of the only European impresario courageous enough to accept the work, the circumstances, and my fatigue made it impossible for me to carry out all my intentions. Yet the piece remains, in my opinion, a window opening upon that which our contemporary theater ought to be.

The score of *Parade* was intended as the musical background for suggestive noises, such as sirens, typewriters, airplanes, and dynamos, placed there like what George Braque so justly calls "facts." Material difficulties and hurried rehearsals prevented these noises from being used. We suppressed nearly all of them. The work was thus given incompletely and lacking the strongest effects. *Parade* was so far from being what I should have wished it to be that I never went to see it from the hall but, instead, confined myself to changing, from the wings, the signs that bore the numbers of the turns. The "Managers' Step-Dance," among other things, rehearsed without Picasso's "skeletons," lost all its lyric force once the "skeletons" were put on the dancers.

One day I was looking at the children's puppet show in the

Champs Elysées when a dog entered the stage, the dog's head in itself as big as two of the other actors put together. "Look at the monster," said a mother. "It's not a monster, it's a dog," said the little boy.

In the theater, men rediscover the violence of children, but not their lucidity.

Fed up with soft and melting music, with frills, the superfluous and the modern hocus-pocus, and often tempted by a technique of which he knew all the resources, Satie abstained voluntarily from using any of these. He modeled in the block and remained simple, clear, and luminous. But the public hates frankness.

Each of Satie's works is an example of renunciation.

Erik Satie's opposition lies in his return to simplicity. This, by the way, is the only possible kind of opposition in an age of extreme refinement. The good faith of the critics of *Parade*, who believed that the orchestra produced a mere din, can only be explained by the phenomenon of suggestion. The word "cubism," mispronounced, suggested to them an orchestra.

The Impressionists thought the orchestra of *Parade* was poor because it had no sauce. . . .

In *Parade*, the public took the transposition of the music hall to be a kind of music hall. . . .

Pelléas is still music to be listened to with one's face in one's hands. All music to be listened to with face in hand is suspect. Wagner's music is the prototype of such music.

One cannot get lost in the Debussy mist as much as one can in the Wagnerian fog, but one still gets sick from it.

The theater corrupts everything, even a Stravinsky. I should not like these observations to affect our friendship; but it is good for our young compatriots to be put on guard against the caryatids of opera—those corpulent golden sirens who caused even so formidable a crew to change its course. I consider *Le sacre du printemps* a masterpiece; but I sense in the atmosphere created by its execution a religious complicity among the initiated, that hypnotism of Bayreuth. Wagner wanted the theater; Stravinsky finds himself embroiled with it by the circumstances. There is a difference, but even though he composes in spite of the theater, the theater has nonetheless infected him. Stravinsky lays hold of us with other means than Wagner. He does not hypnotize us or plunge us into semi-darkness; he hits us rhythmically over the head and in the heart. How can we defend ourselves? We grind our teeth; we feel the cramps of a tree which grows convulsively with all its branches. Even in the haste of this growth there is something theatrical. I don't know whether I make myself clear. Wagner cooks us slowly; Stravinsky does not give us time to say "Ouf!"; but both affect our nerves. This is music of the bowels; octopuses which one must flee if one does not want to be devoured. That is the fault of the theater. There is theatrical mysticism in *Le sacre*. Shouldn't this be music to which one listens with face in hand?

Translated by Ulrich Weisstein from Cocteau's *Oeuvres complètes* (Paris: Marguerat, 1950), by permission of Editions Stock.

IGOR STRAVINSKY (1882-   )

STRAVINSKY's contribution to music in general and the musical theater in particular is too widely known to require a detailed analysis in this context. We simply note, therefore, that ballet and opera were the natural outlets for an artist who "always had a horror of listening to music with his eyes shut," since he felt "that the sight of the gestures and movements of the various parts of the body producing the music is fundamentally necessary" for its understanding. Stravinsky is a tireless experimenter with theatrical forms involving dancers, speakers, actors, and instrumentalists. All of these forms, however, are living proof of the composer's aversion to the music drama *(Gesamtkunstwerk)* which, as he puts it in his *Poetics of Music,* "represents no tradition at all from the historical point of view and which fulfills no necessity at all from the musical point of view," whereas the Russo-Italian opera of the kind represented by *Mavra* and *The Rake's Progress* meets both the above conditions.

Stravinsky's anti-Wagnerian attitude was confirmed in the summer of 1912 when he accepted Diaghileff's invitation to attend a performance of *Parsifal* in Bayreuth. This experience increased his desire "to put an end to . . . this unseemly and sacrilegious conception of art as religion and the theater as a temple." In his operas, accordingly, the audience was to adopt a critical attitude toward the events portrayed on stage. As I have tried to show in the article listed below, *L'histoire du soldat* may well be regarded as the prototype of Epic Opera, to which Brecht's *Dreigroschenoper* and *Mahagonny* are, at least indirectly, indebted.

Following the spectacular success of *Firebird, Petrouchka,* and *Le sacre du printemps,* Stravinsky's first opera, *Le rossignol* (in the making since 1908), was performed in 1914. It was succeeded by *L'histoire du soldat* in 1918; *Mavra,* a comic opera, and *Renard,* a burlesque dance scene, in 1922; *Les noces,* a ballet with songs and choruses, in 1923; *Oedipus Rex,* an opera oratorio written in collaboration with Cocteau, in 1927; *Persephone,* a melodrama with text by André Gide, in 1934; and *The Rake's Progress* (libretto by Auden/Kallman) in 1951.

E. W. White, *Stravinsky: A Critical Survey* (London: J. Lehman, 1947); M. Ledermann, ed., *Stravinsky in the Theatre* (New York: Pellegrini & Cudahy, 1949); C. Mason, "Stravinsky's Opera [*The Rake's Progress*]," *Music & Letters,* XXXIII (1952), 1 ff.; U. Weisstein, "Cocteau, Stravinsky, Brecht, and the Birth of Epic Opera," *Modern Drama,* V (1962), 142-153.

An Autobiography (1936)
IGOR STRAVINSKY

THIS PERIOD, the end of 1917, was one of the hardest I have ever experienced. Overwhelmed by the successive bereavements that I had suffered, I was now also in a position of the utmost pecuniary difficulty. The Communist Revolution, which had just triumphed in Russia, deprived me of the last resources which had still from time to time been reaching me from my country, and I found myself, so to speak, face to face with nothing, in a foreign land and right in the middle of the war.

It was imperative to find some way of ensuring a tolerable existence for my family. My only consolation was to see that I was not alone in suffering from these circumstances. My friends Ramuz, Ansermet, and many others were all in equally straitened circumstances. We often met and sought feverishly for some means of escape from this alarming situation. It was in these talks that Ramuz and I got hold of the idea of creating a sort of little traveling theatre, easy to transport from place to place and to show in even small localities. But for that we had to have funds, and these were absolutely lacking. We discussed this mad enterprise with Ansermet, who was to become its orchestra leader, and with Auberjonois, whose province was to be the *décor* and costumes. We elaborated our project to the last detail, even to the itinerary of the tour, and all this on empty pockets. We had to find a wealthy patron or a group who could be persuaded to interest themselves in our scheme. It was, alas! no easy matter. Refusals not always polite, but always categoric, greeted us every time. At last, however, we had the good fortune to meet someone who not only promised to collect the requisite capital, but entered into our plan with cordiality and sympathetic encouragement. It was Mr. Werner Reinhart of Winterthur, famous for his broad intellectual culture and the generous support that he and his brothers extended to the arts and to artists.

Under this patronage, we set ourselves to work. Afanasyev's famous collection of Russian tales, in which I was then deeply absorbed, provided me with the subject of our performance. I introduced them to Ramuz, who was very responsive to Russian folklore, and immediately shared my enthusiasm. For the purpose of our theatre we were particularly drawn to the cycle of legends dealing with the adventures of the soldier who deserted and the Devil who inexorably comes to carry off his soul. This cycle was based on folk stories of a cruel period of enforced recruitment under Nicholas I, a period which also produced many songs known as *Rekroutskia*, which expatiate in verse on the tears and lamentations of women robbed of their sons or sweethearts.

Although the character of their subject is specifically Russian, these songs depict situations and sentiments and unfold a moral so common to the human race as to make an international appeal. It was this essentially human aspect of the tragic story of the soldier destined to become the prey of the Devil that attracted Ramuz and myself.

So we worked at our task with great zest, reminding ourselves frequently of the modest means at our disposal to carry it to completion. I knew only too well that so far as the music was concerned I should have to be content with a very restricted orchestra. The easiest solution would have been to use some such polyphonic instrument as the piano or harmonium. The latter was out of the question, chiefly because of its dynamic poverty, due to the complete absence of accents. Though the piano has polyphonic qualities infinitely more varied and offers many particularly dynamic possibilities, I had to avoid it for two reasons: either my score would have seemed like an arrangement for the piano, and that would have given evidence of a certain lack of financial means, which would not have been at all in keeping with our intentions, or I should have had to use it as a solo instrument, exploiting every possibility of its technique. In other words, I should have had to be specially careful about the "pianism" of my score, and make it into a vehicle of virtuosity, in order to justify my choice of medium. So there was nothing for it but to decide on a group of instruments, a selection which would include the most representative types, in treble and bass, of the instrumental families: for the strings, the violin and the double bass; for the wood, the clarinet, because it has the biggest compass, and the bassoon; for brass, trumpet and trombone; and, finally, the percussion manipulated by only one musician, the whole, of course, under a conductor. Another consideration which made this idea particularly attractive to me was the interest afforded to the spectator by being able to see these instrumentalists each playing his own part in the ensemble. I have always had a horror of listening to music with my eyes shut, with nothing for them to do. The sight of the gestures and movements of the various parts of the body producing the music is fundamentally necessary if it is to be grasped in all its fullness. All music created or composed demands some exteriorization for the perception of the listener. In other words, it must have an intermediary, an executant. That being an essential condition, without which music cannot wholly reach us, why wish to ignore it, or try to do so—why shut the eyes to this fact which is inherent in the very nature of musical art? Obviously one frequently prefers to turn away one's eyes, or even to close them, when the superfluity of the player's gesticulations prevents the concentration of one's faculties of hearing. But if the player's movements are evoked solely by the exigencies of the music, and do not tend to make an impression on the listener by extramusical devices, why not follow with the eye such movements as those of the drummer, the violinist, or the trombonist, which facilitate one's auditory perceptions? As a matter of fact, those who maintain that they only enjoy music to the full with their eyes shut do not hear better than when they have them open, but the absence of visual distractions enables them to abandon themselves to the reveries induced by the lullaby of its sounds, and that is really what they prefer to the music itself.

These ideas induced me to have my little orchestra well in evidence when planning *Histoire du soldat*. It was to be on one side of the stage, and a small dais for the reader on the other. This arrangement established the connection between the three elements of the piece which by their close cooperation were to form a unity: in the center, the stage and the actors; on one side of them the music, and, on the other, the reader. Our idea was that the three elements should sometimes take turns as soloists and sometimes combine as an ensemble.

At the opening of the New Year (1928) I received from Cocteau the first part of his final version of *Oedipus* in the Latin translation of Jean Danielou. I had been impatiently awaiting it for months, as I was eager to start work. All my expectations from Cocteau were fully justified. I could not have wished for a more perfect text, or one that better suited my requirements.

The knowledge of Latin, which I had acquired at school, but neglected, alas! for many years, began to revive as I plunged into the libretto, and, with the help of the French version, I rapidly familiarized myself with it. As I had fully anticipated, the events and characters of the great tragedy came to life wonderfully in this language, and, thanks to it, assumed a statuesque plasticity and a stately bearing entirely in keeping with the majesty of the ancient legend.

What a joy it is to compose music to a language of convention, almost of ritual, the very nature of which imposes a lofty dignity!

One no longer feels dominated by the phrase, the literal meaning of the words. Cast in an immutable mold which adequately expresses their value, they do not require any further commentary. The text thus becomes purely phonetic material for the composer. He can dissect it at will and concentrate all his attention on its primary constituent element—that is to say, on the syllable. Was not this method of treating the text that of the old masters of austere style? This, too, has for centuries been the Church's attitude towards music, and has prevented it from falling into sentimentalism, and consequently into individualism. . . .

During the rest of the summer and the following autumn and winter, I hardly stirred from home, being entirely absorbed by my work on *Oedipus*. The more deeply I went into the matter the more I was confronted by the problem of style (tenue) in all its seriousness. I am not here using the word style in its narrow sense, but am giving it a larger significance, a much greater range. Just as Latin, no longer being a language in everyday use, imposed a certain style on me, so the language of the music itself imposed a certain convention which would be able to keep it within strict bounds and prevent it from overstepping them and wandering into byways, in accordance with those whims of the author which are often so perilous. I had subjected myself to this restraint when I selected a form of language bearing the tradition of ages, a language which may be called homologous. The need for restriction, for deliberately submitting to a style, has its source in the very depths of our nature, and is found not only in matters of art, but in every conscious manifestation of human activity. It is the need for order without which nothing can be achieved, and upon the disappearance of which everything disintegrates. Now all order demands restraint. But one would be wrong to regard that as any impediment to liberty. On the contrary, the style, the restraint, contribute to its development, and only prevent liberty from degenerating into license. At the same time, in borrowing a form already established and consecrated, the creative artist is not in the least restricting the manifestation of his personality. On the contrary, it is more detached, and stands out better when it moves within the definite limits of a convention. This it was that induced me to use the anodyne and impersonal formulas of a remote period and to apply them largely in my opera-oratorio, *Oedipus*, to the austere and solemn character to which they specially lent themselves.

Reprinted from *Igor Stravinsky: An Autobiography* (New York: Norton, 1962), by permission of the author and M. and J. Steuer.

CHARLES FERDINAND RAMUZ
(1878-1947)

ONE OF THE CHIEF MODERN WRITERS in the French-speaking part of Switzerland, Ramuz was a native and lifelong inhabitant of the Vaud (Waadtland). His novels—*La guérison des maladies, Les signes parmi nous, La grande peur de la montagne, La beauté sur la terre,* to name only a few—are much too little known in the Anglo-Saxon world, and almost no literature on him in English is available. Ramuz is a regional author with a universal appeal who, in the words of the French literary historian Philippe van Tieghem, excels his contemporaries in the ability to "*mêler l'irréel au réel le plus quotidien,*" to mix the unreal with the most common things. At heart he was undoubtedly a lyricist.

Ramuz met Stravinsky in 1915, when the latter moved to Switzerland, where he stayed until 1920. The two artists soon became close friends and collaborators. Ramuz is responsible for the French translations of many of Stravinsky's Russian works: *Pribaoutki, Les berceuses du chat, Renard,* and *Les noces.* The composer, who initiated him "into the peculiarities and subtle shades of the Russian language and the difficulties presented by its tonic accent," was astonished at "his insight, his intuitive ability, and his gift for transferring the spirit and poesy of the Russian folk poems to a language so remote and different as French."

The only original creation which resulted from their collaboration is *L'histoire du soldat,* about the genesis of which Ramuz is speaking in the following excerpt from his *Souvenirs sur Igor Strawinsky.* Ramuz saw in Stravinsky "*un homme complet,*" i.e., a man who was at the same time naïve and sophisticated, a man also who "carried a zone of liberty around with himself." The

Souvenirs are decidedly panegyric in tone and clearly show how deeply attached the writer was to the composer, who, through their collaboration, had taught him to understand himself.

Apart from his creative friendship with Stravinsky, Ramuz' bonds with music were rather tenuous. However, a number of his songs were composed by Ernest Ansermet, the conductor, as well as by his compatriots Jean Binet and Frank Martin.

C. F. Ramuz, *Lettres 1910-1918* (Lausanne: Editions Clairefontaine, 1956), esp. pp. 35-37 and 353-368; *Hommage à C. F. Ramuz* (Lausanne: Porchet & Cie, 1938); U. Weisstein, "Cocteau, Stravinsky, Brecht, and the Birth of Epic Opera," *Modern Drama*, V (1962), 142-153.

From *Memories of Igor Stravinsky* (1928)
CHARLES FERDINAND RAMUZ

THE *Histoire du soldat* was born a little later [than *Les noces*], out of very different and more opportunistic considerations. It was in 1918, and nobody knew when the war would be over. The borders closed ever more tightly around us, which caused Stravinsky's situation to grow increasingly difficult. The *Ballets Russes* had suspended their activities, and the theaters were closed, or nearly so. I myself suffered greatly from the lack of what in the commercial world are called "outlets." And I recall how one day, somewhat naïvely, Stravinsky and I posed the question: "Why not create something simple? Why not collaborate on a piece that requires only a handful of instruments and two or three actors? (We'll soon see how this calculation misfired.) Since the theaters are closed, we'll make our own theater, i.e., settings that can be mounted anywhere, even out-of-doors. We shall carry on the tradition of the trestle stage and the wandering comedians. Thus we may be able to attract all sorts of audiences."

L'histoire du soldat grew out of practical considerations, or rather out of considerations that were meant to be practical but weren't. The show was to make money, and a lot of money at that; but it turned out not to make a lot and, for that matter, no money at all. I think, however, that it owes to the reasons which justified its existence in our eyes (and which are responsible for its failure on the stage) a certain kind of ingenuousness.

Its merits, if it has any, lie in the fact that other than aesthetic considerations are responsible for its creation, that its authors did not use it as a vehicle for theories, that it does not constitute a manifesto, and that it owes everything to the circumstances. We wrote a play—in the broadest sense of the word—that is easy to perform, that belongs to us in spite or because of the circumstances; and we turned the obstacles in the way of its creation into advantages. *L'histoire* is a true *pièce d'occasions* (in the plural), a fact which, naturally, the audience failed to grasp, since it provided too simple an explanation. Each of us had merely sought to remain what he was and to join in the venture without sacrificing his true self.

Since I was not a man of the theater, I suggested that Stravinsky write a "story" rather than a play in the strict sense of the word. I wanted to demonstrate that the theater can be conceived in much broader terms than is usually the case, and that it lends itself perfectly well to what might be called the narrative syle. For Stravinsky it was a foregone conclusion that he would conceive his music quite independently from the text, namely as a suite that could be performed in the concert hall. All we had to do was to find a subject. There was nothing easier than that, however. I was Russian, so the subject would be Russian; and Stravinsky, at that time, lived in the Vaud, so the music would be Vaudois. All we had to do was to leaf through one volume of the vast compilation made by a famous Russian folklorist, whose name I have forgotten. And among the many popular stories in which the devil invariably seems to play a major role, that of the soldier and his fiddle fascinated us the most for several reasons (one of them being its very incongruity). Suddenly I remembered those sheepskin trousers that are now worn by our pioneers; and I imagined how splendid it would be to make one of these soldiers, with his knapsack, sit down at the edge of one of our brooks, pretending that it was the heart of Russia, and to have him play his fiddle, as if this instrument were part and parcel of the military outfit. Stravinsky, on his part, had assigned major roles to the trombone and the trumpet—instruments favored by our military bands—and an even more significant part to the percussion section, which figures equally prominently in these.

Alas! The piece (music and text) once written (which did not take us very long), we realized that the real difficulties were only now to begin. *L'histoire du soldat* existed, but only on paper. It still had to be performed, since this is what it was intended for. Certain musical or dramatic works lend themselves easily to an existence on the library shelf and, in consequence, do not suffer from merely being read. *L'histoire du soldat*, as we conceived it, belonged more to the oral tradition. It was to strike the eye and ear directly and thus was in need of a scenic background. We were lucky in this respect. For [René] Auberjonois took care of the settings as well as the costumes. We were equally fortunate in having found a conductor, because Ansermet was entirely with us. But the musicians and the actors?

A little later we found out that it would have been more practical to work within the framework of an established genre by using traits familiar to both the audience and the actors, whose profession it is to entertain the former. Innovations, even by way of simplification, complicated the matter unduly. We had only a small orchestra of seven musicians. But these musicians, precisely because they were only seven, found themselves taxed with the roles of virtuosi. We also discovered that we had created characters that did not fit into any of the known types, since they belonged to all, although there were only three of them. First of all the reader (we were extremely lucky in finding an excellent one), a completely new species of performer. Then there was the soldier, who occupies the stage but often without speaking. There was also the devil, now man, now woman, who represented all the human types at once and thus had to be a mime as well as an actor. And finally there was the Princess, who did not speak but danced (contradictory genres).

The first performance of *L'histoire du soldat* took place in Lausanne, after many delays, in September, 1918. It was made possible through the help of many devoted people too numerous to mention here but to whom I owe the sincerest gratitude. Eli Gagnebin, a paleontologist, was the reader. The devil was played by two actors, one of them Jean Villard, at present a member of Jacques Coupeau's company, who unwittingly inaugurated his career with this role. A belletrist, Gabriel Rosset, portrayed the soldier. The other half (if I may be permitted to call it that) of the devil was played by Georges Pitoëff, and the Princess by his wife, both luckily still residing in Geneva and doing their utmost to adapt their acting to these roles which were out of keeping with their style. The clarinet, bass, and trumpet came from Zurich, the violin from Geneva, the other instrumentalists from elsewhere. Ansermet had descended from the mountains. Only the painter was found in Lausanne itself. . . . And thus the spectacle took place, for better or worse, at the time and hour specified, nine o'clock being an extremely late hour for Lausanne. But the performance lasted only two hours, and the evening had to be filled.

It was understood, for the rest, that, the troupe having thus constituted itself (and including the musicians), other performances were to follow in other cities. The halls had been rented and posters distributed. It seemed as though we should be able to witness, although in a rather unusual manner, the realization of our project. We had not foreseen that, modest as it was, it would be overshadowed by the circumstances. First there was the grippe, that famous Spanish grippe . . . which deprived us in one fell swoop of our musicians, actors, stagehands, and theaters. It was followed by the Armistice, the Swiss railroad strike, a rash of revolutions in the neighboring countries, an extraordinary unleashing of disorder of every kind. Thus our wagon never came to roll on the routes mapped out by us, and thus we have never acquired the tractor (complete with klaxon, horn, and other accessories) which we had dreamed of owning one day.

Translated by Ulrich Weisstein from Ramuz' *Oeuvres complètes* (Lausanne: Mermod, 1941), by permission of the estate of C. F. Ramuz.

GIACOMO PUCCINI (1858-1924)

THE DESCENDANT of a Lucca family whose members had greatly contributed to the musical life of that city since the first half of the eighteenth century, Giacomo Puccini was cut out for the role he was to play in Italian operatic life. He composed his first opera while studying with Ponchielli at the Milan Conservatory, but did not gain full recognition until after the première of

Manon Lescaut in 1893—the same year in which Verdi completed his *Falstaff*. The role of Verdi's successor was becoming to Puccini, the predominantly lyrical vein of whose music strongly contrasts with Verdi's sense for dramatic values. *Manon Lescaut* spelled the death of short-lived operatic Verism, a style most strikingly illustrated by Mascagni's *Cavalleria rusticana* (1890) and Leoncavallo's *I pagliacci* (1892). According to Grout, it is the aim of Verism "simply to present a vivid, melodramatic plot, to arouse sensation by violent contrast, to paint a cross-section of life without concerning itself with any general significance the action might have." Veristic music thus "aims simply and directly at the expression of intense passion through melodic or exclamatory phrases," everything being so arranged that "the moments of excitement follow one another in swift climactic succession!" Since neither Mascagni nor Leoncavallo had a second triumph, the way was free for their gifted contemporary. Within a decade Puccini had created his three popular masterpieces *La Bohème* (1896)—a subject which Leoncavallo also treated—*Tosca* (1900), and *Madama Butterfly* (1904). In the last twenty years of his life Puccini struggled with subjects less congenial to his talent. Both *La fanciulla del West* (1910) and *Turandot* (posthumously performed in 1926) are, dramatically, too ambitious. The agony experienced by the composer in the prolonged attempt to give shape to the latter work is vividly reflected in the following excerpts from the correspondence with his librettist, Giuseppe Adami.

G. Marek, *Puccini: A Biography* (New York: Simon & Schuster, 1951).
R. B. Marini, *La "Turandot" di Giacomo Puccini* (Florence, 1942).

Letters to Giuseppe Adami
Concerning *Turandot* (1920-24)
GIACOMO PUCCINI

February 7 (?), 1920:

I am sending you the volume of Schiller. We shall discuss the matter by letter, and anyhow the business of the moment is to adapt the story. Choose a style for it, make it interesting, pad it, stuff it out, and squeeze it down again. It is impossible as it is. But worked at and well masticated, it should turn out a kind of Sir Robber, a sort of *taking* gentleman. Hurrah! I am getting some scenic material from Germany. I have a book of [Max] Reinhardt's already, but there is little of *Turandot* in it. I shall get some old Chinese music too, and descriptions and drawings of different instruments which we shall put on stage (not in the orchestra). But at the same time you two Venetians must give an interesting and varied modern form to that relative of yours, Gozzi. Don't talk about it too much, but if you succeed (and you must), you will see what a beautiful and original thing it will be, and how *prenante* (and this last is essential). Your imagination, together with all those sumptuous fancies of the old author, must inevitably lead you to something great and good.

February 8 (?), 1920:

Make Gozzi's *Turandot* your basis, but on that you must rear another figure; I mean—I can't explain! From our imaginations (and we shall need them) there must arise so much that is beautiful and attractive and gracious as to make our story a *bouquet* of success. Do not make too much use of the stock characters of the Venetian drama—these are to be the clowns and philosophers that here and there throw in a jest or an opinion (well chosen, as also the moment for it), but they must not be the type that thrust themselves forward continually or demand too much attention.

February 12 (?), 1920:

Immediately on the receipt of your express letter today I wired to you on a first impulse, advising the exclusion of the masks. But I do not wish this impulse to influence you and your intelligence. It is just possible that by retaining them with discretion we should have an Italian element which, into the midst of so much Chinese mannerism—because that is what it is—would introduce a touch of our life and, above all, of sincerity. The keen observation of Pantaloon and Co. would bring us back to the reality of our lives. In short, do a little of what Shakespeare often does, when he brings in three or four extraneous types who drink, use bad language, and speak ill of the King. . . . But these masks could possibly also spoil the opera. Suppose you were to find a Chinese element to enrich the drama and relieve the artificiality of it?

May 15, 1920:

Turandot! Act I—very good. I like the *mise en scène* too. The three masks are very successful. I am not quite sure about the effectiveness of the close, but I may be wrong. The truth is that is a good act and well laid out. What will the second act be like? Shall we need the third? Or will the action be exhausted in the second? Go ahead with it, using all your imagination and resourcefulness, and the opera will be not only original but moving. And it is on this last that I lay most stress, and this we must achieve.

July 18, 1920:

Your packet to hand. At first sight it seems to me good, except for some criticisms which I might make in both the second and third acts. In the third—I had imagined a different dénouement—I had thought that her capitulation would be more *prenante*, and I should have liked her to burst into expressions of love *coram populo*—but excessively, violently, shamelessly, like a bomb exploding.

October 20, 1920:

And is *Turandot* sleeping? The more I think of it, the more it seems to me the sort of subject that one wants nowadays and that suits me perfectly. But it must have a good comic element and the right kind of sentiment.

November 10, 1920:

I am afraid that *Turandot* will never be finished. It is impossible to work like this. When the fever abates it ends by disappearing, and without fever there is no creation; because emotional art is a kind of malady, an exceptional state of mind, over-excitation of every fibre and every atom of one's being, and so on *ad aeternum*. . . . Is (Simoni)[1] still on his high horse, I wonder?

1. Renato Simoni wrote the librettos for *La rondine* and *Il tabarro* as well as collaborating with Adami on the text of *Turandot*.

I hope not, because for me the libretto is nothing to trifle with. It is not a question of finishing it. It is a question of giving life that will endure to a thing which must be alive before it can be born, and so on till we make a masterpiece. Shall I have the strength to second you? Who can tell? Shall I be tired, discouraged, weighed down by years and spiritual torment, and by my never-ceasing discontent?

December 24, 1920:

I beg you not to forget the cruel Princess. (Don't you think that that golden rose act is rather gentle?)

March 30, 1921:

I have written to Simoni for the finale. How are you getting on with Act III? . . . Pay special attention to Liu in Act III. You will have to adopt an irregular metre. I have the music ready; it has a Chinese flavor, but I shall have to make some changes.

May (?), 1921:

Turandot is groaning and travailing, but pregnant with music. . . . Think of Act III. You must draw upon all your resources of sentiment and emotion. You must move your hearers at the end—and you will know how to do that. Not much rhetoric! And let the coming of love be as a shining meteor while the people shout in ecstasy, their taut nerves vibrating to the pervading influence like the deep-toned strings of a violoncello. I, for my part, will find phrases worthy of your golden numbers.

June 7, 1921:

I am working like a Roman slave. It is terribly difficult, but I am getting on. I am finishing the masks (frightfully good). But I have already done the music for the ghosts and the two songs for Calaf and Liu.

Summer, 1921:

I am not in doubt at all. I think that *Turandot* in two acts is right. The action begins at sunset and ends with the following dawn. The second act is at night, the first rays of dawn appearing at the end. So we come to an end with the rosy dawn and the sunrise.

Why not have an original scene after Calaf's cry, "I have lost her"? A scene a la Shakespeare in front of a special curtain in which they would sing—standing still if you like—a hymn to the risen victory? Or else a dance, and add an epilogue with Liu, slaves, and Turandot? In short, I do not think we should delay long after the riddles. Delay here means weakening the opera. Even the incidents of the second act are not important apart from the duet and the torture. The importance lies in the threat of death to the Prince and the suggestion of flight which precedes it.

September 14, 1921:

I have sent Renato a plan of the second act. Enter Turandot, nervous after the ordeal of the riddles. A short scene ending with the threat: "Let none sleep in Pekin." Aria for tenor. After that do away with the banquet and have instead a scene in which the three masks dominate the action. With bribes of riches, wine, women, they beg and beseech Calaf to speak. "No, for so I lose Turandot." Anxious proposals of flight: "No, for I lose Turandot." Then daggers drawn and threats to his life. Conference of dignitaries, rapid conspiracy, and attack on Calaf. Enter Turandot; flight. Duet, shorter—then torture (and this should be quicker, too) to "I have lost here." Exit Turandot in great agitation. Liu remains to speak to Turandot. Darkness—change of scene. Room in yellow and rose—scene of Turandot and slaves —the cloak. Pangs of jealousy. Darkness. Then the last scene, imposing, in white and rose: Love.

September 21, 1921:

I am still in favor of an imposing and varied second act which will also be the last. Act I: Sunset; Act II: Dawn. One thing is certain: we must inspire the whole thing with life. As it stands, it is absolutely impossible, all wrong, I am convinced. It has no pulse of life, no lightness of movement. I know that the subject is not easily convincing, but just for this reason you must be more sparing of words and try to make the incidents clear and brilliant to the eye rather than to the ear and, above all, give them variety. Every scene must have a beautiful beginning, and a more beautiful ending.

November, 1921:

Turandot gives me no peace. I think of it continually, and I think that perhaps we are on the wrong track in Act II. I think that the duet is the kernel of the whole act. And the duet in its present form doesn't seem to me to be what is wanted. Therefore I should like to suggest a remedy. In the duet I think that we can work up to a high pitch of emotion. And to do so I think that Calaf must kiss Turandot and reveal to the icy Princess how great is his love. After he has kissed her, with a kiss of some—long—seconds, he must say "Nothing matters now. I am ready to die," and he whispers his name to her lips. Here you could have a scene which should be the pendant to the grisly opening of the act with its "Let no one sleep in Pekin." The masks and perhaps the officials and slaves who were lurking behind have heard the name and shout it out. The shout is repeated and passed on, and Turandot is compromised. Then in the third act when everything is ready, with executioner, etc., as in Act I, she says (to the surprise of everyone): "His name I do not know." In short, I think that this duet enriches the subject considerably and raises it to an emotional interest which we have not now attained. . . . My life is a torture because I fail to see in this opera all the throbbing life and power which are necessary in a work for the theater if it is to endure and hold.

November 8, 1921:

I am in black despair about *Turandot*, I wrote that to you before. Perhaps it is the fact that I have returned to the idea of two acts that makes you so taciturn? It could also be a challenge. . . . I repeat that Act II as it stands is a great mistake. After a first act which is so beautiful, so rich and spectacular, and above all so well balanced and convincing, it is absolutely necessary to have a second act which will be the quintessence of effectiveness, and the individual incidents must be clear and telling. I consider the duet as the *clou*—but it must contain some great, audacious, and unexpected element and not simply leave things as they were in the beginning, interrupting them only with cries from within of people arriving. I could write a book on this subject.

November 11, 1921:

I am grieved by your letter. Do you think that I am doing this because I am weary of the subject? God knows it isn't that. But I think that with a more convincing and effective second act our bark will ride safely into harbor. I feel that this act does not convince me and cannot convince the listener. There are certain laws which a theatrical composition must observe: it must interest, surprise, stir, or move to laughter. Our act must interest and surprise. Leave Gozzi alone for a bit and work with your own logic and imagination. Perhaps you could develop it differently, more daringly? One never knows. . . . I have already written the music for Act I, and, good or bad, the act is there. Therefore don't tell me that you see *Turandot* fading away. . . . You will have received a letter of mine from Torre di Lago in which I discussed the duet and was even returning to the idea of one single act, closely packed with incident, to finish the opera. I am still of this mind, although the general opinion is that two acts are not enough for an evening's performance. What does it matter, if the opera turns out more convincing and con-clusive in this form?

November 17, 1921:

Time is pressing, and I think continually of the unfinished *Turandot*. That first act—I am sure of it—is good. Why don't you get on? We must get it finished, and successfully. I have some ideas, extravagant perhaps, but not to be despised. The duet! the duet! It is the meeting-point of all that is decisive, vivid, and dramatic in the piece.

December 21, 1921:

I need the trio scene for the finale of Act I. And with regard to the new Act I, if you find that you can expand it in some directions, do so. This to make it less rapid. And for the first scene of Act II, consider the daughter of the sky, high up beside the Emperor's throne, beseeching and praying that she be not thrown into the stranger's arms.

December 26, 1921:

Yesterday, in the new house, I played the first act of *Turandot*. . . . I liked it. . . . If only you could bring down the curtain after the three masks have finished their pleading and almost exhausted their powers of persuasion! The two—the old father and the slave girl—must say all they can to persuade him, the three masks adding their prayers; then after Calaf's hymns (phrased like the trio in [Gounod's] *Faust*), finished with the beating of the great song.

May 2, 1922:

Turandot is going ahead, if only as far as the orchestra is concerned. I think it is going well. But, of course, I can't be sure.

July 9, 1922:

I have reread Act III. I find much in it that is good. Much—but we shall have to make cuts—many—and the duet too, good at the beginning and in some of the rest, must, however, be touched up in the concluding section. I have some ideas. I am in favor of uniting the first and second parts, but in a rather different way. I should like the icy demeanor of Turandot to melt in the course of the duet, or, in other words, I want a love passage before they appear *coram populo*—and I want them to walk together toward her father's throne in the attitude of lovers and raise the cry of love while the crowd looks on in amazement. She says: "I do not know his name," and he "Love has conquered." And the whole ends in ecstasy and jubilation and the glory of sunlight. The finale should follow on from the duet without a break, and the whole thing be swifter.

November 3, 1922:

I am so sad, and discouraged too. *Turandot* is there with the first act finished, and there isn't a ray to pierce the gloom which shrouds the rest. Perhaps it is wrapped forever in impenetrable darkness. I have the feeling that I shall have to put this work on one side. We are on the wrong track for the rest of the opera. I think the second and third acts are a great mistake as we have envisaged them. I am coming back, therefore, to the idea of two acts, and getting to the end now in one other act. The basis of the act must be the duet. Let this be as fantastic as possible, even if you should exaggerate. In the course of this grand duet, as the icy demeanor of Turandot gradually melts, the scene, which may be an enclosed place, changes slowly into a spacious setting enriched with every fantastic adornment of flowers and marble tracery, where the crowd and the Emperor with his Court, in all the pomp of an important occasion, are waiting to welcome Turandot's cry of love. I think that Liù must be sacrificed to some sorrow, but I don't see how to do this unless we make her die under torture. And why not? Here death could help to soften the heart of the Princess. . . . I am tossed on a sea of uncertainty.

March 6, 1923:

No, no, no! *Turandot* no! I have received part of Act III. It is quite impossible. Perhaps—and maybe there's no perhaps—I too am no longer possible. But about this Act III there is no doubt at all. I am not quite at the stage of crying, *Muoio disperato*, but very nearly. I wonder if you could take it and make something out of it with the help of the old Act III? Is it possible? And shall I be able to do my part?

March 12, 1923:

Here I am—in a house of mourning. I am alone. I am cursing *Turandot*. I want something tender, simple, clear, and—ours. If we can't find it, I'm giving up altogether.

April 14, 1923:

You ask about my work. Slow but good. Turandot's song is nearly finished, but what a labor it has been. Some change will be necessary, however, in the words. This song should not be at all bad, sung while she stands high above the stage at the top of the flight of steps. I am getting on with the trio of the masks too. This scene is very difficult and of the greatest importance, as it has no scenery and is almost purely traditional. And so amid the discouragements and the small and short-lived joys which accompany such work, *Turandot* is advancing, with slow steps, but sure.

September, 1924:

I have written to Renato. We must meet. If you come here we shall fix things up. Bear in mind also our first idea of introducing internal symbolic voices, speaking of liberation for the love which is coming to birth and helping and encouraging it. It must be a great duet. These two almost superhuman beings descend through love to the level of mankind, and this love must at the end take possession of the whole stage in a great orchestral peroration.

October 18, 1924:

I beg you to look at the libretto again . . . and change the stage directions, and please try to make up your minds about *mise en scène* for the trio in front of the curtain. For the staging keep in mind the pictorial ideas of Chini,[2] following the lines of his work where you can. For the trio scene in front of the curtain you could introduce an openwork marble balustrade interrupted in the center like this:

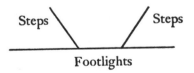

And this could be retained in the following scene with the flight of steps. On this balustrade the masked figures play their part, sitting or lounging on it, or astride it as the case may be. I am not explaining very well what I mean, but I know that in the *Ariadne* of [Richard] Strauss at Vienna they did something of the same sort with the Italian masks; only there the masks climbed up by two stairs from the orchestra. Perhaps that would hardly

2. Galileo Chini (1873-   ) designed the sets for *Turandot*.

do at the Scala—so make the masks come in from descending steps at the sides. It is my opinion that we must invent something special for this trio scene.

Reprinted from *Letters of Giacomo Puccini*, edited by G. Adami, translated by Ena Makin (Philadelphia: Lippincott, 1931).

RICHARD STRAUSS (1864-1949)

RICHARD STRAUSS, Wagner's legitimate successor on the German operatic stage, is principally known for his tone poems in the manner of Liszt and Berlioz and as a composer of operas, at least five of which *(Salome, Elektra, Der Rosenkavalier, Ariadne auf Naxos,* and *Arabella)* are permanently anchored in the repertory. Temperamentally a mixture of Bavarian and Viennese, Strauss sought, and often managed, to combine the realistic strain with the lyrical. His humor, though occasionally coarse, is always compelling, his leaning toward the sentimental at times excessive, and his Baroque liking for the spectacular a little cloying. But where these elements are as happily blended as they are in *Der Rosenkavalier,* the success is overwhelming.

Strauss was not exactly an experimenter, and after the radicalism of his expressionist *Elektra* he settled down to a more conventional manner of composition. Unlike Hofmannsthal, he always thought of opera as performed, and carefully gauged the effect which a given scene or situation might have upon the audience. Much to Hofmannsthal's horror, he demanded librettos in the style of *Die Meistersinger* or *Die Fledermaus.* A masterful orchestrator (he had re-edited Berlioz' treatise on instrumentation), he was often accused of drowning out the voices of the singers on stage. The advice given in the preface to *Intermezzo* is designed to forestall such a misinterpretation of his intentions.

He was lucky enough to find in Hofmannsthal an ideal librettist with whom he was able to engage in a frank exchange of opinions and who would never simply accept directives. When Hofmannsthal died, Stefan Zweig temporarily succeeded him, but was forced to emigrate after the completion of *Die schweig-*

same Frau. Josef Gregor, who took his place, was a historian of the theater rather than a creative writer, and his collaboration with Strauss was not too harmonious. The conductor Clemens Krauss furnished the text for Strauss' last opera, *Capriccio.*

Richard Strauss/Hugo von Hofmannsthal, *Correspondence* (New York: Random House, 1961); H. T. Finck, *Richard Strauss: The Man and His Works* (Boston: Little, Brown, 1937); A. Mathis, "Stefan Zweig as Librettist and Richard Strauss," *Music & Letters,* XXV (1944), 163-176, 226-245.

Preface to *Intermezzo* (1924)

RICHARD STRAUSS

IN CLASSICAL OPERA there are two methods of managing the dialogue which serves to develop the plot: pure prose or the so-called *recitativo secco* with cembalo accompaniment. Only Beethoven and Marschner[1] effectively used an emotional melodrama in important passages. In Mozart's German operas the plot proper is almost exclusively expressed in spoken prose followed without transition by vocal music in the form of songs, ensembles in somewhat freer form, the great finales elaborated into somewhat longer symphonic compositions, and the arias preceded by an orchestral recitative *(recitativo accompagnato)* all of which are inclined to slow down the action. Apart from Gluck's operas and Nicolai's *Merry Wives,*[2] *The Magic Flute* alone contains a recitative passage of greater length which really serves to develop the action: the great scene between Tamino and the priest: a scene which constitutes the zenith of Mozart's dramatic work. In his Italian operas Mozart adopted the *recitativo secco* from the *opera buffa,* with the considerable improvement in *Così fan tutte* of allowing the orchestra to play the accompaniment at times when the dialogue contains lyrical passages.

These brief remarks should suffice to remind experts with what care our great masters treated the dialogue on which the action

1. Heinrich Marschner (1795-1861), German composer and conductor, was active in Hanover between 1831 and 1859. His best-known opera is *Hans Heiling* (1833).

2. Otto Nicolai (1810-49) was a German composer who resided in Rome. His opera *Die lustigen Weiber von Windsor* (1849, after Shakespeare) is still frequently performed in the German-speaking countries.

on the whole depends. But it is striking that none of our classical composers made use of the subtle nuances which may result from the development from ordinary prose via melodrama, *recitativo secco*, and *recitativo accompagnato* to the unimpeded flow of the melody of a song.

Perhaps it was inevitable that the peculiar subject matter taken completely from real life and embracing the whole gamut from the sober prose of everyday life through the various shades of dialogue to sentimental song, should induce me, who had in my previous works taken much care to render the dialogue natural, to adopt the style realized in *Intermezzo*.

I have always paid the greatest possible attention to natural diction and speed of dialogue, with increasing success from opera to opera. While in my first opera *Guntram* the distinction, so carefully observed by Richard Wagner, between passages which are merely recited and those which are purely lyrical, was almost completely neglected, the dialogue in *Salome* and *Elektra* was largely rescued from being drowned by the symphonic orchestra. But it is unfortunately still very much handicapped by instrumental polyphony unless extremely careful observation of my dynamic markings gives the orchestra that pellucidity which I took for granted when composing the operas, and which I know from perfect performances to be capable of achievement.

But since it is indeed rare that we can count on such ideal performances on the stage, I found myself more and more compelled to secure from the start the balance between singer and orchestra to such an extent that even in less perfect performances the action above all should, at least in broad outline, be plain and easily intelligible, lest the opera be disfigured or open to misrepresentation. The scores of *Die Frau ohne Schatten* and *Ariadne* are the fruits of these endeavors.

In the former I attempted, especially in the part of the nurse, to inject new life into the style and pace of the old *recitativo secco* by means of an orchestral accompaniment using mainly solo instruments and filling in the background with light strokes. Unfortunately, this attempt did not succeed in making the dialogue, which is of the utmost importance particularly in these scenes, absolutely clear.

The fault may lie either in a lack of talent on my part, as a result of which even this tenuous and diaphanous orchestra appears still too polyphonic, and the scoring so erratic as to impede the spoken word on the stage, or it may be due to the imperfect diction on the part of the majority of our operatic singers, or again to the unfortunately often guttural tone of German singers, or to the excessive forcing of sound on our big stages.

There can be no doubt that orchestral polyphony, no matter how subdued its tones or how softly it is played, spells death to the spoken word on the stage, and the devil himself is to blame that we Germans imbibe counterpoint with our mothers' milk, to keep us from being too successful on the operatic stage.

Not even our greatest dramatic master succeeded in creating "ideal recitatives" except in *Lohengrin* and *Rheingold*, so that no listener will ever be able to enjoy the poetry of the text, no matter how subdued the orchestral playing, in the great polyphonous symphonies of the second act of *Tristan* and the third act of *Siegfried*.

Anybody who knows my later operatic scores well, will have to admit that, provided the singer pronounces the words clearly and the dynamic markings in the score are strictly observed, the words of the text must be clearly understood by the listener, except in a few passages where these words may permissibly be drowned by the orchestra as it plays with increasing intensity for the purpose of pointing a necessary climax. No praise pleases me more than when after I have conducted *Elektra* somebody says to me: "Tonight I understood every word": if this is not the case you may safely assume that the orchestral score was not played in the manner exactly prescribed by me.

On this occasion I should like to draw attention to the peculiar nature of the dynamic marking I use in my scores. I am no longer content with prescribing pp, p, f, ff, for the whole orchestra, but give a large variety of dynamic markings for individual groups and even individual instruments, the exact observance of which, although it is the main requirement for the correct performance of my orchestral scores, presupposes indeed the existence of a type of orchestral discipline which is somewhat rare today, but is absolutely necessary for a performance of my scores in accordance with my intentions. Special attention should be paid to the accurate execution of *fp* and of every *expressivo* calling for a frequently all but unnoticeable preponderance of one part over its neighbors. Only thus can finely articulated polyphony be clearly represented. If one particular part predominates, important subsidiary strands may be destroyed.

No rendering of the orchestral part, however brilliant and noisy, given by one of the many concert-hall conductors who have unfortunately nowadays taken to conducting opera can silence the just complaints against aural feasts at the expense of the intelligibility of plot and libretto.

It was out of this necessity that the score of *Ariadne* was born. The orchestra has not been relegated to the role of accompanist and yet, in spite of the expressive force of the "chamber orchestra," the sounds and words uttered by the singers are bound to be intelligible in any performance, no matter how heartless the officiating conductor may be.

It was in the first act of *Ariadne* that I first used with full assurance, in the alternation between ordinary prose, *recitativo secco*, and *recitativo accompagnato*, the vocal style which I have now, in *Intermezzo*, carried to its logical conclusion. But in none of my other works is the dialogue of greater importance than in this bourgeois comedy, which offers few chances to development of the so-called *cantilena*. The symphonic element has been so carefully and repeatedly revised and polished that in many instances it is merely hinted at and cannot, even when dynamic markings are carelessly observed, prevent the natural conversational tone, derived and copied from everyday life, from being not only heard but also clearly understood. This applies to the context as well as to each individual word; the lyrical element, the description of the spiritual experiences of the *dramatis personae* is developed mainly in the comparatively long orchestral interludes. Not until the final scenes of the first and second acts is the singer really given a chance of extended *cantilena*.

Wherever the dialogue contains lyrical elements in the other scenes, the singers as well as the conductor should carefully distinguish between *cantilena* and *recitativo*, and the listener must be able to follow the natural flow of the conversation without interruption and must be able to follow clearly all the subtle variations in the development of the characters as portrayed in the opera; if he fails to do so, the performance will have the effect of intolerable tedium since the listener, inadequately understanding the text, will not be able to comprehend the plot in all its details, nor will the musically trained ear find sufficient compensation in symphonic orgies.

The singer in particular should remember that only a properly formed consonant will penetrate even the most brutal of orchestras, whereas the strongest note of the human voice, even when singing the best vowel "ah," will be drowned without difficulty by an orchestra of eighty or a hundred players playing no louder than *mezzo forte*. The singer has only one weapon against a polyphonic and indiscreet orchestra: the consonant. I have myself seen it happen, especially in Wagner's music dramas, e.g. in Wotan's Narration and in the Erda scene of *Siegfried*, the singers with great voices but poor diction were left to flounder impotently in the waves of orchestral sound, whereas singers with considerably weaker voices but decisive pronunciation of consonants, could carry the poet's words victoriously and without the slightest difficulty against the maelstrom of the symphonic orchestra.

I would, on the other hand, ask the conductor when rehearsing *Intermezzo* to pay the greatest attention to the gradual transition from the spoken word to the sung and half-spoken word, to all the subtle turns in the conversation where prose hesitates between *recitativo secco* and the style of the *recitativo accompagnato*, to reach its climax at last in the so-called *bel canto* in which absolute clarity could at times be sacrificed to beauty of intonation. The chief precept for the practical execution of the *Intermezzo* dialogue is that all passages of pure dialogue—in so far as they do not change for short periods of time into lyrical outpourings of emotions—in other words, all passages resembling *recitativo secco*, should be presented *mezza voce* throughout. Practical experience teaches us that with full volume the precision of pronunciation and especially the formation of consonants suffer considerably. This is illustrated by the fact . . . that during orchestral rehearsals even in an empty theater, which is acoustically unfavorable, every word of the singers singing *mezza voce* can usually be understood, whereas barely half the words are understood when they sing with full voice during the performance. . . .

By turning its back upon the popular love-and-murder interest of the usual operatic libretto, and by taking its subject matter perhaps too exclusively from real life, this new work blazes a path for musical and dramatic composition which others after me may perhaps negotiate with more talent and better fortune. I am fully aware of the fact that in breaking new ground unthought-of difficulties will stand in the way of the correct realization of my intentions. May this preface assist and guide the worthy and generous interpreters of my art, the excellent singers and hard-working conductors, in the solution of these problems.

From *Recollections and Reflections* by Richard Strauss. English translation by L. J. Lawrence. Copyright 1949 by Atlantis-Verlag, Zurich. English translation copyright 1953 by Boosey & Hawkes Ltd. Reprinted by permission.

HUGO VON HOFMANNSTHAL
(1874-1929)

ONE OF THE MOST SENSITIVE, intelligent, and versatile writers of the modern age, Hugo von Hofmannsthal, in his writings, embodied, and in many instances successfully recreated, the cultural traditions of Europe from Euripides to nineteenth-century Impressionism. Active primarily as a playwright, he also created a small body of lyrical poetry of a very high quality and was ceaselessly active as critic, essayist, and writer of prose narratives. His skeptical attitude toward language was first manifested in the famous "Letter to Lord Chandos," where the failure of words to convey meaning is cited as the cause for the writer's creative impasse. But subsequently Hofmannsthal learned to use words in such a way as to avoid their surface appeal. Language, for him, became a means of expression rather than remaining one of communication. What mattered to him was not the situation that words delineate but the atmosphere they evoke, not what was said but what was passed over in silence and suggested by the interstices between the words. Reality, in this poet's view, was no more than the arbitrary projection of intangible values upon a social plane. He was thus naturally drawn toward opera, where a framework of conventions gives wider scope to the lyrical, symbolic, and supernatural tendencies.

Richard Strauss, who had set Hofmannthal's *Elektra* to music in 1909, became his trusted collaborator. In the course of the next two decades Hofmannsthal supplied five major librettos: *Der Rosenkavalier* (1911), their most successful and mutually satisfactory undertaking, *Ariadne auf Naxos* (1912), *Die Frau ohne Schatten* (1919), *Die ägyptische Helena* (1928), and *Arabella* (1933). Strauss, who in spite of his lyrical vein was at heart a realist, who wanted to stand with both feet on the ground, felt slightly disconcerted by Hofmannsthal's mythological foreshortenings, and at times would have preferred to write another *Meistersinger*. Only with considerable effort did he manage to complete work on *Die Frau ohne Schatten* and *Die ägyptische Helena*. In *Arabella*, this somewhat weaker offspring of *Der Rosenkavalier*, however, the two once again found an Austro-Bavarian subject congenial to their natures.

R. Strauss/H. von Hofmannsthal, *Correspondence* (New York: Random House, 1961); H. Hammelmann, *Hugo von Hofmannsthal* (Yale University Press, 1957); H. Cohn, "Hofmannsthal's Libretti," *The German Quarterly*, XXXV (1962), 149–164.

Preface to *Die ägyptische Helena* (1928)
HUGO VON HOFMANNSTHAL

To SPEAK ABOUT one's own projects is precarious, but at the same time tempting, and the moment immediately before the launching has a special suspense. Setting out to uncover something one becomes aware how much remains hidden even from him to whom everything should be perfectly clear. Never does the artifact show itself more independent than at the moment when the artist thought he could make use of it without restraint for some trivial purpose. The commentator upon his own work, the one ordinarily assumed to be best qualified, is actually the one most handicapped. He, least of all, has the courage to loosen the texture of the motifs; after all, he has just exerted all his efforts to tie the outside to the inside, to intertwine one thread with another, and nowhere to leave one hanging loose, so that it might be pulled out. He is at a loss as to how to begin.

One speaks of the poet and the musician who join forces and collaborate: Corneille with Lully, Calzabigi with Gluck, Daponte and Schikaneder with Mozart. But apart from the fact that this does happen—it is astonishing how compellingly I have been drawn to this genre. In the section concerning my work in Nadler's *History of Literature*[1] it is said that: "even my first plays unconsciously called for music, a fact which is vaguely implied by the word "lyric." Nadler is absolutely right, except that, in my opinion, the word implies this quite precisely. The French call an opera *un drame lyrique,* and in so doing they have perhaps instinctively always been closer to antiquity than we are: they never entirely forgot that classical tragedy was sung.

Thus our collaboration came about, to which in the course of eighteen years people have gradually become accustomed. But this collaboration had its interruptions, the last one of a duration of eight or nine years. Not that I had become weary of this genre, but other things demanded their creation. However, since 1920, one subject, one group of figures had been mirrored in my imagination—glittering and elusive like a stream which disappears underground only to re-emerge—namely the very subject that I have now carried out: the homeward journey of Helen and Menelaus. Some kind of curiosity had taken hold of my imagination, it was centered on these mythological figures as upon living people whose life one knows in part, while for one important period one is reduced to conjecture.

That night when the Greeks invaded the burning city of Troy . . . Menelaus must have found his wife in one of the burning palaces and carried her out between crumbling walls, this woman who was his beloved, abducted wife and, besides,

1. The reference is to Josef Nadler's *Literaturgeschichte der deutschen Stämme und Landschaften* in four volumes (1912-28).

was the most beautiful woman in the world, the cause of this war, of these frightful ten years, of this plain filled with dead men, and of this conflagration. In addition to all this, she was also the widow of Paris and the love of ten or twelve among Priam's other sons, all of them now lying dead or dying.

What a situation for a husband! It transcends all imagination—no lines, not even lines which Shakespeare might have written, would be equal to it, and I am certain that Menelaus carried this woman, who even in this situation was still the most beautiful in the world, down to his ship in silence. There is no record of what took place subsequently. Several years later, however, we find the son of Ulysses traveling through the Greek kingdoms in search of news of his lost father. He also comes to Sparta—and of what he finds there, we have the clearest picture in the fourth book of the Odyssey, a picture as vivid in color as if it had been painted yesterday. He finds Menelaus in his palace, a hospitable grand seigneur, "beautiful as a god," and Helen as the lady of the manor, as beautiful as ever, the queen of this peaceful land—apparently happy; they are just celebrating the wedding of their children, a son and a daughter; they talk of Troy and the war, as one usually talks of the past, though Menelaus refers to it with calm dignity as to the great experience of his life, while Helen, in that absolutely superior and sovereign manner which Homer always attributes to her, just touches the events and even on her own guilt so elegantly and lightly that she says of the war (just as if to indicate a certain point in time): at the time when the Greeks, because of "my bitchlike coquetry," had gone there to besiege the fortress (1.46).

How amazing to have treated such a famous and awesome event in such a light manner, and—I cannot help but use the word—how modern, how close to the language of our time. Yet, one feels compelled to ask oneself, what happened in the meantime? What is it that for these two people lay between that night long ago and the comfortable situation in which Telemachus encounters them? What may have happened, in order to turn this marriage once again into a peaceful and radiant union? This is extraordinary—even if one makes considerable concessions to heroes and demigods, so far as their way of life is concerned. Even curiosity, if it is only strong enough, can become inspiration. Here was a subject—if curiosity could be turned productive—perhaps a lyric subject calling for music (although this latter fact I did not recognize at once). Ever since 1920 the subject has kept returning to my imagination.

To be sure, there is Euripides' *Helena*, the only ancient work which is concerned with this episode: Helen and Menelaus on their voyage back from Troy. It is here that the motif of a phantom of Helen occurs, that second Helen, not the Trojan, but the Egyptian one. We are in Egypt, or on the island of Pharos which belongs to Egypt, in front of a royal castle; Menelaus appears alone, on his return from Troy. For months, his ship has been drifting aimlessly, tossed about from shore to shore, constantly diverted from its homeward course. Helen, his reconquered wife, he has left behind with his warriors in a hidden bay; he is looking for advice, for help, for an oracle which may reveal to him how to find his way home. There, from the portico of the castle, Helen emerges, not the beautiful, much too renowned Helen, whom he left behind in his ship, but another one, and yet the same. And she claims that she is his wife—the other one over there in the ship, she says, is nobody and nothing, a phantom, an illusion, put in Paris' arm by Hera that day long ago in order to fool the Greeks. It was for this phantom that war was waged for ten years, that tens of thousands of the best men were killed, that the most flourishing city of Asia was turned to ashes. She, however, Helen, the only real one, having been borne across the sea by Hermes, has lived all this time in this royal castle, honored and protected by old Proteus; but now, his son has ascended to the throne, and he has but one desire, to marry her. Thus it is the task of Menelaus, to whom she has always been faithful, to carry her away swiftly and clandestinely, and in fact, the preparation for the flight, the flight itself, and finally the appearance of the Dioscuri [Castor and Pollux] who pacify the enraged Egyptian king, all this forms the content of Euripides' play.

It is understandable that Menelaus does not immediately believe this person who appears before him only to tell him that he spent ten years in a war camp for the sake of a ghost, that for a ghost he shed the blood of tens of thousands of Greeks, for a ghost he set fire to a great city, and that finally he went home with a ghost. They talk back and forth for a long while using pointed arguments, typical of Euripides. And this beautiful and true pronouncement comes from his lips: "I trust the intensity of endured suffering more than I trust you!" And indeed, this denouement of such a terrible involvement in guilt must seem altogether too cheap to him. At this moment, however, a messenger arrives and actually reports that the creature on the ship who was believed to be Helen has dissolved into a thin trail of fiery air.

What choice has Menelaus but to cling to the one who alone remains and who, in addition, is pure and innocent—and to flee with her, before the Egyptian king will rob him of this one, too? So far Euripides.

But if the Trojan War was waged for a phantom, and if this one, the Egyptian Helen, is the only real one, then the Trojan War was nothing but a bad dream, and the whole story falls into two parts: a ghost story and an idyll, which have nothing to do with one another—and none of this is very interesting. I forgot Euripides again, but my imagination kept circling around the episode of husband and wife returning together, and around the question what terrible and eventually redeeming experiences the two might have gone through together. The whole thing seemed so mysterious to me as to be resolved practically only through magic; but magic resolves nothing to our way of feeling. The elements of nature must have had their share in this, the atmosphere of those active elemental beings, who are indifferent and yet helpful at the same time. Not so much in order to save the demi-goddess, as to save him, Menelaus. How deeply disturbed his soul must have been. So much fateful involvement in guilt—and, after all, he was only a mortal. At once, I saw the noble, the tragic in this often ridiculed character. He was to me the embodiment of everything occidental, while in her, I saw the inexhaustible strength of the Orient. He stood for law, marriage, fatherhood. She hovered above all this, uncanny and beguiling, a goddess who could not be bound.

In my notebook I had entered years ago the following sentence by Bachofen:[2] "Not for this was Helen endowed with all of Pandora's charms, to surrender herself to one man only for his exclusive possession." What daemonic power emanates from such a sentence! It could have been put on the first pages of [Frank] Wedekind's *Erdgeist*. He was the man to have considered the substance of such a sentence most seriously in all its implications, and having let it mature within himself to turn it into something extraordinary and formidable.

Two or three years later, I asked [Richard] Strauss to see me in his office at the opera. "I shall tell you," I said, "a plot for a play in two acts. When the curtain rises, we are in a palace by the sea. The palace belongs to a beautiful young sorceress, who is the daughter of some king and the love of Poseidon."

"Does Poseidon appear?"

"No, Poseidon does not appear. No gods at all appear. In fact, take everything as if it had happened two or three years ago, somewhere between Moscow and New York. This young sorceress—I call her Aithra—is frequently left alone by her lover. But it is always possible that he may come; so, every evening she has the table set for two—and so tonight, too, the table is set for two, and the stage is beautifully lit. She has girl servants, and a well-furnished house, but not much company.

Among the furnishings in the large room in which we find ourselves, there is a sea shell, which knows everything that is going on outside upon the sea, and which, in order to divert Aithra, tells everything it knows. On this particular night, the shell reports that something strange is going on inside a ship which is passing by at some distance. A man on this ship, leaving the helm which he passes to another, climbs down into the hold where he looks at an extremely beautiful woman who is lying there asleep; softly, he covers her beautiful face with a cloth, pulls out a curved dagger and is about to kill the sleeping woman. 'Send a storm there,' screams the shell carried away by its own story, 'but instantly! Otherwise, the woman is lost!' "

---

2. Johann Jakob Bachofen (1815-87) was a famous German historian who concerned himself with the religious aspects of mythology and with primitive religion *(Das Mutterrecht)*.

"Can Aithra do that?"

"Yes. The storm flies there, takes hold of the ship, so that it creaks in all its timbers and thus prevents the murder. But just before this, Aithra has asked very quickly who this woman and this man are—and the shell has said that they are Helen of Troy and her husband, Menelaus. Aithra is beside herself with joy and breaks out of her prose into a little aria of jubilation. But afterward, she runs into the next room, hides there and orders one of her maidens to go and meet the shipwrecked people with a torch. For this, too, the shell has reported: the man who had been about to murder his wife, now that both have been washed overboard, is making every effort to stay afloat and save her, and Aithra has immediately commanded the storm to subside.

The stage is empty, then, and now a man appears in the door of the beautifully lit room, a curved dagger between his teeth and dragging behind him (by the hand) an extremely beautiful blond woman. For the minute he felt solid land under his feet, the murderer and avenger has reawakened in him, and he is ready to put his hand again upon the dagger and to make an end. Helen knows this—she knows everything that goes on within him—this is her strength—yet she remains in control of the situation, otherwise she would not be Helen. She goes to the mirror, straightens her hair, and since there is a table beautifully set, with two chairs, as if for a king and a queen, she invites her husband to sit down and eat with her."

"And Menelaus?"

"For nine days and nine nights—it is this long that they have been on their way from Troy—he has neither taken a meal with her, nor touched her with as much as the tip of his finger. For nine days he has pondered whether it would be better to kill her on the ship, or to sacrifice her the day after their return to Sparta. For this much he is certain about, that she must die and by his hand and by the same curved dagger with which he cut Paris' throat. And she knows it as well as he does—just as she knows that he loves her to the point of madness and that he will do it nevertheless. This knowing and understanding of the one whom she loves (and she does love exclusively the man to whom she belongs—as long as she belongs to him), as I said before, is precisely what is her strength. And besides, there is still Aithra."

"How can Aithra save her from this situation?"

"By a ruse. Menelaus is in a condition very close to insanity. He is no longer equal to his experience of the last nine days. Above all, he is not equal to that which he has imposed upon himself. He is torn asunder by the presence of this woman, by the feeling of having her back, and by the inescapable necessity of having to kill her with his own hands. And one little trick of Aithra's is enough to render his derangement complete. Her trick is this: she calls her elves, lemurs, more malicious than benevolent, who squat outside in the moonlight between the rocks on the beach, and she orders them to do something that will confuse Menelaus completely, at least for a moment. For the dagger is raised; it is literally a question of the next minute. The elves are nimble and adroit. They raise a wild warlike clamor. Menelaus thinks he is hearing the Trojan trumpets again, the clanking of Trojan weapons. Very distinctly he hears the voice of Paris who challenges him to battle. His overtaxed mind cannot withstand even this little trick. He rushes out to kill the dead Paris all over again—or, if it is a ghost, to throttle the ghost.

The two women are alone, hostess and guest. A few words suffice to make them understand each other. Aithra has a wonderful potion at hand, a soothing potion without equal, made of lotus and producing quick forgetfulness of every evil. Helen drinks and grows calm like a child; under the touch of her friend's fingers she revives like a half-withered rose when it is put in water. She has almost forgotten what faces her when the man with the dagger returns. But Aithra has enough presence of mind for both of them. She orders Helen to be led away by her maidens; then she turns, and with the calmest expression in the world she intercepts Menelaus. For he comes rushing in just now, brandishing the dagger from which he sees blood dripping down (only he sees this, while we see that the dagger is shiny and dry); for outside he has stabbed two phantoms, taking them for Helen and Paris. How the dead Paris could suddenly have been here again to embrace the living Helen, how all this could be mixed up together, his mind can no longer unravel. He is not insane, but he is in the state of complete shock, which in so many army hospitals has been observed to persist for days and weeks among men who have come out of situations too terrifying to be endured. On the other hand, he is not so completely out of his mind as not to behave with full propriety toward the young lady who approaches him and in whose house he seems to find himself—the more so, since she addresses him by his proper title, prince of Sparta—and asks him to sit down. Now Aithra tells him a story which, with a woman's instinct, she adapts precisely to his condition, the condition of a disturbed person who no longer trusts his own senses or his own mind, since he is under the illusion that he has just committed the most impossible and the most terrible crime. She tells him that for ten years, he has been the victim of a phantom, he as well as all the Greeks; that it was a phantom which he carried from the burning city that night of the conflagration, a phantom for which thousands of Greeks died during those ten years, a phantom which he carried on his shoulders out of the sea a short while ago and which now, just a few minutes ago, he apparently has stabbed with his dagger—and meanwhile she pours him of that potion which so miraculously soothes the nerves and transports one's consciousness into a swaying, gentle, half dreaming state. Then she asks him not to speak too loudly, lest he disturb the sleep of that most beautiful woman who is lying on her bed in the next room.

"What most beautiful woman?"

Why, his wife, Helen of course, the real one, the only one existing,—and at this point she hands him once again the lotus cup—Helen, whom the gods that day, ten years ago, removed; in her sleep, she was carried across the sea here to us, to Egypt, to my father's fortress. Here, she spent those years, carefully guarded, half-slumbering without aging, always the same smile on her lips; she thinks she fell asleep in your arms—and any moment now, she will awake. Prepare yourself to take her into your arms.

The adjoining chamber is suddenly brilliantly illuminated, a curtain is drawn, and on a wide couch Helen opens her eyes, refreshed by sleep, more beautiful and youthful than ever. How could a human heart tormented by self-inflicted pain like Menelaus', resist such an overflow of unexpected happiness? For a moment the thought flashes over the darkened mirror of his soul that this may be the apparition of his real wife, long dead, led before him here by a witch and a conjurer of the dead, but then this bit of darkness vanishes before the splendor of the apparition, the potion takes effect within his veins: he is overcome by gentle oblivion of hideous evil, by inner harmony, by ineffable peace—he walks toward the beautiful creature; exactly like a girl, she leans her head against his shoulder: it is she, Helen of Sparta, who knows nothing of Paris—their voices mingle, and Aithra's bright voice joins in.

"And surely, this must be the end of the play? What could happen after this in the second act?"

"Yes, this could be the end of the play. In this case, it would be a short frivolous comedy, in which a husband after some terrifying adventures is fooled by two women. But this is hardly the way these characters were intended, don't you agree? This Menelaus and this Helen did not look, did they, as if this could be the end?"

"No, but how?"

"The elves are not of the opinion either that the play could be over. These elves are present all the time as an invisible chorus. They watch the whole thing like a show. And this ending seems too cheap to them. They do not think one should get off so easily after such a tangled involvement. They mock invisibly, though audibly, throughout the action. This must not be, they hiss, you won't get away that cheaply."

"Well then, and the second act? I suppose it takes place the next morning?"

"Yes, it does, but not in Aithra's house."

"But where?"

"Somewhere else. Far away. In the desert near the great Atlas mountains. In the first act, just before the end, Helen asked Aithra under her breath, whether she could not use her magic power to remove her and Menelaus somewhere, where no one knew about her, where the name Helen was completely unknown, and where no one had ever heard of the Trojan War. Menelaus did not hear this short and whispered exchange. So the two wake up together in a palm grove at the foot of the Atlas mountains in deep solitude. But I shall not tell you the second act in detail now, only the gist of it. Incidentally, the two do not long remain there alone. In the desert there are sheiks, then, just as today, roaming chivalrous kings, and one of them, with his son and his retinue, comes upon the two lonely strangers—and immediately the most beautiful woman finds herself in precisely the same situation here, as back home, even though no one here has ever heard her name: they fall in love with her, both father and son, they want to snatch her away from Menelaus, they are ready to kill each other for her sake, but this is only a detail—I must come to the point, and the point is Helen: It is the strength of this woman—and this is indeed her genius—that she must possess completely the man to whom she belongs. The seemingly successful deception, however, has given back to her only half of Menelaus, in fact less than half. As he now awakens after this night of love, he glances at her shyly. Actually he is afraid of her. The allegedly dead woman fills his heart entirely; she who caused him so much suffering, for whose sake he endured such hideous nights, for whose sake he murdered Paris and whom he finally killed herself last night over there on the island with the same horrible weapon, his curved dagger. For this is fixed in his disturbed imagination: he is the murderer of the real, the guilty Helen—while this one here, this much too youthful-looking one with her innocent face, this mirage of an Egyptian siren, this is the one whom the sorceress over there has put into his arms, in order to console him. But he himself is Menelaus of Troy, he is the murderer and widower of the Trojan Helen. She is everything to him, to her he is bound by a world of suffering and guilt—the beautiful mirage of a siren before his eyes is nothing to him."

"And Helen?"

"Again, she understands him, understands him more profoundly than he understands himself, and she makes a decision."

"What?"

"She decides to awaken him—as one awakens some one from

a trance; to bring him to the point where he shakes off the de-
lusion, where he recognizes her as the guilty one whom it is
his destiny to punish—in short, to restore between him and herself precisely the situation of last night."

"And does she succeed?"

"She succeeds in everything to which she puts her mind.
She has daemonic powers. Aithra, too, comes to her aid; she
has a potion which cancels out the effect of the other one
causing oblivion. And this is what Helen wants. She faces up
to him, she faces the drawn dagger—convinced that he will kill
her and smiling at the dagger—and at the murderer, in exactly
the same position as twelve hours ago there on the island."

"And he?"

"As soon as he has recognized her, but this time completely,
at the very last moment, he drops the dagger and sinks into her
arms."

"Yes, it is an opera, at least to me, it as an opera, even
though perhaps to no one else. I hope, you have not told the
plot to any one else? By the way, it is surprisingly modern.
Has it not occurred to you to use it for a play in prose?"

"Yes, I do think myself in the hand of a French or American
author it would have turned into a psychological drawing-room
play. It would take only minor changes to remove all the mythical elements; all the little magic tricks are, after all, nothing
but foreshortenings; the potion, the forgetting and remembering—
nothing but foreshortenings of emotional processes. The elves
represent the criticism of the unconscious—all this could have
been projected on to the level of dialectics, and it would have
become a regular psychological drawing-room play: marriage
as a problem, beauty as a problem, an endless train of problems."

"Well, and?"

"I do not like drama to move in the realm of dialectics. I
distrust purposeful dialogue as a vehicle of the dramatic. I shrink
from words; they deprive us of the best."

"But the poet has no means other than letting his characters
talk, in order to bring them to life. Words are to you, after all,
what sounds are to me, and colors are to the painter."

"Surely, words—; but purposeful, sophisticated speech?—no.

Not that which has been called the art of the dialogue, or psychological dialogue of the kind which from Hebbel to Ibsen, and even beyond him, enjoyed such great popularity—and incidentally even with Euripides, and also with Shaw, although with him, it is considerably toned down by his pleasure in witticism which neutralizes the dialectics of the dialogue."

"And how about Shakespeare?"

"Oh no, not a trace of this. With him, the word always conveys expression, never information. In this sense, all of Shakespeare's plays are operas; he is very close to Aeschylus and miles apart from Euripides. But has it never struck you that in life, nothing is ever decided by talking? Never is one convinced of the hopelessness of a situation, as just after one tried to solve it by talking. The twisting power of speech goes so far that it not only distorts the speaker's character, it actually annihilates it. Dialectics dislodges the self from existence. I maintain that a poet has the choice of producing speeches, or characters."

"That is too paradoxical for me. The poet, after all, has no artistic means except speech."

"Oh yes, he has others; the most hidden, most precious, least obvious—the only effective ones. He is capable of everything, if only he foregoes the conventional idea that his characters must make their existence convincing by means of direct communication."

"What kind of artistic means are these?"

"He can through the construction of his plot communicate something without stating it explicitly. He can bring something to life within the spectator without the latter's knowing how this has come about. He can make him feel how complex is the seemingly simple, how closely interconnected that which seems far apart. He can show how a woman becomes a goddess, how something dead can issue forth from something living; he can indicate what a tremendous conglomeration of traits it takes to change the mask of the self into a person; after all, this is the reason why the ancients had the same word for mask and person. He can make audible that which is untold, and make suddenly present that which is distant. He can make his characters grow above and beyond themselves into gigantic proportions, for this is what mortals do in certain rare moments. In a 'natural' dialogue, however, there is no room for all this. The so-called 'natural' is the projection of intangible life upon a most arbitrarily selected social plane. The ultimate of our human nature, which is cosmically conditioned and which comprises time and space, cannot be rendered naturally."

"What kind of artistic means are these? Can't you define them?"

"The way in which I direct the action, in which I intertwine the motifs in which I let the hidden be audible and the audible die down again—through the similarity of characters, through tone modulation which often is more expressive than words."

"But these are my means, these are the artistic means of the musician."

"They are the artistic means of lyric drama, and they seem to me the only ones through which the atmosphere of the present age can be expressed. For if this age of ours is anything, it is mythical—I know of no other expression for an existence which unfolds in the face of such vast horizons—for this being surrounded by millenia, for this influx of Orient and Occident into our self, for this immense inner breadth, these mad inner tensions, this being here and elsewhere, which is the mark of our life. It is impossible to catch all this in middle-class dialogue. Let us write mythological operas! Believe me, they are the truest of all forms."

Reprinted from Hilde Cohn's translation in *The Journal of Aesthetics and Art Criticism*, XV (1956), by permission of the translator and of the editor.

ALBAN BERG (1885-1935)

ALBAN BERG, the most eminent pupil of Arnold Schönberg, with whom he studied from 1904 to 1910, is the author of one of the very few truly modern music dramas that have found a place in the repertories of the larger opera companies. The composition of *Wozzeck* was first suggested to him during a performance in 1914 of Georg Büchner's play of existential anguish and mental aberration. The following three years were spent in selecting and organizing certain scenes from this gripping drama, which its author left unfinished insofar as he did not live to fix the precise sequence of scenes. The music for the opera was written betwen 1917 and 1921; but Berg found it impossible to arrange for a performance of the completed work. It was finally suggested to him that he make an arrangement of excerpts from it for presentation in the concert hall. The "Three Fragments" were successfully performed in 1925, and in the following year Erich Kleiber conducted the premiere of *Wozzeck* at the Berlin State Opera.

Wozzeck has become a classic of contemporary opera largely on account of the unfailing theatrical instinct of its creator, which led him to fashion a series of scenes whose impact is felt by the musical initiates as well as by the listener who is unaware of the intricate musico-dramatic structure of the work. Berg shows himself to be an emulator of Gluck when he states that he wanted to use music in such a way "that each moment it would fulfill its duty of serving the action." One of the most striking features of *Wozzeck* is the persistent use of *Sprechstimme*, which Berg defends in his essay "Die Stimme in der Oper." In his second lyrical drama, *Lulu* (after two "tragedies of sex" written by the proto-Expressionist playwright Frank Wedekind), the musical episodes are all derived from a single twelve-note series related to the principal character. The work was left unfinished at the composer's death and, in this fragmentary form, was first performed in 1937 at the Zürich Opera House.

W. Reich, *A Guide to Wozzeck* (New York: League of Composers, 1931; reissued by W. Schirmer, 1952); W. Reich, "Alban Berg's *Lulu*," *Musical Quarterly*, XXII (1936), 383-401; Kerman, *Opera as Drama*, pp. 221-234.

A Word about *Wozzeck* (1927)
ALBAN BERG

IT IS NOW TEN YEARS since I started to compose *Wozzeck;* already so much has been written about it that I can hardly say anything without plagiarizing my critics. I should like, however, to correct an error that arose in 1925 soon after it was produced and that has spread widely since.

I have entertained the idea of reforming the structure of opera through *Wozzeck*. Neither when I started nor when I completed the work did I consider it a model for further efforts by any other composer. I never assumed or expected that *Wozzeck* should become the basis of a school.

I simply wanted to compose good music; to develop musically the contents of Georg Büchner's immortal drama; to translate his poetic language into music. Other than that, when I decided to write an opera, my only intention, as related to the technique of composition, was to give the theater what belongs to the theater. The music was to be so formed that at each moment it would fulfill its duty of serving the action. Even more, the music should be prepared to furnish whatever the action needed for transformation into reality on the stage. The function of a composer is to solve the problems of an ideal stage director. On the other hand this objective should not prejudice the development of the music as an entity, absolute, and purely musical. No externals should interfere with its individual existence.

That I accomplished these purposes by a use of musical forms more or less ancient (considered by critics as one of the most important of my ostensible reforms of opera) was a natural consequence of my method. It was first necessary to make a selection from Büchner's twenty-five loosely constructed, partly fragmentary scenes for the libretto. Repetitions not lending themselves to musical variation were avoided. Finally, the scenes were brought together, arranged, and grouped in acts. The problem therefore became more musical than literary, and had to be solved by the laws of musical structure rather than by the rules of dramaturgy.

It was impossible to shape the fifteen scenes I selected in different manners so that each would retain its musical coherence and individuality and at the same time follow the customary method of development appropriate to the literary content. No matter how rich structurally, no matter how aptly one might fit the dramatic events, after a number of scenes so composed the music would inevitably create monotony. The effect would become boring with a series of a dozen or more formally composed entr'actes which offered nothing but this type of illustrative music, and boredom, of course, is the last thing one should experience in the theater.

I obeyed the necessity of giving each scene and each accompanying piece of entr'acte music—prelude, postlude, connecting link or interlude—an unmistakable aspect, a rounded off and finished character. It was imperative to use everything essential for the creation of individualizing characteristics on the one hand, and coherence on the other. Hence the much discussed utilization of both old and new musical forms and their application in an absolute music.

The appearance of these forms in opera was to some degree unusual, even new. Nevertheless novelty, pathbreaking, was not my conscious intention. I must reject the claim of being a reformer of the opera through such innovations, although I do not wish to depreciate my work thereby, since others who do not know it so well can do that much better.

What I do consider my particular accomplishment is this. No one in the audience, no matter how aware he may be of the musical forms contained in the framework of the opera, of the precision and logic with which it has been worked out, no one, from the moment the curtain parts until it closes for the last time, pays any attention to the various fugues, inventions, suites, sonata movements, variations, and passacaglias about which so much has been written. No one gives heed to anything but the vast social implications of the work which by far transcend the personal destiny of Wozzeck. This, I believe, is my achievement.

Reprinted from Willi Reich's translation in *Musical Quarterly*, XXXVIII (1952), by permission of the publisher, G. Schirmer, Inc.

The Voice in Opera (1929)
ALBAN BERG

IT IS EVIDENT that an art form which employs the human voice will not renounce any of the possibilities which are open to the latter. Accordingly, the spoken word—either without accompaniment or as melodrama—is just as appropriate in opera as are the various modes of singing, from the *recitative* to the *parlando*, and from the *cantilena* to the coloratura. Thus there exists an opportunity, and the need, for using the *bel canto* even in contemporary operas. For there is no reason why modern melodies consisting of such singable phrases as the following from Schönberg's *Expectation*[1] . . . should not and, if they are to have the proper effect, must not be sung as "beautifully" as the famous *La donna è mobile*.[2]

The fact that here, as almost always in the aria-like forms of Italian music, a single motif suffices which—no matter how often it recurs—is (unlike most women) more or less invariable, certainly gives assurance that everybody can immediately repeat such a melodious idea. It does not justify the assumption that solely by means of the so-called declamatory singing one can do justice to that characteristically German style which, whether tonally or "atonally," is distinguished by a melodic, harmonic, and rhythmical wealth as well as by its suitability for elaborate variation. On the contrary, every composer who conceives of melody in that way will want to have the singer feel and reproduce it as such (if he can find a fitting vocalist). I speak from personal experience when I state how much I was surprised when a reviewer reproached one of the singers in *Wozzeck* (as happened only a short while ago) for being too ambitious to display her voice and to excel by singing. Perhaps not all the resources of the human voice are equally well exploited in my opera (I just notice that it contains no more than a dozen bars of recitative); but it certainly does not renounce the use of the *bel canto*. . . .

That other shortcoming (the lack of recitatives) I hope to have amply compensated for by being the first—and for many years the only—composer to introduce the so-called rhythmic declamation which Schönberg used, almost twenty years ago, in the speaking choruses of his *Glückliche Hand* and in his *Pierrot Lunaire*.[3] As it turned out, this melodramatic way of

1. Arnold Schönberg (1874–1951) composed three operas (plus the unfinished *Moses and Aron*), of which the monodrama *Erwartung* (1909) is the first.

2. From Verdi's *Rigoletto*.

3. Schönberg composed the opera *Die glückliche Hand* between 1910 and 1913. *Pierrot Lunaire* (1912) is based on poems by Albert Giraud in the translation of O. E. Hartleben.

treating the voice constitutes not only the best means of communication (for this is the primary function of language even in opera) but, from the whispered word to the true *bel parlare* of its broadly conceived speech melodies, has enriched opera by a full-fledged artistic technique derived from the purest musical source.

Together with the singing, a welcome musical complement and stimulating contrast of which it is, this melodically, rhythmically, and dynamically fixed manner of speaking is capable of participating in the other types of dramatic music, that is, the duets, tercets, the small and large ensembles, the male, female, and mixed choruses as well as the *a capella* singing and the singing with orchestral accompaniment. It is on account of these possibilities that, like no other musical genre, opera is predestined to serve the human voice and to assert its right—a right it has nearly been deprived of in the last decade of operatic creation when operatic music, in the words of Arnold Schönberg, "was frequently nothing but a symphony for large orchestra with the accompaniment of the human voice."

Translated by Ulrich Weisstein from *Gesang, Jahrbuch der Universal-Edition Wien,* 1929.

PAUL CLAUDEL (1868-1955)

PAUL CLAUDEL'S RELATIONSHIP with music was a profound and lasting one. In his youth he shared the Symbolists' (especially Mallarmé's) enthusiasm for Wagner, with whose works he first became acquainted at the age of eighteen. However, he saw none of these operas performed until 1910. "We belong to a generation that has Wagner in its bones," he confessed to André Suarès. But gradually his objections to the dramaturgical function of music in the *Gesamtkunstwerk* began to mount, although he continued to regard *Die Walküre* as sublime and to speak of the first two acts of *Tristan* as an experience affecting him as strongly as his first communion.

As his friendship with Darius Milhaud, the "young Jew from

Aix," began to deepen, he more consistently aimed at realizing his own theory of the musical drama, which finds expression in the essay "Modern Drama and Music," which is here reprinted. Milhaud, whom Claudel had met in 1912, was to furnish music for the poet's rendition of the *Oresteia* as well as for the play *L'Annonce faite à Marie* and two ballets. However, only *Christophe Colomb* (the opera oratorio that was premiered in May, 1930, at the Berlin Staatsoper, with Erich Kleiber conducting) allowed the two artists to give full scope to their vision of Epic Opera. The subject was suggested to Claudel by the Spanish stage designer José Maria Sert, who had asked him "to write a brief scenario for a choreographic divertissement on music by Manuel de Falla, to be given at the court of Alfons XIII, King of Spain." But Claudel refused "to treat such an enormous subject in a few lines." Having caught fire, he proceeded on his own to develop the subject, and in Milhaud found again a most welcome collaborator. In *Christophe Colomb*, Claudel's own version of the *Bühnenweihfestspiel*, music is used dramatically in many different ways, never "aiming at the realization of a sound picture but giving impulse and pace to [the] emotions through a medium purely rhythmical and tonal, more direct and more brutal than the spoken word." It is music that provides continuity without submerging the listener in the current of the story.

Claudel's other musical collaborator was Arthur Honegger, who wrote the score for the scenic oratorio *Jeanne d'Arc au Bûcher* and the incidental music for Claudel's dramatic masterpiece *Le soulier de satin*.

Paul Claudel/Darius Milhaud, *Correspondance* (Paris: Gallimard, 1961); D. Milhaud, *Notes Without Music* (New York: Knopf, 1953); A. Espiau de la Maëstre, "Claudel et la Musique," *Lettres Romanes*, XIII (1959), 145-176.

Modern Drama and Music (1930)
PAUL CLAUDEL

OFTEN IN THE COURSE of my career as dramatist the problem of the union of music and drama, the word and the note, has inevitably presented itself to me as it had done to many of my predecessors in the most different countries and the most remote ages. Everyone will have in mind the voluminous literature devoted to this question by Richard Wagner, and if any man seemed capable of finding a solution, it was certainly that great genius, who was magnificently gifted both as dramatist and musician. And it would be unjust to say that he totally failed in this immense undertaking. *Tannhäuser* is, on the whole, a grand drama, admirably composed, in which the music poignantly amplifies and colors the emotions of the characters. In my opinion it is the work in which Wagner's soul found its most authentic and complete expression. *Lohengrin* would also be a great success if it were possible to stretch it on new canvas, as is done with old pictures, and strip it of the romantic frippery that renders it nearly unbearable today. As to *Tristan*, I object to its uniform, monochrome tone and also to the dramatic mediocrity of the libretto. When a gentleman and a lady have repeated throughout two whole acts "I love you"—"You love me," the spectator thinks this is enough; if he discovers that in the third act it is all beginning over again, he is driven to despair and seized with a desire to flee that all the solos of the clarinet are incapable of appeasing. . . . The actor who takes the lover's part can do only two things with the prima donna: either hold her at arm's length in order to view his good fortune the better—all the while vigorously shaking his head—or passionately clasp her in his arms. . . . It should be added that the two performers, while they are engaged in these minor gymnastics, have a more serious and difficult task to perform—they must attend to a hard, ticklish score. This somewhat detracts from the sincerity and conviction of unreserved plastic expression, especially when the Isolde that Tristan is to handle has, as is generally the case, a certain amplitude of figure.

But to return to my subject, the union of music and drama.

As the reader has doubtless already become aware, I am not a musician. It is, therefore, not from the point of view of music that I shall approach the question. I go to the opera as rarely as possible, and I have had little experience on this side. So far as I can see, a regular opera is composed of a series of musical numbers, connected by some sort of action: say, solos, choruses, duets, ballets, overtures, trios, septets, and so on, affording an opportunity for the musician to exercise his talent. In short, it is a concert in fancy dress, the intervals and transitions of which are more or less filled up by some vague noise. Only, in a concert, the singers can stand motionless if they choose, while in an opera they feel bound to indulge in conventional, ridiculous gestures of absolutely no use for their essential purpose, such as the long-drawn elaboration of some dizzy F. I shall not speak of the costumes, the scenery, and staging, which are generally wretched and which will before long become insufferable to the most patient audience. A little while ago I was present at a performance of *Carmen*, and I had the feeling that it is soon going to be difficult to make the public believe that all Spaniards are clad in green boleros and sky-blue tights, even though the latter are adorned with a pretty yellow band.

If you prefer another definition of opera, I might say that it is a dramatic action offering an occasion for several situations upon which the orchestra and the actors comment lyrically. For whatever a singer may do, his business is not to act but to sing and to express the movements of his soul with his voice rather than with his limbs.

Of course, there is no form of art, however mediocre and absurd, that will not yield to genius or to that mysterious force, often so oddly applied, which we call "conviction." And genius and conviction sometimes manage to do something even with the opera. Of this strange outcome I can give a few examples, such as Gluck's *Orpheus*, Beethoven's *Fidelio*, Berlioz' *Trojans*, Wagner's *Tannhäuser*, Verdi's *Rigoletto*. Recently, however, I had an experience which gave me pause. I was present at a performance of *Don Giovanni* at the Metropolitan Opera House, and after a few moments devoted to a refreshing nap, I found, to my great amazement, that I was following the piece with some interest. And yet it would have been difficult to imagine a form of art and, I must own it frankly, a kind of music more repugnant to my taste. That mysterious force called "conviction" was operating upon me, and I regretted having to leave before this experience had reached a decisive stage.

Wagner had a clear idea of the hybrid, artificial character of the opera and of the kind of suffering caused an audience by the fact that their minds are divided and that they do not know whether they have been invited to a play or a concert. He tried to increase the importance of the drama, to immerse the actors more deeply in it (forbidding them to turn toward the spectators), and to carry all the action along on an orchestral flood, a continuous torrent of passion and desire sustained by remembrance and a sort of nostalgic remorse. In fact the lyrical commentary, which the old opera simply assigned to a tenor or a soprano, Wagner reserved entirely for the orchestra. Let us suppose, for instance, that the composer wants to express this idea: "How beautiful the weather is today; I believe it is a good time to take a walk." In an Italian opera, the tenor would come to the footlights, with a hand on his heart, and supported by a few discreet chords, would have no difficulty in imparting his feelings. Wagner, on the contrary, would paint for us with the orchestra all surrounding nature in a mist of sonorous dreams, the singer playing a part in them and his voice emerging, as it were, accidentally. In reality a Wagner drama is a vast symphony, in which the true characters are the leitmotifs, and human beings intervene—in general, pretty laboriously—only to explain where we are, what has happened, what is happening, and what will happen. The human mouth therein is far less important than the silver mouth of the flute or the golden one of the trumpet, and it completely disappears in the continual breaking down of the harmonic superpositions in which the great artist delights. There remains only a submerged gesticulating image.

I am far from wishing to suggest that Wagner did not have a dramatic temperament; on the contrary, he had a very profound, if not an unerring, one. But every situation called forth in him sonorous upheavings which swallowed up all the rest, and which subsided somewhat only to swell again into new waves a little farther on.

On the whole, I think that it would not be giving a bad definition of a Wagner drama to say that it is a symphony with a continuous programme and less an action than the sonorous memory of an action.

I have said enough of the way in which musicians have made use of the drama in the practice of their art. My real purpose is to examine what use dramatists can make of music.

One use we can discard at the outset: it is the introduction of music in the guise of a prelude or a detached piece as, for instance, when one of the characters sings a little song or when some vocal or instrumental concert must, for some reason or other, take place. Nothing is more dangerous. The musician is never given his share, and he, as a rule, does not care a straw for the play, his only idea being to find a place for a little score. The action is kept standing still, on one leg, so to speak, until the performers make an end of their pleasant noise. Moreover, between the atmosphere of the spoken word and that of music there exists an almost distressing difference, and the passing from one to the other results in a complete destruction of the spell which the poor poet has been at such pains to cast over the spectators.

How is it, then, that not only the Greek theater but all primitive theaters, up to and including the stage during the period of melodrama from 1840 to 1880, used music?

I got my first explanation of this fact at a performance of [my drama] *L'Annonce faite à Marie* given in Paris at the *Comédie des Champs-Elysées*, with the assistance of M. Gémier. There is a scene in this play in which the head of a family, on the point of undertaking a long journey, breaks bread for the last time with his children and his servants gathered around the table. This is an idea which looks natural on paper, but it is difficult for it to escape ridicule when presented on the stage. And indeed at the first performances I never witnessed that touching picture without feeling a shudder run along my spine as if I had heard a false note. Gémier, prompted by his vast dramatic experience, did not hesitate a moment: "We must have some music," he exclaimed. They set going a *glockenspiel* of some sort, and the scene passed off triumphantly, the sound of the bells at once conferring upon it the atmosphere, the ambient, the dignity, and remoteness, which the words alone, in their thinness and bareness, were unable to provide. And the cinema, of course, offers many instances of the same kind. Any pantomime or dumb show is simply impossible without musical support.

I had carried the recollection of this incident to Japan where, for several years, I occupied a diplomatic post, and where I was a constant spectator at the admirable national theater called "Kabou Ki," now unfortunately on the way to disappearance, like all things of beauty in this world, under the influence of our coarse, materialistic civilization. The long hours which I spent at the Imperial Theatre watching with emotion the unfolding of the heroic epics of the Genrokou period were for me a true professional school of drama. Unluckily this was rather late, at a time when I had given up all dramatic ambitions—the more so as the modern stage, taken up by ecstatic debates of amorous psychology, would collapse under the heavy buskin of a hero or demi-god. I then understood what dramatic music is, that is to say, music used by a dramatist, not by a musician, not aiming at the realization of a sound-picture but giving impulse and pace to our emotions through a medium purely rhythmical and tonal, more direct and more brutal than the spoken word. We are, let us say, at the denouement of a play. The atmosphere is stormy. Somebody arrives. Something is going to happen. It is one of those situations where in Europe a whole orchestra would be used. In Japan you have only a little yellow man perched on a platform, with a tiny cup of tea by his side and in front a tremendous drum, which it is his role to beat. I will call him the director of thunder. Those single hollow thumps, repeated at first at long intervals, then more vigorously and rapidly until the frightful, expected apparition comes at last, racking our nerves, are enough without any orchestra or score to put us in the desired ambient. In the same way, when anger rises and two human cocks are on the point of coming to blows, or when some peremptory intervention occurs, three or four hard, sharp clacks, with a bat on the stage floor are enough to silence speech and to make way for authority. So a teacher raps his desk with his ruler to call his class to attention.

To take another example: in *Tristan and Isolde*, when the lovers, after drinking the fatal potion, cast on each other distracted looks and suddenly feel burning passion take the place of the hatred in their souls the tremolo of the violin, like the vibration of a soul on the verge of breaking, is all the dramatist needs to have, and the rest of the orchestral commentary seems useless. The sound, the rhythm, the tone of cymbals or a bell do not form with the spoken word so sharp a contrast as does music which belongs to another sphere. On the other hand, the directing of a modern orchestra, whose path is implacably traced by little black signs and measure bars on the rigid stave, has not sufficient life and suppleness. On the Japanese stage the musician is himself an actor. He watches the development of the drama, which he freely punctuates, at the right moment, with whatever instrument, guitar, lyre, or hammer, may have been placed in his hand, or simply with his voice—for this is a magnificent element in the Japanese theater that I have failed to mention. Side by side with articulated voice goes the inarticulate voice—grumbling, exclamation, doubt, surprise, all the human feelings expressed by simple intonations in charge of those official witnesses of the play sitting squat in their little boxes. When we are in the grip of the play we are grateful to the anonymous fellow who utters cries for us and assumes the task of expressing our feelings by something less conventional than plaudits or hisses.

Music in the classical drama of Japan and of China has also another role, which is to express continuity. It is the *current* of the story, as we speak of the *current* of a river. It is the latent revenge of narration upon action, of duration upon incident. Its business is to give the sensation of the flow of time, to create an ambient, an atmosphere, for in life we not only speak or act, we listen, we are surrounded by something vague, diverse, and changing to which we must needs give attention. According to this conception, music does not aim at sustaining and underlining the words; it often precedes and provokes them, it invites expression through feeling, it sketches the sentences leaving to us the task to finish them. It follows a path parallel to our own. It attends to its special business while we, our ears filled with its murmurs of memories, forebodings, and counsels, read at sight *our* score. When necessary it weaves behind the drama a tapestry of sounds, the colors of which both divert and relieve the spectators, and suffuse with their pleasing suggestions the dryness of a description or of an explanation. Such music is to the ear what a back-scene is to the eye. In the same way the sound of a waterspout or of cages full of birds agreeably mingles with our conversation and carries along on a stream of reverie the prose of our everyday affairs. . . .

For a writer theories are only the—often temporary—scaffolding that serves to prop his productions. And so it seems to me that instead of keeping to the domain of dreams and doctrines it might be more interesting if I were to add a few words about a work to which the various ideas just stated served as accompaniment and support. I have in mind a play for which I received an order from a producer who, after showing intemperate enthusiasm, refused to accept it. This fact, by the bye, only resulted in advantage to me, for my play, *Christopher Columbus,* thus abandoned by Herr Max Reinhardt,[1] was eventually performed with Darius Milhaud's music at the Staatsoper in Berlin. It is of this play . . . that I should like to speak before bringing this article to a conclusion. The conditions of the contract, laid upon my desk by the invisible powers whose virtual and imperious agent Herr Reinhardt had consented to be, contained interesting possibilities. The work was to be an historical drama, and, up to that time, I had written only works of pure imagination. Music and, it was specified, choruses were to play an important part. So all through the writing of the drama I had to bear with some implied collaborator, a collaborator who, naturally, could be no other than my friend Darius Milhaud, with whom I have been for years on terms of close intimacy in both ideas and feelings. My role, then, consisted in looking on Christopher Columbus, in turning over the leaves of his history and legends, in evoking the principal scenes, one after the other, and in waiting for the questions, objections, and comments which the musician, through the collective medium of the orchestra and chorus, would have to present in the name of the public—that audience surrounding a great man and a great event which is composed of all peoples and of all the generations.

---

1. For the story of Claudel's relationship with Max Reinhardt, the famous theatrical producer, see pp. 211-12 of Milhaud's autobiography.

A life, a work, a destiny, the most sublime that can be, that of the inventor of a new world and the welder of God's earth, is unfolded on the stage, and the reactions and emotions provoked in us by that spectacle do not remain unexpressed. By turns murmuring applause and issuing a challenge, the public follows all the incidents of the drama—that anonymous power which we call Opinion, the opinion of which the press today has become the mouthpiece, the opinion of posterity which supports, espouses, opposes, or reinforces the opinion of Columbus's contemporaries.

In such a drama music plays an entirely different part from what is previously played down in front of the stage. It is no longer a simple resonator; it does not merely accompany a song; it is a true actor, a collective person with diverse voices, whose voices are reunited in a harmony, the function of which is to bring together all the rest and to disengage little by little, under the inspiration of a growing enthusiasm, the elements of the final hymn.

Pascal has very justly said: "Prolonged eloquence is tedious." I am inclined to modify his thought thus: "Prolonged music, prolonged poetry are tedious." The soul is not all the time in the same state of tension, and this applies to the spectators as well as to the actors on the stage. It needs, now and then, to come down to earth, if only to find a new base from which to spring again. For the author, and with him the spectators, it is advantageous to do as the wine-tasters do in France, who, at intervals, suck a piece of lemon to wash out their mouths and so be better prepared to appreciate the next sip of nectar. A drama thus understood is not a monotonous flight amidst the uninterrupted purring of the orchestra or the versification. It is a series of outbursts and abatements.

I mentioned Wagner earlier in this article. The glory of that great man was his understanding that all things which partake of sound, from speech to song, are bound together by subtle links reaching across different realms, and that music is inherent in whatever is realized in time, whether it merely imposes rhythm upon those realizations or gradually colors them with various tones and raises them at last to the full expression of the orchestra and of the song. His only mistake was in not establishing degrees between reality and the lyrical state, and by this impoverished his palette of sounds and narrowed the scope of his flight. With him we do not penetrate little by little a conquered or deserved world; we are placed at the outset, through an enchanted blending of tones and the incantation of the brasses, in a narcotic atmosphere in which everything happens as in a dream.

Milhaud and I, on the other hand, have tried to show how the soul gradually reaches music, how the sentence springs up from rhythm, the flame from fire, melody from speech, poetry from the coarsest reality, and how all the means of sonorous expression, from discourse, dialogue, and debate, sustained by simple beatings of the drum, up to an eruption of all the vocal, lyrical, orchestral riches, are gathered in a single torrent at once varied and uninterrupted. In a word, we wanted to show music not only in the state of full realization, as a cryptic language portioned out among the pages of a score, but in the nascent state, rising and overflowing from some violent feeling.

Christopher Columbus is seen dying in the Valladolid inn, whither he has crawled to ask the King for the means to sail once more. And at that moment, as all his past on the point of reaching its final issue reappears before his eyes, the hero, so to speak, divides into two and becomes for us both spectator and judge of his own epic. Scene follows scene. We see the line of the horizon toward the West! The dove, image of the Holy Ghost, crosses the sea and comes to Genoa, bringing to the hands of a child its fluttering message. The sailor at the Azores receives intercepted revelations from beyond the Ocean and from beyond the Tomb. Genius strives against creditors and courtiers, against the envious and the skeptic. The captain quells rebellion. And then comes the hour of the Passion: the censure and bickering of petty minds; the Discoverer of the Globe lashed by a cook to the mast of his ship and buffeted by the rage of men and the fury of the elements; the prodigious ingratitude of the whole world, one woman excepted. Death approaches and, finally, the dove, that, as in the days of the Flood, escapes and bears a branch plucked from the newly risen world to the bosom of the Pantocrator [Christ].

All this is not performed in the void. Every voice, every word, every act, every event calls for an echo, an answer. They bring about and diffuse a kind of collective, anonymous roaring as of a sea of generations following one another, looking on and listening.

This I have called the Chorus. It is not the Chorus of the ancient drama—that troop of commentators and self-appointed advisers that no protagonist, if he were ever so little eloquent, had any difficulty in enlisting on the Mediterranean quays. It is, rather, the Chorus which the Church, after the triumph of Christianity, invited to enter the sacred edifice to become an intermediary between the priest and the people, the one *officiating*, the other *official*. Between the speechless crowd and the drama developing on the stage—and, if I may say so, on the altar —there was needed an officially constituted interpreter. . . .

Christopher Columbus, as it was given in Berlin and may be given some day in America, may be interesting also because of another novelty. This novelty originated from a desire to have no walls and for eyes or for ears to submit to no ready-made stage spectacle, so that instead we might evoke for ourselves our own music and scenery and paint its ever-changing surges on the panels of the magic box in which we are confined for an instant. In a musical drama whose characteristic is the transformation, under the action of time, of disconnected events into one melodic line, why should we admit immobile scenery? Why not let the images suggested by poetry and sound be exhaled like smoke and be caught for a moment on the screen, gradually to disappear and give place to other visions? Why, in a word, not make us of the cinema?

Reprinted from the *Yale Review*, XX (1930), by permission of the editors. Copyright Yale University Press.

KURT WEILL (1900-50)

KURT WEILL, the musical collaborator of Bertolt Brecht in the latter's pre-Communist phase, has been called "the poor man's Verdi" because of his concerted attempt to reform opera by making it into a popular, modernized version of the *Singspiel—*

the antithesis of Wagner's through-composed *Gesamtkunstwerk*. Weill, who was a student of Busoni from 1921 to 1924, started his career as a writer of serious orchestral, vocal, and chamber music. His first opera, *Der Protagonist*, was performed in 1926. Its libretto, like those of *Der Zar lässt sich photographieren* (1928) and *Der Silbersee* (1933), stems from the pen of Germany's leading Expressionist playwright, Georg Kaiser.

In 1927 Brecht and Weill embarked on the first of a series of projects for the musical stage that extended until their emigration immediately after Hitler's rise to power. The original *Singspiel* version of *Mahagonny* was staged at the Baden-Baden music festival in the summer of that year. It was followed by the smash hit of the *Dreigroschenoper* (1928), the less successful *Happy End* and the expanded, operatic version of *Mahagonny* (both premiered in 1929). Weill also wrote the music for Brecht's radio cantata *Lindberghflug*, his school opera *Der Jasager*, and the ballet *Die sieben Todsünden des Kleinbürgers*.

After settling in America in 1935 Weill became strongly interested in the musical and collaborated with the playwright Maxwell Anderson in the creation of several works of that type. The first great success in the medium came with his version of Elmer Rice's *Street Scene* (1947). Subsequently Weill composed the folk opera *Down in the Valley* and the musical drama *Lost in the Stars* (after Alan Paton's novel *Cry the Beloved Country*). His role in the development of the *Zeitoper* (modernistic opera) was considerable; and his influence can be felt in many European and American works belonging to that genre.

<hr>

John Willett, *The Theatre of Bertolt Brecht* (New York: New Directions, 1959), pp. 131-137.

On the Composition
of the *Dreigroschenoper* (1929)
KURT WEILL

ACTUALLY, the success of our piece proves not only that, artistically speaking, we chose the proper moment for the creation and promulgation of the new genre, but also that the public seemed to expect a rejuvenation of this popular type of theater. I do not know whether our genre is going to replace that of the operetta. After all, there is no reason why, after Goethe's return to earth in the form of an operetta tenor, other historical characters or, at least, members of the nobility should not also have their tragic moment at the end of the second act. This matter will take care of itself, and I don't believe that there will be a gap that is worth while filling. More important for all of us is the fact that, for the first time, an inroad has been made into the entertainment industry, which was hitherto reserved for a completely different type of writer and composer. With the *Dreigroschenoper* we reach a public which either did not know us at all or thought us incapable of captivating listeners whose number far exceeds the size of concert hall and operatic audiences.

Seen from this point of view, the *Dreigroschenoper* is part of a movement which affects almost all of our young musicians. The renunciation of the *l'art pour l'art* principle, the rejection of individualism in matters artistic, the present concern with music for the cinema, the newly established connection with the movement sponsoring music for young people, and the simplification of the musical means of expression which results from all this, are all steps in one direction.

Opera alone persists in its splendid isolation. The operatic audience still constitutes a coherent group of people who seem to exist apart from the average theater fans. *Opera* and *theater* are still regarded as two completely different phenomena. Dramaturgically as well as in the use of language and choice of subject matter, modern opera remains totally anachronistic. How frequently one hears it said: "This may be possible in the theater, but not in opera." Opera was founded as an aristocratic form of art, and all operatic conventions serve to emphasize the sociological nature of the genre. But no other such genre is now in existence; and the theater in particular is bent on reshaping society. If the framework of opera is unable to withstand the impact of the age, then this framework must be destroyed.

The above reasons cogently explain why, basically, the nature of all recent operatic experiments was destructive. In the *Dreigroschenoper*, reconstruction was possible insofar as here we had a chance of starting from scratch. We wanted, most of all, to restore the primitive form of opera. Every new work for the musical stage raises the question: how is it possible that music and, especially, song can be used in the theater? We solved the problem in the most primitive manner possible. I was faced with a realistic action and had to use music in opposition to it, since I do not think that music can achieve realistic effects. Thus we either interrupted the action in order to introduce music or deliberately led it to a point where singing became necessary. Add to this that the piece gave us an opportunity to treat opera as the principal theme of a dramatic presentation. At the very beginning of the play, the audience is told: "Tonight you will see an opera for beggars. Since this opera was to be as sumptuous as beggars alone can conceive of, and since it was to be cheap enough for beggars to afford, it is called the *Dreigroschenoper*." The last finale, accordingly, is by no means a parody, since here the concept of opera forms an inherent part of the action and had to be dealt with in the purest and simplest manner.

This return to a primitive form of opera entailed a drastic simplification of the musical language. I had to write music that could be sung by actors, i.e., laymen. But what originally seemed to be a limitation, soon turned out to be a real blessing. For the creation of a new type of musical theater, such as we have in the *Dreigroschenoper*, became possible only through the use of easily grasped and identifiable melodies.

Translated by Ulrich Weisstein from *Bertolt Brechts Dreigroschenbuch* (Frankfurt: Suhrkamp, 1960), by permission of Lotte Lenya-Weill-Davis.

BERTOLT BRECHT (1898-1956)

THE MOST INFLUENTIAL and controversial German playwright of the twentieth century, Bertolt Brecht first gained prominence with his Expressionist drama *Trommeln in der Nacht*, for which he received the Kleist Prize in 1922. It was followed by a host of *Lehrstücke*, radio plays, operas, and *Schulopern*. Brecht's international reputation dates from the Berlin première of the *Dreigroschenoper* (1928), his modern version of John Gay's *Beggar's Opera*. However, it was in exile that he made his greatest contribution to dramatic literature. *Galileo, Mutter Courage, Der gute Mensch von Sezuan,* and *Der kaukasische Kreidekreis* were all written between 1937 and 1945.

As a theatrical reformer Brecht sought to establish a non-Aristotelian poetics. The keyword of this new dramaturgy was *Verfremdung* (alienation), a term that implies both the detachment of the audience from the drama and the separation of the dramatic ingredients from each other (Epic principle). Brecht went so far as to suggest that from time to time the actor should step out of his role in order to make any identification between himself and his role impossible. The performance of a play, that is, was no longer to give the illusion of reality. In the field of opera Brecht relentlessly battled the Wagnerian concept of the *Gesamtkunstwerk* and demanded that the music should liberate itself as much as possible from the drama. The theory of Epic Opera, touched upon in the notes to the *Dreigroschenoper,* was fully developed in those appended to *Mahagonny.* Brecht's chief musical collaborators were Kurt Weill, the composer of the *Dreigroschenoper, Happy End,* and *Mahagonny;* Hanns Eisler; and Paul Dessau. Paul Hindemith collaborated in the radio cantata *Lindberghflug* and the *BadenerLehrstück vom Einverständnis.*

John Willett, *The Theatre of Bertolt Brecht* (New York: New Directions, 1958), pp. 126-143; U. Weisstein, "Cocteau, Stravinsky, Brecht, and the Birth of Epic Opera," *Modern Drama,* V (1962), 132-143.

Notes to the *Dreigroschenoper* (1931)
BERTOLT BRECHT

WHEN SINGING, the actor effects a change of function. Nothing is more appalling than for the actor to behave as if he didn't notice that he had just left the level of ordinary speech and was already singing. The three levels—ordinary speech, heightened speech, and singing—must always be separated from each other; and on no account must heightened speech denote an intensification of ordinary speech, and singing an intensification of heightened speech. Under no circumstances, that is to say, does song make its appearance where words fail due to an excess of feeling. The actor must not only sing but must also demonstrate that he is singing. His main concern is not so much to express the feelings expressed in his song (can one offer to others food one has already eaten?) as to produce gestures which, in a manner of speaking, are the customs and habits of the body. To this end it is preferable for him, in learning his part, not to use the actual words of the text but common, vulgar turns of speech which convey a similar meaning but in everyday language. As for the melody, he must not follow it blindly: there is a manner of speaking against the melody that can be very effective on account of a stubborn, incorruptible matter-of-factness that is independent of both music and rhythm. When he rejoins the melody, this must be an event the significance of which the actor may underscore by openly betraying how much he enjoys it. It is good for the actor if the musicians are in evidence while he sings and if he is permitted to make visible preparations for his act (by moving a chair or putting on make-up). In singing especially it is important that the manifestor be manifest.

Reprinted from Eric Bentley's translation in *From the Modern Repertoire*, Series One (Denver: University of Denver Press, 1949), by permission.

The Modern Theatre is the Epic Theatre
(Notes to the opera *Aufstieg und Fall der Stadt Mahagonny*)
BERTOLT BRECHT

Opera—With Innovations

For some time past there has been a move to renovate the opera. Opera is to have its form modernized and its content brought up to date, but without its culinary character being changed. Since it is precisely for its backwardness that the opera-going public adores opera, an influx of new types of listener with new appetites has to be reckoned with; and so it is. The intention is to democratize but not to alter democracy's character, which consists in giving the people new rights, but no chance to avail themselves of them. Ultimately it is all the same to the waiter whom he serves, so long as he serves the food. Thus the *avant-garde* are demanding or supporting innovations, which are to lead to a renovation of opera; but nobody demands a fundamental discussion of opera (i.e., of its function), and probably such a discussion would not find much support.

The modesty of the *avant-garde's* demands has economic grounds of whose existence they themselves are only partly aware. Large institutions like the opera, the stage, the press, etc., impose their views as it were incognito. For a long time now they have taken the handiwork (music, poetry, criticism, etc.) of intellectuals who share in their profits—that is, of men who are economically committed to the prevailing system but are socially near-proletarian—and processed it to make fodder for the public entertainment machine, judging it by their own standards and guiding it into their own channels. Meanwhile the intellectuals themselves have gone on supposing that the whole business is concerned only with the presentation of their work, is a secondary process which has no influence on their work but merely wins influence for it. This muddled thinking which overtakes musicians, writers and critics as soon as they consider their own situation has tremendous consequences to which far too little attention is paid. For by imagining that they have got hold of an apparatus which in fact has got hold of them they are supporting an apparatus which is out of their control, which is no longer (as they believe) a means of furthering output but has become an obstacle to output, and specifically to their own output as soon as it follows a new and original course which the apparatus finds unsuitable or opposed to its own aims. Their output then becomes a matter of delivering the goods. Values evolve which are based on the fodder principle. And this leads to a general habit of judging works of art by their suitability for the apparatus without ever judging the apparatus by its suitability for the work. People say, this or that is a good work; and they mean (but do not say) good for the apparatus. Yet this apparatus is conditioned by the existing society and only admits what keeps it in that society. We are free to discuss any innovation which doesn't threaten the social function of this apparatus—that of providing an evening's entertainment. We are not free to discuss those which threaten to change its function, which assign to it a different role in society by connecting it with the educational system or the organs of mass communication. Society absorbs via the apparatus whatever it needs in order to reproduce itself. This means that an innovation will pass only if it leads to the rejuvenation of existing society, but not if it is designed to change it—irrespective of whether the form of the society in question is good or bad.

The *avant-garde* don't think of changing the apparatus, because they fancy that they have at their disposal an apparatus which will serve up whatever they freely invent, transforming itself with each of their ideas. But they are actually not free inventors. The apparatus fulfills its function with or without them; the theatres play every night; the papers appear so many times a day and absorb what they need. All they need, however, is a certain amount of material.[1]

You might think that to reveal this situation (the creative artist's utter dependence on the apparatus) would be equal to condemning it. It is so modestly hidden.

And yet to restrict the individual freedom of invention is in itself a progressive act. The individual becomes increasingly drawn into events that transform the world. No longer can he simply "express" himself. He is urged and enabled to solve problems of more general interest. The trouble, however, is that at present the apparatuses do not yet work for the general good, that the means of production do not belong to the producers, and that, as a result, the works take on the character of merchandise and are governed by the laws of mercantile trade. Art is merchandise, not to be manufactured without means of production (apparatuses). An opera can only be written for the Opera. (One can't just think up an opera like one of Böcklin's sea monsters, then hope to exhibit it publicly after having seized power—let alone try to smuggle it into our dear old zoo. . . .) Even if one wanted to discuss the opera as such (i.e., its function), one would have to write an opera.

Opera

The existing opera is a culinary opera. It was a source of pleasure long before it turned into merchandise. It serves pleasure even where it requires, or promotes, education, for the education in question is one of taste. It approaches every object

---

1. The creative artists, however, are completely dependent on the apparatus, both socially and economically; it is the only channel for the realization of their work. The output of writers, composers and critics comes more and more to resemble raw material. The finished article is produced by the apparatus.

hedonistically. It "experiences" and serves as an "experience."

Why is *Mahagonny* an opera? Because its basic attitude is that of opera: that is to say, culinary. Does *Mahagonny* adopt a hedonistic approach? It does. Is *Mahagonny* an experience? It is. For *Mahagonny* is a piece of fun.

The opera *Mahagonny* pays conscious tribute to the absurdity of the operatic form. The absurdity of opera lies in the fact that rational elements are used and three-dimensional reality is aimed at while at the same time everything is neutralized by the music. A dying man is real. If he sings at the same time, we have reached the sphere of absurdity. (If the audience sang at the sight of him, this would not be the case.) The more confused and unreal reality is rendered—a third, very complex and in itself quite real element comes into being, which may have quite real effects but is utterly remote from the reality it treats—the more pleasurable the whole process becomes: the pleasure grows in proportion to the degree of unreality.

The term "opera"—far be it from us to profane it—leads, in the case of *Mahagonny*, to everything else. The intention was to make something absurd, unreal and flippant annul itself when properly placed.[2] The absurd which here appears fits the place in which it appears. Such an attitude is purely hedonistic.

As for the content of this opera, *it is pleasure*. Fun, that is to say, not only as form but as subject matter. Enjoyment, at least, should be the object of the inquiry if the inquiry is to be an object of enjoyment, which here appears in its current historical role: as merchandise.[3]

It is undeniable that, at first, this content will be provocative. In the thirteenth section of *Mahagonny*, for example, where the

2. This narrow limit would not keep one from introducing directly a didactic element, and from basing everything on the *Gestus*. The eye which looks for the *Gestus* in everything is the moral sense. In other words, a moral tableau, but a subjective one.

> *Jetzt trinken wir noch eins*
> *Dann gehen wir noch nicht nach Hause*
> *Dann trinken wir noch eins*
> *Dann machen wir mal eine Pause.*

The people who sing this are subjective moralists. They describe themselves.

3. Romanticism here is also merchandise; but it appears as content, not as form.

glutton stuffs himself to death, he does so because there is a famine. Although we do not even hint that others were going hungry while he stuffed, the effect was provocative all the same. For while not everyone who is in a position to stuff himself dies of overeating, many are dying of hunger because he stuffs himself to death. His pleasure provokes because it implies so much.[4]

In similar contexts, opera as a means of pleasure has provocative effects today, though not, of course, on the handful of opera goers. The provocative element reinstates reality. *Mahagonny* may not taste particularly agreeable. It may even (thanks to guilty conscience) endeavor not to be so. Yet it is culinary through and through. *Mahagonny* is nothing but an opera.

With Innovations

Opera had to be brought up to the technical level of the modern theatre. The modern theatre is the epic theatre. The following table demonstrates certain shifts of emphasis from the dramatic to the epic theatre:[5]

Dramatic Theatre	*Epic Theatre*
plot	narrative
involves the spectator in an action on stage	turns the spectator into an observer, but
wears down his capacity for action	arouses his capacity for action
provides him with sensations	forces him to make decisions
experience	world view
the spectator empathizes with something	he faces something
suggestion	argument
feelings are preserved	brought to the point of cognition
the spectator is in the thick of it, shares the experience	the spectator stands outside, studies
the human being is regarded as a known quantity	the human being is the object of the inquiry

---

4. "A dignified gentleman with an empurpled face had fished out a bunch of keys and was making a piercing demonstration against the Epic Theatre. His wife didn't desert him in this decisive moment. She had stuck two fingers in her mouth, screwed up her eyes and blown out her cheeks. Her whistle was louder than the key" (Alfred Polgar on the first production of *Mahagonny* in Leipzig).

5. This table does not show absolute antitheses but mere shifts of accent. In a communication of facts, for instance, we may choose to stress the emotional or the rational element.

Dramatic Theatre (continued)	*Epic Theatre (continued)*
he is unalterable	he is alterable and able to alter
eyes on the conclusion	eyes on the course of action
one scene makes another	each scene for itself
growth	montage
linear development	in curves
evolutionary determinism	leaps
man as a fixed point	man as a process
thought determines being	social being determines thought
feeling	reason

The intrusion of the methods of the epic theatre in opera leads mainly to a *radical separation of the elements*. The great struggle for supremacy between words, music and action (which always brings up the question "which is the pretext for what?": is the music the pretext for the events on stage, or are these the pretext for the music? etc.) can be resolved by the radical separation of the elements. So long as "Gesamtkunstwerk" means that the integration is a muddle, so long as the arts are to be fused together, the various elements will be equally degraded, and each will act as a mere "feed" for the rest. The process of fusion extends to the spectator, who is also fused and becomes a passive (suffering) part of the "Gesamtkunstwerk." Such magic must, of course, be fought against. Whatever is intended to produce hypnotic effects, sordid intoxication or confusion, has to be abolished.

Music, Words and Setting Had to Acquire More Independence.

a) *Music*

For the music, the change of emphasis proved to be as follows:

Dramatic Opera	*Epic Opera*
the music dishes up	the music mediates
music which heightens the text	music which interprets the text
music which proclaims the text	music which presupposes the text
music which illustrates	music which conveys a point of view
music which paints the psychological situation	which depicts an attitude

Music is the most important contribution to the theme.[6]

---

6. The large number of craftsmen in the opera orchestras allows of nothing but associative music (one barrage of sound breeding another); and so the orchestral apparatus needs to be cut down to thirty specialists or less. The singer becomes a reporter, whose private feelings must remain his private business.

b) *Text*

In order that it should not be merely absurd, we had to invest our joke with the didactic. The form employed was that of the moral tableau. The tableau is constituted by the characters in the play. The text was to be neither sentimental nor moralizing but was to exhibit morals and sentimentality. In the titles, the written word became as important as the spoken one. Reading seems to encourage the audience to adopt the most natural attitude toward the work.

c) *Setting*

Showing independent works of art as part of a theatrical performance is a novelty. Neher's projections comment on the events on stage; as when the real glutton sits in front of the painted glutton. In the same way the stage unreels the events that are fixed on the screen. Neher's projections are quite as independent a component of the opera as are Weill's music and the text. They are its visual aids.

Of course such innovations also presuppose a new attitude on the part of the audience frequenting the opera houses.

Effect of the Innovations: A Threat to Opera?

Undoubtedly, certain wishes of the audience, which the old opera easily satisfied, are no longer taken into account by the new. What is the audience's attitude toward opera, and is there any chance that it will change?

Bursting out of the subway stations, eager to become wax in the magicians' hands, grown-up men, their resolution proved in the struggle for existence, rush to the box office. At the cloakroom they leave their hats and, with them, their normal behavior, the attitudes of "everyday life." Leaving the cloakroom, they take their seats with the bearing of kings. How can we blame them? You may think a grocer's bearing better than a king's and still find this ridiculous. For the attitude that these people adopt in the opera is unworthy of them. Is there any possibility that they may change it? Can we persuade them to take out their cigars?

Once the content becomes, technically speaking, an independent component toward which text, music and setting "take an attitude"; once illusion is sacrificed for the sake of discussion; and once the spectator, instead of being urged to have an experience, is forced to cast his vote, a change has been initiated which goes far beyond matters of form and which, for the first time, affects the social function of the theatre.

The old opera categorically excludes any discussion of its content. If a member of the audience, during the representation of certain situations, happened to voice his opinion about them, the old opera would have lost its battle: the "spell would have been broken." Even the old opera, of course, contained elements which were not purely culinary. One has to distinguish between the period of its development and that of its decline. *The Magic Flute, Figaro, Fidelio* contained activistic, political elements. But the political element, a kind of daring, in these operas was so subordinated to the culinary principle that the meaning was actually decaying and subsequently absorbed in pleasure. Once its proper meaning had died away, the opera was by no means left bereft of sense, but had simply acquired another one, that of opera. Content was gone from the opera. Our modern Wagnerites are satisfied with remembering that the original Wagnerians had posited a meaning familiar to them. Those composers who stem from Wagner still insist on posing as philosophers. Their philosophy, being of no other use, can only be disposed of as a means of sensual gratification. *(Elektra, Jonny spielt auf)*. We still retain the whole highly developed technique which made this attitude possible: the *petit bourgeois* strikes a philosophical pose throughout his petty everyday existence. It is only from this point, from the death of meaning (which implies that this meaning could die), that the continual innovations which are inflicted on opera are understandable: as desperate attempts to invest this art with a posthumous meaning, a new meaning, the result being usually that the meaning comes ultimately to lie in the music itself. The sequence of musical forms, for example, acquires a sense simply *qua* sequence, and certain proportions, shifts, etc., turn from a means into an end. This progress has neither cause nor effect, which does not spring from new requirements but satisfies the old ones with new titillations, thus furthering a purely conservative aim. New material, which is unfamiliar in this context—since when this context was evolved it was not known in any context at all—is absorbed. (Train engines, factories, airplanes, bathrooms, etc., act as a diversion. The better composers choose instead to deny all content by presenting—or rather smothering—it in the Latin tongue.) This sort of progress only indicates that something has been left behind. It is achieved without change in the overall function; or rather with a view toward keeping any such change from taking place.

And what about *Gebrauchsmusik?* At the very moment when starkest Art for Art's sake took the field (it came as a reaction against the emotional element in musical Impressionism), the idea of utilitarian music, or *Gebrauchsmusik*, emerged like Venus from the waves. Here music was to make use of the amateur. The amateur was used as a woman is "used." Innovation upon innovation. The punch-drunk listener suddenly wanted to play. The struggle against idle listening turned into a struggle for keen listening, then for keen playing. The cellist in the orchestra, father of a numerous family, now began to play no longer for philosophical reasons but for pleasure. The culinary principle was saved.[7]

What is the point, we wonder, of chasing one's own tail like this? Why this obstinate clinging to pleasure and intoxication? Why so little concern with one's own affairs outside of one's own home? Why this refusal to discuss matters? Answer: nothing can come of discussion. To discuss the present form of society, or even one of its least important ingredients, would lead inevitably and at once to an outright threat to the form of this society as such.

We have seen that opera is sold as evening entertainment, and

---

7. Innovations of this kind must be criticized as long as they are helping to renovate institutions that have outlived their usefulness. They represent progress as soon as we set out to effect radical changes in the function of these institutions. Then they become quantitative improvements, purges, catharses which acquire meaning by the change in function which has been or is about to be made.

True progress consists not in having progressed but in progressing. True progress is what enables or compels us to progress. And that on a broad front so that the adjacent categories are also set in motion. True progress has its cause in the untenableness of an actual situation, and it results in a change of the latter.

that this places definite limits on all attempts to change it. We see that this entertainment has to be ceremonial and devoted to illusion. But why?

In our present society opera has its distinct place. Its illusions have an important social function. Intoxication is indispensable; and nothing can be put in its place.[8] Only in the opera does the human being have a chance to be human. All his mental capacities have long since been reduced to those of painful distrust, defraudation of others and selfish scheming.

The old opera survives not only because it is old but chiefly because the condition it serves is still the old one, although not entirely so. And here lies the hope for the new opera. Today we can begin to ask whether opera hasn't come to such a pass that further innovations, instead of leading to a reform of the genre, will bring about its destruction.[9]

Perhaps *Mahagonny* is as culinary as ever—just as culinary as an opera ought to be—but one of its functions is to change society. It brings the culinary principle under discussion and attacks the society that needs operas of this sort. It still perches happily on the old bough, but at least it has started (out of absent-mindedness or bad conscience) to saw it through. And that, with their singing, the innovations have done. Real innovations attack the roots.

For Innovations—Against Renovation

The opera *Mahagonny* was written two years ago, in 1928-29.

8. The life imposed on us is too hard; it brings us too many agonies, disappointments, impossible tasks. In order to be able to endure it, we have to have some kind of palliative. There seem to be three types of those: powerful distractions, which cause us to belittle our own sufferings, pseudo-satisfactions, which reduce it, and drugs which make us insensitive to them. The pseudo-satisfactions offered by art, if compared with reality, are illusions; but they are nevertheless effective, thanks to the part played by the imagination in our inner life (Freud, *Das Unbehagen in der Kultur*, page 22). Such drugs are sometimes responsible for the wastage of great stores of energy which might have been used for the improvement of the human lot (*ibid.*, page 28).

9. Such, in the opera *Mahagonny*, are those innovations which allow the theatre to present moral tableaux (revealing the commercial character both of the entertainment and the person entertained), and those which put the spectator in a moralizing frame of mind.

In subsequent works attempts were made to emphasize the didactic more and more at the expense of the culinary element and so to develop the luxury into an object of instruction by converting certain institutions from places of entertainment into organs of mass communication.

DIMITRI SHOSTAKOVICH (1906-   )

LIKE SERGEI PROKOFIEFF—whose *Love of the Three Oranges* (1919) comes close to being an operatic masterpiece—Dimitri Shostakovich, the present composer laureate of the Soviet Union, has repeatedly explored the possibilities of lyrical drama. A student of Glazunov at the Leningrad Conservatory, he composed the first of his symphonies in 1925; it clearly betrays the influence of Paul Hindemith. Shostakovich, whose technical mastery is unchallenged, remains essentially a composer within the tradition. Three times he turned to classical Russian literature as the basis of his compositions for the stage. *The Nose* (1928) harks back to Gogol's famous story, as does the unfinished *The Players;* and *Lady Macbeth of Mtzensk* (1932) is based on Nikolay Leskov's novel by that name. Shostakovich's melo-dramaturgy is quite conventional. He writes primarily for the voice but uses the orchestra symphonically, thereby producing a kind of through-composed opera. In *Lady Macbeth*, a dramaturgic dilemma results from the composer's need to make his heroine sympathetic and yet to treat the subject "from our modern point of view," i.e. from the point of view of social realism.

Shostakovich, who, apart from his symphonies, is mainly known for his chamber music and his ballet and film scores, has also re-orchestrated Mussorgsky's *Boris Godunov.*

V. I. Serov, *Dmitri Shostakovich: The Life and Background of a Soviet Composer* (New York: Knopf, 1943); I. Martinov, *Dmitri Shostakovich: The Man and His Work* (New York: Philosophical Library).

My Opera *Lady Macbeth of Mtzensk* (1934)
DIMITRI SHOSTAKOVICH

I BEGAN TO WRITE the opera *Lady Macbeth of Mtzensk* at the end of 1930 and completed it in December of 1932. Why did I select just this novel by Nikolai Leskov for its subject?

First, because very little of our heritage in Russian classic literature had been utilized in the development of Soviet opera. Second—and this was most important—because Leskov's narrative is imbued with rich dramatic and social content. There is, perhaps, no other creation in all Russian literature which so vividly portrays the position of women in old, pre-revolutionary Russia.

But I have given *Lady Macbeth of Mtzensk* a different treatment from that of Leskov. As will be seen from the title itself, the novelist approached his subject ironically. The name indicates an insignificant territory, a small district; and the characters are little people, with passions and interests not comparable to those in Shakespeare's play. Moreover, Leskov, an outstanding representative of pre-revolutionary literature, gives us no illuminating interpretation of the incidents which are developed in his story. As a Soviet composer, I determined to preserve the strength of Leskov's novel, and yet approaching it critically, to interpret its events from our modern point of view.

Accordingly, the subject itself has been somewhat altered. In Leskov's novel, Ekaterina Lvovna Izmailova, the heroine, commits three murders before she is sentenced to hard labor in Siberia. She kills her father-in-law, her husband, and her nephew. As I proposed to justify the action of Ekaterina Lvovna and create an impression of a definite personality, deserving of sympathy, I omitted the third murder, undertaken solely to make herself the heir of her slain husband.

Now to arouse sympathy for Ekaterina was no simple matter. She has committed a number of crimes against accepted moral or ethical laws. Leskov presents her simply as a cruel woman who "wallows in fat" and murders innocent people. But I have conceived Ekaterina as a woman clever, gifted, and interesting.

Set by fate in gloomy, miserable surroundings, belonging to a merchant class which is hard, greedy, and "small," her life is sorrowful and pitiable. She does not love her husband, she has no happiness, no recreation. There now appears Sergei, a clerk hired by her husband, Zinovy Borisovich. She falls in love with this young man, an unworthy and negative creature, and in her love she finds joy and the purpose of her existence. In order to marry Sergei she commits her series of crimes. When Boris Timofevich, her father-in-law, catches Sergei after a meeting with her and orders him to be lashed, she is inspired by a desire for revenge. She poisons her father-in-law for the sufferings inflicted upon her lover. Sergei now urges her to marry him, and, together with Ekaterina, he strangles her husband. Thus, in her love for Sergei, Ekaterina sacrifices all of herself. On the discovery of the crimes they are sentenced together to Siberia "at hard labor." When she finds that he no longer loves her and has turned to the prostitute Sonetka, she drowns her rival and herself. With Sergei's love, life has lost its only interest.

It is unnecessary for me to relate the action further. For I have justified it chiefly by the musical material. It is my belief that in opera music should play the principal and the deciding role.

I have tried to make the music of the opera as simple and expressive as possible. I do not agree with the theories, at one time current among us, that in the modern opera the vocal line must be absent, or that it should be no more than speech in which the intonations are accented. Opera is above all a vocal production and singers should occupy themselves with their real duty—that is, to sing, and not to speak, recite, or intone. Thus I have built all the vocal parts on a broad *cantilena* taking into account all the possibilities of that richest of instruments, the human voice.

The musical development progresses constantly and on a symphonic form; in this respect I have abandoned the old operatic formula of construction on individual parts. The musical stream flows unbroken and is interrupted solely by the ending of each act; it resumes its course in the following one, not piece-wise, but by developing further on a grand symphonic scale. This must be taken into consideration during the production of the opera, as in each act, except the fourth, there are several scenes and these scenes are separated not by mechanical pauses but by musical entr'actes during which the change of scenery take place. The entr'actes between the second and third, fourth and fifth, sixth and seventh, and between the seventh and eighth scenes are merely the continuation and further development of preceding musical ideas and play a great part in the characterization of what takes place on the stage.

And now a few words in regard to the principal personages and their musical characterization. The most important is, of course, Ekaterina, a dramatic soprano. Her musical language is shaped completely by my idea that she must by every means evoke sympathy. In her music there are a tender and warm lyricism, a sincere, profound sorrow in suffering, and also joy in moments of happiness. The musical language given to Ekaterina Lvovna has been designed for the one purpose of justifying this "criminal." To quote the famous words of Dobroliubov[1] about Leskov's character, she is "a ray of light in a kingdom of gloom."

The suffering folk of that epoch are presented in the fourth act—"at hard labor." There is no darker picture of the old days than that of the halting place of convicts, of broken people moving under guard through the far off expanses of the former Russian empire, to penal servitude. How unforgettable is the picture drawn by Dostoievsky in his *Memoirs of the House of the Dead:* the little girl who gave him, a convict "at hard labor," a kopeck and the peasants in the villages who sacrificed their bread to the unfortunates. Such reactions I intended to arouse for the prisoners in the fourth act of my opera.

All the remaining members of the cast—Boris Timofevich, Zinovy Borisovich, Sergei, etc.—are but expressions of the dismal and hopeless existence of the merchant class of that period. Izmailov's clerks are potentially the same future merchants as the Izmailovs, they cheat and short-change so that in time they themselves may open their own little shops and become real merchants. These characters I have endowed with negative traits.

Sergei, the clerk, is the evil genius who turns up in Ekaterina

---

1. Nicolai Dobroliubov (1836-61), famous Russian critic, is best known for his essay on Gontcharov's novel *Oblomov.*

Lvovna's hard life. He is a small scoundrel whose aim in life is to attain security and, as he says, "to satiate himself with woman's sweet flesh." Because of him Ekaterina murders her father-in-law and her husband. When she is no longer a rich merchant's wife, but a common convict, without a moment's thought he throws her aside and finds a new woman. He has picked up a little culture, reads books, and expresses himself in high-sounding language; his outlook upon the world is servile and mean.

Thus for Sergei the music is insincere, showy, theatrical; his sufferings are affected; through his handsome, gallant exterior peers the future kulak. He is a Don Juan, not in the sense of the famous legend, but a cruel, cunning criminal. Even in Siberia "at hard labor" he still remains a "small" coarse person.

Boris Timofevich, Ekaterina's father-in-law, is a solid and powerful old man, who stops at nothing to gain his desires. His son, Zinovy Borisovich, Ekaterina's husband, is a pitiable wretch, the "frog that longed to be an ox." When he tries to speak authoritatively as the master in his home, the music exposes him and we see a weak, pathetic specimen of the merchant class.

The task of the singers in these roles is both difficult and exacting, they must act as well as they sing to "carry" the opera to the audience. A great role is played by the chorus, which is one of the most active elements in the opera; its movement must be genuine and convincing.

A final word in regard to the general musical character of the opera. As previously stated, it is written from first to last note upon a symphonic form; the orchestra must therefore never be reduced to a mere accompaniment. On the other hand it must not be elevated to such a position that it will distract from and stifle the action on the stage.

Reprinted from *Modern Music*, XII (1934), by permission of the League of Composers of the International Society of Contemporary Music.

ERNST KRENEK (1900-   )

BORN IN VIENNA, Ernst Krenek at the age of sixteen became a pupil of the then highly regarded composer Franz Schreker, author of such now completely forgotten operas as *Der ferne*

Klang. In 1920 he followed his master to Berlin but parted ways with him to turn his attention to modernistic opera. *Zwingburg* and *Der Sprung über den Schatten* were both performed in 1924. The premiere of *Orpheus und Eurydike*, based on Oskar Kokoschka's Expressionistic play, occurred during Krenek's tenure as musical assistant at the opera houses of Kassel and Wiesbaden between 1925 and 1927. Krenek's most famous *Zeitoper*, the jazz opera *Jonny spielt auf*, was first heard in Leipzig on February 10, 1927. It antedates Brecht/Weill's *Dreigroschenoper* by more than a year. In 1928 the composer moved to Vienna, where he was increasingly influenced by Arnold Schönberg and his method of composition with twelve tones, a method he himself embraced in his opera *Karl V*. "The New Music and Today's Theater" was written in conjunction with this work, which was staged at Prague in 1938. Krenek calls *Karl V* an Epic Opera in the manner of Claudel/Milhaud's *Christophe Colomb* and stresses its inherent "tendency to divide the dramatic action between diverse simultaneous scenes and the device of an all-enclosing treatment." In 1938 Krenek emigrated to America, where he is presently living.

H. Rosenwald, "Ernst Krenek" in *The Book of Modern Composers* (New York: Knopf, 1942)

The New Music and Today's Theater (1937)
ERNST KRENEK

IF OPERA IS TO FOLLOW a new path, if it is to continue along the new direction developed in the last twenty years, it must take its bearings from the new, the really new music; that is to say, opera can find a really new path of its own by taking this new music for a guide.

The new music has attained a superlative degree of sincerity and truth by climactic power of expression, boldness and logical consistency of structure. At the same time it has been remarkably spiritualized by these characteristics and therefore stands directly opposed to the currents of the external world. In brief, it is the "atonal" music that Schönberg, his school, and a few other musicians practice and continue to develop in the face of outside opposition.

The twelve-tone technique is, as we know, a remarkably individual and ingenious artistic resource which this music has perfected. It has directed the creation of music into new channels and given it a new content. However, its meaning cannot be grasped if it is regarded only as an external procedure of craftsmanship which may be used with a whole series of other working methods in the same sense and to attain traditional ends.

Only a composer who makes the effort to build adequate creative designs, ideas, and form conceptions, out of the special characteristics of the twelve-tone technique or, more precisely, out of the great reservoir of ideas behind it, who willingly acknowledges the legitimacy of this technique, and makes the most strenuous intellectual effort to discover its innermost meaning, can hope, through its application, to find the way to new and individual forms.

This is not the place to develop a theory of the new music. I can only point to a certain peculiarity of form intrinsic in the essence of this music, and most significant in its application to dramatic ends. By their very nature the principles of the new music lead away from the closed form, and realize instead the idea of "fragments." This does not imply the production of artificial, incomplete structures. But those forms of the new music which are most complete in artistic development are "fragmentary," not only in size, but in structure. Their abruptness, lightness, transparency are reflected in the sonority, in the instrumentation with its simple superposing of tonal strata, with its pronounced accentuation of single colors and its lack of connective material and "filler."

Though abrupt and compressed into small areas over a few points, these forms have an abundant musical vitality; just as the fragment of an ancient statue often reveals the intense and secret life which might emanate from the work were it seen whole. If at times hearing such music leaves us unsatisfied and troubled, it is perhaps because we cannot entirely grasp it, perhaps because some inner instinct finds its unusual mixture of intensity and melancholy particularly appropriate.

Applied to drama, this music does not develop closed forms in the old sense, either. Intermittently it may be interrupted by the spoken word; it reappears, almost as if by chance; it dies away with no real ending. Illustrations of these principles appear in Alban Berg's *Wozzeck* and, more distinctly, in his *Lulu*. I have applied them in my opera *Karl V.*, where I have attempted to give the procedure an especially dramatic sense.

It is my belief that all artistic methods should be inherent in the thing itself, not attached as externals. In the old opera, interrupting the music by the spoken word served to emphasize the outline of the closed form. These interruptions in the new opera have quite a different function; they are real interruptions, preventing the development of the closed form. What is the vocal instance most clearly exercising such functions? It is the reflective question, and as a matter of fact, in *Karl V.*, the meaning of the drama depends on the occasional interruption of the historical accomplishments of the Emperor which serve to justify him, by questions of persons who analyze these deeds, who probe their political and religious implications. In this way, I have tried to continue along the road pointed out by Paul Claudel in his magnificent *Colomb*.

I believe that it is not by chance that my composition, which carries still further the idea of interrupting form by reflection, has a fundamental Catholic idea. The spiritual gains of the new music inspire a closer relationship with religious motives, quite apart from the fact that the latter provide especially strong inducements to dialectic and reflection.

A second formal characteristic arising from this ideology of the music drama is the tendency to divide the dramatic action between diverse simultaneous scenes and the device of an all-enclosing treatment. Reflection, an absolute anti-realistic force, always penetrates from an outer to an inner circle, which explains the practice of placing the circles within each other spiralwise and finally reducing them to a point quantitatively small, but of the greatest spiritual concentration. In *Christophe Colomb*, this reflection proceeds from a chorus representing posterity, the other world; while next to the stage, where the earlier life of the hero has been played, there is a film which introduces still another, a third level. In *Karl V.*, it is the people in attendance at the hero's deathbed who put the question and start the action on a second plane. The simultaneous scenes as well as the idea of an enclosing frame recall Calderón's dramatic technique and the old mystery plays. The urge for reflection, analysis, and commentary represents intellectual speculation just as much as it does the age-old, naïve hunger of man for truth. And since the new music presents the result of a ruthless critical appraisal of tradition, it is most apt and most powerful when applied to theatrical material which also represents the force of criticism.

It is therefore easy to understand why the new opera has frequently made use of historical subjects and will continue to do so. Shunning the old illusionistic conceptions of history, it searches out the true political significance of events, and develops the conflicts that are essential to dramatic construction.

Obviously the dramaturgical technique of such works has been influenced by the films. The straight use of motion pictures, as in *Colomb*, may perhaps not even be desirable, since films and realistic dramatic action do not blend easily. But the quick change of locale, the compressions of dialogue into a few decisive phrases, the epic course of the scenes, are all devices closely related to film technique.

It is no wonder that such an art should encounter special external difficulties. To the technical problems of the new music itself must be added the spiritual hazards met by every kind of truth. The new idea first of all meets the preconception that opera should be dedicated to non-serious subjects presented in agreeable form, that it is merely an arrangement of play, song, and dance that aims to please; whereas the new method would link opera with important ideas, transforming empty trifling into real achievements, with results commensurate with the heavy labor and expenses of preparation. For quite a long time to come, it will be the fate of many genuinely new operas to go unperformed. The most numerous and best prepared opera houses— the German—bar the development of this kind of work; the theaters of the rest of the world are neither technically nor spiritually equipped to solve such hazardous problems. Indeed the most important operas of our day lie in the drawers of their writers and publishers, to the loss of the whole art of the drama.

We can only hope that composers, by some miracle, will summon enough resistance to continue this new hopeless industry. At least a later age, surely deeming itself better than the present one, will be grateful to them.

Reprinted from *Modern Music*, XIV (1936/37). Copyright © 1937 by the League of Composers, Inc. Renewed 1965 by the League of Composers—ISCM U.S. Chapter, Inc. Reproduced by permission.

WYSTAN HUGH AUDEN (1907-)

WYSTAN HUGH AUDEN, the most influential poet of the English-speaking world since T. S. Eliot, has always been involved with music, especially since the days of the Group Theatre (in the late thirties) when he actively collaborated with the composer Benjamin Britten. Britten wrote incidental music to plays like *The Ascent of F. 6* and *On the Frontier* (both by Auden and Isherwood), set a number of Auden's lyrics to music, and composed an operetta *(Paul Bunyan)* as well as a radio play *(Hadrian's Wall)* to texts furnished by his older contemporary. More recently, the author of *The Age of Anxiety* (1947), a collection of poetry whose very title evokes the spirit of our times, has contributed to operatic literature by preparing the libretto for Igor Stravinsky's *The Rake's Progress* (1951) and by translating Schikaneder's book of Mozart's *Zauberflöte* (both with the help of Chester Kallman). In addition, Auden and Kallman have given us an English version of Brecht's ballet cantata *Die sieben Todsünden*.

In a rejoinder to an English critic, who had taken exception to his views on opera, Auden reiterated that these views were based on the following principles: 1) "that opera is an art form of great value," 2) "that the primary element in opera is vocal," 3) "that the libretti should not be entrusted to literary hacks," and 4) "that nothing, however musically or poetically valuable in itself, should be admitted in opera if it interferes with the singing."[1] Judging by the course of operatic history in the second half of the nineteenth and the first half of the twentieth century,

1. In *Opera, III* (1952), pp. 34-35.

Auden's melo-dramaturgy would seem to be somewhat old-fashioned. Even Mozart and Verdi would repudiate such statements as "In opera the orchestra is addressed to the singers, not to the audience" and "The verses which the librettist writes are not addressed to the public but are really a private letter to the composer." Nothing, certainly, could be more remote from the theory underlying the various guises of Epic Opera.

Some Reflections on Music and Opera (1952)
WYSTAN HUGH AUDEN

ALL OF US have learned to talk, most of us, even, could be taught to speak verse tolerably well, but very few have learned or could ever be taught to sing. In any village twenty people could get together and give a performance of *Hamlet* which, however imperfect, would convey enough of the play's greatness to be worth attending, but if they were to attempt a similar perform-ance of *Don Giovanni*, they would soon discover that there was no question of a good or a bad performance because they could not sing the notes at all. Of an actor, even in a poetic drama, when we say that his performance is good, we mean that he simulates by art, that is, consciously, the way in which the character he is playing would, in real life, behave by nature, that is, unconsciously. But for a singer, as for a ballet dancer, there is no question of simulation, of singing the composer's notes "naturally"; his behavior is unabashedly and triumphantly art from beginning to end. The paradox implicit in all drama, namely, that emotions and situations which in real life would be sad or painful are on the stage a source of pleasure becomes, in opera, quite explicit. The singer may be playing the role of a deserted bride who is about to kill herself, but we feel quite certain as we listen that not only we but also she is having a wonderful time. In a sense, there can be no tragic opera because whatever errors the characters make and whatever they suffer, they are doing exactly what they wish. Hence the feeling that *opera seria* should not employ a contemporary subject, but con-fine itself to mythical situations, that is, situations which as human beings we are all of us necessarily in and must, therefore, accept, however tragic they may be. A contemporary tragic situation like that in Menotti's *The Consul* is too actual, that is, too clearly a situation some people are in and others, including the audience, are not in, for the latter to forget this and see it as a symbol of, say, man's existential estrangement. Consequently the pleasure we and the singers are obviously enjoying strikes the conscience as frivolous.

On the other hand, its pure artifice renders opera the ideal dramatic medium for a tragic myth. I once went in the same week to a performance of *Tristan und Isolde* and a showing of *L'eternel retour*, Jean Cocteau's movie version of the same story. During the former two souls, weighing over two hundred pounds apiece, were transfigured by a transcendent power, in the latter a handsome boy met a beautiful girl and they had an affair. This loss of value was due not to any lack of skill on Cocteau's part but to the nature of the cinema as a medium. Had he used a fat middle-aged couple the effect would have been ridiculous because the snatches of language which are all the movie permits have not sufficient power to transcend their physical appearance. Yet if the lovers are young and beautiful, the cause of their love looks "natural," a consequence of their beauty, and the whole meaning of the myth is gone.

"The man who wrote the Eighth Symphony has a right to rebuke the man who put his raptures of elation, tenderness, and nobility into the mouths of a drunken libertine, a silly peasant girl, and a conventional fine lady, instead of confessing them to himself, glorying in them, and uttering them without motley as the universal inheritance" (Shaw).

Shaw, and Beethoven, are both wrong, I believe, and Mozart right. Feelings of joy, tenderness, and nobility are not confined to "noble" characters but are experienced by everybody, by the most conventional, most stupid, most depraved. It is one of the glories of opera that it can demonstrate this and to the shame of the spoken drama that it cannot. Because we use language in everyday life, our style and vocabulary become identified with our social character as others see us, and in a play, even a verse play, there are narrow limits to the range in speech possible for any character beyond which the playwright cannot go without making the character incredible. But precisely because we do not communicate by singing, a song can be out of place but not out of character; it is just as credible that a stupid person should sing beautifully as that a clever person should do so.

If music in general is an imitation of history, opera in particular is an imitation of human willfulness; it is rooted in the fact that we not only have feelings but insist upon having them at whatever cost to ourselves. Opera, therefore, cannot present character in the novelist's sense of the word, namely, people who are potentially good *and* bad, active *and* passive, for music is immediate actuality and neither potentiality nor passivity can live in its presence. This is something a librettist must never forget. Mozart is a greater composer than Rossini but the Figaro of the *Marriage* is less satisfying, to my mind, than the Figaro of the *Barber*, and the fault, is, I think, Da Ponte's. His Figaro is too interesting a character to be completely translatable into music, so that co-present with the Figaro who is singing one is conscious of a Figaro who is not singing but thinking to himself. The barber of Seville, on the other hand, who is not a person but a musical busybody, goes into song exactly, with nothing over.

Again, I find *La Bohème* inferior to *Tosca*, not because the music is inferior, but because the characters, Mimi in particular, are too passive; there is an awkward gap between the resolution with which they sing and the irresolution with which they act.

The quality common to all great operatic roles, e. g. Don Giovanni, Norma, Lucia, Tristan, Isolde, Brünnhilde, is that each of them is a passionate and willful state of being. In real life they would all be bores, even Don Giovanni.

In recompense for this lack of psychological complexity, however, music can do what words cannot, present the immediate and simultaneous relation of these states to each other. The crowning glory of opera is the big ensemble.

The chorus can play two roles in opera and two only, that of the mob and that of the faithful, sorrowing, or rejoicing community. A little of that goes a long way. Opera is not oratorio.

Drama is based on the Mistake. I think someone is my friend when he really is my enemy, that I am free to marry a woman when in fact she is my mother, that this person is a chambermaid when it is a young nobleman in disguise, that this well-dressed young man is rich when he is really a penniless adventurer, or that if I do this such and such a result will follow when in fact it results in something very different. All good drama has two movements, first the making of the mistake, then the discovery that it was a mistake.

In composing his plot, the librettist has to conform to this law but, in comparison to the dramatist, he is more limited in the kinds of mistakes he can use. The dramatist, for instance, procures some of his finest effects from showing how people deceive themselves. Self-deception is impossible in opera because music is immediate, not reflective; whatever is sung is the case. At most self-deception can be suggested by having the orchestral accompaniment at variance with the singer, e.g. the jolly tripping notes which accompany Germont's approach to Violetta's deathbed in *La traviata*, but unless employed very sparingly such devices cause confusion rather than insight.

Again, while in the spoken drama the discovery of the mistake can be a slow process and often, indeed, the more gradual it is the greater the dramatic interest, in a libretto the drama of recognition must be tropically abrupt, for music cannot exist in an atmosphere of uncertainty; song cannot walk, it can only jump.

On the other hand, the librettist need never bother his head, as the dramatist must, about probability. A credible situation in opera means a situation in which it is credible that someone should sing. A good libretto plot is a melodrama in both the strict and the conventional sense of the word; it offers as many opportunities as possible for the characters to be swept off their feet by placing them in situations which are too tragic or too fantastic for "words." No good opera plot can be sensible, for people do not sing when they are feeling sensible.

The theory of "Music-drama" presupposes a libretto in which there is not one sensible moment or one sensible remark: this is not only very difficult to manage, though Wagner managed it, but also extremely exhausting on both the singers and the audience, neither of whom may relax for an instant.

In a libretto where there are any sensible passages, i.e. conversation not song, the theory becomes absurd. If, for furthering the action, it becomes necessary for one character to say to another "Run upstairs and fetch me a handkerchief," then there is nothing in the words, apart from their rhythm, to make one musical setting more apt than another. Wherever the choice of notes is arbitrary, the only solution is a convention, e.g. *recitativo secco*.

In opera the orchestra is addressed to the singers, not to the audience. An opera lover will put up with and even enjoy an orchestral interlude on condition that he knows the singers cannot sing just now because they are tired or the scene-shifters are at work, but any use of the orchestra by itself which is not filling in time is, for him, wasting it. *Leonora III* is a fine piece to listen to in the concert hall, but in the opera house, where it is played between scenes one and two of the second act of *Fidelio*, it becomes twelve minutes of acute boredom.

In opera the Heard and the Seen are like Reality and Appearance in philosophy; hence the more frankly theatrical and sham the sets the better. A realistic painted backdrop which wobbles is more satisfactory than any conscientiously three-dimensional furniture or suggestive non-representational objects. Only one thing is essential, namely, that everything be a little over life size, that the stage be a space in which only the grand entrance and the grand gesture are appropriate.

If the librettist is a practicing poet, the most difficult problem, the place where he is most likely to go astray, is the composition of the verse. Poetry is in its essence an act of reflection, of refusing to be content with the interjections of immediate emotion in order to understand the nature of what is felt. Since music is in essence immediate, it follows that the words of a song cannot be poetry. Here one should draw a distinction between lyric and song proper. A lyric is a poem intended to be chanted. In a chant the music is subordinate to the words, which limit the range and tempo of the notes. In song, the notes must be free to be whatever they choose and the words must be able to do what they are told.

Much as I admire Hofmannsthal's libretto for *Rosenkavalier*, it is, I think, too near real poetry. The Marschallin's monologue in Act I, for instance, is so full of interesting detail that the voice line is hampered in trying to follow everything. The verses of *Ah non credea* in [Bellini's] *La Sonnambula*, on the other hand, though of little interest to read, do exactly what they should, suggest to Bellini one of the most beautiful melodies ever written and then leave him completely free to write it. The verses which the librettist writes are not addressed to the public but are really a private letter to the composer. They have their moment of glory, the moment in which they suggest to him a certain melody: once that is over, they are as expendable as infantry is to a Chinese general: they must efface themselves and cease to care what happens to them.

There have been several composers, Campion,[2] Hugo Wolf,[3] Benjamin Britten,[4] for example, whose musical imagination has been stimulated by poetry of a high order. The question remains, however, whether the listener hears the sung words in a poem,

2. Thomas Campion (1567-1620), an Elizabethan poet and composer of songs, was the author of several Books of Airs.

3. Hugo Wolf (1860-1903), an Austrian composer, is best known for his songs on poems by Goethe, Heine, Eichendorff, Mörike, and Paul Heyse. He wrote one opera, *Der Corregidor* (1895).

4. Benjamin Britten (1913-), the most popular and prolific British composer of his generation, is the author of approximately ten operas, among them *Peter Grimes* (1945), *Billy Budd* (1951), and *A Midsummer Night's Dream* (1960).

or, as I am inclined to believe, only sung syllables. A Cambridge psychologist, P. E. Vernon, once performed the experiment of having a Campion song sung with nonsense verses of equivalent syllabic value substituted for the original; only six per cent of his test audience noticed that something was wrong. It is precisely because I believe that, in listening to song (as distinct from chant), we hear, not words, but syllables, that I am violently hostile to the performances of operas in translation. Wagner in Italian or Verdi in English sounds intolerable, and would still sound so if the poetic merits of the translation were greater than those of the original, because the new syllables have no apt relation to the pitch and tempo of the notes with which they are associated. The poetic value of the words may provoke a composer's imagination, but it is their syllabic values which determine the kind of vocal line he writes. In song, poetry is expendable, syllables are not.

The golden age of opera, from Mozart to Verdi, coincided with the golden age of liberal humanism, of unquestioning belief in freedom and progress. If good operas are rarer today, this may be because, not only have we learned that we are less free than nineteenth-century humanism imagined, but also have become less certain that freedom is an unequivocal blessing, that the free are necessarily the good. To say that operas are more difficult to write does not mean that they are impossible. That would only follow if we should cease to believe in free will and personality altogether. Every high C accurately struck demolishes the theory that we are the irresponsible puppets of fate or chance.

Originally published in the *Partisan Review*, XIX (1952). Reprinted by permission of the author. Copyright 1952 by *Partisan Review*.

CONTEMPORARY OPERA

UNFORTUNATELY, the youngest generation of operatic composers is not represented among the participants in the following symposium, all seven artists questioned having been born between 1880 and 1905. One should have liked to hear also what Hans

Werner Henze, Giselher Klebe, and other European and American melodramatists of their age-group have to say about the genre.

Luigi Dallapiccola (1904-   ) was influenced by Alban Berg and Anton Webern, and makes consistent use of Schönberg's method of composition with twelve tones. He is the author of *Volo di notte* (Night Flight) based on the book by Saint-Exupéry and *Il prigionero* (The Prisoner) on texts written by Charles de Coster and Villiers de l'Isle Adam.

Ildebrando Pizzetti (1880-1968) developed an interest in opera in the course of his acquaintance with Gabriele d'Annunzio. He has occupied chairs in harmony and composition at the conservatories in Florence, Milan, and Rome. He has set to music dramas by Aeschylus and Sophocles as well as Shakespeare's *As You Like It* and, more recently, T. S. Eliot's *Murder in the Cathedral*.

Gian Francesco Malipiero (1882-   ), another traditionalist, is deeply imbued with the spirit of Baroque music. He has edited the work of Monteverdi and helped to renew interest in Vivaldi. A few of his numerous operas have won international recognition. He is also the composer of much choral, symphonic, and chamber music.

Werner Egk (1901-   ), one of the leading German composers of our day, has been unusually successful with his operas. The first of these, *Die Zaubergeige* (1935), enjoyed considerable popularity, and both *Peer Gynt* and *Columbus* still appear occasionally in the repertory. His latest contribution to the lyrical stage is a setting of Gogol's *Inspector General*.

Boris Blacher (1903-   ), of Baltic origin, occupies an equally prominent place in the musical life of contemporary Germany. Presently director of the *Hochschule für Musik* in Berlin, he has specialized in the writing of scenic oratorios.

Marcel Delannoy (1898-   ) studied painting and architecture at the Ecole des Beaux-Arts in Paris, and in music is largely self-taught. His reputation as an operatic composer dates from the première of *Le poirier de misère* (The Pear Tree of Want) in 1927.

Sir Arthur Bliss (1891-   ), Master of the Queen's Music since 1943, has written only one opera, *The Olympians;* with a libretto by J. B. Priestley.

Composers' Forum: Subject Opera (1953)

SEVEN DISTINGUISHED composers representative of contemporary Europe here join in a symposium of six topics which may be considered basic to any contemplation of operatic thinking in our time. The composers are Luigi Dallapiccola, Ildebrando Pizzetti, and Gian Francesco Malipiero (Italian), Werner Egk and Boris Blacher (German), Marcel Delannoy (French), and Sir Arthur Bliss (British). The round-up was made by [the magazine] *World Theatre*, published under the auspices of UNESCO, of which René Hainaux is the editor.

I: *What Impels You to Compose an Opera?*

Werner Egk résumés the general feeling as follows: "Because I am convinced that opera is the fullest form of artistic expression, uniting as it does music, drama, and the plastic arts." Luigi Dallapiccola adds: "It is a means of expressing feelings and passions with a precision and high relief unknown in pure music." Marcel Delannoy gives a detailed answer: "1) I believe in the ideal of a *complete entertainment* of which present-day opera is the prefiguration. 2) For the last fifty years the genius of composers has been almost entirely devoted to the search for a new musical language and now we are reaching a dead end. On the other hand the lyrical drama of the future offers immense perspectives of development as soon as we start to consider it from a structural point of view. 3) At a time when contemporary music is wilting in suffocating conservatories, lyrical drama constitutes a battle ground where composers are obliged to resume contact with the public. The impact is certainly rough at times for music which aims at pleasing without prostituting itself. But we must do or die."

II: *Do you Consider the Libretto as a Support for the Music? Or the Music as a Complement of the Poem?*

Egk is categorical: "The libretto is a support for the score." This is also the opinion of Dallapiccola, who adds: "My ideal is therefore a short libretto of not too literary a quality." Sir Arthur Bliss is not far from agreeing: "Any play or story may be considered suitable for operatic treatment. There are however subjects which music can weaken or destroy. I do not think, for instance, that plays whose interest lies in discussion and argument, or naturalistic drama of contemporary life make very happy libretti. Opera is for the ear as ballet is for the eye." Boris Blacher prudently declares "that one cannot generalize," while Delannoy, Francesco Malipiero, and Ildebrando Pizzetti qualify their answers.

Delannoy: "At the outset the libretto is certainly the woof upon which the composer weaves his score, and it is what first attracts the public. But subsequently the work will live only through the flesh and soul of its music. It is a commonplace to say that music is unnecessary to drama which is sufficient to itself. But any libretto worthy of the name needs and calls for music. It presents itself as a framework and an inspiration. The ideal would be if it were sufficient to see the performance in order to understand it, for words in lyrical drama are fragile and the least thing will efface them."

Malipiero: "When I started it was the libretto that suggested to me lyrical forms which were not those of official Italian 'melodrama.' At that time I knew nothing of *Boris Godunov* or *Pelléas et Mélisande.* . . . Poetry above all things: which does not mean that poem and music are two contrasting forces; on the contrary they form together the integrated whole of lyrical drama."

Pizzetti: "In 'melodrama' the libretto is a support and the music a complement, but in true opera poetry and music are inseparable. Neither should be considered in themselves, both are equally necessary to the dramatic expression."

III: *How, in Your Own Work, Do You Envisage the Relationship Between Words and Music?*

This question, closely related to the last, has given the composers an opportunity to reconsider their ideas and give them more precision. Thus Pizzetti describes libretto and music "as one plus one which make, not two, but one." Bliss, who had expressed the opinion that "the words of a libretto are of secondary importance," maintains his position. "Even with good diction singers only succeed in making about seventy-five per cent of the text intelligible. In opera the music must take charge from the first bar to the last."

Egk: "The text must be so conceived that it allows, or still better, provokes, the musical form."

Malipiero: "In my work, words and music, far from seeking to eliminate each other, are on the most cordial terms. Where poetry reaches its climax the word prevails by translating itself completely into music. In certain cases it is actually necessary to understand the words, as for instance when their object is to explain the situation or elucidate the subject." Dallapiccola is of the same opinion: "So long as the action is not completely sketched out, the text must remain clear. In an aria, which as a rule expresses simply a feeling (of joy, distress, etc.), the audibility of each word is no longer indispensable."

Delannoy: "In the last resort it is the lyrical translation of the situation which carries the day. But, in order to give a work of large dimensions the necessary aeration, one is obliged to provide successive planes which lead from ordinary speech to absolute song, by way of poetic diction, and the varieties of recitative, from *secco* to *sostenuto*. It is naturally possible to make this progress in reverse, or to break the chain of transition, according to dramatic requirements. For my part I used this method with discretion in *Puck* [1946][1]; in the choreographic drama *Abraham* I make a tragedian's dialogue with the orchestra. The field of experiment is wide, but at all events music, even when it is invisible, must always be present or rather implied."

IV: *Do You Agree With the Proposition That the Essence of the Spoken Theater is Action, and That of the Lyrical Theater Emotion?*

Dallapiccola and Delannoy answer yes. Malipiero and Pizzetti consider that, whether spoken or sung, drama is always action and emotion combined. Blacher and Egk answer with a downright no, and Blacher, to contradict this excessive generalization, instances the work of Chekhov and Giraudoux in straight theater, and that of Mozart and Verdi in opera.

---

1. An opera based on Shakespeare's *A Midsummer Night's Dream.*

V: *Are the Traditional Forms of Opera Founded on Funda-
mental Necessities and Still Valid in Our Days? Or Should They
Be Considered as the Offshoots of a Tradition that Grew out of
Temporary Circumstances?*

Bliss believes that every new opera poses new problems of
style, and that therein lies the fascination of this greatest of all
forms of music. He is joined in this opinion by Blacher, who
considers that the form of all good operas is always new. Dallapiccola desires a definition of the term "traditional forms."
They serve to establish a clear differentiation "between moments
of lyrical expansion and moments in which the action is unfolded.
I therefore consider the obligation of providing arias, choruses,
duos, etc., well-founded. Moreover neither Wagner, Moussorgsky, Berg nor anyone else has ever repudiated such an obligation."
Delannoy: "The traditional forms constitute an order which
is still valid. We must catch hold of them again, over the heads
of Wagner and Debussy, but in order to carry them much
farther ahead." This opinion is echoed by Egk: "The traditional
forms of opera always allow of a new declension. But under the
most novel, personal, and apparently revolutionary forms the
primitive prototypes are always clearly discernible."
Malipiero: "The life of the mind perpetually renewed is our
only challenge to death. Under the Second Empire the opera with
grand arias, duos, trios, etc., was necessary to Paris, as Wagner
was necessary beyond the frontier. But if the form of opera
that flourished at the turn of the century continues to be fairly
well received today, it is simply because the singers play
a similar part in it as the spoiled champions of the sporting
world."

VI: *Among the Operatic Productions of Recent Years which
Do You Think Have Contributed Most to Renewing the Art?*

Out of five answers (Bliss and Pizzetti having abstained) it is
significant that Berg should be mentioned three times; Ravel
and Kurt Weill twice. Here, however, are the answers in full.
Blacher: *Wozzeck* (Alban Berg), *Oedipus Rex* (Cocteau-

Stravinsky). Egk: *Dreigroschenoper* (Brecht/Weill), *Oedipus Rex*. Dallapiccola: *Wozzeck, Lulu* (Berg), *L'enfant et les sortilèges* (Ravel), *Doktor Faustus* (Busoni), *Christophe Colomb* (Milhaud), *Le sette canzoni, Il torneo notturno* (Malipiero), *Erwartung* (Schönberg).

Delannoy: "Attempts to reform the structure of opera have remained exceedingly timid. Nevertheless very interesting signs are discernible in such spectacular oratorios as *Jeanne d'Arc au Bûcher* (Honegger) and *Columbus* (Werner Egk) despite their static character, and in Kurt Weill's *Mahagonny*, Jacques Ibert's *Angélique*, and Benjamin Britten's *The Beggar's Opera* in a lighter vein. The most audacious is perhaps Malipiero's *Allegra Brigata*, but audacity does not always spell success. With *The Consul* Gian Carlo Menotti has shown extraordinary ability both as a composer and as a man of the theater, but he has not renewed anything."

Malipiero: *Wozzeck, L'enfant et les sortilèges.* "These masterpieces are floating islands that lie at a certain distance from the mainland of lyrical drama."

From *Musical America,* LXXIII (1953). Reprinted by permission of *Musical America/High Fidelity* magazine.

INDEX

11/1/12